The Complete Literary Works of Lorenzo de' Medici

The Complete Literary Works of Lorenzo de' Medici
"The Magnificent"

Translated with an Introduction
by Guido A. Guarino

Italica Press
New York
2016

Copyright © 2016 by Guido A. Guarino

ITALICA PRESS, INC.
595 Main Street, Suite 605
New York, New York 10044

Italica Press Medieval & Renaissance Texts

All rights reserved. No part of this publication may be reproduced, stored in a retrieval system, or transmitted, in any form or by any means, electronic, mechanical, photocopying, recording, or otherwise, without prior permission of Italica Press. For permission to reproduce selected portions for courses, please contact the Press at inquiries@italicapress.com.

Library of Congress Cataloging-in-Publication Data
Medici, Lorenzo de', 1449–1492.
[Works. 2015]
The complete literary works of Lorenzo de' Medici, "the magnificent" / translated with an introduction by Guido A. Guarino.
volumes cm -- (Italica Press medieval & renaissance texts)
Includes bibliographical references and index.
ISBN 978-1-59910-230-6 (hardcover : alk. paper) --
ISBN 978-1-59910-231-3 (pbk. : alk. paper) -- I
SBN 978-1-59910-229-0 (e-book)
I. Guarino, Guido A., 1925- II. Title.
PQ4630.M3 2015
858'.209--dc23

2015030257

For a Complete List of
Medieval and Renaissance Texts
Visit our Web Site at
www.ItalicaPress.com

CONTENTS

INTRODUCTION
Lorenzo's Life vii
Lorenzo's Reputation as a Poet x
Lorenzo's Works xxv
Note on the Translation xxxv

I. LOVE POEMS
Lyrics 1
Commentary on Some of His Sonnets 79
Eclogues 197
Corinth 197
Apollo and Pan 203
Ambra 209
The Loves of Venus and Mars 220
Sylva I 224
Sylva II 231

II. COMIC WORKS
Nencia da Barberino I 263
Nencia da Barberino II 268
The Hunt with Falcons 279
Symposium 289
Ballads for Festive Occasions 315
Carnevale Songs 343
Three Epistles 359
Short Stories 362
The Story of Giacoppo 362
The Story of Ginevra 371

III. PHILOSOPHICAL AND DEVOTIONAL WORKS
Disputation 381
Devotional Poems 413
Sonnets to Ginevra de' Benci 430
Hymns of Praise 432
The Mystery Play of Saints John and Paul 447

BIBLIOGRAPHY
Editions 485
General Background 489

INDEX OF FIRST LINES 497

a Maria

INTRODUCTION

Lorenzo's Life

Lorenzo de' Medici was born in Florence in 1449 to Lucrezia Tornabuoni and Piero de' Medici. His grandfather Cosimo was the founder of the political power of the Medici[1] and was also much interested in culture and education. Among other things he established a library in San Marco, which was to be at the disposal of anyone who needed it. At his death the library had 400 manuscripts and continued to grow. Lorenzo's mother, Lucrezia, wrote religious poems and created a friendly atmosphere for her son and artist friends.

Lorenzo's family, then, had a cultural tradition and interest in humanism that explains the care taken in his education. His first tutor was the humanist Gentile de' Becchi from Urbino. This was a small city under the dukes of Montefeltro that came to represent the Renaissance city par excellence, as may be seen in Baldassare Castiglione's *Book of the Courtier* (1528). The learned dukes of Montefeltro had other ties with Florence in that the mercenary armies they led were hired by the Florentines on various occasions.

Lorenzo, then, was exposed to humanistic thought from the beginning, and his education continued when he attended the lessons of Cristoforo Landino (1424–98), Marsilio Ficino (1433–99) and others at the Studio Fiorentino. At the same time he participated in another tradition, that of the "brigate" that existed long before Giovanni Boccaccio (1313–75), who mentions it in the *Decameron*. The "brigate" were made up of groups of young aristocrats who banded together to look for adventures and entertainment. Lorenzo's father Piero, who was sickly, needed his son's help and used him for embassies and other confidential matters from the time he was an adolescent.

---

1. William Roscoe, *Life of Lorenzo de' Medici Called the Magnificent* (Liverpool: J. M'Creery, 1795); Cecilia M. Ady, *Lorenzo dei Medici and Renaissance Italy* (New York: Collier Books, 1966); Vincent Cronin, *The Florentine Renaissance* (New York: Dutton, 1967); Sara Sturm, *Lorenzo de'Medici* (New York: Twain, 1974); Paul Oskar Kristeller and Michael Mooney, *Renaissance Thought and Its Sources* (New York: Columbia University Press, 1979); Concetta Carestia Greenfield, *Humanist and Scholastic Poetics* (Lewisburg, PA: Bucknell University Press 1981); Jack Lang, *Laurent le Magnifique* (Paris: Perrin, 2002).

Probably during his jaunts with the "brigata," he met Lucrezia Donati (1449–1501) and was in love with her for the rest of his life, or at least she became the one he loved in his love poems. As part of his youthful activities Lorenzo participated in a joust and was declared the winner. In 1469 he married Clarice Orsini (c.1453–88), a member of that powerful Roman family.

With the death of his father that year (Dec. 2, 1469) came the end of what may be called his "careless" years, for the most important citizens came to offer their condolences and at the same time asked him to take over the leadership of Florence and Tuscany. This was a ritual, of course, which had been already played for his father at Cosimo de' Medici's death in 1464. Be that as it may, he accepted reluctantly, as he said at the time and often thereafter, for the protection of his family and friends, as well as of Florence.

From then on we have individual highlights within a general policy whose aim was to strengthen his hold on power in Florence and protect the state through alliances that were to maintain a balance of power and also impede invasions of Tuscany by foreign powers. Events of a personal nature were the birth of his children, of whom three males were to have an historical role in the future: Piero, heir to his father, in 1471; Giovanni, the future pope Leo X, in 1475; and Giuliano, duke of Nemours, in 1479.

Throughout his life Lorenzo maintained a court of exceptional artists, poets, philosophers and men of letters and of science, which made of Florence a center of cultural activities. He befriended these and even defended the philosopher Pico della Mirandola (1463–94) who had incurred the displeasure of a pope and was accused of heresy. Lorenzo's efforts and expenditures to beautify his city were incredible. Even more unbelievable is the fact that in the midst of all these occupations he participated in the creative activities of the members of his cultural coterie by being an estimable poet.

In 1472 Lorenzo reopened the University of Pisa, which had fallen on hard times. In that period he had to put an end to the rebellion of the city of Volterra in which he succeeded by means of the duke of Montefeltro's mercenaries. Two years later, threatened by the designs of Pope Sixtus IV to aggrandize the papal state, Lorenzo concluded an alliance with Milan and Venice. As a result there was an attempt by the Pazzi family to assassinate Lorenzo, probably with the pope's approval. On April

26, 1478, during the mass attended by Lorenzo the attempt was carried out. Lorenzo's brother Giuliano was killed, but Lorenzo escaped with a slight wound by locking himself in the sacristy. The rebellion was put down with many casualties, but on June 1st the pope excommunicated Lorenzo, and on June 20th he issued an interdict against Florence. Then the pope, allied with the king of Naples, moved against Florence, which was not ready for war. Here came Lorenzo's "finest hour" in defense of Florence. He dared to go alone to see the king of Naples putting his life in his hands. He succeeded in convincing the king to break the alliance with the pope. On his return to Florence he was received as the hero who had been ready to give his life in order to save his city.

Although there were other conspiracies and assassination attempts, none was successful. Among other cultural projects, in addition to the rebirth of the University of Pisa, there was the further strengthening of the Studio Fiorentino, where his friend Poliziano taught the Greco-Roman classics in accord with his humanistic thought. With the aid of Pico della Mirandola and Poliziano, he founded a great library that today bears his name (the Laurentian Library). As for guiding the state, Lorenzo had many other diplomatic successes and was able to maintain various alliances necessary for his balance-of-power policy.

We cannot here follow his political career except to say that it was most successful in that he survived long enough to come to be regarded as the shrewdest statesman in Italy. He was seen as a sort of genius who was able to maintain a political balance among Italian states that was most beneficial. He did indeed watch over his family's interests, although not so well on the economic side because of his enormous expenditures for artistic purposes.

To counter his statement that he became the political leader of Florence in order to protect his family's interests first of all, there is the fact that he was capable of sacrifices to ensure the welfare of Florence. His personality and his achievements were such that his greatness was recognized even by those who, like Niccolò Machiavelli (1469–1527), condemned the Medici as the usurpers of power who had put an end to the free republican government, for he was also seen as the one who had enriched Florence artistically in an incredible way.[2]

2. "Machiavelli e Guicciardini," ed. by Maria Sarena Sapegno, in *Storia e antologia delta letteratura italiana,* ed. A. Asor Rosa (Florence: La Nuova Italia, 1979), 7: 187ff.

Lorenzo died on April 8, 1492 while still young. His friends Poliziano and Pico were with him at the end, which has been described for us by Poliziano. Lorenzo *il Magnifico* was buried in the church of San Lorenzo in the Medici Chapel in a tomb sculpted by *il Divino* Michelangelo.

Lorenzo's Reputation as a Poet

When we turn our attention to Lorenzo's works, rather than his political career, we see that critics have been stymied by the fact that Lorenzo's poetry touched so many different motives that one could hardly see any of them as having greater weight than the rest. The reason for this seemed to be that since he had a state to lead he could not be expected to devote much time to his poetry and thus he found it easier to refer to other poets and imitate various schools. This feeling continued across the centuries and then in the twentieth century found someone (Enrico Nencioni, 1837–96) who gave it a name that seemed to attract many: Lorenzo was a "dilettante." Since he had a state to govern we can easily deduct that he could not have been a professional, full-time poet. Of poets who could be said to be professional in this sense there is a great scarcity. There was, of course, Petrarch who insisted on it, and later some wealthy ones who could afford to be full-time, but even these had other interests. We must note that to say that someone is a dilettante always brings out the idea of inferiority in comparison to "professionals," even when the phrase "absit iniuria verbo" is added.

The critics who found it difficult to come to a decision about Lorenzo's poetry cited the fact that Lorenzo was inspired by and imitated other poets and poetic schools. This is quite true, but one must see what the meaning of this is. The great Poliziano also imitates; in fact, he has been known to lift an entire verse from Dante. Yet that verse is no longer Dante's, for it has become something new. Petrarch, who in the fifteenth and sixteenth centuries was seen as model and guide in literary matters, had insisted that to be original one must first assimilate all that has been produced in the past, and only then one can take his own strides and be original. And original means being different, but not cut off from the past.

It is well known that Lorenzo took an interest in the history of Italian literature — an interest that is well documented in his works — which he saw as capable of holding its own alongside the Greek and Roman. What the humanists had said, and were saying, about the loss of Greek and Latin works due to the "criminal" lack of care and interest during the Middle Ages obviously affected Lorenzo. He feared that the same situation might develop for Italian literature in the future. Wanting to help preserve this great inheritance, he, with the help of Poliziano, put together the famous *Raccolta aragonese*[3] (1476–77). This interest in and reverence for the past is present in his works, particularly in his *Commentary,* where he discusses this literary tradition and the history of the language.

Given his humanistic environment[4] and his concern for the Italian (but also classical) tradition, it is not surprising that Lorenzo consciously imitates or is inspired by the great works of the past. He is taking possession of his heritage in the Petrarchan sense, and at the same time he is learning his art. In fact, an attentive eye will soon see that he was fully aware of the "tricks of the trade" and could use them as well as any other. Lorenzo's interest in past literary expression and its influence on him are important and of much interest. But more important still is that he was also able to find his own voice and add something to what he had received from the past. As was said above, we can easily see Lorenzo's links with the past and point out that the Sicilian School,[5] or Dante Alighieri (1265–1321) and Guido Cavalcanti (1255–1300), or Francesco Petrarch (1304–75) are a constant background. But also present is his own realistic note that is never lost. It might seem absurd to say that while he flies, he also keeps his feet on the ground. But this is what he does,

3. The *Raccolta aragonese* was a collection of texts from Italian literature that Lorenzo put together with Poliziano's help. He states that because of negligence many Greek and Latin texts had been lost,and that he wished to preserve Italian literature from a similar fate. The letter that accompanies these texts when sent to Federico d'Aragona was probably written by Poliziano.

4. See Myron Piper Gilmore, *The World of Humanism: 1453–1617* (New York: Harper, 1952); Paul Oskar Kristeller, *Renaissance Thought II: Papers on Humanism and the Arts* (New York: Harper & Row, 1965); Charles Edward Trinkhaus, *Adversity's Noblemen* (New York: Octagon Books, 1965); Eugenio Garin, *Italian Humanism,* trans. Peter Munz (Oxford: Basil Blackwell, 1965; rpt. Westport, CT: Greenwood Press, 1975).

5. The Sicilian School was a philosophical and literary movement centered around the emperor Frederick II (1194–1250) in the first half of the thirteenth century. Its importance was based on innovative poetic modes like the sonnet. It contributed to codifying the Italian language.

and so we find that while he gives us a perfectly ethereal version of the *stil novo,*[6] he also does not forget reality, and so to explain or exemplify the spirit, he finds a way of doing it by observing the flight of bees and their working methods,[7] and to express an idyllic sense of peace, he contrasts it with a realistic assessment of his own life in Florence.[8] There was also, among other traits, the evolving view of neo-Platonism.

Towards the end of the fifteenth century when an escape from death, that is a fantastic disregard of death, is found either in a philosopher's flight of imagination, as in Ficino, or in a poet's myth of eternal youth and spring, barely tinged by a trace of melancholy, Lorenzo adheres to the dream, but with eyes wide open. And so in the composition that became the symbol of the Quattrocento love of life and invitation to joy, written to celebrate the Mardi gras, we find the continuous toll of death that seems to negate the positive statement:

> Oh how beautiful is youth
> That from us so swift does flee:
> To live happy do not wait
> For tomorrow may be late.[9]

In the refrain we are told constantly that youth is beautiful, but the note that remains is that it disappears. Yes, be happy, but then we are told that happiness too, if ever one is happy, abandons us. The "happiness" presented in this composition is more a search for forgetfulness through frantic passion and wine, rather than a positive happiness. Reality here is infinitely stronger than the veil of melancholy mentioned above in reference to other poets like Poliziano.

Another humanistic myth that opposed medieval expressions of the powerlessness and worthlessness of man was that of man as the maker of his own destiny, as in Pico della Mirandola, and as a marvelous being, a god on earth who gave voice to Nature and ruled over all, as in Ficino, Poliziano, and countless others. In one of his poems, the *Ambra,* Lorenzo begins with a very long description of the power of nature, a nature unbridled whose destructive force is tremendous, a nature that seems conscious and malignant in its attack on man. And where is the man who is all

6. See p. xxv, n. 28.
7. *Love Lyrics* CXIX, 18–41, pp. 75–76.
8. *Commentary* XXI, pp. 144–46; *Love Lyrics* CXVIII, 1–17, pp. 72–73.
9. *Carnevale Songs* VII, pp. 352–53.

powerful and dominates nature? He is reduced to the condition of poor wretches who try to save their lives by climbing on the roof of their house from where they see their poor belongings and animals swept away by the flood. And then we have a god who attempts to seize beauty, but it escapes from his fingers, leaving him to bewail our fate. Our ideals are unreachable, all we succeed in doing is soiling them in our attempt to seize them. But even more interesting is the fact that instead of a poetic attempt to hide death behind the myth of eternal youth and spring, here we have Lorenzo who presents a god who, not only bewails the impossibility of achieving what he desires, but curses the fact that he is immortal, for eternity means nothing but eternal suffering.[10]

In trying to arrive at a rational view of a person as complex as Lorenzo, our task is made easier if we recur to the views and works of two men, one of whom, Poliziano, was his contemporary, and the other, Machiavelli, nearly so. Both of them loved Florence, but Machiavelli, the philosopher and historian, saw Lorenzo as the tyrant whose family had brought an end to the glorious free republic of Florence, which he had served loyally, while Poliziano, the poet and also historian, was pleased to spend almost his entire adult life at Lorenzo's court.

Both these men played an important role in the history of Florence, and their works help clarify different aspects of Lorenzo and Florence itself. In his *Istorie fiorentine,* Machiavelli speaks of Lorenzo as "two different persons united by an almost impossible union" ("due persone diverse, quasi con impossibile coniunzione congiunte").[11] Machiavelli is referring to the contrast between the poet and patron of the arts and the statesman and he correctly sees that there is a union, in that whatever Lorenzo did as citizen and head of state penetrated his poetic vision. And so we have a politician and a poet, but just try to separate the two, even in some of his works like the *Carnevale Songs* and the supposedly religious drama he wrote for his children where Machiavelli's future teachings would seem to be at home.

Machiavelli's view of Lorenzo as "two different persons united by an almost impossible union" can be applied to many aspects of his life and works. We have the tyrant, but a "tyrant" who makes his city great at his own expense, and even risks his life for the sake of Florence. We have the idealist who can easily

10. *Ambra,* 50–51, p. 210.
11. "Machiavelli e Guicciardini," p. 189.

be seen as a realist, the traditionalist who breaks with tradition, etc. If we take the last as meaning someone who is in full accord with his times, but is also an innovator, we have a fundamental trait of Lorenzo and the "almost impossible union" too. But for clarification of the situation we must turn to Poliziano.

In Quattrocento Florence humanism was triumphant and so was its central call for the return to the ancients and the reconstruction of antiquity. Petrarch had given life to the movement in the previous century by first of all rejecting medieval Latin and resurrecting classical Latin based on the study of ancient works. The refusal of medieval Latin was implicitly the abandonment of the ways and mores of those who had used it Petrarch insisted on the necessity of returning to our ancestors and assimilating their culture. Then, and only then, there is for us the possibility of originality; as he puts it, the son must resemble the father, but be different. There seems to be need for another "almost impossible union."

In Quattrocento Florence, then, the return to the ancients meant returning to our Greco-Roman cultural ancestors. However, these humanists believed that their "revolution" was marred by the difficulty of doing for our Greek ancestors what had been done, and was being done, for the Latins, in that experts in Greek were particularly rare in Italy. This had been felt by Petrarch and Boccaccio who had even tried to learn it, with little success, with the help of someone who seemed to have a little knowledge of Greek. Their valiant efforts even involved sacrifices in that this person may have known some Greek, but had no notion of the basic rules of hygiene. From this grew the myth (?) that Petrarch had been found on his death-bed with a Plato manuscript on his breast and tears on his cheeks because he had never been able to read it.

To a Florence in which humanism was rampant among men of letters, but was regrettably limited in its application to Greek, there came a youngster from Montepulciano whose father had been killed there, and he himself had been sent to Florence to avoid the same fate. We can imagine what the reaction must have been in Florence when it became known that this youngster (Angelo Ambrogini by name, but known as Poliziano from his birth place) who came from the provinces had brought with him a partial translation of the *Iliad* from Greek to Latin. It soon became known that he could use these languages and could express himself in them as well as the ancients themselves. In fact he later pretended to have found ancient works, though in reality he had written them. The result was that he became tutor to Lorenzo's son and professor of classical literatures at the Studio Fiorentino. He remained with Lorenzo all his life except for a brief period. Perhaps it would be useful to mention the reason for his temporary absence, since it serves to show that humanism was not quite all-triumphant after all, since in Florence there was still the force of religion.

As tutor to Lorenzo's son, Poliziano tried to instill in his pupil the love of the humanities that he himself felt. For the Latin lessons, he used to write original pieces in that language on whatever was of interest to him, the Latini. Lorenzo's wife, Clarice Orsini, who came from the famous Roman family, was traditionally religious. Poliziano's lessons were in conflict with her religious upbringing and did not please her. This caused Lorenzo to keep Poliziano away from his court for a brief period.

As stated above, the humanists aimed to restore their Greco-Roman heritage, to find what the Middle Ages had allowed to be either lost or damaged. They had to find what seemed lost and restore what had been damaged. Some of them seemed to have a special sensitivity when it came to decide where a particular manuscript might be found. When one of these "lost" works came to light, the news seemed to travel with the speed of lightning, and the members of this elite fraternity rejoiced, for a member of their community had been brought back to life (Renaissance). But we must stress that all this was limited to the ancient world that they wanted to make their own. We must not forget that Petrarch went so far as to write letters to the ancients in which he did not hesitate to scold Cicero or praise others as if they were alive. In fact all of this was a two-way phenomenon, for Petrarch tells us that Cicero, after being scolded, punished him by letting a heavy tome of his orations drop on his toes.[12]

We now come to the problem of Lorenzo's various, and at times contrasting, sources of "inspiration," which have seemed so inexplicable to many critics. In the introduction to his edition of Lorenzo's works (well-worth reading), Paolo Orvieto states that the central problem of Lorenzo criticism has been how to judge the many divergent paths taken by him in his works.[13] This has led critics astray ever since Machiavelli saw two persons in

12. Petrarch is not known for humor, but at times he surprises us.

13. Lorenzo de' Medici, *Tutte le opere,* ed. P. Orvieto, vol. I (Rome: Salerno, 1992).

Lorenzo because they also sought the "almost impossible union." In the nineteenth century, Francesco de Sanctis (1817–83) apparently believed he had found the union. The two persons that Machiavelli had seen were both negative for the critic, as was his judgment of Lorenzo's poetry. He could unite the two persons by means of what seemed to be Lorenzo's most efficacious quality: hypocrisy. Given de Sanctis' authority, his judgment was echoed by others even in the twentieth century. Walter Binni (1913–97), for instance, who does a great service to Lorenzo in his discussion of the text of the *Nencia,* also reflects de Sanctis' opinion in regard to poetry. But we shall return to de Sanctis later.

It is now necessary to remember what has been said about humanism and turn our eyes to a most important document that may enlighten us in this matter. This is the *Epistle to Federico d'Aragona,* attributed to Lorenzo, but almost certainly written by Poliziano. Whether it was written by Lorenzo or Poliziano does not really matter very much, since it must have been commissioned by Lorenzo and approved by him, for it certainly bears his name.[14]

The *Epistle* begins with the statement that glory has always spurred man to act and that the ancients must be praised most of all for not letting worthy deeds go without reward. So many excellent traits of these worthy "ancients" will never be without fame, as our Tuscan Poet, Francesco Petrarch, says so well: "if the universe is not first dissolved" ("se l'universo pria non si dissolve).[15] And then we have Alexander the Great who mourns before Achilles' tomb: "O happy you that found so clear a voice / And he who did of you so lofty write."[16]

We must note here the fact that greatness and excellent deeds are attributed only to the ancients, and that although Homer is mentioned, the poet cited in this case is not an ancient, but Petrarch. And he is referred to as "our Tuscan Poet" and implicitly there is a link between "our Tuscan Poet" and Cicero.[17] In other words there is something curious here: we have the ancients praised for their greatness, and then someone who is *not*

14. Mario Santoro, "Il Poliziano o il Magnifico?" in *Giornale italiano di filologia* 1 (1948): 139–49.

15. Petrarch, *Rime sparse* LIII.

16. "O fortunato che si chiara tromba / trovasti e chi di te si alto scrisse!" (Petrarch, *Rime sparse* CLXXXII, 3–4).

17. Cicero, *Pro Archia* 10.

ancient, but "our Tuscan Poet"; and he is praised, as the ancients were, although he belongs to a new era: he is not just a poet, but a Tuscan Poet, and the pride of country or region is shown by that "our." We may even see here a civic role for poetry. We are told that had Homer not lived, Achilles' fame would lie buried together with his body. Thus we have the poet as the giver of glory and assuming the role of "conscience" of the state. Since the ancients had ceased to perform and appreciate worthy deeds, memory of Homer himself had almost disappeared. It would have died altogether had it not been for a worthy Athenian who resurrected and raised him to heaven. Homer's work had been dismembered and scattered throughout Greece, but this worthy prince, Pisistratus,[18] offered rewards to those who would bring him any part of the text, and thus, having saved it, he proceeded to restore it. There is no need to say that this was the general program of the humanists: first find the texts and then restore them with the aid of philology.

The world of the ancients where great deeds abounded had come to an end. It was separated from the contemporary by centuries of disregard for the heroic ages of the Greco-Roman world, and thus the sacred poets themselves were forgotten. The result was the great loss of so many Greek and Latin writers, to man's eternal sorrow. But in this great "shipwreck in stormy waters many venerable poets began to cultivate the barren field of the Italian language so that in our own times it has become all adorned by spring flowers and grass."[19] Thus we have the decline of states through the loss of civic spirit and the consequent languishing of poetry for lack of inspiration. We have centuries of almost total neglect (the Middle Ages) and then the humanist efforts to save what could be saved. The poets in this situation draw inspiration from the ancients and wish to be linked to what they recognize as their roots. Thus we have Petrarch's image of the son resembling the father, but being different at the same time, and that of the bees drawing the essence of diverse flowers and then producing their honey. Also important is the fact that in the Quattrocento the basic literary language is Latin.

We could say that what is described above is the "traditional" view of the humanists with which Lorenzo is in agreement. But

---

18. Pisistratus, ruler of Athens (VI century BCE), known for his passion for Homer.

19. Angelo Poliziano, "Epistola a Federico d'Aragona," in *Il Quattrocento,* ed. Giovanni Ponte (Bologna: Zanichelli, 1966), pp. 680–85.

he also moved in another direction, far beyond the centuries of total neglect of culture: he sees the birth of a new language, Italian, that is praised as the equal of the languages of antiquity and a new literature that is great, or at least well on the way to greatness. This opens for Lorenzo, and Poliziano a new direction that is at first spurned by most humanists. This new interest brings Lorenzo and Poliziano to seek and value popular poetic forms native to Tuscany. Like good humanists who had advanced further, they both sought their roots not only in Greco-Roman culture, but in what was native to them. And so we must not be surprised to see the range of their interests and the links in their work with all the different poetic currents, not only of the ancients, but of those that are their new "ancients." It is not a question of lack of motivation, lack of focus, or lack of an all-embracing interest that can cause dismay in critics. Lorenzo is a "traditionalist," but has added a new branch to his traditionalism. And with Lorenzo we have Poliziano, who brought part of the *Iliad* to Florence, but also searched for popular Tuscan lore. The *Epistle to Federico d'Aragona* accompanied the *Raccolta aragonese,* which is a collection of works in Italian literature, from the beginning to Lorenzo's day, including some of Lorenzo's own sonnets. This collection is necessary because these two humanists do not want Italian literature to have the same fate as Greek and Latin, that is, being dispersed and lost. And so we have a Humanism that cares not only for the past, but for the present and the future. No longer do we have an historical view of human culture that stops after the Greeks and Romans before the insurmountable void of a medieval period that has done nothing but lose our cultural heritage. Yes, there is a vacuum, but with the aid of the new humanists our ancestors have leaped across the emptiness of the "Dark Ages" and a new culture has been born with its Guido Guinizelli (1240–76), Cavalcanti, the three giants of the Trecento — Dante, Petrarch and Boccaccio — and many others that by means of a new language have reached the present where we can find Lorenzo himself. And with this new language new problems have arisen. The present is linked to our past and we have Petrarch's concept of imitation, that, as we have said, does not mean "copying," but assimilating in order to produce anew and achieve originality. But some have not understood and believe that the son must not just resemble the father, but be the exact copy of the father. And there can be but one father, the one who on earth has approached nearest to the ideal of perfection that is in heaven. As a consequence, Cicero is idealized and becomes the model for some.

Fortunately there are those who oppose this concept, and once again we can turn to Lorenzo and Poliziano. The latter theorizes on the nature of poetry, while the former puts in action the *variatio* that seems to guide both. The refusal to accept a single model as perfect and then try to become the model is to be found in various works like Poliziano's academic discourse on Quintilian and Statius in 1480. There is, however, a brief letter that contains the same vehement condemnation and gives us a clear understanding of the problem. This is Poliziano's epistle to Paolo Cortese (1465–1510). The epistle begins with an unusually strong condemnation: "I am returning the letters that you diligently collected. To be sincere, I am ashamed that I wasted so much useful time in reading them. In fact, with very few exceptions, they are not worthy of being read by a cultured person, nor of being collected by someone like you." He then states that there is something about style in his letters with which he must disagree: "In fact, you are accustomed, as I understand, to approve only those who reproduce Cicero. As for me, the aspect of the bull or lion is much more honorable than that of the ape, although the latter resembles man more."[20] He then gives several examples of ancients who condemn the above practice. Should someone accuse him of not reproducing Cicero, his answer would be simple: "I am not Cicero, I express myself."

20. Remitto epistolas diligentia tua collectas, in quibus legendis, ut libere dicam, pudet bonas oras male collocasse. Nam praeter omnino paucas, minime dignae sunt quae vel a docto aliquo lectae vel a te collectae dicantur. Quas probem, quas rursus improbem, non explico. Nolo sibi quisquam vel placeat in his, auctore me, vel displiceat. Est in quo tamen a te dissentiam de stylo nonnihil. Non enim probare soles,ut accepi, nisi qui lineamenta Ciceronis effingat. Mihi vero longe honestior tauri facies aut item leonis quam simiae videtur quae tamen homini similior est. Nee ii,qui principatum tenuisse creduntur eloquentiae, similes inter se, quod Seneca prodidit. Ridentur a Quintiliano qui se germanos Ciceronis putabant esse, quod his verbis periodum clauderent: *esse videatur.* Inclamat Horatius imitatores, hac nihil aliud quam imitatores. Mihi certe quicumque tantum componunt ex imitatione, similes esse vel psittaco vel picae videntur, proferentibus quae nee intelligunt. Carent enim quae scribunt isti viribus et vita; carent actu, carent affectu, carent indole, iacent, dormiunt, stertunt. Nihil ibi verum, nihil solidum, nihil efficax. Non exprimis, inquit aliquis, Ciceronem. Quid turn? non enim sum Cicero; me tamen, ut opinor, exprimo.

Here in this epistle we see again why Poliziano or Lorenzo would condemn the idea of a model, be he Greek or anything else. Before us is the vast panorama of human accomplishments, which has been broadened by the inclusion of the contemporary period. All this is ours and we have the duty not to copy any single model, but to assimilate all this and then proceed to make our original contributions. We assimilate everything because it is our history, be it ancient or modern. We can turn to some Greek poet, or a contemporary, and in so doing we express our freedom; we are the children of all these, and we resemble our fathers, but we are not our fathers. Thus Lorenzo does not lack direction or motivation as he roams through our cultural history and is inspired to make original contributions. No whimsical person, no "dilettante" ever showed Lorenzo's mastery of writing nor the ability to change from one subject to another without undue effort. He could turn from the Greek to his own florentine lore and poetic form without strain and with what Castiglione in the next century would call "grazia."

Lorenzo's reputation was to suffer for many years because of his characterization as whimsical and not serious and because of repeated comparisons with Poliziano, who was seen as a serious poet, greater by far than a mere whimsical lightweight. Little did they know that Lorenzo had a more important role in the poetic history of Florence than Poliziano and was as good a poet, if we can make such judgments. The negative view of Lorenzo was generally prevalent across the centuries and well into the twentieth century. There were individual attempts to rescue Lorenzo, at least partially, from his fate. One was made in the nineteenth century by a fellow poet, Giosuè Carducci (1835–1907), but it was squelched by the critic de Sanctis, who was held in great esteem in Italy, but was particularly prejudiced against the Renaissance. Of all the critics of the Ottocento, or of any other century, he was the fiercest by far, for he did not limit his savage attacks to Lorenzo's poetry, but subjected the poet himself to the most offensive insults. No other critic did even approach de Sanctis in his attempt to destroy poetry and poet.

He states that Lorenzo did not have the culture, the education and the idealism of Poliziano. He was more a Florentine than all Florentines, not of the old type, of course. He was Christian and Platonic in abstract, but in reality Epicurean and indifferent. He enjoyed the pleasures of the spirit and of the flesh. He frequented churches and taverns. He alternated between night orgies and academic disputations. He was corrupt and a corruptor. He perfected the new art of the state. He governed a society in which feasts and literature itself had become means of governing. Corrupt people and corrupt prince were worthy of each other.[21]

It is obvious that de Sanctis is continuing with Machiavelli's depiction of Lorenzo as two persons, but only as a means to redouble or triple the fierceness of his attack on the statesman, the poet and the person. He springs from one thing to another, and as was said above, he participates in nightly orgies and academic discourses. If this is his character, can his poetry be any better? This is not just literary criticism, but a vehement moralistic attack with not only Lorenzo as the target, but the Renaissance as a whole. We must not forget that we are in the age of Romanticism and de Sanctis and Romanticism do not see their roots in the Greco-Roman world and humanism, but in Christianity. So the Renaissance becomes an age in which cold intelligence is admired, but has no moral foundation; it would revive a pagan view of life and is completely godless. Dante becomes the poetic god of Romanticism, not Petrarch, nor Lorenzo. But not even the power of religion can explain the fierceness of the attack, which strikes not only Lorenzo's poetry, but the poet himself. To the dual stream of contrasting vices is added hypocrisy, a necessary quality if he was to corrupt the people. Probably it was this hypocrisy that makes de Sanctis so fierce in his condemnation: Lorenzo had succeeded in making the Florentines in his image, and thus a corrupt prince and a corrupt people deserved each other. But what he sees as the corruption of Florence, others may see as the transformation of a not-too-remarkable city into a cultural powerhouse that almost everyone admires. As for his own poetry and poetic influence, Lorenzo had drawn Florentine poetry from its local, provincial milieu and given it broader horizons.

In the twentieth century most critics followed the lead of the previous century in giving Lorenzo's poetry unfavorable attributes. This time, however, the adoption of a certain point of view of the nineteenth-century scholar Nencioni made Lorenzo's poetry more acceptable and attractive. Nencioni said that Lorenzo's particular style was the result of his being a "poetic dilettante,"[22] and of course he must be a "dilettante" for

21. Francesco De Sanctis, *Storia della letteratura italiana,* ed. Niccolò Gallo, introduction Giorgio Ficara (Turin: Einaudi-Gallimard, 1958 and 1996).
22. Enrico Nencioni, "La lirica del rinascimento," in *La vita italiana nel rinascimento,* ed. Ernesto Masi (Milan: Fratelli Treves, 1893), p. 273ff.

he had the care of the state and of his family, and therefore he could hardly find time for becoming anything but a dilettante in poetry. In fact, De Sanctis had said that he did not even receive a good education. Poor Lorenzo, he had had to be content with the likes of Landino, Ficino and Pico della Mirandola as teachers.

This attractive tag of "dilettante" caught on like wild fire. Most of those who adopted it did not seem to realize that it is a name that brings with it the condemnation to inferiority, particularly in this case where the "dilettante" is in close contact with a "professional" of the likes of Poliziano. The comparison was often made, of course, and not in favor of Lorenzo. What everyone seemed anxious to preserve as "real" poetry is the famous "Quant'è bella Giovinezza..." ("Oh how beautiful is youth..."). Here all good qualities seem to have given themselves a rendezvous: true sincerity, positive realism, strong motivation, etc. One of the qualities lacking in Lorenzo's poetry, according to these twentieth-century critics, was poetic evolution. They did not seem to realize that it was they themselves that had made any evolution seem impossible by putting all these qualities together as if they had all sprung together at the same time, thus denying each a time and space of its own and its possible relation to others. Otherwise they would have noted various changes in Lorenzo's poetry that would have denoted a slow but sure movement towards neoplatonism with Ficino as his teacher. In this he passed through many stages including the thought of various philosophers and the teachings of Duecento poets like Guinizelli and others.

Here we should mention a revised *Raccolta aragonese* (1476–77) sent to Federico d'Aragona, son of Ferrante, king of Naples. Among other things it contained 449 rhymes, including some of Lorenzo's own, and a special importance is given to Dante by including Boccaccio's *Vita di Dante* and Dante's own *Vita nova*.[23] He stresses the nobility of the origins with the presence of early Tuscan poets who had been neglected and forgotten during the previous fifty years. These appear in the noble assembly of the *Raccolta*, and since at the same time he evicts from this assembly the contemporary poets and stresses the fact by his own presence, it becomes clear that he is condemning them for the betrayal of

23. The revised *Raccolta aragonese* stressed the poets of the first centuries of the vernacular and gave greater importance to Dante and Cino. It included some of Lorenzo's works, but not those of many he blamed for a certain decadence.

the sacred art of poetry and its faithful practitioners. At the same time this collection presents as noble models the poets from the origins to Lorenzo himself. We must resemble our fathers and yet be ourselves if we are to aspire to originality, and thus what had been the program of the humanists in regard to Greek and Roman culture now became the program for the vernacular. Tuscan literature abandoned its easy ways of irony, sarcasm, a provincial note and ambient, in order to follow Lorenzo in his call to dignity and nobility.[24]

Nencioni's formula of dilettantism was not accepted by everyone. Some saw the focus of Lorenzo's poetry in his "realism." Among these was Edmondo Rho who also speaks of "momentary nature" ("la natura momentanea.")[25] He views Lorenzo's "realism" in a positive light, thus cleansing it of De Sanctis' negative assessment. A third current may be seen in those who, like Emilio Cecchi, (1884–1966) have abandoned the search for a dominant motive and speak of a "volubile eclettismo" that in the end shows its relationship to Nencioni's "dilettantism."[26] As for the specific character of Lorenzo's poetry, scholars have produced discordant notes and even antithetic qualities. For example, we have a Lorenzo humanist and one anti-humanist. We have chosen this particular case of discord since it should have proven the easiest for us to arrive at a conclusion. But a look at what has been written, accompanied by some reflection, has shown that we were wrong. We relied on the famous *Raccolta aragonese* of 1476–77 to make the needle move towards a Lorenzo humanist, but others have relied on the fact that Lorenzo has used the vernacular, not Greek or Latin, to make the needle go in the opposite direction.

We thought that a Lorenzo humanist was so obvious, as we mentioned above in regards to Lorenzo the traditionalist who broke with tradition by applying all the views of humanism to a new language; while classical humanism limited itself to the ancients and mainly to Greek and Latin, Lorenzo had seen that a new language had been born and had acquired the possibility of expressing all there was to be expressed. The literature in that

---

24. Lorenzo spent much effort in his attempt to bring contemporary literature to abandon its easy provincial qualities and move towards the "nobility" of the poets of the Duecento.

25. Cf. Edmondo Rho, *Lorenzo il magnifico* (Bari: Laterza, 1926).

26. *I classici italiani nella storia della critica,* ed. Walter Binni (Florence: La Nuova Italia, 1956), 1: 268.

new language was vast and noble, and like a good humanist Lorenzo called out to all Florentines and others to make that new literature their own, assimilate the old and proceed to the new. He was also proclaiming that the time had come to abandon the provincialism of a literature that by now had become appropriate only for a merchant era and to adopt the noble literature of the poets of the Duecento and the Trecento. Florence was no longer governed by merchants, but had adopted the rule of noble princes; it was time that everything in Florence reflected that nobility.

And so we believe that with Lorenzo a new humanism was born, one that did not abandon the noble work of classical scholars who intended to bring about the complete rebirth of Greco-Roman culture and restore it by using the new science of philology. This was being done by the expenditure of great sums to strengthen the Studio Fiorentino and the University of Pisa. With the help of eminent scholars, Pico and Poliziano, Lorenzo founded a distinguished library in Florence that today justly bears his name. But he, who has been called "anti-humanistic," also believed in the value and achievements of the new world, and so accomplished much towards its appreciation by extending the purposes of classic Humanism to include the contemporary, and by adding his own work to that of the "new ancients."

We have finally come to the point where we believe that our discussion has cleared the air around Lorenzo's poetry. Far from being an "insincere," unfocussed "dilettante," we have a man who firmly believes in the new humanism and therefore is not interested in one solid, never-changing view of nature and reality, but in the variegated and changing aspects of our world. Variety and change seem to be the guiding words for part of the Trecento, Quattrocento and the early Cinquecento. In opposition to Dante's world where everything is known, firm and unchanging on earth, as depicted in the *Divine Comedy,* we come to the other great poet of the Trecento,Petrarch, who is very different. The name he gave his *Canzoniere, Scattered Verses (Rime sparse),* was intended to show that his world no longer had the solidity found in the *Divine Comedy.* His world had lost that quality because he had introduced a new factor, time. In the opening sonnet he makes it clear that a man is ever-changing and that nothing in our world is ever finished or permanent. When he was old, his friend Boccaccio, who worried about his health, asked him in a letter to stop working so hard. What do you want to do, he asked, do you want to do everything yourself? Don't you want to leave something for others to do? Petrarch answers that culture is a continuum that is never ending and changes with the years. All of us have the obligation to contribute to it.[27]

This is Lorenzo's world also, ever different and attractive. He is not unfocused, but tries to focus on different aspects of an ever-changing reality. And as reality changes, so does he change and move from one object of interest to another. This is not a weakness, however, it is the strength of his poetry and also Poliziano's.

Lorenzo's Works

And so we can now turn our attention briefly to Lorenzo's individual works, starting with the *Lyrics.* In the first part of the *Lyrics* Petrarch's presence is dominant. Lorenzo is influenced by both Petrarch's style and by his concept of love. We have a love that while idealized is still human and well-planted in this world. Fortune, time, memory and other Petrarchan themes are prevalent, as is the bitter-sweet concept of love. In the second part we have the addition of the presence of Dante, Cavalcanti, and the *stil novo.* The attention seems to shift to a more rarefied, ethereal concept of love with the aid of all the philosophical and psychological elements of the school mentioned above that he presents in great detail.[28] Here we find that the poet is distancing

27. Francesco Petrarch, *Letters of Old Age,* XVII.2, trans. Aldo S. Bernardo, Saul Levin and Reta A. Bernardo (New York: Italica Press, 2005), 2: 644–54.

28. The *dolce stil novo* was not a native of Tuscany, but came to Florence early and was adopted by Florentine followers of Guido Guinizelli (1240–76), who is considered the father of this style. This new style of poetry was based on the concept that everything has a value, which love brings out. The ultimate objective was to reach God by means of a sort of fantastic love ladder with many rungs. It was believed by these poets that love enabled man to rise from a lower rung to the highest. Since the highest rung meant loving the highest beauty, and this beauty, on earth, belonged to women, loving the female form was no longer considered sinful, since it would bring to God. Having, through love of creation, reached the ultimate objective and shed his interest in earthly things man can then join in the vision of God. To make a difficult notion more understandable, I shall refer to its noblest practitioner, that is, Dante Alighieri. In the *Divine Comedy* Dante experiences all earthly things in his travels through hell, purgatory and paradise. Having experienced all there is to experience, he is ready to shed all earthly interests and finally he gains vision of God.

himself somewhat from contact with a personal experience and is seeking refuge in a less invasive, impersonal, and almost clinical vision of love. We must remember, of course, that in addition to the literary influence of the past there was also a very powerful living one. The neo-Platonic philosopher Ficino was one of Lorenzo's teachers and was much admired by him, as can be seen in his works. Since the stilnovistic tenets of love appear in various ways in Ficino's works, we can be sure that some of this current and of Ficino's neo-Platonic ideas found their way into Lorenzo's mind and works.

All this also applies to Lorenzo's *Commentary.* The idea of having a series of poems connected by a comment or explanation in prose goes back to Dante's *Vita nova*. The great psychological interest shown in the second part of the *Lyrics* finds here full scope in the explanatory prose. We have a Lorenzo who likes to use psychology, who faces the mystery of human feelings and must penetrate them at all costs. To do this he makes full use of ancient myths, references to philosophers and specialized language. But the reader welcomes the fact that together with the above there is also a human being who draws on his experience and observation. To tell the truth, some of the explanations where the poet goes to extremes in his efforts to find rational causes for something are far-fetched indeed. But in general, the evidence is that there is a serious mind at work and also a highly cultured one.

Of different inspiration, although still dealing mostly with love, are the two eclogues — *Corinth* and *Apollo and Pan* — *The Loves of Venus and Mars,* the *Sylvas* and the poem *Ambra*. In these we find a much greater classical influence than is noticed in the works already discussed. Although no precise date can be given to most of Lorenzo's works, one can say with assurance that these belong to his later period.[29] In other words, with greater maturity came a greater interest in classical antiquity, with Lorenzo being probably influenced by the renowned classical scholar and exquisite poet Poliziano, whose works were written in Greek and Latin as well as in the vernacular. But he differs from Poliziano in what we have said was characteristic in Lorenzo, a strong realism and an almost pessimistic consideration of life.

In the *Corinth* Lorenzo creates very skillfully a bucolic atmosphere where everything is harmonious and at peace, except

29. *Corinth, Apollo and Pan* and *The Loves of Venus and Mars* were probably written before 1486; the *Sylvas* and *Ambra* after 1486.

poor Corinth, the shepherd who is at odds with the peace that surrounds him for he loves, but his love is not requited. In the darkness of the night he bewails his fate and speaks to the moon and the elements. It is not necessary to point out the elements of the classical bucolic tradition, which that Lorenzo continues here. In line with the humanistic tradition we find here references to the power of words and of poetry that Lorenzo evokes through ancient myths. And so the breeze and the swaying tree-tops will bring his laments to his loved one. But they also bring a warning, for in harmony with the Quattrocento tradition Galatea is presented with the lesson that the rose imparts by blooming and dying in so brief a time. Lorenzo very skillfully creates the scene of the illumination, where all at once the roses Corinth had seen so many times seem to change and give him a warning. And Corinth then learned that "the flowering of youth a vain thing is."[30]

Lorenzo is not content to leave the matter here, as Poliziano does in his exquisite version of this warning, but finds it necessary to explain to us the meaning of all this by giving us a representation of the cycle of life through reference to the cycle of the seasons. This reminds us of the *Commentary* where the need to explain is triumphant. But this is also in line with his greater realism, as was pointed out previously. And so the warning imparted so lightly by a rose's petals becomes heavy with the weight of the falling fruit. But Lorenzo is also capable of an ironic light touch when his own physical characteristics seem to be those of Corinth.

The *Ambra* has been mentioned above in particular for its strong realism and pessimistic view of life, nature, and man's destiny,[31] which separate Lorenzo somewhat from the generally optimistic views held by the humanists almost to the end of the fifteenth century. This work bears the strong stamp of classical influences. Classical references and reminiscences are used to make the poet's passionate participation less immediate and to distance him somewhat from the savage and brutal struggle he follows with such attention and describes with such care and variations of tone. Like his ancient predecessors, he is creating a myth. We could call it the myth of beauty and the beast, except that while Ambra is lovely, poor Ombrone, who is a god, turns out to have very human feelings and could represent all mankind

30. "...che vana cosa e il giovenil fiorire..." (*Corinth,* 180, p. 202).

31. See p. XII.

in his suffering. Actually Lorenzo has created a myth by which to explain the origins of a place he loved and in which he had a villa where he often sought a respite from the cares of life in the city.

Like the *Corinth,* the second eclogue, *Apollo and Pan,* is steeped in classical references, myths and scenes. With Apollo punished by being exiled to earth for having avenged his son's death by killing the Cyclops Sterope, Lorenzo proceeds to provide the god, now more human, with a paradise on earth. He takes us to a far-away place suitable for the creation of an earthly paradise, but still very clearly named in geographic terms. There he describes a marvelous nature that makes the place so wonderful, for it is the seat of eternal spring. We do notice that in this marvelous setting of eternal qualities there are still tears. The river god Peneus has his daughter, Daphne, turned to a laurel, on the river bank, and by crying "he makes the waters rise so he can caress her. Apollo loves this place because the Daphne he had lost and still bewails is there. And Pan had lost his Syrinx who had been turned to a tree, in whose shade he now sits to find comfort. It is there that to begin his contest with Apollo he sings of the death of Daphnis. The poem was not completed, but we may be sure that when Apollo would have begun his song, he would have bewailed his loss also.

The Loves of Venus and Mars, which Lorenzo left unfinished, is of some interest because of its dramatic form in which there are separate parts each with its protagonist, and because of its depiction of a love which differs from both that of the love lyrics and of the songs composed to celebrate the Carnevale. It is a love which is physical and passionate and which, at least on Venus' side, leaves no room for anything else in its deep yearning. In the songs written for Carnevale we have an invitation to love which is certainly not spiritual, in fact at times it reaches licentiousness, but it is not so intense as to exclude a humorous note, a smile or laughter that preclude passion. Although in the love lyrics there may be a yearning for even a physical love, this yearning is never without a note of gentleness and of something that goes beyond the physical. With Venus love, as stated above, takes the form of a deep, passionate yearning that leaves room for nothing else.

Also produced in Lorenzo's mature period are the two love *Sylvas* on which he seems to have concentrated all his poetic ability with excellent results. In line with the eclogues and other compositions of classical inspiration, the *Sylvas* also have bonds with the Greco-Roman world. The genre itself, of course, goes back to Statius and had been recently taken up by Poliziano.[32] It permits a variety and a change from one motive or topic to another in accordance with the poet's fancy and imagination, which seem to suit Lorenzo very well. While the Laurentian theme of the vanity of life is as present here as in his other works, yet life seems to be filled with the joy of love, beauty and gentle feelings. If the mind seeks relief from sorrow, as in the case of the beloved's absence, it does not abandon the world for fantastic journeys of love as in Ficino, but finds a sense of peace in the hope of the beloved's return and the imagination of the effects of that event. It seeks to oppose to the brutality of reality a vision of idyllic life and peace and beauty, but the idyll is firmly planted in this world in a vision of spring, of shepherds and their peaceful life opposed to his own burdened with the cares of state.

This vision of life is idealized, of course, but also realistic enough to include the peaceful sleep of the shepherds with their loud snoring, and if there has to be a mare, that mare will be pregnant to recall the cycle of life. Links with the classics are evident, particularly with Ovid and Virgil. Various myths are re-presented, and there are interesting personifications of some feelings like jealousy. Also present is a long evocative reminiscence of the Age of Gold when, among other things, man was not tormented by his thirst for knowledge. But most of all there is an exquisite representation of love.[33]

Most of the *Ballads for Festive Occasions* were written in Lorenzo's late period, as were the *Carnevale Songs*.[34] Both of these reflect a closer affinity with the popular Florentine tradition, rather than with the literary tradition of the love poems or the classical of the eclogues and most other compositions of the late period. It has been said that this is due to the "social" aspect of Lorenzo's political position. Be that as it may, we can easily see that these ballads are in harmony with the ballads in Florence, where in the early fifteenth century they had assumed a light,

---

32. For concise information on meters used in Italian, see *Princeton Encyclopedia of Poetry and Poetics*, ed. Alex Preminger (Princeton: Princeton University Press, 1965); *Dictionary of Italian Literature*, ed. Peter and Julia Conway Bondanella (Westport, CT: Greenwood Press, 1979).

33. *Sylva I*, 17–20, p. 224; *Sylva II*, 18ff., pp. 231–61.

34. It is almost impossible to date Lorenzo's works precisely. While the *Carnevale Songs* and the *Ballads* are mostly of the late period, some go back as far as 1467.

playful, and comic note. The topics dealt with include first of all physical love with its pleasant aspects, but also the annoyance felt when the time for its fruition becomes exceedingly long. There is also the rejection of a love that once had seemed attractive.

Themes which had appeared in Lorenzo's other works reappear here with insistence: time that waits for no one, fortune that seems to enjoy ruining our plans, the invitation to enjoy youth while one can, useless repentance for time lost and, more frequently in this tradition, the invective against those who envy us and interfere with our enjoyment of life. The motive of time and loss of youth, with later useless repentance, appears repeatedly with great effect:

Time does so swiftly fly.
The flower of our life will soon be gone.
A gentle heart remember must always
That time with it will sweep all things away.[35]

And the following expresses a stronger sense of sadness and regret:

How many things in youth we justly value!
How beautiful in springtime flowers are!
But when old age so useless does arrive
And nothing but more ills we can expect,
We see the day we've lost when night is near,
And for time lost we can now but repent.[36]

We must add that several of these ballads are as licentious as the poet's compositions celebrating Carnevale.

An important note in Lorenzo's works is the comic one, which ranges from the *Carnevale Songs* to three longer poems of another type. Of these three poems the *Nencia da Barberino* is the most famous.[37] In this work we have the transference of ideals, sentiments, and imagery from a most refined cultural level to the world of the humble, poor peasants and shepherds. It is as if Lorenzo sets out to study the poor people who are

---

35. "Vola l'etate e fugge / presto di nostra vita manca il fiore: / e però dee pensar il gentil core / ch'ogni cosa ne porta il tempo e strugge..." (*Ballads* II, 5–8, p. 315).

36. "O quante cose in gioventù si prezza! / Quanto son belli i fiori in primavera! / Ma quando vien la disutil vecchiezza / e che altro che mal più non si spera, / conosce il perso di quando è già sera / quel che il tempo aspettando pur si strugge" (*Ballads* IX, 9–14, pp. 320–21).

37. The *Nencia* was composed in the period 1473–76.

his subjects and wonders what they must think and feel. And so Lorenzo manages to give us this poem which is a veritable comic masterpiece. The ideals and modes of courtly love are lowered into the every-day world of shepherds with startling and wonderful effects in the way the imagery of one is adapted to the other. At he same time the characters do not become caricatures. Their sentiments are real and as important in their humble lives as the much refined others may be to the poet at his lofty cultural level. Lorenzo understands this and shows much sympathy for these poor people. It is this that separates his work from that of some well-known poets who tried their hand at providing further episodes in this love story, but did not rise above the level of caricature.

The second of these poems, *The Hunt with Falcons,*[38] is also written with an eye to the particular foibles of the characters who appear in it. It is a realistic work in the sense that it is an unassuming description of a hunting party on one of their expeditions. The party is made up of Lorenzo's friends who are presented with a sure touch that manages to single out some particular aspect of their character that is then pounced on to create comic effects. So we have a poet, Luigi Pulci, described as the one with the long nose, whose disappearance from the hunt is seen as a withdrawal into his bizarre poetic world where he is probably writing some venomous sonnet about one of the party. These comic notes are all inserted into what is a matter-of-fact account of a day spent hunting with friends. The hunt is vividly and realistically described with many details so that we feel we are there witnessing these events. It has no abstruse or symbolic meanings; it is simply a day spent with friends. There are no strange encounters or magic transformations as in another famous hunt in Poliziano's *Stanze per la giostra,* in which the hero is Lorenzo's brother. As the poet says at the end, this is simply the way they manage to pass the time pleasantly.

The third of these poems, *Symposium,*[39] also known as *The Topers,* is a parody of Dante's *Commedia* and uses the same *terza rima* employed by the other two poets. Here, too, we have a traveler who narrates his encounters with "sinners," but whereas Dante's sinners span the rainbow of sins, Lorenzo's are all drunkards. Although this at times tends to become somewhat monotonous, there are scenes that are truly comic, such as the

38. *The Hunt* was probably written in 1478.
39. The *Symposium* is from the 1473–78 period.

one that describes a high prelate's method for drinking while proceeding in a procession. The comic effects, of course, would be enhanced if we were familiar with the sinners as Lorenzo and his readers were at that time. The sure comic effects depend on the use of language and of the parody of Dante's work. We must say that the very fact that Lorenzo can be so very irreverent in regards to the *Commedia,* whereas all others seem to approach it as if it were sacred, adds to the enjoyment. And he does not forget Petrarch, who is also made a target of parody, but much less. Since we have mentioned Dante and Petrarch, we should also turn to the third member of the triumvirate, Boccaccio. There are two short stories attributed to Lorenzo — *The Story of Giacoppo* and *The Story of Ginevra* — that are decidedly modeled on stories from the *Decameron.* Both the situations and the style remind us of Boccaccio, although the stories do not develop with the crispness and sagacity of the model.

The *Carnevale Songs*[40] also belong to the late period as shown by the poet's mastery of poetic forms. For comic effect the poet depends mostly on double meanings and a skillful use of a popular, far-from-refined language. Bakers, for instance, vaunt their wares and explain the secrets of their art, an art that is not that of baking bread and biscuits as it turns out. All the situations are openly salacious and ribald with the exception of the seventh song, that of Bacchus and Ariadne, which has become almost symbolic of this entire period, as we said above. Love here has no Petrarchan tones or references to courtly love. It is candidly physical, but with no salacious effects. It is the desperate attempt to seize happiness in a reality that steals it from us. Bacchus and Ariadne embrace each other frantically, "since time flees and us deceives." And then there is the refrain that cannot allow for the coarseness of the other songs. It invites us to be happy, but the final note is always one of regret that negates the rest: youth is beautiful, but time destroys it; be happy now is the invitation, but how can we since happiness is so precarious? As mentioned above, the love of Bacchus and Ariadne is given as the result of their consciousness of time. It is a desperate attempt to wrest happiness out of a reality that denies it. Wine provides another way to seek happiness and make us forget old age, but all it can

40. Although no precise date can be given for the *Carnevale Songs,* most of them seem to be from the late period both because of the technical skill with which they have been composed and for the "social" aspect they share with some of Lorenzo's late works.

do is to create an illusion; reality is always there, as shown by the repeated "in spite of all" that accompanies each attempt at happiness.

Works inspired by philosophical and religious interests can be safely assigned to either Lorenzo's youth or to his mature period, with the *Disputation* and the *Devotional Poems (Capitoli)* written in 1473–74, most of the *Hymns of Praise* in his mature period and the mystery play just a few months before his death in 1492. Lorenzo's philosophical interest was nourished mostly by one of his teachers, the philosopher Ficino, whose influence has already been noted in the discussion of the love lyrics. Lorenzo's *Disputation,*[41] in fact, is almost a paraphrase of two of Ficino's epistles, *De felicitate* and *Oratio ad deum theologica*. The main theme also goes back to Ficino, regarding the primacy of will over intellect. There are also other themes and motives that recur throughout Lorenzo's works. He states that he has left the city with all its cares and sought to restore his spirit in nature, which for him represents all the peace and tranquility he loves, but cannot find in Florence. He proclaims all this to a shepherd he meets in the woods and speaks with bitterness of his burdens of state and family, the dangers he faces,and how he is persecuted. He envies the shepherd for his bucolic existence, which he describes as if it were the mythical Age of Gold. But then Lorenzo's sense of reality penetrates the illusion, which is shattered by the shepherd's realistic presentation of his life with all its hardships and misery. At this point Ficino appears, who is immediately asked to act as judge in the controversy. Ficino, of course, will find that they are both wrong and will then embark on a discourse that will identify happiness with God. And Lorenzo's long work in *terza rima,* the form used by both Dante and Petrarch, will present a paraphrase of Ficino's work.As mentioned above, this is a youthful work that has all the traits of a disciple's awe and respect for his teacher's knowledge.

Psalms, religious hymns, and neo-Platonic texts form the *Devotional Poems* and the *Hymns of Praise.*[42] In these works Lorenzo follows the popular religious tradition, and thus they are the documents of what has been called his "social" aspect and of his relations to the people he governed. In the hymns he usually proceeds as if he were writing a sermon, that is, he

41. The *Disputation* is from the 1473–74 period.

42. The *Devotional Poems* are from the early period, 1473–78, while most of the *Hymns of Praise* were probably written around 1486.

takes some passage from the Bible and then builds on that by explaining and paraphrasing. Of greater interest in the *Devotional Poems* is the sixth, specifically written to bring him out of his own slothfulness. While most of these works of a religious nature seem to be an echo of this popular tradition, in some the poet does reach remarkable poetic expression. The overall impression created is that Lorenzo's desire for peace and tranquility seen in his other works makes him look towards God as a last resort for finding what has escaped him on earth.

Lorenzo wrote the *Mystery Play of Saints John and Paul* to provide his son, member of an acting company of young people under church tutelage, with a play in which to act. It was presented for the first time on February 17, 1491, not long before Lorenzo's death. It is a play well written and of much interest for various reasons. As demanded by this type of composition, human feelings, particularly of a religious nature, do not seem to be very complicated, but are the expression of simple souls, whose basic beliefs and faith are their only guide. In strict relation with this, of course, is the appearance of miracles and their acceptance. Their faith is such that they can accept without blinking the idea, and the materialization, of an army sent by God in answer to the prayers of a defeated general, who is then suddenly converted and turns to God for a new army.

At the same time we have assessments of political life which are well in line with Lorenzo's realistic comments on this subject found throughout his works. We have an emperor who abdicates in his sons' favor because he is too old and tired to continue and tells them that to rule is to live in constant peril and worry, and then proceeds to impart his final lesson.[43] This lesson has nothing new and consists of those ethical concepts and realistic assessments of a ruler's perilous life found here and there in Lorenzo's works. But the real figure of the "prince" is that of Julian the Apostate, whose character is the opposite of the simplicity of the others. His ideas on the state are the result of a cold, clear mind and heart. It is interesting to note that he blames Christianity for Rome's decadence as Machiavelli would do later.

Lorenzo tried his hand at many different genres, not always with the same success, of course. But even in the least of these he was able to give his work literary dignity, and in the more successful he reached real poetic expression and left his stamp on the achievements of a century that was one of the greatest in the

43. *Mystery Play of Saints John and Paul*, 98–101, p. 471.

history of civilization. In addition to his own work, he was at the center of a remarkable group of artists, poets and scholars that he promoted and held together. And what seems most remarkable was that in spite of the cares of state and the successes he achieved as a statesman he was able to hold his own in this genial group of artists. He did indeed earn the title the world bestowed on him: the Magnificent.

NOTE ON THE TRANSLATION

In regards to the translation, the main concerns were to remain as faithful as possible to the original and produce a version both readable and poetic. It soon became apparent that this could not be done if attention was to be paid to rhyme. In the introduction to his *Commentary* Lorenzo himself speaks of the difficulty posed by rhyme: "And as those who have practiced this know, rhyme disrupts many beautiful thoughts, nor does it permit one to express them with ease and clarity." Since there was no desire to disrupt once more Lorenzo's "beautiful thoughts," and the need for clarity seemed paramount, the problem of rhyme, even more difficult in English, had to be resolved. A series of experiments showed that the various metrical forms used by Lorenzo could well survive even if rhyme was greatly reduced, in fact they did not seem to suffer at all. The decision was then made to use rhyme only where it seemed to have an important function, that is, in the last two verses of each *ottava,* where it is necessary to give the sense of completion, and in some of the refrains. To reproduce the rhythms of the Italian verses, iambic pentameter has been used for the Italian endecasyllable, and for the shorter verses of seven or eight syllables three iambi or a combination of an anapest and two iambi have been found to be most satisfactory. The sestina has been retained in its original form. It is a type of poem that has no rhyme, but revolves around the number six, with six words which are used one each at the end of each verse. It consists of six stanzas of six verses each. At the end instead of six, we have a stanza of three verses, each of which contains two of the basic six words. The use of the six words which repeat themselves in each stanza has the forceful effect of hammering. Two of the poets who used the sestina were Dante and Petrarch. The latter, to press his great technical skill, once wrote a sestina not with six, but with twelve stanzas, while meeting all regulations.

The translation of Lorenzo's literary works is complete. It does not concern the epistolary of more than one thousand items because it is not *literary.* The basic sources for the translation are three and have been chosen for their reliability, scholarship and general reputation. They are:

1. Lorenzo de' Medici II Magnifico. *Tutte le Opere.* Ed. Gigi Cavalli. 3 vols. Milan: Rizzoli, 1958.
2. Lorenzo de' Medici. *Tutte le Opere.* Ed. Attilio Simioni. Bari: Laterza, 1939.
3. *Scritti scelti di Lorenzo de' Medici.* Ed. Emilio Bigi. Turin: U.T.E.T, 1965.

Some other editions have been consulted as well.

It is a pleasure to express my thanks to Peter L. Frattarelli for his masterly management of production difficulties. I am also grateful to Carla Adabbo and Antonio Frattarelli for their patience and invaluable technical help. Finally I owe a debt of gratitude to my wife Maria, who not only encouraged my undertaking this work, but patiently listened when difficulties arose and provided most useful suggestions. The author of the translation wishes to express his appreciation to the editors of Italica Press for extending their scrupulous cooperation and for using all their considerable skills and technical knowledge in bringing this book to completion.

The Complete Literary Works of Lorenzo de' Medici

I. LOVE POEMS

Lyrics

I

So cruel and inhumane the first wound was,
So savage was the arrow and so fierce
That had my heart not been by hope sustained
So sweet would death itself have seemed to me.

The young of tender age do not refuse
To follow Love with ever-growing need:
This joyful evil willingly they follow,
For destiny has this allotted them.

But since you wish that I shall serve your flag
With diligence, O Love, you will so act
That my own illness will not others teach.

For merciful you'll be to one who serves
And will a fire instill in that proud woman
So that she will then know what me does ail.

II

The year's sweet time had come when old Tithonus[1]
Completed had a third of all his labors:
His golden rays already did one prick
With gentle warmth that not unpleasant was.

The mountains and the plains were decked in green,
The meadows brilliant were with all their flowers,
The bushes their young leaves did display,
In vain in sorrow Philomel did cry."[2]

And I, who at one time would not have feared
If Hercules himself had here returned,
Was taken by a pair of charming eyes.

---

1. Tithonus was the husband of Aurora (Dawn). He was given the gift of immortality, but not of youth, so that his name is usually accompanied by the adjective old. He is used here to signify the passage of time.
2. The nightingale.

So sweet it was to enter Love's own maze,
But no way out does now the maze provide,
And I am where I must forever burn.

III

Tithonus seven times our hemisphere
And heavy globe already circled has;
For me on earth no sun has there appeared,
No light or splendor has there been for me.

In bitter tears I've seen my joys all change,
And bitter most of all for me has been
That while at first placated Love did seem,
He grew more fierce and cruel and still more cruel.

A sad beginning this for our love is.
Already my first venture I repent.
But only now when I can't help myself,

For in my heart a flame I now feel burning,
A flame that now so fiercely has grown.
Let all beware before by Love they're seized.

IV

Sonnet Written for a Lady Who Had Gone to the Country

O happy countryside, green fields and woods,
Bountiful trees and those that bear no fruit,
Green grass and shrubs and thickets dense with thorns,
And joyful meadows that reflect my love.

Tall, shady, craggy mountains, hills and slopes.
And rivers that collect the flowing springs;
All animals together tamed and wild,
And you, O nymphs, O satyrs, fauns and gods:

The time has come to heed no more Diana[3];
Your realm now sees another goddess come
Who also holds a bow and quiver bears.

---

3. Diana was the goddess of chastity and of the woods, so that nymphs, satyrs, and other inhabitants of her domain were her subjects.

Her prey she takes where Pan does not hold sway,[4]
And those she injures she then turns to stone,
Just as Medusa once was wont to do.[5]

V

The sun that your dark way did brightly light,
And such a comfort was to your poor sight,
Is now no longer there, nor will it be.
Cry then forever since deprived you are.

To bitter winter has my joyful spring
Been now transformed. The season that more joy
I thought would bring, now only grief does offer.
And only now I see what Love's face is.

And if so sweet at first the arrow seemed,
And the first blow so sweet did once appear,
And if at first Love's service joy did bring,

To sorrow has that happiness been changed.
To a blind pit a pleasant road did lead,
Where I have fallen and must ever burn.

VI

O happy land where still my lady dwells,
Who holds in her two hands my heart's own fate,
And she ordains my sorrow and my joy:
A thousand times each day I live and die.

At times she gives me pain, at others joy.
Now joy, now pain does ever fill my soul.
And so my doubtful heart she does maintain
In joy, in tears, now it must live, now die.

Happy are you above all other lands
For you do see two suns arise each day.
So bright is one, the orb feels envy rise.

My eyes have seen six moons all come and go
But have not seen the light that soothes my heart,
Yet like the Phoenix my true sun I'll follow.

---

4. Among men, since Pan held sway over flocks and herds.
5. Medusa was a Gorgon who would turn to stone anyone who looked in her eyes.

VII

My eyes could not withstand at any time
Those rays so bright that from her own did come.
My own poor eyes could never firmly stand
The light emitted by her lovely eyes.

Admiring them against all reason seems.
From heaven they descend and are so bright
That they do not permit a mortal mind
To gaze upon and the divine embrace.

From earth she does not come, from heaven yes.
To man has she been sent: a gift divine.
To earth she has descended, here to dwell.

To look at her is then to be at peace,
But I for sure in sorrow do remain.
To others peace she gives, to me just war.

VIII

This weak and frail poor little bark of mine[6]
So tossed and battered is by stormy waves,
So filled with water it already is
That it will sink, so heavy are my thoughts.

Since plaints in vain have been for such a long time,
And since our prayers Neptune does not hear,
How safe her course can be we all can see,
Threatened by reefs and tossed by tallest waves.

I see the winds oppose me more and more.
Fortune and Love, who firmly steers the boat,
Told me that fear docs not help us at all:

Adversity requires that we still hope.
The same advice it seems that reason gives
For he shall win who to the end endures.

IX

Fortune with ease could happiness bestow,
But she did me deny, deaf to my prayers.
Nor did she want to favor me at all —
Lest one should say that happiness he found —

6. Cf. Petrarch, *Rime* 189.

And did not favor her for whom so hard
Did Nature labor then to make it clear
That she who mortal had to me appeared
Could not a denizen of our world be.

But here she now appears, she lacks just breath.
As real and live and close to her true form
As master's skill could only her portray.

But if the master who portrayed her true
The virtue she embodied could reveal,
Where would then Phidias be or Polycletus?[7]

X

O gentle lady mine, who all surpass
Among the moderns and the ancients, too,
Your journey did leave me without my star
And deep in grief my stricken soul then was.

To comfort me did Fortune take me then
To that small temple that you did adorn.
A ray of light appeared that was so bright,
That other things dark seemed to be to me.

I could not bear to look, so I then thought
Of light so bright the source a gem must be,
A precious stone, a jewel of such deep splendor

You to adorn, but you did it surpass.
But then to me the truth did come: your eyes,
Only your eyes could stars so brilliant be.

XI

Sonnet Composed in Reggio on Returning from Milan Where I Had News That a Woman Was Ill

Afraid that Jove again to love would fall,
The Thunderer's own sister then did act[8];
And Venus was afraid that fiery Mars,
Her old dear lover, would astray then go.

7. The original has a third name, Praxiteles, omitted for reasons of meter. The three were great Greek sculptors.

8. Juno was both sister and wife of Jove, the Thunderer.

The goddess of the woods, the chaste Diana,
So envy did the beauty great and new.
And Pallas[9] could not stand that mortal woman
More beautiful and chaste on earth could be.

The sacred limbs they made both weak and feeble.
Honored they should have been, not made to suffer.
In heaven, too. O envy, you hold sway!

If you remember still your first true love
And pity moves you still, O blond Apollo,[10]
Restore my happiness. You can I know.

XII

To this beloved place I often come
From which my wounded soul cannot depart,
For here I once would find both rest and peace.
Flint it once was, my flame it now does feed.

And this the reason was that by degrees
I moved away from Love and turned my back
To gain the laurel I so much desired,
In search of which I have so hoarse become.

Her face have I seen here splendid with light,
Her sacred eyes such brilliant rays gave forth
That mortals never could their light sustain.

This place joy gave me once, now only woe.
Bereft it is and all I love it lacks:
Thus often gains do losses turn to be.

XIII

These eyes of mine will ever have no tears?
This flood of tears will never be curtailed?
I do not know, but if my heart speaks true,
Afraid I am her back has Fortune turned.

So sweet my life once was, in feast I lived
And in the rays of my warm sun I basked.

---

9. Athena.

10. Apollo loved Daphne who fled from him and begged the gods to save her. They did by turning her into a tree that bears her name, the laurel.

While up above of love the god did smile
And all propitious was to happy living.

The sacred light has now from me been taken
That in the maze the way to me did show,
And in confusion, blind I now remain.

And if this path the way to death should be
I'm not surprised for I can't sec my end,
And what the future holds a secret is.

XIV

The tree Apollo once did love so much,[11]
To which no other plant can e'er compare,
More happy for itself and for its lover
So green and shady was once here on earth.

And then, I don't know why or through whose fault,
Apollo did remove his sacred rays
From both the happy plant and lovely visage,
So that now tears and sorrow reign supreme.

The green and happy leaves their color changed.
The laurel, once so shady, so luxuriant.
Then wilted as it lost the sacred rays.

Always are pain and sorrow here at hand.
How easy 'tis for smiles to change to tears.
'Tis better not to hope in future joys.

XV

I wish and seek what I do most dislike.
For greater love of life, I seek my end.
To save myself from death. I do death call.
I do seek quiet where peace there never was.

I do pursue what harms and what I flee.
My foe I love more than I love myself.
Of bitter food I never sated am.
I do want freedom, but to serve I like.

In fire I do ice seek, in pleasure pain.
And life in death I seek and war in peace.
To flee I wish and do myself tie down.

---

11. See n. 10 above.

In stormy seas my little bark I steer.
To stay at sea I can't nor head for shore,
And fear has driven out reason and care.[12]

XVI

With bitter sighs and deepest sorrow filled,
With various thoughts so bowed, so sad and weary,
I lead my life, what years do still remain,
As pleases one who still my mistress is.

If Fortune will proceed ahead on course,
I think I shall soon come to such a pass
That sorrows will no longer wrack me so,
And she who is their cause will then have pity.

And so among sad sighs and wistful tears
I shall go on with life until the moment
When Clotho and her sisters the thread cut.[13]

My heart will then not suffer any pain
If her desire by dying I obey,
For death at her command is life to me.

XVII

SESTINA I

How many times for having too much hope,
Since first I found myself a slave of Love,
A flood have I then shed of bitter tears.
Mow often I. while I did hope for peace,
Did beg those sacred eyes to give me life;
As lesser evil then, I begged for death.

In such a state I'm now that if dear death
Abandons me, so will my only hope,
So wretched, so unhappy is my life.
Is this what you did promise us, sweet Love?
Is this what we invoke, our dreamed-of peace?
If we can peace call woes, sad plaints and tears.

To hope of finding more in Love than tears,
Or life that wretched is much less than death,

12. Cf. Petrarch, *Rime* 134.

13. The Fates: Lachesis assigns the lot, Clotho spins the thread of life, and Atropos severs it.

Or to enjoy if but one hour of peace,
To live in dreams it is, fallacious hope.
For nothing else it is to be in love
Than dying a thousand deaths each day of life.

So peaceful once, so tranquil was my life!
One cannot know the bitterness of tears
If first become one doesn't a slave of Love.
He will then know a life that is like death,
And how a fool one is to harbor hope,
And how denial awaits desire for peace.

To call this life is then to banish peace
Forever more from this our mortal life.
And judge that evil stems always from hope.
For hope subjects us all to bitter tears,
And hope does make us bear a living death,
And worst of all it makes us slaves of Love.

As soon as gentle heart does welcome Love,
Desire is joined by strongest hope for peace
That can be driven out by only death;
I do not mean the death of this our life,
But of that love that causes mortal tears:
This of a better life is our sole hope.

I, who don't hope to have the grace of Love
And must live on in tears and with no peace,
Shall find a belter life, I'm sure, in death.

XVIII

Canzone I

O Love, I see that satisfied you're not
With my eternal grief,
For other bonds and chains
You forge more bitter still and ever stronger
Than those you had before; and so my hope
For favor and your grace.
The wind has swept away
And death to me remains as my last hope.
Unwary, dull and blind
Is a poor lover's mind!
In eyes so pure and lovely

That fierceness did there dwell who could believe?
Nor did it seem that harshness
In such a lovely face from us could hide.
My life I did so put in alien hands,
And I do think myself I'll never be.

My ancient freedom now I appreciate.
The fair and happy time.
The tranquil state of mind
That Fortune's favor once bestowed on me.
Then like good things that can't forever last.
Did Fortune take it back,
And she and Love together
To now torment and hound me did agree,
As if of such a force
A part would not suffice
Against just one who strives
To tie his bonds himself always more tight.
Naive and simple fool.
Beyond the golden glow I did not look.
My hands did weave the cord for binding me
So that a slave I could of myself make.

A simple animal, a little bird
If e'er a snare or trap
That threatens them discover
That will for sure disturb their future peace
Will keep their eyes wide open all the time,
For nature does command
That we our life defend.
Yet while I see that Love deceitful is,
I do pursue my way,
Though I do know the past
And evil yet to come,
And also know the fate of hundreds more.
But Love has so succeeded
To kill in me all vestiges of reason.
That I don't want a remedy to find
To take from me the wish in love to burn.

So overwhelming Love's deceit has been,
And so my age-long woes,
That I cannot now find
A threat to peace of mind, if not myself.

For nothing do I look, nor ever strive,
If not to fool myself,
And to my woes I add,
And as an evil thing my safety see.
With sighs and sorrow ever
I do enjoy to be.
I hate all those who try
The yoke to take from me and leave me free.
If one to tie me tries.
It seems to me as if he would free me.
Thus harm I do enjoy, of good complain.
Of what I seek I do myself deprive.

Thus Love and Fortune, enemies of mine,
In doubt and frail hope
And sure and deepest sorrow
For more than five long years have held me bound;
And in the midst of fraud and bold deceit.
Under so cruel a mistress,
The best sweet years of youth
I have consumed and now no joys remain.
O Love, you know how true
How faithful I have been,
So surely I should see
Some signs of mercy that you meant for me.
So near is now the realm
Of her who only fools hope to avoid,
That should by joy at last my years be crowned.
It still would not make up for what I've lost.

My dear song now our plaints do secret keep
And bitter dire laments
You must not show in any place at all.
Your bitter torment you must secret keep
Till Fortune, Love, or Death do us assist.

XIX

I do not know what destiny of mine
To me opposed or planet bearing evil
Has made my life resemble death itself,
A life as happy once as it should be.

Love knows quite well how constant I have been.
Firm as a rock and like a diamond hard.

If false opinions love do take from me,
I bear the onus with no fault of mine.

Though evil Fortune can oppose me so[14]
And cause strong rage and scorn in me to rise,
It never can make me my path abandon.

In tears and sorrow I prefer to stay
And my true Lord and first old flag obey,
Rather than tired of tears another serve.

XX

Love promised me at peace one day I'd be
And in his realm to keep me full of joy,
But evil Fortune all our plans destroys
And future hopes does all for me make vain.

A lovely face that pity does adorn
To meet my death now happy makes me go,
But Fortune hates both me and what mine is
And does leave me my sighs and all my pain.

How this long war will end, I do not know,
What its outcome will be, whose prey I'll be
Despite my hopes and all that I have borne.

The heavens Love did conquer after all,
On earth alone does Fortune have its way.
I can then hope my tears will dried soon be.

XXI

Love that is ever paired with jealousy
My every thought did guide and step by step
Led me where happiness had once been mine,
But now decided has it must not be.

As I my eyes did turn a glimpse I caught
Of golden tresses that did float on air[15];
The sun intent in admiration was,
And he did stop his rolling chariot there.

---

14. The theme of Fortune is an important one in Petrarch's poetry, and equally so in that of the Petrarchan poets of the fifteenth and sixteenth centuries.

15. Cf. Petrarch, *Rime* 90.

An evil thought at once then came to me:
I feared that love once more had Phoebus struck.
A short time only did suspicion last.

I soon did see that rival he was not.
A brief time only did he stop and tarry,
In awe or envy hard to tell it is.

XXII

The sun has now its ancient course resumed.
His wonted splendor Phoebus[16] has regained.
Now one and then the other sun so shines
That icy winter has like spring become.

If only mine would gracious, friendly be
Just like the one whose rays the earth does brighten,
My soul an end would find to all its grief,
An end to bitter life so cruel and dire.

Resplendent more than ever Phoebus is,
His rays more brilliant are than is his wont,
More strong and hot and bright his flames do burn.

His change was wrought by fear that two bright stars
Would him outdo in beauty, light and splendor.
And that the earth could boast a greater boon.

XXIII

Five times the sun its course completed has
Since thoughts of love my soul did first besiege
And since did Love hold me in bonds and chains,
And Fortune still, alas, the same course steers.

As fate has now decreed and I can see,
Cancelled have been my tears, my sighs and prayers,
Verses and words that ink cannot express
And hope that my poor heart did once sustain.

Only one comfort now remains to me,
For all the rest does make me wish for death,
That most unjust was Love in treating me.

---

16. Apollo, the Sun.

A gentle soul can have no happier fate
Than knowing well that life of use has been,
And that each hour so brief has well been spent.

XXIV

Sonnet Written for a Certain Matter That Every Day Showed Itself in a Thousand Different Forms

The jeers of Fortune ever follow me;
Always she offers hopes, but all in vain.
A sudden change then comes and she does show
That all we see or think mere shadows are.

Benevolent at times, and then so bitter,
With heavy cares she burdens me, then frees.
Vain fears and shadows tear my soul apart,
But unaware it is of pressing danger.

By nature we do fear, grow sad and cheer
A thousand times a day or even more.
We are by evil cheered, saddened by good.

For harm we hope and our own good we fear,
So little wisdom do we show in life.
How vain are cares and thoughts the end will show.

XXV

Growing in me from day to day I feel
The ardent flame that ever burns my heart.
While hope that once sustained now feeble grows,
And with that hope all joy abandons me.

Life flees from me and hurries fast away.
Fortune opposes all for which I strive.
So I return to days and nights ill spent,
And there I dwell with my sad tears and sorrows.

The grief that always was so sweet to me,
The plaints, the sighs, the tears that followed Love,
Hope sweet for me did make and made me cherish.

But now that hope no longer is with me,
My grief must grow and be no longer sweet,
And death of all the sorrows least will be.

XXVI

Those lovely eyes that give or take away
Power from Love, as they may wish or please,
Have made and make me hate so much my peace
That I see it as source of all my grief.

And though of my eternal harm I think,
And time that flees and does abandon us,
And evil thoughts of mine, vain and fallacious,
I do not recognize a clear deceit.

My fatal way I blindly still pursue,
Nor will I stop unless my love or death
Turn me aside from this dire path of mine.

The time of life that Fate to me does grant
To her I give for only she can aid
My troubled heart some sort of rest to find.

XXVII

I do not know who is my greatest foe.
Malignant Fortune, Love most fierce and cruel,
Or can it be excessive hope[17] that makes
The sweet old lire of love burn high and grow?

Fortune disrupts for me all friendly thought,
My fiery ardor Love does still increase.
My hope my soul does help to keep alive,
And I with sweetness always feed my heart.

Asperity so bitter never was
As is such sweetness now, or death so cruel.
As is my life for all its burning hope.

Benignant more to me let Fortune be
Or Love or hope show less hostility,
Or let then death take me and all these, too.

XXVIII

A simple little bird that nature guides,
On seeing the snare that ready is to spring,
Will flee at first, but later will succumb,
Recalled by tender songs of other birds.

---

17. For the theme of excessive hope, see *Sylva II,* 67–83, pp. 232–33.

Just so I, too, do flee those loving eyes
Where snares are set against my peace of mind.
Sweet words and glances then will make me run
To meet my grief as if to joy I went.

And what in others time will bring about,
In me accomplished is through diverse ways,
For less than ever my own ill I know.

Mindless and blind, I let myself be guided
By my blind foe through treacherous dark ways.
So in the end I've reached a dark blind pit.

XXIX

I did my lady see among green leaves
Close to a brook with happy women stay.
Never was she more beautiful or kind
In all the time my heart for her has burned.

This did indeed desire just sate in part
And gave my soul to be consoled good reason,
But when she left. I felt my heart would stop
And even more my thoughts and sorrow grew.

The sun was slowly setting towards the west,
Dark shadows did the earth already cover,
And my own sun herself elsewhere did hide.

That first sweet sight my mind more sad did make.
How short a time good things on earth do last,
But memory a longer lime prevails.

XXX

Canzone II

I thought, O Love, that now the time had come
To put an end to my eternal tears
And bitter grief of mine;
And you and Fortune, that so evil is,
Would not my ill pursue yet further now.
For if you should then want,
As proper is for such a mighty lord,
To grant at least what you did promise me
(So much, so many times!)

It would be hard, though you almighty are.
My soul, my flesh, my bones.
Your promise all of them did bind to you.
You know how long, and even more do I.
For this great hope of mine
I did in youth serve you, and now I'm old.

I lived well satisfied with such a fate
And my poor troubled heart, only sustained
With sight of my beloved.
Her splendor so divine, her lovely eyes,
My soul did calm though sorrowful and sad.
This sweet the hardships made
That I so long for love did undergo.
Our hopes for future happiness will make
Our present ills seem less.
But evil Fortune that my good did envy
All things did then upset.
My tranquil state, my happy fate from me
Did take and sight of her for whom I pine.
Better would death have been
Than being denied of bright eyes the sight.

Sustain my soul is all that I can do
With memories of her most lovely face.
To her divine ways now
A thousand times a day I turn my mind.
Though Fortune takes from me those lovely eyes
And my tranquility,
My eyes always in woods, in vales, in streams
And where my soul my body may transport,
At night or light of day.
Always their only splendid sun do see.
The words so sweet she said
Still now to me resound always so clear,
For memories of what we justly love,
Though we grow old and weary,
In gentle heart never can time destroy.
The highest and loneliest hills I always seek[18]
And always there my poor tired eyes I turn
Where I did leave my love,
There where my heart does sadly still remain.

18. Cf. Petrarch, *Rime* 129.53–65.

Of this I nourish it and with the hope
That sated soon will be
My eyes that tears have shed for such a long time
(Unless I am all wrong and death will come).
This thought now helps to soothe
My grief in part and comfort gives my soul.
I patiently support
My bitter fate and my unjust exile
Until once more will happier times return.
Should evil longer last,
An hour can us repay for all lost days.

There, O my song, do go
Where my heart is unless shut is the way
As it to me now is. The trail do follow.
Do say my life is happy,
Since I have heard my absence she laments.

XXXI

If Love should happen some brief joy to offer
My soul to comfort after such long trials,
The more I value this so wanted good
The more content I'd be and should rejoice.

If some event does favor me some time,
My hope on high does rise beyond belief.
As much as my desire my grief docs grow
And multiplied my thoughts and worries are.
If comfort I received that day there when
My love I saw with other ladies 'round
Amidst green leaves and near an icy brook,

Now that I'm far away, of her deprived,
To my old tears I turn, and what I did
Most like now most my heart does burn and grieve.

XXXII

Sestina II

I feel returning that so sweet a time,
Which I cannot recall if not with tears,
That a beginning gave to my harsh life
And never more I saw my own sweet freedom.

To bring it back again into my mind,
Remember it I must forced now by Love.

His victory always remembers Love 2
And so he wants that both season and time
In verses be extolled and kept in mind.
Content he's not with all my sighs and tears,
But happy I must be of my lost freedom
In this abysmal, sad and tearful life.

If he in fact the lord is of my life, 3
I must perforce the bidding heed of Love
And bid farewell to my old cherished freedom,
Which let itself be overcome that time,
When it was not accustomed yet to tears,
Submit it will, with now my slavish mind.

If I to others body gave and mind 4
And so for this afflicted is my life,
I only can myself blame for the tears.
And must not ever think of blaming Love,
For if he did hold me for such long time,
It is because for this I gave him freedom.

No more can one its own call my lost freedom: 5
A present then of it did make my mind.
If Love wants me to celebrate that time
And of all this be happy in my life,
He'll have his way, and I'll accede to Love,
And happy as he wants I'II be of tears.

Not only am I happy in my tears, 6
But I do hate and so renounce my freedom.
I should not ever wish to not serve Love,
And if a thought arrive should in my mind
Once more to gain my freedom in my life,
I'd hate it and deem lost all other time.

Happy and gay the time and sweet the tears 7
In which my life abandoned its own freedom:
So deems my mind and so demand does Love.

XXXIII

O blessed home that then accustomed were
My plaints to hear and my most bitter tears,

Preserve the sacred image of her eyes,
As worthless scorn all other things around.

O waters, O clear spring that so sweet are
And with your murmuring did share my grief
Just a short time ago, your tears abandon.
Do join me now and change them all to song.

O bed, of my eternal tears true witness,
With sorrowful, deep sighs I did fill you;
O study mine that shelter gave my grief,

Our sorrow Love has now to joy transformed
By showing us her visage most serene,
And I know not why death I now delay.

XXXIV

The time I've waited for is now approaching.
My faith is now about to be rewarded.
The time for granting mercy fast arrives,
And my poor soul does quake and fear the more.

As if it were a stranger to itself,
It seems to be all lost in disbelief,
For in the past deceived it had oft been,
Though true it seems, my soul to doubt inclines.

All this because it does unworthy feel
Of such a boon, and so all pale it trembles
When it compares itself to such a beauty.

Or Love himself has shown and taught my soul
To be in doubt as it desires and fears,
For one can faint when sweetness will exceed.

XXXV

By Love conducted, I the top had reached
Of all my hopes as time was fast approaching.
What one desires and hopes was then so near
For which I have so sighed and have shed tears.

And then a voice I heard that makes me quake,
Most cruel and unjust, severe and rigid:
"Mad is your hope and mad your proud desire
For seeking that which stands alone supreme.

Let it suffice for you to see my eyes
And hear the harmony of words and voice
And contemplate the lofty, sacred virtues.[19]

If more than that of me you wish to have,
It is in vain; if more your heart will want,
Let it then blame not me, but mad desire."

XXXVI

Sonnet Composed for a Friend

The One who lifted was on up to heaven[20]
Did not there see a thing of such great beauty,
Nor was such harmony then heard when Argus[21]
The other heard to his own detriment,

Nor does the phoenix at its end collect
So many fragrances for its own pyre,[22]
Nor was so sweet the fruit that Adam ate
And so did bring us down on earth to grieve.

Nor with such sweetness Love did ever grace
A lover he did wish to satisfy,
As mine is now, and other thoughts it bans.

The bow, the sacred arrows I do bless
And the just cause that did my freedom take,
Since such a recompense you grant me now.

XXXVII

Never to taste your sweetness, O my Love,
Or by your grace be blessed better would be,
For, if to grief a soul accustomed is,
All sorrow's will it bear without complaint.

And so does one desire and value more
The good he knows and will then grieve much more

---

19. Cf. *Commentary* VI, pp. 105–7.

20. 2 Cor 12:2–4.

21. Argus of the hundred eyes was put to sleep by a melody and killed by Mercury.

22. Mythical bird from Arabia. Every five hundred years it prepared its own pyre with fragrant wood, burned itself to ashes and was immediately reborn.

If Fortune bans, destroys or interrupts
That which he holds and has for long possessed.

What I desired when yet I knew it not
And sought when new and hazy it still was
So very near death had then brought me.

I have now seen it, understood and known.
Just think, O Love, how dire my fate must be
Now that deprived I've been of such a treasure.

XXXVIII

Sweet thoughts of mine, do not as yet depart.
Where will you leave me. O sweet thoughts of mine?
Is this the way my tired feet you will guide
To the sweet arbor where my love resides?

Not here is Zephyr, nor does Flora dance.[23]
No grass, no flowers do the slopes adorn.
Cold sleet and wind, dark shadows, deepest fear,
Woods, rocks and rivers do my feet impede.

You leave me now and go to her who still
Your safe, sweet harbor is and of my heart,
And I remain alone in these dark shadows.

To my blind feet does Love point out the way,
For with me are always those two bright stars
That are the only light to strike my eyes.[24]

XXXIX

Sonnet Composed before a Canvas with the Portrait of a Woman

O my dear image, you the haven are,
The harbor of my thoughts and of my cares;
With you I cry and comfort find in you,
When I can hope and when I suffer fear.

At times as if you were alive and present.
Of wrongs and all deceits I will complain.

---

23. Zephyr is the wind of spring, and Flora the goddess of flowers.

24. See the explanation to verse 13 of Sonnet IX in the *Commentary*, pp. 111–13.

So my vain thoughts do carry me away
That if that state could last, I'd be content.

But then new sighs from my poor heart arise.
Of tears my eyes a very river shed
And all my sorrows quickly are renewed.

At last my wretched soul does realize
That both my prayers and my words are vain,
And to my old desires I must return.

XL

Canzone III
Written during a Woman's Illness

Through many paths and many varied ways
My loyalty to him oft Love did test,
As he did please and I did often tell;
And though a thousand bonds he added on
He still had doubts of my fidelity:
More tightly bound he wanted me to be.
At first in early times the thought he had
That if that pure, celestial, glorious face
Would turn hard eyes on me,
In fear my quest I would abandon soon;
And so the fire of love
Never did burn within my lady's heart,
And so rejoice she seemed at my deep sorrow.
No greater grief there is
Than seeing another laugh as we shed tears.

And for a time like this did Love keep me
So that I never felt another joy
Than seeing celestial beauty here on earth.
This is what bind and constrain me did:
Content I was to be before such grace,
In peace and happy in the midst of war.
Since I most firm remained and did not waver,
As he could see, new plans Love did then forge:
With a small flame he warmed
The proud and haughty heart of my fair lady,
Not much, but just enough
To give some cause for raising hope in me
And in the midst of woes keep me alive.

And then with stronger verve
His treachery and fraud he did redouble.

How painful was my sorrow at that time
And what a torment was my cruel harsh fate
Is difficult to say or to believe.
My sighs and tears my only comfort were.
Of all my hopes just death did then remain
And only there I thought I should find mercy.
But my full constancy and perfect faith
Did not for sorrow fade and were not lost,
But greener yet they grew,
As greater grew my sorrow and torment.
Amidst such great harsh woes
Her beauty present was to give me aid
And make me deem a trifle all my woes.
Love soon became aware
And thought of something new and a new game.

And so he did most gently Fortune beg
To look and find all possible new things
That would my lady bother and dismay,
And she, who ready is to importune,
The ultimate trial did decide to make,
And so her heart she filled with various ills.
My lady was so sad and so in grief
And ever more she would have been aggrieved,
But she of this was freed,
As Love and Fortune did together want.
Her health and her well-being
In her true lover's hands they willed to put,
And then it was that Love true proof received
Of his eternal love
And what his constant faith from him deserved.

When he had done all this, his golden arrow
Love put aside and drew a leaden one
That love does kill and pierced my lady's heart,
And from that time my poor green hopes did not
Ever again my sun's warm rays enjoy.
Bereft of any hope was my poor soul.
And so the love that in my heart did burn
That gentle makes the soul and worthy, too,
Almost to scorn did turn,

And such a wrong was difficult to bear.
So great was the chagrin
At such ingratitude the heart then felt
That it almost abandoned Love's own colors,
But once again it burned
At thought of how unique her beauty was.

When Love then saw that all his tricks were vain,
Of a new one the thought he entertained:
The cause he would remove for my firm faith,
For if remove he would her loveliness,
He thought, there would no reason be for faith,
And to this end he did his mind then turn.
Of her great beauty he a part did take
By making her sweet face become so pale
That heaven did show us
Down here on earth and where all good resided.
My grief did this increase,
But my true faith of old decrease did not,
For neither sorrows, tears nor labors can
From me my faith remove,
Nor can you, Love, her beauty take away.

If you deprive then will of all her beauty
This gentle flower most beloved, pure
And of this lovely phoenix take the plumes,
You take your own preeminence away,
Yourself deprive of your supreme distinction,
Of the foundation of your happy state,
The very thing that happiness gave you.
This beauty of your reign the pillar is,
She gives you fame and vaunted daring, too.
Your name she will transmit
To future generations ever more.
While she on earth endures
Of this blind world of ours leader and guide,
So will your strength endure, so will your valor,
But if that splendid light
Extinguished is on earth, so will Love be.

Do not, O Love, with others ever share
What is yours only, honor real and true.
Do pit your own great strength against blind death!
Prevent, O Love, what both of us will rue,

Do remedy at once your empire's ruin.
For this do now defeat malignant fate
So that this gentle soul with her own body,
That has made you content and worthy both,
Will here on earth remain,
As I will, too; my life from her depends.
By now you must well know
That my fidelity is whole and firm.
Of me no more do now, O Love, seek proof.
My loyalty true is.
Your powers and your plans do elsewhere use.

Dear song do go beg Love
Not to delay himself to aid and save
For in dire peril I his empire see.
So near is his destruction
That it will be too late if he delays.

XLI

Sonnet Composed While Going along the Seashore in Maremma

With heavy steps and slow and troubled mind,
I seek through every path so hard and steep
The dens of savage beasts so wild and fierce
Where the Tyrrhenian sea the shore does bathe,

To see if sight of new and varied things
Can calm my soul and give some rest to me,
For always present are before my eyes
The ones that open did my ancient wound.

If to the left I look in some dark den
Among the leaves I then see her appear,
A new Diana that dark places brightens,

And to the right I see the salty waves
Where Thetis'[25] reign it seems she has usurped us
And so with me is ever my sweet sorrow.

---

25. A Nereid, mother of Achilles, here presented as a goddess queen of the sea.

XLII

Sonnet Composed Because of a Dream[26]

More beautiful than ever but less proud.
My dearest foe did Love then bring to me,
When all the cares and worries brought by day
Deep sleep at night in kindness did remove.

To me she seemed as she had always been
With only her old harshness laid aside,
Replaced by her embracing Love's warm rays.
More true than truth the dream to me did seem.

At first I was so slow, afraid to speak
As I was wont to be, but then desire
Did overcome my fear and I then spoke.

But as I said, "My lady," like the wind
She fled, and thus from me she did at once
Herself, my sleep, my just reward then steal.

XLIII

That proudest look so lethal to our eyes
That did all beauty cancel by her presence,
To have a few days' respite I had fled
And blind Love's arrows in my war with him.

But Love himself or fatal destiny
That did resent my respite from my sorrow
With pious mien my basilisk did show me.
How vain it is, alas, with Love to struggle.

That time of year when farthest from us is
The chariot Phaeton[27] drove so very ill,
When our minds see what they would most desire,

Her lovely visage scorn did not express.
The touch of beauty that before she lacked
Pity did add to that proud visage then.

---

26. See Petrarch, *Rime* 302.

27. Phaeton, son of Apollo, tried to drive the Sun's chariot, but did so badly. Because of the damage he caused, he was hurled down into the Po river.

XLIV

Of your uncertainty, O Love, am I
So certain that by not resting I rest.
I see though blind I am and you affirm
Most steadily your great mobility.

Most clear to me suspicions are and doubts,
I laugh when tears I shed, my woes I sing;
No pleasures do I have but woes and sorrows,
Bitter is sweet and harsh most gentle is.

Only my darkness does on me shed light,
Desire I know not what I want
And for excessive courage often fear.

My eyes are dry and yet I cry a flood.
I change my ways and as I'm used to act,
And to desire my death I stay alive.

XLV

I'm leaving you, O sweet dear thoughts of mine,
And I abandon all my cares of love,
For Fortune so unjust and harsh with me
Compels my doing that which I don't want.

Sweet tears and sighs so tender yet so cruel,
Vain hopes and doubtful most uncertain fears
That my frail nature did in turmoil set,
Abandon her, to other hearts do move.

Verses and rhymes in which all my laments
Sweet were and which did comfort my deep sorrow
While I remained in happy servitude,

Against my will I leave you but consent
To the foreseen deceit since I am forced,
But so be it since such my dire fate is.

XLVI

What I once loved with my most strong desire
Does now displease and even more disturb.
What once did give me happiness and peace
Now wages war on me and my grief causes.

Happy times now dire and most grievous are,
Now dead is my desire that once did bum.
And my fond hopes that once so fervent were
To fear have turned and fear becomes desire.

Time, which to me once seemed to move so slow,
Now swiftly flies away more than swift leopard.
Thus Fortune upside down has turned my world.

To bitter, sweet has turned, to tears has joy,
So lazy I am now. in all things slow,
Bui more than ever swift, towards death I fly.

XLVII

Sestina III

Love has so held me tight from time to time 1
With promises that false all are and vain,
That I have just become of waiting tired,
And of his false deceit now more than certain
And of my long and ever bitter labor
Grief now is my reward, shame, ire and scorn.

And what does add to my most bitter scorn 2
Is that I have so lost my youthful time
That I regain cannot for gold or labor.
That our desires now are and were all vain,
If ever I had doubts, I am now certain,
And this has made me grieve and made me tired.

Of other things, too, but of thought I'm tired, 3
And now against myself I feel my scorn.
Of good in doubt I am, of evil certain.
The punishment for one who wastes time
Is to repent for having lived in vain,[28]
And our deep shame the fruit of all our labor.

Vain is of all poor mortals their own labor, 4
But he who follows Love and is not tired,
Drawn by false flattery and all so vain,
And as unworthy holds all else in scorn
More than all others wastes efforts and time,
And his mistake clear is and is most certain.

28. Cf. Petrarch, *Rime* 1.12–13.

If I had been, as now I am, so certain 5
How vain it is to strive and to do labor
At Love's command, and how is lost the time,
I might perhaps of striving soon have tired,
But I the bonds and chains now only scorn,
Now that all hope to free myself is vain.

To what extent our passions are in vain, 6
To what extent are grief and tears all certain,
And how most useless is our mortal scorn,
To what extent is lost all human labor
Is shown by what of flight is never tired
And all things steals and sweeps far away: time.[29]

Away sweeps time, and all my works are vain. 7
And I am tired, but I am also certain,
And all my labor and myself I scorn.

XLVIII

How vain it is for us to ever hope,[30]
How wrong it is for us to ever plan,
How our world is with ignorance so filled
Death does show us and all of us does teach.

With song and dance and jousting some do live,
Others their minds will turn to noble tasks,
Others the world and all its things do scorn.
Others what burns within do never show.

Vain cares and thoughts and diverse roles and fates,
Diversity that Nature offers us,
Are always seen in this, our erring world.

All things are fleeting. Little do they last
For Fortune here a constant evil is.
Here Death alone forever more firm is.

---

29. For the theme of the flight of time and the vanity of human action, see *Disputation* II.112ff., pp. 388–91, and III.1ff., pp. 391–96; also Sonnet XLVIII, p. 30; and *Canzone* IV (XLIX), pp. 31–33.
30. See n. 29 above.

XLIX

Canzone IV

Ever from us time flies.
My youth, my cheerful age, is now fast passing.
And my old hopes do fail me more and more.
But that most fierce desire
That in my tired and my afflicted soul
Death only can remove is not yet still.
Love still holds me with his so ancient bonds
And through long custom he my own ill does
Through natural desire still make me want.
O fate so harsh and cruel,
Against myself you did make me so bold,
And help myself I can't!
Would that the hope that in her lovely eyes
I seem to see fail me completely,
For with these weapons Love offends me still.

At least if one couldn't see
In her dear face of pity any signs,
Or that her words were not so sweet to me,
And so her gentle smile
Would from my eyes and ears now hidden be,
And my sweet sun would hide herself from me!
My soul does not know how, nor can it flee.
Nor wishes to, from what its life sustains,
Or rather to a happier death does lead.
My doubtful fate does not
Let me despair nor yet with reason hope,
So that I do beg Love
Fallacious hope to take away from mc.
Or succor my poor, sad, afflicted heart
To satisfy or error drive away.

Alas, I did believe
That diverse age and other varied cares
Would make me change both my desires and hopes.
Happen it must, I'm sure,
That other thoughts time brings and some deletes.
While new impressions rise, the old do fade.
What adds more sorrow to my grieving heart
Is that the mind, as over things it runs.

Of myriad thoughts that ever gather there,
At once it swiftly runs,
Never to others, but this one alone
Where tired some rest it finds.
And thus does Fortune lead it to its fate.
In this so bitter, tedious life of mine,
My doubtful thoughts and grieving soul do lie.

O Love, do tell me please
Why does my poor tired soul still have some hope,
Though you to us no signs do give of aid.
The length of my travail
To Nature's law a custom may have changed,[31]
And so the straight true path now lost has been.
Nor does it think it is what once it was:
Only desire it follows where it leads.
Since hope does it maintain, it comes and grows
Together with desire.
Thus if desire will never be restrained,
Always will hope be there.
For even if from some unknown fresh spring
Water did come to quench the fire in part,
New guiles and cunning Love would surely find.

Thus I myself deceive,
And it is there my soul some comfort finds
Whence my age-long and cruel woes do come.
Such sweetness have those eyes
Given my heart that hope they make it still.
To its own death this makes it give consent
And where desire most vain may ever lead
It follows what it neither sees nor knows.
It yet knows not the malady it has.
All that it wants and seeks
To his well-being a foe most lethal is.
As Love does it entice,[32]
In that which kills it mercy thinks there is,
Nor can it help itself or find some aid
For of his life to others guidance gave.

Itself it must then blame
Or else the lovely eyes that lead it did

31. See Petrarch, *Rime* 7.3–4.

32. Verse taken from Petrarch, *Rime* 129.7.

To the blind error whence its death was born.
To this they led it then,
So let it not believe they'll set it free
For what once we did like cannot displease.
From the first day that there in it arose
The great desire, it from its mind did drive
All other thoughts and seized it to itself.

If no defense it made
It will not now when to its ill consents.
If now my fate decrees
That so it must now be, at once or later
As my desire commands the path I'll follow
Till in the end I reach the final crossing.

At night, my own dear song,
Were you then born. Avoid the light, the sun.
Alone your fate bemoan.
Avoid the sight of those so lovely eyes.
Let your own fatal destiny proceed.
Since otherwise to do of no use is.

L

I did once cry as Love commanded me
For how so slow he was to keep his word
And the result of this to both of us:
To me the grief, to him his honor stained.

As my own lady wants I now shed tears
For time does flee and never more returns,
And what once was I see cannot now be.
This is what kills and what my heart does break.

Greater than were the first, my new woes are,
For at that time there was some hope at least,
But only vain repentance there is now.

Now my mistake I measure in my mind
And for our human destiny I cry:
More bitter are these tears than all the others.

LI

Those first sweet thoughts that nourish did my heart
In its most grievous sorrows and its woes,

I now returning feel and old deceits
Along with all my bittersweet desire.

What a great fool I was to ever think
That weightier thoughts and wiser, riper years
Would set me free from all the woes of love.
How little my desire I understood!

Just as in some dark woods a savage beast
By poisoned arrows wounded flees and thinks
It now safe is while towards its death it runs,

Thus I believed while running fast away
I would escape that evil I didn't know.
Now that I know, to fate I do consent.

LII

Just as in spring the sun and morning dews
From time to time do make green plants produce
New flowers and new leaves so that the earth
A new appearance takes and is renewed,

So do my sun and those two stars so bright
And my eyes' dew that from the heart does spring
Make Love new leaves and flowers then produce
When there returns that time I can't forget.

Into my mind return those two bright stars,
Those ways, those words that once did brave make me
Against myself, but cowardly with Love.

The old and the new flames does Love redouble,
And I so fear and hope at the same time,
But pity is so slow: nine years have fled!

LIII

Just as a lantern in the early hours
When lacking is the fuel that feeds the flame
Extinct does seem, but all at once it flares
And burns more bright as to its end it goes,

So in my vague and still wandering mind
The fuel of ancient hopes now lacking is
And if a greater fire there still does burn,
It means its illness near the end now is.

So now I do not fear your new insults,
No more the ardent flame does frighten me,
The end has come of wrath and of desire.

My beautiful Medusa into stone
No longer can turn me, no siren beckon,[33]
For heaven now calls me to worthier love.

LIV

Sonnet Composed at Rimaggio

Leave your beloved isle[34] so dear to you.
Your graceful, lovely kingdom do now leave,
O Cyprian goddess. Do come to this brook
That bathes the tender grass so green and new.

Come and enjoy this shade, the sweet cool breeze
That makes all these green leaves so softly murmur,
And the sweet songs of all the birds in love.
Your chosen haven this let ever be.

And if you come to stay in these green meadows,
Do bring with you your dear beloved son,
For here his valor one does not yet know,

And her chaste nymphs do from Diana[35] take,
Who now do freely wander in no peril
And do not value Love's eternal force.

LV

Sonnet Composed at Rimaggio for Certain People Who Were There on Holiday

A beautiful and gentle, graceful nymph,
More than the ones Apollo ever loved,
With her sad tears has made the cool brook rise
There where the poor sad girl abandoned was.

There she bewails now this, now other cause
Of her sad life that harsh and bitter was.

---

33. See p. 3, n. 5 above for Medusa. The Sirens were mythological beings whose song fascinated sailors and made them lose their direction, often leading them to death.

34. Cyprus, a sacred island where Venus dwelled.

35. See above, p. 2, n. 3.

From the time she did leave Diana's service
Her wish has been to serve the third star well.[36]

Nothing can be of comfort to her grief,
Unless the one who did love take from her
Her dear beloved treasure does restore.

A sole doubt does arise that this sad heart
That has to crying turned with flowing tears
Might not first turn into a brook or laurel.[37]

LVI

CANZONE V

O Love, so many trials you set for me
And you your servants scorn
In spite of ever true and constant faith.
So that your unjust laws I will obey
No more, but through new ways
Set forth to seek new paths in this my quest;
For in the old I can
For nothing hope but sighs and fear and scorn,
Instead of pleasures, only woes and shame.
Would that I had your kingdom
Known well and what a lover's life is like
That day when my pure thoughts
To you I did then turn.
For signs you gave you would peace offer me.
When I to you myself
Did give: a distant day I now must rue.

Without condition I did give myself
And for the truest sign
Of my complete and pure and strongest faith
No treasure, but my heart as pledge I gave.
Direction and command
Love freely took of me and still maintains.
For pity I did hope
For my deep grief and anguish so extreme,

36. Diana here is the goddess of chastity. The third star indicates love, since it refers to the third heaven consecrated to Venus.

37. Reference to Arethusa, loved by the river Alpheus, and to Daphne loved by Apollo; when pursued by Apollo, Daphne called on the gods to help her escape, and they did so by turning her into a tree.

And that of many promises he made
At least one true would be,
And Fortune would some time direction change.
My efforts now and years
I see I have all lost
And my sweet youth and all my greenest years,
Fruitless and with no joys
For time we lose we never can regain.

That I was caught no marvel was it then
For I so simple was
And with fine bait you did the hook so hide.
No mortal object did you offer me
The day and hour when you
A slave did make of me, as I still am,
For she who made me suffer
A being divine did seem that time to me,
Nor do I think deception there was then,
So that the tears and grief
I suffered to serve her until today
For six long years already
Did please me then, but now
That all my hopes have proved to be so false,
And I have been redeemed,
The bonds and chains, O Love, I do cast off.

My sails I set before a better wind.
For in so cruel a tempest
To sail was not without a mortal peril.
I leave my life of sorrow and of tears
And my laborious striving.
New paths I take, and a new course I set.
With reason as a guide,
I sail this ship of mine through salty waves
That once was headed straight towards a sharp reef.
Through other seas I'll sail,
For other shores now will my tired prow head
Where hidden from me aren't
Sure rest and a safe harbor
That a short time ago were out of reach.
From my dire past I've learned
And from fatigue and time all lost in vain.

My blood with fear does freeze in all my veins
When I do now recall
My hard and sinful life so filled with danger.
Just as one can his senses almost lose
If on a fearful snake
He steps without his knowing as he walks,
But when it over is
His fear does grow much more than it had been,
For then the present danger he didn't know
And that frightening snake
He had stepped on without a thought or fear.
Although he now safe is.
He sees with greater fear.
Thus I now look upon my previous life
So grievous, harsh and sinful.
And do not know if happy or in fear.

Since now our style has changed, dear song of mine,
Do not the old path take.
This gentle soul do help its freedom find.

LVII

Sonnet Composed for a Friend in Love Once More Who Sent It to the Lady

Faster than Jove can make the heavens bright
When showing off his weapons, or an eye
Can blink, did seem to me the time it took
For me with love to burn on first seeing you.

If not less powerful will those eyes be
In giving peace than when they did find me,
And if they will their promise to me keep,
I can then hope my tears to joy will turn.

Though Love does often prove to be deceitful,
And hope all vain, and poor and simple lovers
A path do tread that with deceit is filled,

Yet I do know her eyes that promised peace
Will not keep me for long to sink in grief,
But will give me what I do hope and yearn.

LVIII

Sonnet Composed for the Duke of Calabria[38] in the Name of a Woman

Enough it was that you my freedom stole
And then away drew me from my chaste life.
You did not have to want my cruel death
In anguish and at such a tender age.

You did abandon me without compassion,
And I at your departure pale and sad
Was more than sure that life would soon leave me
And did no longer care for my own beauty.

Of nothing can I think but of that hour
That was the cause for all my tender tears,
Of my sweet martyrdom and my sad gift.

And if remembrance did not always come
To comfort poor, afflicted and sad lovers.
Death would by now an end have put to grief.

LIX

Sonnet Composed for Some Poetaster Who Claimed Bartolomeo Colleoni[39] Would Be the Author of Great Deeds, Which in the End Turned Out to Be Only Smoke

An impious fury now in Janus's temple[40]
With blood is stained and horribly does roar.
The strongest cords do hold him tightly bound
As he now tries to free his own two hands.

He surely strives and labors all in vain,
For he who has for him his sword drawn out
So many times defeated now has been
That though a coward, mad he really isn't.

38. The duke of Calabria (Alfonso d'Aragona) was in Florence in the period 1467–68 on the occasion of the war against Venice.

39. Bartolomeo Colleoni, referred to offensively as "Coglioni" (meaning testicles and used to call someone a fool) was in command of the Venetian forces.

40. Cf. Virgil, *Aeneid* 1.294–96.

So then Parnassus and the sacred font[41]
If they depend on him will dry remain:
A poet's glory won't with him be won.

One knows by now that theirs is Echo's voice,
Nor will they better fare than Phaeton[42] did
When he did try to lead the fiery chariot.

LX

Sonnet Composed for the Duke of Calabria When S Went Away to the Shore

"But a short time ago you did know joy
And now of all your honors are deprived,
O country mine that bears a flower's name.[43]
What fate does you bereave of such a treasure?"

"Alas, the one who saddens me so much
Always kept Love within my city walls.
She has now left and so with her has gone
All that is good, and I remain bereft.

Thus sad will I remain until the treasure
That she did steal restore to me will Fortune
And my lost happiness bring back to me.

My honor, all my good in her does lie.
Gladden our days she can or make them sad,
Nor can we happy be with her away."

LXI

If Love their lovely sun to my eyes shows,
Or if my mind presents it to my heart,
If the celestial music of her speech
In truth I hear or do imagine it,

My soul that still does suffer for the past
Does tremble so in fear of future ill
Because a flame that recently was snuffed
Can easily be lighted once again.

---

41. Parnassus and the font Hippocrene, sacred to the Muses, will be denied to the poetaster, who will not gain the poet's laurel.

42. See above, p. 27, n. 27.

43. The poet is addressing his city, Florence, in the first quatrain, and then receives an answer.

And if the tinder of my ancient hope
Is now all gone, the promise is there still
Of her sweet smile and tender words and eyes.

But then my wrath does break the bonds and chains
Together with the bow and golden arrows
When all my former ills I do remember.

LXII

To Feo Belcari[44]

Unto itself the spirit draws at times
And to a tranquil port and safe does flee
From the most perilous, tempestuous seas
And thinks, has doubts, and wants the truth to learn.

If it is true that all proceeds from God
And nothing without him can be but sin,
And through his grace it is that we all can
Sow here and then eternal fruit will reap,

And that this grace effective is in one
If well-disposed he is it to receive,
What is it then that makes us well-disposed?

What I should like to know is what comes first,
Is it our wanting it or is it grace?
Resolve for me the problem that I pose.

LXIII

Sestina IV

The ardent rays I flee of my bright sun 1
Like a wild beast beneath the shady leaves
And I do seek those little brooks and fonts
On slopes and valleys and the highest hills
Where all the nymphs that pledged are to Diana
Go to pursue wild animals in woods.

Though in the shade of trees in the thick woods 2
I do myself defend and flee the sun,

44. Although codices state that the sonnet was addressed to Feo Belcari (1410–84) — a Tuscan author of some religious poetry and drama — there is evidence that it may have been sent to Giorgio Benigni Salviati. See A. Fabroni, *Laurentii Medicis Magnifici vita* (Pisa: Jacobus Gratiolius, 1784).

All this green world belonging to Diana
Cannot protect me under the green leaves
From this fire that defies the shade of hills,
Nor is it quenched by water of clear fonts.

But from my tears there spring so many fonts, 3
Which irrigate so often those green woods,
And paths do carve anew through highest hills,
But not for this does fire from my clear sun
Grow tepid while more green the loving leaves[45]
Are born and grow forever for Diana.

I thought that through devotion to Diana[46] 4
My sorrows would soon end and that the fonts
Would quench the fire and that the shade of leaves
That I go seeking through so many woods
Impede the rays would now of this bright sun
That would so weaker be in dales and hills.

Hot is the breeze that blows on highest hills — 5
My worries grow though present is Diana[47] —
The more it burns, though farther is the sun,
And hot the water is of all fresh fonts.
Hot is the shade although in darkest woods,
And hot the waves all are, and trees and leaves.

For though so well deep in the midst of leaves 6
My body is and over all these hills
As I the game do follow through the woods,
And I do roam the fair fields of Diana
And seek a remedy in shade and fonts,
Yet never far my heart is from the sun.

While with bright rays the sun does bathe the leaves, 7
And play will fonts on high over the hills,
My own Diana I'll pursue in woods.

---

45. "Loving leaves" *(l'amorose fronde)* is a metaphor for thoughts of love. Petrarch used it to refer to Laura.

46. Hunting.

47. In spite of practicing Diana's art, that is, hunting.

LXIV

Sestina V

From many sides am I attacked by Love 1
And by most evil and most cruel Fortune,
So in an hour I many times feel death
And many times then rises my poor soul,
Which is attracted by a vain desire
And lives and dies as pleases her who rules.

But if it happens that the one who rules 2
Does not disdain sometimes to heed dear Love
And lets herself be governed by desire
And with auspicious wind along comes Fortune,
And so cheered is somewhat my wretched soul,
It later is the cause of harsher death.

Thus living does please us the more when death 3
A threat does pose, and yet hope ever rules
In a hard case and does keep firm the soul.
This has kept me a faithful slave of Love.
Though change her ways decide should evil Fortune,
Woes didn't, and never will, change my desire.

Before I ever could change my desire. 4
My poor limbs cold would be and stiff in death,
Nor so much can be done by cruel Fortune
That I won't guided be by she who rules.
Can anyone from what does please dear Love
Ever his thoughts remove or change his soul?

In vain reward awaits my poor sad soul 5
That must take as its own a strange desire.
But even if I were left free by Love
And my frail body did approach its death,
To her who honored is and does me rule
Faithful I'll be in good or evil Fortune.

At no time ever can one boast that Fortune 6
Can ever force a change in my firm soul,
For he who heaven, world and Pluto rules
To us did give it free, and free desire.
You surely can advance the time of death,
But you cannot undo the bonds of Love.

The bonds of Love will never loosen Fortune;
Not even death can ever change my soul
If afterwards desire itself still rules.

LXV

Canzone VI
Composed for Lauretta, Pierfrancesco's Lady, at His Request[48]

That graceful sweetness Love was pleased to place
In those most lovely eyes where he resides,
And to be there he the third heaven[49] left.
The lilies, violets and those fresh roses,
The pure and lovely face that its compassion
Hidden does keep beneath a graceful veil,
Now when my hair and ways
Should change, do always make me there return
In those same bonds of Love where I was kept
Till he did pity me,
Poor wretched soul, and so to compensate
For all my past deep grief,
As proper is for all most loyal lords,
He did that clearest sun[50]
To me present and thoughts forbade of others.

The purest beauty there can ever be
He did bestow on her, and to me gave
The love one can for peerless beauty have.
No flame did ever burn as bright as that
Which burns and does consume my lucky heart
That happily at peace in fire does rest.
Life spent in serving Love
Did once. alas, lead me myself to hate.
To it I now return, but oh so changed,
For happier would death seem
To me today than my old previous life,
For when I'm with my love
No pain or sorrow do I ever feel.

---

48. Pier Francesco de' Medici.
49. The third heaven consecrated to Venus, Love's mother.
50. "Clearest sun" is the beloved.

My sole regret is when
Her beauty is denied to my poor eyes.

How glad that lovely valley makes my heart
Where often does the sun come drawn by Love,
Or stops perhaps to marvel at the sight.
I low happy does the breeze my soul now make
And fills my heart with ardent hope and joy.
So sweet and tenderly does it now sigh
That of the sea the tempest
When it in wrath does boil it would soon tame.
More clear the waves here are than brightest crystal
And here in this love's chamber
With their sweet murmur soothe me so at times
And sweetly moan at others,
And as my own heart does, they cry and smile.
Just so my wrath and ire
Love calms and so much peace in me instills.

I think that Love as he once was would be
Once more towards me, and all his cruelty show,
As always has his ancient custom been,
If she did not with her most soothing words
To greater pity towards me, move him now,
For no match is his strength for her great beauty.
Such power now she has
That not alone am I by her now ruled,
But so amazed is Love at her great beauty
That he himself has fallen.
I now can see the proof that all great powers
Will fall to greater ones:
To her I fell, but then she fell to Love,
But then resist Love couldn't
Before her strength and bowed before her valor.

Just as on golden curls a garland's green
The gold stand out will make and shine much more,
And curls of gold will make the green more bright,[51]
So that compassion Love instilled in her
Her beauty does enhance and make resplendent,
And beauty pity makes so much more welcome.

---

51. The effects of colors and their combination is discussed in Lorenzo's *Commentary* XXXIX, pp. 189–92.

The help each gives the other
More dear and worthy will make both of them,
For small the value is of that compassion
Where beauty absent is.
Without compassion beauty has no life,
And most of all we scorn
The good desired if pity alien is.
With beauty and compassion
Together Love and Nature did her bless.

Together both such harmony create,
So sweet that nothing can with it compare,
And I past grief forget and my own self.
Endowed my lady is with many virtues
That can my soul make happy when most weary,
For joy so great does follow great desire.
Since merciful you are,
No matter what your reason is, O Love,
For such a happy fate I do thank you.
My only fear now is
My life may shorter be than I would want
And too much joy will kill
The root of my well-being and so bring death,
But grievous it won't seem
To end it so, for it in joy would end.

Do go to that dear valley
Where spring always does reign: my heart is there.
There near the brook, my song,
And there alone and happy you will dwell.
Don't speak, don't say a word.
Stay where that gentle breeze does softly murmur.

LXVI

Who can that be there in my lady's eyes?
Can that be Love, alas, that I now see?
My dazzled eyes did him in them perceive,
Though blinded by their splendor my sight was.

"O Love, why don't you speak to her for me?"
Aware of my mistake he answered me:
"Because my bow and arrows she did take
And with her lovely tresses did bind me.

With sheer and willful violence she made me
Against myself my own sharp arrows turn.
Because of her I hate my ancient star.[52]

Two in exchange for one I did then get,
Each one more beautiful, but I do fear
For now dry is the font of her compassion.

LXVII

Most tenderly does Love beg me at times,
Speaking before my poor afflicted heart:
"'Oh do come back to see that lovely face
Where once I did accompany your heart.

He left because of his excessive grief.
In those beloved stars I did remain
Where to past harshness I'm a witness still,
Which now at last to kindly ardor turned.

To your old faithful splendid stars come back
For by Love's favor they are now all yours
And by the courtesy of your sweet lady.

Their beauty now by pity is enhanced."
My woeful heart does not to this respond;
In silence he remains in doubt and fear.

LXVIII

Sonnet Composed in Volterra

If in some sunny, sweet and lovely site
My tired and weary body takes my soul,
Always with me Love is there step by step.
With him I cry and of my grief I speak.

If I in shady woods or wild peaks go,
I do see Love who sits there on a rock;
If in some dark, low place or in some valley,
I think I hear, I see no one but him.

No longer does my heart know what to do:
In those so lovely eyes should he seek death
Or far from them a thousand deaths do suffer?

---

52. Venus.

"If in those eyes," he thinks, "I once did burn,
My fate yet happy was and so my dying.
So better burn and happy there now die."

LXIX

"Why in my heart do you return, O Love,
That had regained its peace once you had left?"
"I do return to my engraved seal there
Set by her lovely eyes that pierced your heart."

"Much time has now gone by since he was freed.
So I did think you had forever gone."
"Do not think so. The arrow that her eyes
Into your heart did send is there forever.

"I did so feel a sign of my old flame
There in the ash that once my heart had been
And in the tears that from my eyes did flow."

"You will then see that this minute spark will
Soon stir and grow into eternal flame.
Your eyes you must now blame for your misfortune."

LXX

If someone tunes two instruments so that
In harmony one voice they will both have,
Vibrations from one string the other move
Since they will both to the same note respond.[53]

Thus in my heart, the image there impressed,[54]
To our sighs deaf, yet to awaken seems
If I someone will see who does resemble
That face that is beyond the human mind.

How you the heart retake, O mighty Love,
For fleeing the presence of her lovely face
With a mere portrait feeding my poor heart,

Maybe my eyes see her and not an image.
Maybe the painter her did see in heaven,
But her I saw. How can you flee from Love?

---

53. See *Commentary* XXXIII, pp. 174–77.
54. *Commentary* XXIV, pp. 153–56.

LXXI

I ever used Endymion to deride,
Accuse Narcissus that he was a fool.
Pygmalion did always amaze me so
That at the image he had wrought he stared.[55]

Alas my madness ever greater is:
For a mere painted face I've come to love
That in my heart a great desire instills,
But can no comfort give with words or smiles.

The eyes I flee and her so lovely hair
At least could always then some help give me.
A mere resemblance this can never do.

O Love, how infinite your power is!
Mad indeed must be those who deny it.
For I have seen love grow without a hope.

LXXII

If when I'm close to her so lovely face
My blood grows cold and to my heart returns,
And if a sudden pallor blanches me,
I know what all my strength does take from me.

That face in which all goodness ever is
Amazing rays does have of such great splendor
That they instill their own ethereal force
Into my heart that ready is for love.

In my sad heart she will then ever dwell
So that the presence of her real true form
Completely destroys her unreal image.

It's not surprising then to see that force
That from her image came from me now flee,
So that it can return where born it was.

LXXIII

How can I leave you or you stay with me,
O face so dear that my own fate do rule.

---

55. Endymion, a shepherd in love with Diana; Narcissus fell in love with his own image; Pygmalion fell in love with the statue he had sculpted of a woman.

How can I elsewhere live or elsewhere die.
Do tell me please, O Love, for I don't know.

Who forces me to leave if I don't want?
If from my sun I flee, whereto and how?
Alas, what darkness stops her finding me
If to my eyes dark night it never is?

The truth is that if her real form I see,
She seems most beautiful, though ever proud,
Beyond words graceful, though most scornful, too.

If I'm away from her, a new springtime
With grass and flowers in the meadow blooms,
So charming I see her and also gentle.

LXXIV

Sonnet Composed in Naples

My tender thoughts together all the time
Of that so charming lady mine do speak.
So sweetly do they speak that my heart moves
To go to her and then my soul does follow.

Love, who forever dwells in my own heart,
Did see my soul as it was leaving me.
To pity moved he was and so showed me
The graceful, pious gem of all his kingdom.

The eyes and hands, the lips and lovely face
Of my most charming lady Love did take
And with them all adorned he has another,

So that on seeing her I think I see
My own two sacred stars, and so Love does
My heart restrain from flight and saves my life.

LXXV

If one should have so powerful a sight
That at my lady he could firmly gaze,
Such beauty he would see in her sweet face,
Enough to make all souls contented be.

But Love endowed has her with such bright splendor
That heaven is denied to mortal eyes,

So that those who from such a good are banned
With nothing but amazement will remain.

Love only favors those who gentle are,
Gives them the strength to gaze at this great beauty
By lowering the splendor of her rays.

One who does once this great beauty admire
And of this special honor worthy is
Cannot but give her love forever more.

LXXVI

O truly sacred and most happy night
That to such joy divine a witness were,
O blind soft steps in darkness sweetly led
By that light hand so delicate and soft,

My heart and you and Love, you only know
And my dear lady (no one else can know)
The sweetness no man ever felt before
And is beyond all human understanding.

O silence, more than harmony of song
And music sweet, O shadows blind that had
The privilege of tears and light of love,

O happy sighs and sweetest tears of love.
O proud desire that did the daring have
To a supreme reward there to aspire.[56]

LXXVII

Sonnet Composed "Ex Tempore ad Saxum in Lucu Repertium"[57]

Some time ago I was a poor sad lover.
Transformed I now have been into hard stone
By the great charm of eyes that magic are
Of a sweet nymph among young tender trees.

If by me should some gentle heart now pass,
May my sad story serve to make him wiser.

---

56. The same situation is described in *Sylva II,* 58–62, p. 232.

57. "To a stone found in the forest." It is the stone that speaks in the sonnet.

Let not the eyes rebel against true reason
For traps are laid always on every side.

Although a stone I am, yet I feel pity
And wish to warn all those who pass me by
And make them wiser through my own sad fate.

With lowered head and eyes and with much care
Let those pass by who are as I once was,
For of these places Love the god remains.

LXXVIII

As once you seemed to me, O eyes, you are
More beautiful than any I have seen.
The other graceful charms that I admired
And your ways are most beautiful and pure.

Never can I of these, alas, complain,
But thank them all and honor them most highly,
But you, false Love, I blame for you did know
A heart of stone she had, but didn't tell me.

I did the eyes then ask in which you dwelled,
And you did put some words on her sweet lips
That mountains could have moved, not just my heart.

Her sighs did then bring me to understand
Her loving thoughts and pity in her heart,
But I knew not with what fierce fire it burned.

LXXIX

A bitter thought at times possesses me
And in my mind above all others rules.
If it endures I'll die, but if I drive
It out, it will return more strong and bold.

It tells me that my hopes are all fallacious
And so is love and so my lady's faith.
It does tell me the various thoughts I had
Before in her my good did Love all place.

On Death I call for help when this I think,
And merciful she would reprieve me now,
But Love knows well that my complaints are wrong.

Her lovely eyes to me he shows and so
My bitter thoughts and my complaints all flee
Like night does flee before the light of dawn.

LXXX

Those tearful stars to my own eyes have given
So sweet a model of how one should weep
That from them now two ceaseless rivers flow,
So great is the desire I have to cry.

How beautiful they were, alas, when I
In a most wretched state did them then leave.
O memory how you do burn me, yet
You dare to promise worse. O wicked fate!

For such a fault mild punishment are tears:
Sweet tears, and they are sweet since I did see
The tears those lovely eyes did shed for me.

So then my eyes that did presume so much
Did want to be like those with their warm tears,
And I do want that Death will soon them close.

LXXXI

My thoughts always and only do admire
The eyes with which my love last looked at me.
At first my eyes do envy feel and wrath,
For not so swift they are to reach their love.

But then though I do look at diverse things,
My thoughts that power have to draw them in
Into her image do transform them all,
And my mistaken eyes a brief joy feel.

Just as the sun through rest does always get
New virtue and new force forever more,
And with its heat then warms and lights the earth,

So then when various things through my own eyes
Into my mind arrive, Love gives them form
And to my eyes my lady will present.

LXXXII

My lady's sacred feet Love did then guide,
As he did please, to that most charming place

Where her white hand she first did offer me
As her heart's pledge of constancy and faith.

Once in that place she turned her eyes about
And looked for me, but since I was not there.
Her heart such pity filled at once for me
That her tears came and did enhance her beauty.

Her pledge of love and those dear early days
She did recall and looked at where she was
So all alone and so she did then sigh.

With all her sighs her soul then tried to leave,
But she retained the soul that wished to flee
By calling out the name that so pleased her.

LXXXIII

Let not the earth that did well nourish you,
O lovely sylvan flower, now complain,
If I take you and from her do pluck you,
Or fear that you your vigor will now lose.

A gift for my dear lady you shall be.
If then she should in her white hand take you
And gently turn her loving eyes on you,
Restored you'll be at once by their great virtue.

If she should cry and her warm tears of love
Your languishing, poor petals should then bathe,
For paradise on earth you fit would be.

Do not then fear or marvel at all this,
For I, now being so far away from her,
Alive alas am kept and fed by tears.

LXXXIV

Not from the well-cared-for, ornate, green gardens
Beneath the sweet and sunny Paestum sky,
Do we, my lady, come in your white hand,
But from wild woods and shady meadows plucked,

Where Venus running was, but all in vain,
Worried and grieving at Adonis's fate,
When a vile thorn and sharp her bare foot pricked,
And in thick woods her sacred blood was shed.

Beneath her foot our petals we did place
So that her sacred blood the ground didn't reach:
Our candid color crimson then became.

No summer breezes or cool distant streams
Have nourished us, but sweetest sighs of love
Have been our breezes and warm tears our streams.

LXXXV

When from her lovely face my soul had left
Full of laments as she was used to do,
Love who does grieve to hear my many sighs
Saw that my eyes had firmly turned to tears.

And so with sweet and most desired oblivion
He put an end to tears, sad sighs and words,
And while I slept he made my lovely sun
More beautiful and happy come to me.

She offered me her hand and said to me:
"Do you not recognize this place at all?
It is the place where Love gave me to you."

Then upward step by step she went away.
The pleasure I did feel awakened me,
And I was left in tears with my desire.

LXXXVI

In shadow through long, steep and savage ways.
With Love as guide for my bereaved blind thoughts,
Over an unknown path, my feet I moved,
With my desire by now to heaven turned.

With great fatigue and through so many errors,
Of our own hemisphere the end I saw,
And to a loftier proud place taken was
So far beyond the earth away already.

To the third ring of the great stairs arrived,[58]
To his dear mother Love entrusted me.
At first the sun we could not clearly see,

58. See above, p. 44, n. 49.

But then I was to brighter parts soon led,
And at the sun I looked with mortal eye.
No earthly thing could afterwards please me.

LXXXVII

The young and tender leaves in warm springtime[59]
All trees and bushes do always adorn,
And Flora[60] to the sun her womb does offer,
And then gives birth to you and other flowers.

The riper season now has made them all
Into seed change and fruit that is so luscious.
What marvel then makes you alone appear.
Flowers of love, so beautiful and fresh?

Just this I do believe, my dearest violets,
You have by Nature destined been to seek
The warm bright rays of this, my lovely sun.

All wonder will soon cease if you will come
Into her hands, and she will hold you so.
For you will see a miracle on earth.

LXXXVIII

Those beautiful and perilous bright stars
Were far away from my afflicted soul.
Though very timid, she did then decide
To free herself and seek to distance Love.

Hidden from Love, she then did call my thoughts
And in a low, soft voice her wish related.
Of all those there, for all just one did answer:
"It is too late, the effort now in vain."

My poor sad soul he guided as he spoke
To the now desert place where my heart dwelled,
For he had lied with the rebellious spirits.

My wretched soul did then become aware
Of being alone and so gave up her plan,
And Love is all that still keeps me alive.

---

59. Cf. *Commentary* XVI (both sonnet and explanation), pp. 131–34.
60. See above, p. 22, n. 23.

LXXXIX

A thought that does of Love so often speak
Alone in me now lives, and I do listen,
And if another in my mind does rise,
Just like a stranger, long it does not stay.

My wretched soul so all my spirits sees
Against life turn, as do my other thoughts,
In fear into herself she then withdraws
And does accuse that face that lovely is.

Hearing of these complaints from Love's own spirits,
That lovely face with words most true and pious
Herself excuses to my poor, sad soul:

"Of beauty just and gracious duty is
Pleasure to give; your own desire then blame
If I please all and only you displease."

XC

Alas, how much desire Love has now placed
Within my poor and sorrowful sad breast,
And since for such a bundle space is tight.
In guise of sighs it often does escape.

So much oppressed does my wise heart now feel
That space to make himself for such a crowd
He has now gone on that so lovely hill
Where my love is and there with her remains.

Although desire its source no longer has
Since my heart left, yet all that in me lives
By custom will always my love desire.

From that proud hill my heart does let me know
Through Love's own messenger just sent to me
That in that lovely breast does pity sigh.

XCI

My tired and moist eyes often do tell me:
"We should now like to go as did the heart
To those bright eyes like stars where all sight dies
And dying becomes more lovely and more clear.

The way is known quite well to our slow steps,
For just as lightning will the night make clear,
So will of Love the spirits make most bright
The happy path that to the lady leads."

I grievous find refusal or compliance,
So to the top I take them of high hills
And from afar the place I do show them.

If one is parched, but does not fully drink
And only wets his lips, thirst will increase,[61]
So grow the tears and in the breast the fire.

XCII

"When will Hope die, sweet enemy of mine,
That my sad life sustains that bitter is
And dies when of my life the sweet clear light
To me returns and nourishes my heart?

The Faith that given was, sister and friend
Of dearest Hope, of sorrow full and tears,
Most gentle Faith so rare today on earth
When will it die? O Love, do tell me now!

O Love, to live these do enable me.
But you don't speak and will my death now cause.
Yet death I beg for them, for you long life.

What a mistake!" Love smiles and answers me.
"Sweet is my fate, their life a martyrdom.
Soon they will die, but Love forever lives."

XCIII

In your swift waves you carry away with you,
O willful and clear river, the sad tears
Shed by my lady from her lovely eyes
That evil Fortune does from me now hide.

The sad soft murmur that I used to hear
And that to my laments so sad responds
Certain makes me. On your green banks her tears
A river form that sheds itself in you.

---

61. See the explanation to Sonnet XX of the *Commentary*, pp. 142–43.

Your rapid course, swift river, do restrain.
And I do hope for you that Sirius's dog
Will never you offend with rabid teeth.

May you with Ganges vie and with Euphrates!
But you do flee and do your help deny.
No news you bring to me of my dear sun.

XCIV

O lovely violet, you were born there
Where my desire of love first came to life.
Beautiful, sad tears were your only waters[62]
That nourished you and often did you bathe.

My lady's love did mercy nourish there
Where the plant lay in that most sacred earth.
Her lovely hand plucked you and then was pleased
To make mine happy with so dear a gift.

That you to flee did want it seemed to me
To that most lovely hand, so I hold you
Against my bare breast tenderly and tight.

Grief and desire my poor bare breast does hold
In my heart's stead, for my poor heart scorns me[63]
And there remains whence you just came, O violet.

XCV

If all intent it happens that my sight
Steadily points at her warm flaming eyes,
My breast with desire will then burn and sigh,
Smoke of my fire that does torment my heart.

The path will thus quite easy then become
From fire to fire through my continuous sighs,
Just as a new flame seems the smoke to draw
Of a dead candle that just now was snuffed.

---

62. See *Commentary* XVI, pp. 131–34.

63. The theme of the heart fleeing to stay with the beloved is a fairly common one in various poets, including Petrarch. It is used extensively by Lorenzo. See *Commentary* XII, pp. 118–21; XVI, pp. 131–34; XXX, pp. 166–69; and XXXI, pp. 169–71, etc.

If one so wants, one then can clearly see
Of Love the spirits there in that sweet smoke
That the sweet fire one to the other gives.

From heart to heart they do come and then go,
And none of them aware of his ill is,
For tenderly and willingly they die.

XCVI

Of that so loving breast the lofty sighs
Do always bring me news of my dear love.
Still warm they are as when her lips they left
As by my heart they are in me received.

The words that Love told them they retell him
In lovers' amorous and silent speech.
My spirits then do all to hear them rush
And thus the heart oppressed and tight remains.

Against his own desire the heart then must
The spirits drive away with his deep sighs.
Love's troop he pushes back whence it had come.

From life and death they equally did come.
Thus every other spirit moved is by
A living that partakes of life and death.

XCVII

O hill so proud, though humble in appearance.
More fortunate and more superb than those
So favored and so fabled hills of Rome,[64]
Though they were sung in a more lofty style.

Those more than once did see such great men triumph
As Scipio and Aemilius and Marcellus.
Of those so lovely eyes you see the triumph.
With Love in chains and so all gentle hearts.

Unkempt the Graces, Pity and so Beauty
Before the chariot in chains they all do come,
And Virtues that in gentle heart reside,

64. The original gives the names of three Roman hills, which have been omitted for reasons of space and tonality.

Defeated and in triumph led, but happy.
So much more so since they can see themselves
In my sweet lady's face more beauty gain.

XCVIII

Love did, on that triumphant day that still
Remind does me of when I first fell ill,
Happily climb the mountain great and proud
With all his brothers dear and with the Graces.[65]

The noble mantle that adorned him so
He laid aside; to me the wings and band
He gave, to her in her right hand the bow,
Dart in her left and quiver on her shoulder.

My amorous Diana a dress wore
So candid, thin and clinging that it let
The form be seen of beautiful bare limbs.

Her eyes and hair did Phoebus then adorn,
So that no human art, no mortal hand
The beauty did create that I first saw.

XCIX

In my poor heart my soul does seem to move
Many harsh thoughts of my deep grief all born.
If they should die, to sighs they'll be transformed
And by my endless sorrow renewed be.

I know not how, but only by experience
The heart does with desire forever burn
For its own death, and yet from such harsh thoughts
The food it draws that does keep it alive.

"Do tell me now, O Love, and how these thoughts
That dying are can yet her image still
So sweet, immortal in my heart create?"

Love smiles and then an answer does give me:
"No good can so sweet be as is my illness.
Sweet miracles no one but I perform."

---

65. The Graces (Aglaia, Euphrosyne and Thalia) were daughters of Jupiter and Eurynome and goddesses of favors, loveliness, grace, etc.

C

So beautiful my lady is and such
Sweet charms she has that never have been seen,
That we prefer to be with her in vain
Than our desires with anyone fulfill.

Sorrows and tears, both hopes and all desires
That from so great a beauty have derived
Are such that they with them salvation bring,
And he whose life they take forever lives.

O lovely death, O sorrows that sweet are.
O thoughts that while I sigh you do bring me
Such sweetness in my heart that no one knows,

How can one ever be by grief so burdened,
Although afflicted, if before his eyes
And in his thoughts there reigns beauty supreme?

CI

Never a cruel god, O Love, you'll be
Since from my lady's lovely, sacred eyes
The tears so warm did spring and did bathe you:
Beautiful tears, sweet tears and pious tears.

That pity that was moved by sweet desire
And her so sacred tears did then make you
Merciful be: then let all lovers raise
In honor of my grief the happiest songs.

Happy and safe has my own grief made you.
No longer fear, O lovers pale and wan,
That tears of love will make your heart so weary.

And if you did now cry, my gentle lady,
So sweet has now made tears by her sweet crying
That gentle hearts will all now wish to cry.

CII

Alas, how beautiful were all those tears
That of desire the cloud did then exude,
When the just sorrow that the heart did strike
Aloft did rise, up towards the stars of love.

Those beautiful sad tears on her soft skin
Drew lines on her white cheeks just touched by red,
As a clear brook would do in a green field
Sprinkled around with flowers white and red.

Love stood most happy in the loving rain
Like a bird, happy when the sun has gone,
Receives sweet drops of dew so much desired.

In those sweet eyes then where he dwells he cried
And from those lovely tears that so sad were
He then made tender sparks be seen to rise.

CIII

A lovely, pleasing work our eyes do see
That in no one but you one could expect,
By one made who, though with no eyes, can see,
Neither in ink inscribed, or paint, or stone.

I seem to see Love happy to show me
That first sweet time that birth did give to love,
To so much gentleness and so much faith,
To our sweet sorrow and desires so high.

That first and happy fear does shake my heart.
Towards me you move your steps so quick and happy,
Your hands, your lips, those merciful bright stars.

Though Love does show this beauty everywhere,
In those high mountains where they were first born
Your sweet tears do enhance and make it truer.

CIV

Annoyed with Love, my lady did pretend
To be disturbed and in a sweet way said:
"No more fire now, my breast does burn too much,
For my poor heart that there does sigh have pity."

Love laughs at this. The heart that to burn wishes
Finds in the greater fire a greater pleasure,
Like perfect gold that in the furnace is,
By fire he is not harmed but gains in beauty.

New tender sighs did Love from my heart move,
Sweet and mad sighs with which he made fire burn
In that sweet breast as high as fire can go.

This fire that splendid shines in her bright eyes
And her most ardent words when she does speak,
Wherever they arrive new flames they light.

CV

When for my greater sorrow blind desire
The hours that once swift were now counts so slow,
Just like a snake that by a wheel oppressed
Its sleek spine moves, but can no headway make.

Thus Phoebus slowly leads his golden chariot
In which he envious seems with him to have
Of my desires so bitter their sweet death
And of my hopes the end that gives such pain.

No new and sweet thoughts does my heart permit,
Nor sweet oblivion for my tearful eyes
That would now make the sun more swiftly move,

And as I wait, what makes me grieve much more
Is that now slow is Phoebus, but tomorrow
He'll swiftly take away what joys I'll have.

CVI

O nights so brief and clear, days long and dark.
O shining shadows, light profoundly dark,
Light that from open eyes away take sight,
Shadows that with bright light closed eyes do cheer!

O dark deep sleep that my tormented thoughts
To visions does transform of bright pure light.
Image of death that while it lasts I see,
I hear. I feel and my desires fulfill!

O my excessive sweetness, mortal foe
Of your own self that do before desire
My true good place and flee, and I must grieve.

O sad unhappy dreams of all poor lovers!
For when I tightly hold what I most want
From me it flees just when it nearest is.

CVII

Against the power of those proud new eyes
So brilliant and from which desire derives,
Who will make strong and constant my own eyes,
Wretched and happy in defeat and death?

O Love, why don't you succor my mad eyes?
Through them you did first enter in my breast.
They made me yours and you they made my god.
Why do you then not offer them some aid?

My anguished breast do leave where you reside
Just like a gentle image in clear mirror
Of beauty that with you in her does live.

My breast do leave and to my eyes do mount
That armed by you and beautiful made will
In safety then her lovely eyes confront.

CVIII

If in my eyes at times my lady looks,
Not them she likes, but her own self in them.
So lovely does she seem that she admits
That for a gentle object my heart sighs.

So towards my own her eyes she often turns
Where well and true so real she is reflected
That such great beauty or one just like it
She cannot see or wish if not in them.

When she herself in them does see so lovely,
A flight of amorous and ardent spirits
Her graceful face does frame and goes along.

When she my heart does reach, which even more
For her does burn, my sluggish Hope expels
And my own grief and happy makes my spirits.

CIX

When the light of her eyes to me arrives,
The various thoughts that in my mind do crowd
Before her loving eyes do take to flight.
And so do Pity and my lifeless Hope.

Impressions that appear to be all real
My memory abandon that weak is.
Sweetness and marvel only do remain
And drive away whatever else there is.

From me my spirits flee and happy go
To meet that splendor marvelous and sweet
And there they know that Love will kill them all.

If my sight flees or does in me remain,
Though dead in me, will it in others live?
That is the doubt a gentle soul should clear.

CX

O memory so harsh, why don't you leave,
For present you do so torment my heart?
O memory so harsh that now you offer
Deceit and scorn and wrath in my sad thoughts.

Alas, unhappy day when you do try
My pleasant, sweet desires to now disturb.
And you such evil do permit, O Love,
So that your rule no one will dare reject.

My grievous thought does now suggest to me
A thing I dare not tell, but to my heart,
At once the spirits flee that it have seen,

And finding in my heart that evil thought
More strong and fierce, they all one by one die.
My poor heart trembles and calls them in vain.

CXI

Why be surprised, O my gentle Cortese,
If though you have a white, cold, flowing mane
A new volcano Love did bring to life
With fiercest fire in your cold, dormant breast?

Poisoned and dying some did their life preserve
By countering one poison with another:
Thus did the icy mane of yours thaw out
The ice in your cold heart and lit the fire.

This fire at times in all the veins the blood
Does freeze; ourselves we hate and others love;
Some live without a heart and death invoke.

This life of love great marvels does present;
The lover often in himself will feel
What he would not of others have believed.

CXII

Why is my lady not here with my thoughts,
My sweet lady who is my very life,
In this sweet shade and near this flowing brook
That my laments and sighs joins and reflects?

Why does her gentle foot not press this grass?
Why does she not my sad laments hear now,
And my deep sighs that my desire does move,
Which an untimely hope instilled in me?

Perhaps that pity promised me by Love
So long ago, a promise now renewed,
In my heart written with his golden arrow,

Would show itself before my dying breath.
If she could only hear my sweet lament,
My lady's beauty pity would enhance.

CXIII

All happy places to my heart do bring
A thousand bitter sighs and painful thoughts,
For it does not seem I can, or know
How to be happy far from my bright star.

To find some rest, my soul does now lead me
Into dark woods or craggy mountain slopes,
Away from trodden paths and human signs.
Some comfort in all this she now does find.

Among the trees thus all alone I stay.
Not really so alone, for with me are
A thousand sweet and gentle thoughts of Love.

With sweet tears here my breast always I bathe,
And with these tears I nourish my sad heart
That death or better times does wish would come.

CXIV

On a cold rock and hard I often sit
And with my arm I do support my cheek,
And I do think and in my thoughts I view
My lover's journey step by step again.

I first do see the day and hour when Love
Into his kingdom did take me, alas,
And then events that happy were and sorrow
Until I find myself in present time.

Of my age-long affliction I do think
And of the days and nights that I have spent
In bitter tears as Love of me demanded.

And since no end I see to my great grief,
I do my fate accuse, but what does pain
Me more is being away from my bright stars.

CXV

I do thank you, O Love, for all my woes,
And if a cruel Lord I did call you,
As one who by his fury guided was,
I do repent for all my faults today.

The one for whom I now do feel my heart,
My very lucky heart, in sweet fire burn
Of honors worthy is on earth and heaven.
To pine for her I'll be more than content.

To serve a gentle and most worthy lady
And in her seek tranquility and peace
A fortunate and happy fate it is.

A thousand times already I've sought death,
Yet though she does me scorn, content I am,
So much do I enjoy to be her slave.

CXVI

It does not honor you, O Love, that you
When I was young deceived and did seize me,
For at that age one is disposed to fraud.
No glory can you gain by such weak fires.

If I gave up, wronged me you should not have,
....
Your arrows and your bow you should reserve
For heavy armor, not for flimsy dress.

Powerful being the winner, weak the loser,
Glory must then perforce go to the latter.
Thus does your glory fade little by little.

As prisoner a god you did once hold.
Heaven and earth you kept in trembling fear
And Hades too. Go now and light your fires.

CXVII

CANZONE VII

When a warm ray of light
Through a minute small crack
Enters of bees the dark and gloomy house,
When spring is sweet, it warms and stirs them all.
Then by new urges driven, out they come,
And through the lovely woods,
Preying they all do go on this or that
Species of flowers that the earth adorns.
They back and forth do go
All laden with perfumed and lovely prey.
Some do incite and spur
Those that are slow or that do idle seem,
Others the lazy drone,
That would on others' labors live, urge on.
From many various flowers, leaves and grass,
Frugal and wise, they honey make and save
For when on earth no violets there are.

Into my breast in darkness[66]
First through my eyes did come
Of love the ray that from her eyes did shine
And all the dormant spirits did awake
That in my breast carefree and idle dwelled.
But as the lovely light
Went down until my very heart it reached,
Alight my spirits in that lovely ray

66. See *Love Lyrics* CIX, pp. 65–66.

Down to the heart did run.
They did there stay enchanted for some time,
Then seeking a new pleasure,
They rushed to see from where the light was coming.
In my afflicted breast
They left the heart that still in flames is now,
And to my eyes they went, through which this new,
Gentle, and ever-welcome flame had come.
From there my lady they did all admire.

Then in that lovely face
Love they did see who there
In arms proud dwells and threatens all vile hearts.
Away he drives them far from that bright light
So that no one but gentle hearts it warms.
Sadly my spirits dropped
Their quest to reach the source of that bright light
And full of fear in my own eyes remained.
Some spirits they then saw
Come full of pity from those eyes where Love
Resides. To mine they said:
"Do come to the sweet font of truest light.
With us most safe you'll be.
Although that gentle lord does flames ignite.
He does not burn or lead to evil death.
The heart ignited by that light does shine,
And if it does not live, it happier dies."

These sweet and tender words
To my poor spirits gave
The courage to move on with their slow steps.
Accompanied by those that lovelier were,
In doubt and fear they went where Love resides.
Little by little they,
Secure in this most beautiful, sweet fire,
Spirits of Love became in fear no more,
Confused and mixed with those
My pious lady to their aid had sent,
Only the sharpest lynx
Apart one from the other could them tell.
In those so lovely eyes
So sweet and dignified some then do gaze,
While others from her features strength derive.

At her white throat and breast do others stare.
Still others seem her golden hair to seize.

If one should wish to tell
About the lovely grace
And the diverse and beautiful and many
Flowers that Flora in the springtime shows,
He would have to describe them one by one.
Nor from my breast as yet
Of Love so many spirits have been born
That there are not of beauties myriads more.
Through them eternal sparks
sends to my heart this beauty ever new.
Now this, now that the spirits
Compete to bring my heart right through my eyes,
Oh beautiful, sweet prey
That loving spirits on their back do carry!
Forevermore they burn with great desire,
And from her lovely eyes to my own heart
They come and go and never do they stop

Though many beauties does
Always each spirit bring
To see my poor sad heart, by great desire
Possessed, he always thinks he's being deprived,
And if so lazy should a spirit be,
"What are you doing," he says,
"You know how sweet your burden is." By fury
Taken and by desire, he threatens him
That he with his sighs will
Send him outside, a slave to all the winds.
If a strange thought should come,
The heart at once will then chase it away,
For on that lovely path
That from her charming eyes leads to my heart
No one can tread if not to Love devoted,
For no vile thought must then with gentle mix.
This makes my heart content who wants just this.

How will you nourish life
Grieving and wise heart now?
Since the most beautiful of Love's exchanges
To my poor spirits now has been denied,
And the sweet springtime now has fled away,

And other sites now warms
That gentle sun whence came that fire of yours.
Those loving spirits that now shut in are
Their prey so sweet in thoughts
Have now transformed in my afflicted mind
And often show the heart
The lovely flowers that so long ago
The frugal spirits saved
In that most joyful time when flowers bloom.
Now that my beautiful sweet light has fled,
With these sweet thoughts my heart my longing feeds
That with new life always reborn will be.

O my new song so young,
These sad and grieving verses
That into sighs by now my thoughts have changed
And into words, of sorrow full, my sighs,
Do bring to that most beautiful sweet meadow
Of colors full, where Love
Happy did stay and in the grass did hide.
And if the way to her you do not know.
Be led by the deep traces
That on the path my thoughts then left impressed.
The road to Love do follow.
Perhaps on it you will her own thoughts meet,
For they too like that path
So sweet. When all alone you will see her,
Tell her that my poor heart no hope has left
Of finding more sweet thoughts himself to nourish.
For him remains or Death or her sweet light.

CXVIII

Canzone VIII
Composed on a Certain Day When I Was Where There Were Certain Ladies, and Not without Personal Danger

To open once again an ancient wound
That in my heart had healed
Through cooling ardor or through Love's own fault,
The ancient object and those lovely lights
That so reflected pity
To my eyes Love gave and through them my heart.

Her pious expression did not seem to show
That she felt sorrow for my own harsh fate,
But seemed with humble words
That she my pardon begged for my hard fate,
As proper is for such unjust offenses.
To persuade my heart, she was then saying
That harsh it is a pardon to deny.
Her lovely face thus spoke without a word.
No one could understand if not a lover.

Like one whose wounds had then not healed so well,
I was at once oppressed
By such great force, that careless I forgot
How more effective and more easy 'tis
The roots soon to destroy
Of what is later difficult to cut.
I could not help myself, but gladly lent
To such a lovely messenger my ears,
For of that evil custom
In such short time my heart I could not free.
Although almost still present were the wrath,
The scorn, the shame and my most sad repentance,
On such a scale more heavy was desire,
And I did nothing else but what one does
Whose will is overcome by alien forces.

But then — like one who well-accustomed is
In dubious strife to triumph
Well knows the state in which the victor is —
In part the old lost glory to regain,
In part not to act so
As in another's hands myself to put,
And thinking of my previous state of love,
My worthy soul was of itself ashamed,
So that a shield of scorn
Oppose it did to that so lethal blow.
Against such strong force I did then resist.
And so much greater did my own prove then
That it annulled the arrow's lethal blow.
But my defense could not so thorough be
That I am not by the result still hurt.

For in my breast there did incised remain,
As in soft wax a seal,

That kind and humble visage that pious was.
That first assault of Love was then so strong
That thought of it didn't let
My poor afflicted heart have peace again.
Wherever I may be, there is that thought!
I see those eyes adorned with such great pity,
And what I once desired
I seem to see return always to me.
These words forever in my mind resound:
"That good that you did seek amidst such tears
To you Love offered. Look, it is now here."
Though present is this thought, another says
That from afar my lady wounds me still.

This thought made me recall the past to see
What once my life had been
When my well-being I blindly had opposed
And made me see that her sweet, happy eyes,
And her pretense of aid
Would in the end my servitude prolong.
And since that virtue of much use is not
That sees ill coming, but does not provide,
I thought the knot I'd sever
That to my soul a good life had denied
And the old freedom then to her restore.
And pity for myself then stronger was
Than that her lovely face for me did show.
An end thus I did put to errors past,
And a free spirit once again became.

The son of Venus, my dear song, do beg
For me to lay aside
His flaming arrows and his ardent torch.
Quenched is his fire, though warm the ashes are.
Pretense of no use is
For fully adamant my heart now is.
Disturb my wandering mind let him not
With his false hopes, or think he can in me
Instill once more that base desire that once
Enslave did me. When hold me then he could
He did refuse, let him now give up hope
When he cannot, although he may so wish.
Let him no longer try with me in vain
And somewhere else his bow and arrow aim.

CXIX

Ballad[67]

From my breast light and fast
The thoughts do now depart
That my sad soul does send as her envoys
To Love's own charming mountain,
To that most gentle breast where dwells my heart.

Pursuing the path of Love.
Each one of them at every step does meet
Some thoughts that are most pious
That from my lady's breast do seem to come
And to my soul now comfort wish to bring.
They do together stop and all when asked
Of her will say what always does seem new
About the sense of mercy
That makes her send them out
From her kind breast where handsome stays my lord.
Alone my heart would stay,
But Love and Mercy also there reside.

From all these ancient caverns,
Ardent and clear the sun's bright flame draws out
All those so little ants.
Wise and solicitous, one does find out
And tells the others where a mound of wheat
The frugal peasant hide had tried now is,
And so the black and eager troop moves out.
To that rich mound they rush,
From it they do return.
In mouth and hand they bring their prey most dear.
They go so light and quick,
But slow and laden they return inside.

Their little steps they stop
As on the way they meet and while they rest
One does the other tell
Of that great prey, so that desire more eager
The other does entice to join the labor.
Trodden and crowded the long path now is,
And though the self-same thing they all do carry,

67. See *Commentary* XXXII, pp. 171–74.

More dear it is and welcome,
As it should surely be,
For if without we are, no life there is.
Most light the burden is
If die the little beings without it would.

Thus my own thoughts more lightly
Go to my lady who so lovely is.
As they her own encounter
They stop and with the others they all chat.
With them they bring a burden heavy but
Also so sweet from her immortal treasure.
Unique it is and lovely ever more,
For from that lovely breast
Where Love and Pity reign
By grievous sighs it is sent out to me.
My soul at once thus feels
Anger and joy, and also grief so sweet.

Happy if she does feel
That Love and Pity reign in that white breast.
My grieving mind complains
That hard harsh thoughts the gentle drive away,
And that so sad and sorrowing always
My lady is because of me, and mixed,
Desire and sorrow a sweet poison make.
And thus my soul acquires
Sweet death or evil life,
Saddened at her own good, at her ill joyous.
Heavy with this dear burden,
New vigor do my thoughts instill in me.

When on that lovely mountain
They do arrive where that great beauty is,
They like it so that none
To my sad soul so lonely does return,
As my wise heart and cruel did show them,
Whom they so happy see at journey's end,
As he my soul forgets and with Love stays.
And if I didn't get help
In such dire straits and grief
From those my star in pity does send me,
Since by my own betrayed,
My poor sad soul all valor would then lose.

I do excuse my thoughts
If in the presence of so great a beauty
They all remain confused,
For on a quest one of the end does think.
This was their object that did them elude:
Bewildered by the presence of such sweetness,
They cannot evermore to us return.
I do thank you so much,
Merciful, charming thoughts
That help my heart in his mistaken ways.
If it were not for you,
In this too high a quest the heart would die.

CXX

As Love had wished, reduced almost to ashes
Were the bright flames of all my ardent hopes.
My heart did seem to be without his power,
So that he had all lost his boldness then.

When Love, whose power does unchallenged go,
A golden arrow from his side did take
And that so proud, unconquered heart did pierce
With such a force that could all firmness break.

....
.... and would have taken more
if the deceits of Love he had not feared.

Well hidden a taut cord in the tall grass
He thought he could then see. I do not now
Know whether hope or fear in me grew more.

CXXI

With one farewell content I cannot be
As I do now abandon all Love's flags.
For all at once you can't a great flame snuff,
Nor can an age-long sorrow soon be healed.

....
....
Appropriate worthy words and sweet desires
From my own early thoughts I myself steal.

O tears of mine of every sweetness full,
O tender sighs that rose in various forms
That other fates and thoughts in me induce,

May I be granted only this one grace:
Remembering at least until my death
That live and clear, angelic light of mine.

CXXII

What wonder can it be if evermore
That gentle fire in which I burn does grow?
The more that face so lovely I do see,
The more her charms it to my eyes reveals.

My heart in which this beauty does descend
Is so surprised and then my eyes reproaches
For always being so tardy, dull and lazy
In seeing the virtue of those lovely stars.

Through my own lady's eyes Love then does see
My own poor eyes and to my heart then speaks
By means of the sweet rays from her kind eyes:

"Infinite is the power from which comes
To your own eyes a sweetness ever new.
Mortal the eyes, may fire eternal be."

Commentary on Some of His Sonnets

I have been in doubt for quite some time whether I should undertake the present interpretation and commentary on my sonnets. Even though at times I was inclined to do so, the following reasons against it would occur to me and keep me from this project. First of all there was the question of presumption of which it seemed to me I should be guilty if I commented on my own works. This because it would seem I thought too much of my own self, and also because I should assume the task of judging, which would better be left to others. Moreover, it would seem that I thought that those in whose hands my verses should fall lacked the intelligence to understand them.

In addition to all this, I thought I could easily be reprimanded by someone for lack of judgment in that I had wasted my time in composing and commenting on verses whose subject was for the most part a love passion. And this would be more reprehensible in my case since I had continuous personal and public duties, which should have made me abstain from such thoughts. And some deemed that these thoughts were not only frivolous but actually pernicious and harmful to both our soul and our worldly honor.

If this is true, then, to think of such things is a grave error and to put them in verses a greater one. But to comment on these verses does not seem to be a lesser fault than that of one who has become hardened by long practice of evil deeds. And especially because commentaries are reserved for theological or philosophical matters of great consequence either for the benefit and consolation of our mind or for the utility of mankind.

In addition there are some, perhaps, who even if the subject were nobler in itself, would condemn the use of the vernacular in which I write, because our mother tongue wherever it is spoken and understood, being of common use, may seem to be somewhat vulgar. Moreover, in those places where it is unknown, it cannot be understood, and thus in this respect our work and labor seem vain and as if they had not been done.

These three difficulties have until now delayed what I had intended to do long ago, that is, the present commentary. Better reasons in my opinion have now made me decide to undertake this project, thinking that if this slight labor of mine will be appreciated and give pleasure to someone, then it will have been worthwhile and not completely in vain. If it is not appreciated, then it will be read by few and by few condemned, and since its life span will be short, so will whatever condemnation it may encounter.

In regards to the first reason and to answer those who would blame me as presumptuous, I say that it doesn't seem presumptuous to me to interpret my own works, but rather to lighten the burden of others. No one is more fit for the task of interpretation than the author of the works, for no one can know better or reveal the true meaning of his words. This is clearly shown by the confusion that arises from the variety of commentaries, in which most times the critic follows his own inclination rather than the true intention of the author. Nor does it seem to me that in doing this I think too much of myself or that I deprive others of the faculty of judging me, for I believe it is the duty of all men to act always for the benefit of mankind, whether his own or that of others. And since not everyone is born with the capability to undertake those things that are deemed of highest value in this world, one must assess his potential and see in which occupation he can best serve humanity and then practice it. For the diversity of human minds and the necessities of our lives do not permit that all have the same occupation even if it is the most excellent that man could have. In fact, it seems that contemplation, which is without controversy deemed to be the first and most excellent[1]...because of this we conclude that not only intellectual occupations, but also lower trades contribute by necessity to the perfection of human life, and that the true duty of all men — no matter in which rank they are placed by heaven, nature or fortune — is to be useful to humankind

I should have liked to be able to do greater things. In spite of this, in so far as my ability and strength permit, I do not wish to fail those, be they one or many, who have encouraged me to proceed, perhaps more to please me than because my work pleases them, but their authority and friendship are important to me. If my verses will not be very useful to those who read them, at least they will derive some pleasure from them, for perhaps they will find a mind commensurate and in harmony with theirs. If someone should laugh at my verses, it would please me that he derives that pleasure from them, though a small one, since it seems to me that by publishing this interpretation I have submitted myself to the judgment of others. Had I myself judged my verses not worthy of being read. I should have avoided the

1. Although there is a lacuna in the text, the meaning is that notwithstanding the fact that contemplation is the most proper activity of man, it would not suffice by itself. Cf. Aristotle, *Politics* 1.2 and *De anima* 2.19.

judgment of others. By publishing and commenting on them, I avoid in a much better way, it seems to me, the presumption of judging my own work.

I now shall answer the calumnies of those who may wish to accuse me of having wasted time in both writing and commenting on things that do not justify the expenditure of time and labor since their subject is a love passion, etc., especially since I have many necessary occupations. To these I say that I could be justly condemned if human nature were so excellent that all men could always undertake and perform perfect tasks. But since this degree of perfection has been granted to very few, and to these only on rare occasions in their lifetime, it seems to me that we can conclude that, given the imperfection of humankind, those things are best in this world that cause the least harm.

Judging rather by the common nature and universal customs of men, I believe, though I should not dare to affirm it, that human love, not only is not reprehensible, but almost necessary and a sure sign of gentleness and nobility of mind.[2] Moreover, it is above all a spur for men to worthy and excellent things and to act and put into practice those virtues that are potentially in our soul. For those who search diligently for the true definition of love will find that it is nothing else but a desire for beauty.[3] If this is so, then all deformed and ugly things will necessarily displease one who loves. For the time being I shall not speak of that love, which according to Plato, is the means by which all things reach their perfection and will finally rest in the Supreme Beauty, that is, God.[4] I shall speak only of that love which is limited to loving a human being, and I say that although this is not that perfection of love that is called "the highest good," we see at least that it contains many good things and avoids so many of the evil. So that in accordance with the common judgment of men, it is to be considered good, especially if it is adorned by those conditions and circumstances proper to a true love. These, I believe, are two: the first is that the object of love be one, and the second that it be forever. These two conditions cannot be realized if the loved one is not of the highest perfection, always

---

2. Here Lorenzo links his work to the *Dolce stil novo* of Guinizelli and Dante and to the philosophical interpretation found in Ficino, *De amore* 1.3, and 6.10. Lorenzo presents Ficino as his mentor in the *Disputation.*

3. The definition is from Plato through Ficino, *De amore* 1.3 and 2.9.

4. Love of God and earthly love. Lorenzo treats the former in the Disputation. Here again the source is Ficino's *De amore* 2.7.

with respect to human possibilities, and in addition to natural beauty, does not have an excellent mind, proper and charming manners and customs, elegant ways and gestures, skillful use of proper and sweet words, love, constancy and faith.

All these things necessarily pertain to the perfection of love, for even though the beginning of love originates in the eyes and in beauty,[5] its continuity and perseverance nevertheless necessitate those other conditions. For if through illness, age or other causes the face should become pale and beauty disappear totally or partially, there would still be those other attributes that are no less pleasing to heart and soul than beauty is to the eyes. All these conditions would still be insufficient if the lover did not have a true perception of them, and this presupposes perfection of judgment in the lover. Nor could love be reciprocated if the lover did not merit to be loved, and this presupposes perfect judgment in the one loved.

Thus to speak of a true love is by necessity to speak of great perfection in both lover and loved one, always in relation to human possibilities. Thus, as is true of all perfection, I believe that this love has been very rare in this world, and this is proof of its excellence. One whose love is focused on one person and forever is necessarily incapable of loving others, and thus he avoids all errors and lust to which men are usually subject. And loving a person who is capable of true perception, one strives in every way to please and thus will in all his actions try to make himself deserving of her love. He will strive to excel among others and will be worthy in all his actions to become as deserving as possible of the one he loves, whom he esteems as the most worthy. It seems to the lover that just as the loved one, whether present or absent, is always present in his heart, so is she a witness to all his actions, which she praises or condemns according to their nature as a judge not only present at the action, but also cognizant of his thoughts.[6] Thus repressing evil through shame

5. Again a reference to the *Stil novo.* Ficino *(Sopra lo amore* 6.2) states: "La figura dell'uomo lo quale spesse volte per la interiore bontà felicemente concessa da Dio e nello aspetto bellissimo, per gli occhi di coloro che la riguardano, nel loro animo transfonde il raggio del suo splendore." ("Human form, which often through the interior goodness happily granted by God is most beautiful in appearance, through the eyes of those who see it transmits the ray of its splendor into their soul." Trans. is mine.)

6. Ficino, *Sopra lo amore* 1.3.

and pursuing good through desire of pleasing, these lovers always act, if not perfectly, at least in a way that the world considers least evil, which with regard to human imperfection is considered good.

This then was the subject of my verses, and if in spite of all these reasons I do not satisfy those who wish to condemn and slander me, at least with those who have experienced what love is, as our Florentine poet said: "Pity I hope to find, as well as pardon,"[7] and the judgment of these will sufficiently satisfy me. For if it is true, as Guido from Bologna[8] says, that love and gentleness are but one thing, I then believe that it is sufficient to have and to desire only the praise of lofty and gentle minds, paying no attention to others, for it is not possible in this world to do something that will be praised by all. And so those of good judgment will strive to earn the praise of those who deserve praise and will disregard the opinion of others. It seems to me that one can hardly condemn what is natural. There is nothing more natural than the desire to be united with what is beautiful, and this desire has been willed in man by nature for human procreation, which is most necessary for the preservation of the human species.[9] The true reason that should move us in this matter is not nobility of birth or hope of property, wealth or other goods, but only natural selection not influenced or coerced for any other reason, but moved only by a certain fitness and proper relationship between lover and loved one for the purpose of propagation of the human species. Thus all those whose appetite moves them to love strongly objects that are beyond the natural order and true scope we have mentioned are to be condemned absolutely, while those who within this scope love one person only always and with firm constancy and faith are to be praised.

It seems to me that an ample answer has been given on this subject. Since this love is good, as we have stated, it doesn't seem necessary to delete that part that in me would seem more than reprehensible because of my diverse public and private occupations. For if it is good, the good does not need to be excused for it has no faults. And if a scrupulous judge should not

---

7. Petrarch, *Rime* 1.8.

8. Guido Guinizelli, credited as the founder of the *Dolce stil novo.* Lorenzo refers to "Al cor gentil repara sempre Amore" (Love will always go to a gentle heart).

9. Ficino, *De amore* 2.7.

want to accept these reasons, let him at least concede this slight license to youthful and tender age, which does not seem to be so much subject to censure and the judgment of men. At that age no error seems so serious in that the young are more prone to take the wrong path because of lack of experience and so can least oppose those things that nature and the universal ways of others encourage. I say this in case it should be deemed wrong to love deeply and with the greatest sincerity one who because of her perfection compels her lover's love, and I certainly do not say that this would be wrong.

If this is correct, either for the reasons given or with regards to age, then neither composing nor commenting on my verses written on this subject can be seen as a grave error on my part. If it should be true that a comment on such matters is inappropriate because the subject is trifling, of little importance for the edification or pleasure of our mind, then I should say that the task of this commentary is particularly proper for me in order to avoid that another mind of greater excellence than mine should tire itself or waste time on such lowly things And if this subject is lofty and worthy, as it seems to me, it will be most useful to everyone to make it clear, linear and intelligible, and for this and for the reasons given above no one can do it with a clearer expression of its true sense than I myself can. Nor am I the first to comment on verses on similar love subjects, for Dante himself commented on some of his *canzoni* and other verses.[10] And I have read that Egidio from Rome and Dino del Garbo,[11] both excellent philosophers, did the same for that most learned poem of Guido Cavalcanti,[12] who in his time was reputed to be the greatest logician on earth and who was also an excellent poet in the vernacular, as shown by all his works and in particular in the above-mentioned *canzone* that begins: "Donna me prega...."[13] This poem is about nothing else but the way in which love is born in gentle hearts and its effects.

If neither the above reasons nor the examples given are sufficient to excuse me, at least compassion should justify me.

---

10. See Dante's *Convivio* and *Vita nova*.

11. Egidio Colonna (1246–1316), theologian, and Dino del Garbo (d. 1327), physician and philosopher.

12. Guido Cavalcanti (circa 1240–1300) was greatly esteemed by Lorenzo as poet and thinker and much praised in particular by Boccaccio and Ficino. He was a friend of Dante who mentions him in the *Commedia*.

13. Guido Cavalcanti, *The Complete Poems,* translated by Marc Cirigliano (New York: Italica Press, 1992), pp. 58–67.

Since in my youth I have been much persecuted by men and fortune, I should not be denied some relief, which I have found only in loving ardently and in composing and commenting on my verses, as we shall make clearer when we come to the explanation of the sonnet that begins: "If with my sighs that from my breast do come. . . ."[14] The malicious persecutions to which I have been subjected are well-known since they were public.[15] The relief from these and the joy found in my most sweet and most constant love no one but I can possibly know. For even if I had told someone about them, it would have been as impossible for him to understand as for me to do them justice. And so I return to the above-mentioned verse of our Florentine poet that among those who understand love through experience — the love I have so praised and some particular love and charity shown towards me — "Pity I hope to find as well as pardon."[16]

There now remains to answer only the possible criticism that I have written in the vernacular, which according to some is not capable or worthy of expressing any lofty matters or subjects.[17] To this one answers that nothing is less worthy because it is more common. On the contrary one can prove that every good is much better as it is more common and universal — as it is by its nature what is called the "highest good" — for it would not be the highest if it were not infinite, and nothing can be called infinite except what is common to all things. So then the fact that our mother tongue is common to all of Italy does not deprive it of dignity, and one should rather think of the perfection or imperfection of the said language, considering what are the attributes that give dignity and perfection to any language or idiom. I believe they are four, of which one, or at most two, are truly praiseworthy qualities of a language, while the others depend either from the customs and opinions of men or from fortune. That which is a truly laudable attribute of a language is having an extensive and abundant vocabulary and

14. Sonnet X ("Se tra gli altri sospir ch'escon di fore"), p. 114.

15. Lorenzo refers to various conspiracies, in particular to the one known as the "congiura de' Pazzi" (the Pazzi Conspiracy) in which his brother was killed in 1478, and to the difficulties of various wars.

16. See above, p. 83, n. 7.

17. A defense of the Italian language as being equal to all exigencies of expression and ennobled by great writers, whose importance Lorenzo emphasized by compiling the famous *Raccolta aragonese,* a collection of works of the great poets in Italian with an introduction probably written by Poliziano.

being capable of expressing well the sense and concept of the mind. For this reason it is deemed that Greek is more perfect than Latin, and Latin than Hebrew, for one more than the other is capable of expressing the thought of one who has spoken or written something.

The other attribute that gives dignity to a language is its sweetness and harmony, which some have more than others. Although harmony is natural and in relation to the harmony of our soul and body, it seems to me that this is a matter of opinion rather than reason because of the variety of human minds, unless they are all well-proportioned and perfect. Those things, which are judged according to whether they please or don't please, seem to rest on opinion rather than reason, especially those in which pleasure or displeasure is determined by desire and not reason. Nevertheless, in spite of all this, I do not wish to affirm that this cannot be a real merit of a language, for as I have said, since harmony is in relation to human nature, it may be inferred that the judgment of such sweetness and harmony should be proper for those who are similarly well proportioned and able to perceive it, and the judgment of these has to be accepted as true, be they many or few, for the affirmations and judgments of men are to be pondered and not counted.

The other condition that renders a language more excellent is when in it are written subtle and grave matters necessary to human life, both for our mind and for usefulness to mankind and the health of the body. This may be said of the Hebrew language for the admirable mysteries it contains, useful or rather necessary to the infallible truth of our faith. The same may be said of Greek, which treats many metaphysical sciences, natural and moral, very necessary to humanity. When this is the case, one must admit that the subject is worthy rather than the language, for the subject is the end while the language is the means. Therefore one cannot think that such a language is more perfect in itself, but rather that the matter it treats is more perfect. Those who have written about theological and metaphysical matters, both natural and moral, seem to think that, in so far as the value of the language in which they have written may draw from these matters is concerned, merit is to be attributed to the subject matter, while the language is the instrument, which may be good or bad in accordance with the end.

There is only one more condition that adds to the reputation of a language and that is when the course of events is such that it renders universal and almost common to the entire world what naturally pertains only to a city or a province. This may be seen as the favor of fortune rather than a true merit of a language, for the happy reputation and celebrity of a language in this world depend on the opinion of those who value and appreciate it. One cannot deem a true good what depends on others and not on ourselves, for those who now value it could easily change opinion and scorn it. Also conditions could change, so that since the reasons for valuing it would come to an end, so would easily end the reputation and fame of the language. This condition of being valued because fortune has smiled on events is very true for Latin, for the spread of the Roman empire made it, not only common throughout the world, but almost necessary. For this reason we shall conclude that these external values that depend on the opinion of others or on fortune are not true merits of a language.

So then, if we want to prove the dignity of our own language, we must insist only on the first condition, that is, whether our language can easily express all our mind's concepts and to this end no better proof can be produced than experience. Dante, Petrarch and Boccaccio, our own Florentine poets, with their noble and sweet verses and prose, have clearly shown that all things can be easily expressed in this language. Those who read Dante's *Commedia* will find much theological and philosophical matter expressed with skill and facility. They will also aptly find in his writings the three types of style praised by orators, that is, the humble, medium and high. In fact, Dante by himself has perfectly practiced what is found in diverse authors, both Latin and Greek. Who will deny that in Petrarch's work one finds a noble, tender and sweet style, and love matters expressed with such a lofty style and beauty that without doubt one cannot find equaled in Ovid, Tibullus, Catullus, Propertius or any other Latin writer? Dante's *canzoni* and sonnets are of such gravity and subtlety and so adorned that they find no comparison even in prose. Those who have read Boccaccio, a most learned and eloquent man, will easily judge him to be unique in this world, not only for his imagination, but for the eloquence and extent of his work. If we consider his *Decameron,* we shall note the great diversity of the subject matter in high style at times or medium or low at others, and the presentation of all perturbations that may occur to man in questions of love, hate, fear and hope and so many different wiles and ingenious inventions and tricks and the expression of all the character and passions of those who live in this world. And having noted all this, one must judge without doubt that no language is capable of full expression more than our own. And Guido Cavalcanti, whom we mentioned earlier, was able to join gravity and sweetness so wonderfully that it is hard to describe, as shown by the above-mentioned *canzone* and some of his sonnets and most sweet ballads.

There are still many other noble and elegant writers whom we shall not mention for the sake of brevity, although they are worthy of being remembered. And so we shall conclude that there has been a lack of men to practice our language rather than that men have lacked a language for their thoughts and subjects. All those who have become acquainted with our language through practice find its sweetness and harmony to be really great and very capable of affecting our emotions. These qualities, which are proper merits of a language, as some will perhaps agree, seem to me to be abundantly present in our own. And our language seems to be highly useful because of what has been treated in it until now, especially by Dante. It seems to me that it is not only useful, but necessary to read his verses because of their important and noble effect. This is shown by the fact that famous and most learned men have written many commentaries on the *Commedia* and that every day we hear its verses cited in the public sermons of holy and excellent men. Perhaps other subtle and important things worthy of being read will yet be written in this language. This is especially true since we could say that this language has been in its adolescent stage until now and is growing more gentle and elegant. And so it could easily be that in its youth and adult stages it will achieve greater perfection; and this would be even more probable if there would be some great success and development of the Florentine state,[18] as good citizens must not only hope, but help to bring about with all their intelligence and strength. Yet, since this is in the hands of fortune and the infallible judgment and will of God, it is not right for us to affirm it, just as it would not be just to despair of its being accomplished.

For the time being, it is sufficient to conclude as follows: that our language abounds in those qualities for which a language can be praised, and it would be unjust on our part to complain of it. And for these same reasons no one can reprimand me for having

---

18. According to Lorenzo, the fortunes and development of a language are linked to political conditions.

written in the language that is mine by birth and development, especially since in their time Hebrew, Greek and Latin were the natural mother tongue of those who used them, although spoken or written more accurately and with the observance of rules by those who have been valued and honored for it, than was the case generally for the common people.

It seems to me that it has been sufficiently proved that our language is not inferior to any of the others. Since I have demonstrated its perfection in general terms, I think it proper now to descend to particulars and come from generalities to some specific properties, as if from the circumference to the center. Since my first purpose is to interpret my sonnets, I shall strive to show that among the other forms of style in the vernacular, customary to those who have written in this language, the form of the sonnet is not inferior to the *terza rima* or the *canzone* or other forms in the vernacular, arguing from the point of view of difficulty, since according to philosophers virtue's worth consists in the difficulty.[19] Plato stated that to narrate many things briefly and clearly is not only admirable among men, but is almost divine. The brevity of the sonnet does not permit the use of a single word in vain. Therefore, the real subject matter of the sonnet must for this reason be some brilliant and dignified thought properly told, restricted to a few verses and avoiding obscurity and harshness. This type of composition is similar to the epigram in respect to the brilliance of the subject matter and the agility of its style, but the sonnet is capable of heavier thoughts and therefore becomes that much more difficult. I admit that the *terza rima* is a loftier and grander form, nearly similar to the heroic, but this does not make it more difficult, for it has a broader field, and the thought to which in the sonnet the poet cannot devote more than two or three verses without committing a fault, in the *terza rima* can be given more ample space.

The *canzoni,* it seems to me, are very similar to the elegies, but I believe that, because of either the nature of our verse forms or of the customs of those who have written them until now, this form would hardly admit without shame many things, not only light and frivolous, but exceedingly tender and lascivious that are commonly found in Latin elegies. Since the *canzoni* have broader space for wandering, I believe that this form is not as difficult as the sonnet. This can easily be proved by experience. Those who have composed sonnets and have restricted themselves to

19. Plato, *Republic* 2.366, *Laws* 4.718.

a certain subtle matter have with great difficulty avoided lack of clarity and harshness of style. And there is a great difference between composing sonnets in which rhyme governs contents and those where content governs rhyme.

It seems to me there is much more freedom in Latin verses than in those in the vernacular, for in our language in addition to observing the feet, which are regulated more by the nature of the language than anything else, there is also the difficulty of rhyme. And as those who have practiced this know, rhyme disrupts many beautiful thoughts, nor does it permit one to express them with ease and clarity. That our verses have feet is shown by the fact that one could compose many verses of eleven syllables without their sounding like verses or being different from prose. We shall then conclude that verses in the vernacular are very difficult and that the sonnet among other forms is the most difficult and for this reason to be prized as much as any other in the vernacular. But with all this I do not mean to infer that my sonnets are of the perfection I have prescribed for this form. But as Ovid says of Phaeton,[20] for the time being it is sufficient for me to have tried that style which is the most excellent in the vernacular, and if I did not succeed to reach its perfection and steer the sun's chariot, at least let me have the merit of my daring to try this form, even though my powers were not sufficient for such an enterprise.

Perhaps some will judge the beginning of my verses to be improper since I begin, not only differently from those who have written similar verses until now, but, as it seems at first sight, by reversing natural order in that I place at the beginning what in the course of human life comes at the end. This because my first four sonnets were composed for the death of one who, not only caused me to write these sonnets, but was also the cause of the universal tears of all men and women who knew her.[21] So then, though it may seem absurd that I begin with her death, to me it seems very just for the reasons we shall give later.

It is the opinion of good philosophers that the corruption of one thing is the creation of another, and the end of an evil is the

20. Ovid, *Metamorphoses* 2.327–28: "Hic situs est Phaeton, currus auriga paterni. / Qui si non tenuit, magnis tamen excidit ausis" ("Here lies Phaeton, driver of his father's chariot. / If he did not do so well, he yet fell in attempting something great"). The chariot, of course, is the sun's.

21. Simonetta Cattaneo (1453–76) who was loved by Lorenzo's brother Giuliano, and apparently by Lorenzo also. Poliziano makes her a central figure of his *Stanze*, and she was also celebrated by many others.

beginning of another.[22] This happens of necessity for according to philosophers, since the form and species are immortal, then one must necessarily begin with matter, and from this perpetual motion then necessarily is born a continuous generation of new things. These being without any intermission of time and with a most brief presence of the being of things and its condition in that state or form, one must admit that the end of one thing is the beginning of another. And according to Aristotle, privation is the beginning of created things, and thus one concludes that in human things end and beginning are the same thing. I do not mean end and beginning of the same thing, but that which is the end of one thing is at once the beginning of another. And if this is so, death is most proper as the beginning of this work. So much more so because if one examines this more closely, he will see that the beginning of a love life proceeds from death, for one who lives for love does first die to other things.[23] And if love has in itself that perfection we have mentioned, it is impossible to reach such perfection if one does not die first in reference to less perfect things. This same judgment seems to have been followed by Homer, Virgil and Dante, of whom Homer sends Ulysses to the infernal region, Virgil sends Aeneas and Dante himself explores hell to show that through this path one reaches perfection. But after acquiring knowledge of imperfect things, it is necessary to die in so far as they are concerned, so that after Aeneas reaches the Elysian fields and Dante is led to Paradise, they never afterwards remember hell. And Orpheus would have conducted Eurydice from hell to the world of the living, if he had not turned back towards hell. This may be interpreted to mean that Orpheus had not really died and therefore did not reach the perfection of his happiness, that is, of having his dear Eurydice. Thus the beginning of true life is the death of the untrue life. For all these reasons it does not seem that death has been put at the beginning of our work without good cause.

Perhaps this preface of ours has been too long and a greater preparation than required by the subject. But it seems to me that this has not been without necessity, for considering the trifling nature of these verses of mine, I thought they needed some ornaments, which are necessary for those things that in themselves are little adorned, nor was a lesser defense needed against faults that perhaps would be attributed to me. Thus having

22. See Ficino, *Theologia Platonica* 4.
23. Ficino, *De amore* 2.8.

completed this part, we come to the comment on the sonnets, first discussing things that seem necessary to the first four.

As we said above, in our city a woman died who gave rise to the pity of the entire Florentine people. This is not very surprising for she was adorned with beauty and human gentleness more than anyone before her. Among her other excellent virtues, she had such sweet and attractive manners, that all those who had some slight acquaintance with her believed they were much loved by her. Women in general and the young of her own age, not only did not envy her for this great virtue of hers, but highly extolled and praised her beauty and gentleness so that it seemed impossible to believe that so many men loved her without being jealous and that so many women praised her without envy. Although in life she was dear to all for her worthy condition, in death pity for her green years and for the beauty that she in death had greater than anyone alive ever showed gave rise to a burning regret at her loss. Since from her house she was brought to the burial place with her features uncovered, all those who gathered to see her shed many tears. Among these, those who had been acquainted with her, in addition to feeling pity, were amazed that she in death had surpassed the beauty that when alive seemed unsurpassable. Those who had not known her before felt grief and almost remorse at not having known such a beautiful woman before being deprived of her and knowing her only now so that they would forever grieve. In her was really seen what Petrarch said:

> "Lovely did death seem in her lovely face."[24]

When this woman had so died, Florentine minds gave expression to their grief at such a public calamity in different ways, as was proper. Some grieved in verses and others in prose for the acerbity of this death, and everyone strove to praise her according to the power of his mind. And I willed to be with them and accompany their tears with the sonnets below, the first of which begins:

> "O brilliant star that with your own bright rays."

It was night. A dear friend of mine and I were walking and talking of this common calamity. The weather was clear, and as

---

24. Petrarch, *Trionfo della morte* 1.172 ("Morte bella parea nel suo bel viso"; "Lovely did death appear on her lovely brow").

we talked, I turned my eyes towards a very brilliant star that could be seen towards the west. It was of such splendor thatø not only it surpassed the other stars by far, but was so bright that shadows were formed by objects struck by its light. At first I was amazed, but then turning to my friend I said: "We must not be surprised: the soul of that most gentle woman has either been transformed into this new star, or it has been joined with it. If this is the case, the splendor does not seem surprising. Just as her beauty was a great comfort to our eyes, let us comfort them now with the vision of this most bright star. And if our eyes are too weak to sustain such light, let us pray the deity, that is, her divinity, to strengthen them by deleting part of its splendor so that we may contemplate it without injury to our eyes. Being adorned with that woman's beauty, it certainly would not be pretentious of this star to want to outshine the other stars, for it could contend with Phoebus and demand his chariot so that it would be the one to give birth to the day. If this is so and this star can do all this without being presumptuous, then death showed great presumptuousness in striking such beauty and virtue." These thoughts seemed to me to be very good material for a sonnet, and so I left my friend and wrote this sonnet in which I speak to the above-mentioned star:

I

O brilliant star that with your own bright rays
Of all your neighbors you obscure the light,
Why more than you are wont do you now shine?
Why do you wish with Phoebus to contend?

Perhaps those lovely eyes that Death so cruel,
Grown so presumptuous, has from us now taken
You have in you received and so adorned
You can from Phoebus take his golden chariot.

Whether 'tis so or a new star you are
That with new splendor do the sky adorn,
When begged, O goddess, listen to our voice:

Enough do you remove from your bright splendor
So that our eyes, to tears eternal bound,
Will then see you so clear and most content.

This most excellent woman died in April, a time when the earth clothes itself with varied flowers beautiful to look at and of great comfort to the soul. Moved by pleasure in this, I walked alone and in thought through some beautiful meadows of mine. All taken by my remembrances and thoughts of her, it seemed that I saw everything in relation to her. As I looked from flower to flower, I saw among the others that little flower that we in our vernacular call "sunflower," which the Latins called *clytia.* According to Ovid,[25] a nymph called Clytie was transformed into that flower. She had loved the sun so ardently that, once she had been changed into a flower, she ever since faces the sun and cherishes her lover as much as she can. As I looked at this pale amorous flower, characteristic of lovers, and since it is really pale, being yellow and white, I felt sorry for its fate, because evening was near and I thought that soon she would lose the most sweet sight of her lover, since the sun was approaching the horizon that deprived Clytie of her vision. Her grief was even greater since what was denied to her was common to many others, that is, to the eyes of those who are called "antipodeans," for whom the sun shines when we are deprived of it, and their night is when it is day here.

This thought gave rise to another, that although for one night she lost sight of her lover, at least she would see the sun the next morning, for just as the western horizon deprives her, the eastern would restore him to her, and kindly dawn, feeling pity for her love, would show him to her again. And I still thank for this the eastern horizon, for it is most natural and human to have compassion for those who suffer, especially for those whose suffering is in some ways similar to ours. Clytie's fate, different and alternating, made me think of how much harsher and wicked was the fate of one who greatly desires to see something, whose view is necessarily impossible, not for a night, but forever. I see which dawn restores her sun to Clytie, but I do not know what other dawn can render to the world this other sun to, that is, the eyes of her who died. And if this sun cannot by necessity return, then for those whose eyes have no other light, it must perforce be eternal night, for night is nothing else but being deprived of sunlight. It is a very harsh fate that of one who greatly desires and waits for what he cannot have. Nor can he find any other respite than to remember and keep his mind's eye fixed on what he has most loved and has been most dear to him. I think this is the case for Clytie, who at night remains facing the western horizon, which is the one that deprived her of the sun's vision,

25. Ovid, *Metamorphoses* 4.169ff.

until morning when the sun makes her turn to the east. In a like manner, this new Clytie cannot have greater relief than keeping his mind and thoughts fixed on the last impression and dearest things of his own sun, which can be said to be like the western horizon that deprives one of his beloved vision.

We can also say that this last horizon stands for the death of this most noble woman. For "horizon" means nothing but last boundary, beyond which the human eye cannot see. Meaning that if the sun sets, it is the last place beyond which the sun can no longer be seen, and when it rises, the first place where the sun appears. Thus we can properly call death the horizon that took away the sight of her eyes, towards which this new Clytie, that is, the lover of those eyes, must keep his eyes fixed and still, considering that all things, although beautiful and most excellent, must by necessity die. This last consideration is a great and effective remedy for consoling one of any grief and showing men that mortal objects must be loved as finite things subject to the necessity of death. One who considers this in others can easily understand that this condition and necessity are also his own, observing that most wise saying that was written in the temple of Apollo: *"Nosce te ipsum."*[26] One must persevere in this thought until death comes and will render his sun to this new Clytie, just like the dawn renders it to Clytie transformed into a flower, for then the soul freed of its body will be able to consider the beauty of the soul of this woman, much more beautiful than that which before was visible to the eyes, for the light of human eyes is like a shadow in comparison with that of the soul. Thus, just as this woman's death was the horizon of the setting of the sun for his eyes, the death of this new Clytie will be the eastern horizon that will render to him his sun, just as dawn renders it to Clytie already transformed into a flower. Since this thought seemed to me to be proper for rendering in verse. I composed the following sonnet:

II

When the horizon sees the sun descend,
I look at Clytie whose face is so pale,
And I decry her fate that her deprives
Of seeing the one who then for others shines.

---

26. "Know thyself."

Then when with us is Phoebus once again
And with new fire lights flowers, plants and grass,
I turn to give my thanks then to the East
And gracious dawn that him to her returns.

Alas, poor me, I know not what new dawn
Will give my world its sun. Oh harshest fate
That in eternal night does cover us!

To see him now you hope in vain. O Clytie.
Till death docs close them, do your eyes keep fixed
To the horizon that took him away.

The universal nature of lovers is such that they feed their amorous hunger on sad and melancholic thoughts, with many tears and sighs. And this is their greatest happiness and sweetness. I believe that this is due to the fact that love, which is lonely and compelling, proceeds from a strong imagination, and this could hardly be if the melancholic humor did not prevail in the lover, whose nature is such that he is always suspicious and converts all events, whether beneficial or harmful, into grief and passion. If this is the nature of lovers, then their grief is certainly greater than that of other men when to their natural characteristics is added some event that is painful and causing tears in itself. Nothing can happen to a lover that causes more grief and tears than being perpetually deprived of the object of his love. From this one can deduce what grief the death of this woman caused in those who strongly loved her, a grief greater than many a man can feel.

It is in the nature of melancholic people, to which category we have said lovers belong, to seek no other remedy for pain than to accumulate further pain and to hate and avoid all sort of relief and consolation. Therefore, if at times as a remedy for this most bitter sorrow death appeared to me as a way of putting an end to this painful passion, I scorned it and hated it so much more because it had been in the eyes of that woman and could therefore be said to have become more sweet and gentle. This because, having been in contact with a most gentle person, it necessarily acquired the qualities it had found so abundant in her. Thinking how through this event death had become gentle and noble, I thought the gods would want to change their fate so that they, too, could taste the gentleness of death. This being so, and by nature wishing only for grief and not to enjoy anything sweet, to increase my grief I determined to continue living. I came to this decision so that my grief would become more compelling, my eyes could shed tears for a longer period of time, and my heart could sigh longer for the sunset, that is, the death of my sun, and so that my eyes, deprived of their most sweet sight, and my heart, of every hope and comfort, would continue to cry and sigh in the company of Love, the Graces and the Muses, to whom tears and grief are as proper and fitting as they are to my eyes and to my heart. Just as my eyes and my heart have lost the end for which Love had ordained and destined them, so must Love also cry for he had chosen her eyes as the seat of his empire and of his purpose, and the Graces had endowed her beauty with their own gifts and virtues, and the Muses had spent the glory of their choir in singing her most worthy praises. Therefore tears are proper and fitting for all of them, and if anyone did not cry with them, he must perforce be without a particle of love or grace. Since everyone must cry, some because they are not and some not to seem to be opposed to such gentleness, I should have wanted to express these sentiments in the following sonnet:

III

Of life the sweet light I would now abandon
For that all others Death do always call,
But noble Death so beautiful is now,
I think the gods do wish to die today.

Death noble is because she did her touch
That in the sky the brightest star now is.
I who no longer wish for any joy,
Now that she's dead, will my sad years live out.

Always my eyes will cry and my sad heart
Will for the setting sigh of our own sun.
My eyes have lost their sun, my heart all hope.

The Muses on Parnassus and the Graces
With me and Love will now so sweetly cry.[27]
And who would not all these in tears now join?

No one whose heart has burned with love will be surprised on finding in these verses diverse passions and sentiments, which are contrary to each other. For since love is a gentle passion, it would

27. See n. 65 to *Love Lyrics*, p. 61. The Muses, daughters of Zeus and Mnemosyne, were deities of the arts and intellectual activities.

be a greater cause for surprise if a lover had a moment's peace or an untroubled life. Therefore, if in our love verses or those of others one often finds this variety of contrasting objects, this is a privilege of lovers who are free of human restrictions,[28] for one cannot give reasons or find order and rationality in those things that are ruled only by passion.

The present sonnet seems to be in opposition to the preceding one since that one refuses all sorts of consolation and seems to dote on present grief and hope it will increase, while this one seeks diverse forms of consolation and has tried many things, though without success, in the hope of driving away the bitter memory of the death of that woman. Furthermore, in the end it shows some desire for death, which is alien to the preceding one. A person who feels excessive grief usually tries to mitigate it in two ways, that is, either to sweeten grief through something beautiful, sweet and pleasant, or to drive it away with some serious and important thoughts, and in general one elects first the remedy that is easier and sweeter. Therefore, since I felt the bitterness of this memory, I sought some solitary or shady place or the beauty of some green meadow, as mentioned in the comment on the second sonnet, or I stayed near some clear running stream or in the shade of some young trees. But I was like one seriously ill who, since his taste has been destroyed, although fed most delicate foods, from them receives the same sensation that converts into bitterness the sweetness of those foods. Thus the more pleasure these diverse and charming things should have given my heart, since my taste was damaged and my soul disposed to tears, the more they multiplied my sorrow, and the memory of the woman, who was present everywhere and always made all these things seem more bitter than ever.

As we have said of the sick that all his food tasted bitter, yet it nourished him and kept him alive, just so the most bitter food of her memory, although most painful and harsh, sustained my life. Actually no better remedy or antidote against this illness could be found than the illness itself. Nor could one overcome that thought if not with the same thought, for no sweetness remained for the heart except this most bitter memory, and this alone was useful in my illness. Since it was necessary to recur to the second remedy, I fled from these charming places into the stormy waves of civil occupations. This remedy also proved scarce, for since that most gentle creature had taken possession

28. See Petrarch, *Rime* 15.12–14.

of my heart and made it her own, the thought and memory of her were central in my heart among all others and, in spite of all other cares, consumed it as its own, for "care" means nothing else but "that which burns and consumes the heart." Therefore, finding it impossible to free myself from such bitterness and grief with any of the two methods, there remained no other remedy and hope than death, which hears one too late. This may be interpreted that death had previously refused to listen to the prayers of so many who wished to preserve her life, or that the sorrow felt after this woman's death was so great and had no remedy but death, so that any delay and postponement seemed unbearable, even though slight.

IV

Where shall I go where I shall not find you,
Sad memory of mine? In what dark corner
Where you will not be always there with me
Shall I then flee, for harm you do bring me?

If in a meadow with new flowers filled,
If in the shade of green young trees I go
And see a flowing brook, with it I cry.
What is there that will not my tears renew?

If to my woeful native nest I go,
Among a thousand cares this one will reign
There in my heart and gnaw and it devour.

What shall I ever do? What shall I trust?
In Death alone can I for mercy hope,
But Death, alas, will only too late hear.

I have completed the explanation of the previous four sonnets. Those that follow are very different and therefore, in order to make things clearer, it seems necessary to discuss a new topic that is common to all the following sonnets. This will show the aptness of what we said above, that is, that death was a proper beginning for this new life, as I shall strive to demonstrate below.

All men are born with a natural desire for happiness,[29] and all human works tend towards this as a true end. But since it is difficult to know what happiness is and in what it consists, and since even if one knows it, it is no less difficult for men

29. Ficino, *Theologia Platonica* 11.2.

to achieve it, it is sought in diverse ways. So that since men have in general and confused ways proposed this as the proper end for man, they try to achieve it in one way or another. Thus moving from the general proposition, they restrict themselves to the particular that is personal, and they strive in different ways, according to their character and disposition. From this is born the variety of human studies and the ornamentation and greater perfection of the world through diversity, in a way similar to the harmony and consonance that results from diverse voices in concordance. Perhaps it is to this end that He who is infallible has made the way to perfection dark and difficult. And thus we know that our works and human intelligence proceed from what is better known and goes to what is less known. Nor is there any doubt that it is easier to know things in a general way rather than in detail and singly. I mean in accordance with human intelligence that cannot have a true definition of anything if it does not proceed from the knowledge of its general and universal principle.

The life and death of the woman we have mentioned was then the general universal principle and the confused knowledge of what human passion is. From that universal cognition I then came to the particular knowledge of my own most sweet and amorous sorrow, as we shall discuss later. After the above-mentioned woman died, she was by me praised in the preceding sonnets and her fate regretted as a public calamity and common misfortune, and I was moved by a grief and compassion that many in our city felt, for it was a universal and common grief. Although in the preceding sonnet there are some things that seem to have been dictated by a personal and private passion, to better satisfy myself and those whose grief at her death was great and private, I strove to imagine that I also had lost a most dear person. In my imagination I tried to introduce all the effects that would be apt to move me in order to better move others. Being in this frame of mind, I began to think how much more harsh was the fate of those who had most loved that woman, and I tried in my mind to determine whether in our city there was any other woman worthy of such love and praise. Judging that it would be a great happiness and sweetness for one who had either by intelligence or fortune the grace to serve such a woman, I spent some time seeking, but not finding, anyone worthy, in my opinion, of a true and most constant love. Having almost given up hope of finding such a person, chance in an instant did more than my most accurate search had done in such a long time. Love, wishing perhaps to better show me his power, showed me such a great good at the moment when it seemed to me that there were no more possibilities.

There was a festival in our city, and many men and most young ladies, noble and beautiful, participated. Almost against my wishes, but I think it was fate, I went to the festival with some friends and companions because for some time I had kept away from such festivities. If at one time I had liked them, it was more from a certain common desire to do what other young men did than because I derived great pleasure from them. Among other women there was one I thought had great beauty and such a sweet and attractive appearance that, on seeing her, I began to say: "If only this one had the same delicacy, intelligence and ways as the one who died as stated above, for her beauty, charm and brilliance of the eyes are certainly greater." Speaking later with someone who knew her somewhat, I saw that those particulars, which were not very common, were perfectly in harmony and corresponded with her beauty, and especially with her eyes in which one could see what Dante had expressed about his lady's eyes in a canzone:

> "She brings there Love as if he were at home."[30]

In truth, when nature created them, it created not only two eyes that would be fixed on others in accordance with whether loved or hated, but the true site of Love together with the death or the life and happiness of men. At that moment I began to love the beauty that was apparent, and as to the beauty that did not appear, my impression and the indications given by her sweet and unusual appearance gave rise in me to an incredible desire. While before I marveled that I could not find anyone whom I thought worthy of a sincere love, I now marveled even more at having seen a woman who exceeded in beauty and grace the one who died. In truth, burning with love for her, I strove diligently to investigate how gentle and intelligent she was in words and deeds. I found all her conditions and attributes so excellent that one could with difficulty determine which was more beautiful, her body or her mind and soul.

Her beauty was admirable, as we have said: beautiful and proper size; her skin white, but not pale, with color, but not bright; her aspect serious, but not proud; sweet and pleasant, but

30. Dante, *Convivio, Canzone* 2.58.

not light or vulgar in any way: her eyes lively, but not wandering and without any sign of levity or pride. Her body was so well-proportioned that among other women she showed dignity without any signs of clumsiness or ineptitude. Nevertheless, in walking, dancing and other acts, where it is permissible for women to use their bodies, she was elegant and beautiful; indeed she was so in all her movements. Her hands were beautiful above all others that nature ever made, as we shall say in some sonnets inspired by them In dressing and in her ways she was very elegant and properly adorned, avoiding all the styles that are not proper for noble and gentle ladies, and preserving seriousness and dignity. Her speech was most sweet, indeed, with good and intelligent remarks, as we shall show later, for some words and subtle questions provided subject matter for some of my sonnets. She spoke at the proper time, briefly and concisely, and one could not wish to add to, or delete from, her words. Her witticisms and jokes were intelligent, humorous and sweetly sharp, but did not offend anyone. Her mind was truly marvelous, much more than is necessary in women, and this without presumption or showing off and avoiding a certain fault found in most women who think they know a lot and wish to be the judges of everything, thus becoming unbearable and earning the name of "know-it-all" in the vernacular. She was quick-witted, so that many times one word or a single gesture was enough for her to understand another's mind. In her ways she was sweet and pleasant beyond measure, but without anything sensual or that would provoke ill effects in others. In everything she was wise, careful and circumspect, avoiding however any sign of shrewd malice or duplicity and giving no reason to infer little loyalty or faithfulness. A full account of her excellent virtues would be much longer than the present commentary, and so we shall conclude with few words by saying that nothing one could desire in a beautiful and gentle lady would be found not to abound in her.

These excellent attributes had so bound me that I no longer had thoughts or limbs that were free And with regard to my eyes, I can say that the woman who died, of whom we have spoken, was the star Venus that the Romans called Lucifer, which precedes the sun, but then gives way and goes out when that greater splendor arrives, just as if her function were to notify men that the sun was coming and not to shed light on the world. This star goes out and dies when the splendor of the sun arrives, and nevertheless it is called Lucifer that means something that bears light, and light does not shine on the world until its light goes out. And so to the Romans the death of that star seemed to be the beginning and the life of the light of day. Therefore, their authority also verifies that the death of that woman was the proper beginning of this day that was brought to my eyes by the new sun of the eyes of this woman. Although we have praised her extensively, this praise cannot do justice to her excellence and her merits. Dead Lucifer showed me that soon would come this new sun of mine, and guided me while I was blind, as I have said, to the vision of this immense splendor. And once it had accustomed my eyes to seeing the splendor of that star, that is, celestial splendor, and seeing the sun arrive, it went out, and I who had turned my eyes heavenward for her, was able to turn my eyes from the light of the star to the splendor of the sun with less harm to my sight

V

Alas, poor me, when in the presence of
That proud, most sweet, angelic face I am,
Around my heart my poor cold blood then gathers,
And all the color from my face departs.

Her eyes then seem so merciful to me
That back my courage comes and so my spirits.
Love that in her bright eyes did always dwell
To my sad heart then shows the blind dark path.

To him he speaks and says: "I swear to you
By the sacred light of her sweet eyes,
Of my darts' power, of my reign high honor,

That I always with you shall be, and I
Tell you that most sincere her pity is."
My heart did him believe and fled from me.

My heart, alas, was all taken by and ardent for the beauty and gentleness of this lady of mine. If any part of me did not agree with this, it was due to the doubt that with her great beauty and most gentle ways there might be also some hardness and little pity. For I already knew how great was my desire and expected grief and intolerable torment if this most gentle lady had no pity. This doubt still held back my heart and did not give it the assurance to depart. And so if I was in her presence, her face really seemed angelic to my heart, sweet and proud. Sweet because it really was so, proud because of the fear my heart had of a lack of pity in her, and so at first I would become all pale, for my heart, already burning with love and with the above-mentioned doubt, could not help but make me be in great fear. Because of its fear, my heart would pant and thus the vital spirits, rushing to assist the heart, would leave my face without color, pale and lifeless, and together with the spirits a great quantity of blood flowed to the heart, as nature has ordained.[31] This generated much more heat than usual in that place, and since this heat had no vent and since the space was too small for such a mass, there occurred almost a suffocation of the spirits and blood. Not being able to expel the blood, the heart was forced to cool and mortify itself. This is shown by our experience of those who die through fear, in whose bodies is found a quantity of coagulated and cold blood, while in the rest of the body there is still some heat.

But then, looking at her face, it seemed to me there were many signs of pity, and thus the heart would lose its fear and recover some courage. For this reason the vital spirits returned to the place whence they had come, and with them there returned the color and the strength that had been lost earlier. The more so since looking in her eyes I would see Love, enveloped in the rays of those beautiful eyes, who would show my heart the way it could flee from me into my lady's eyes. That way could be called blind because my heart had no certainty except Love's words, and thus walked in darkness and enveloped in doubt; the more so in that Love who escorted it on the way is himself depicted as blind. To make my heart have more faith in him, he swore by my lady's eyes that the pity they showed was real, and also that he would always stand by my heart. For where Love and pity concur there could be no room for suspicion or fear in my heart, and since Love swore by the eyes of my lady, he could make no more effective promise. For swearing is nothing else than producing as witness of what you affirm the object by which you swear. For, so to say, one who swears by Jove wants Jove to be a witness and almost a guarantor of the observance of what is sworn, and

---

31. According to Ficino, the heart with its warmth generates a thin and clear vapor from the most thin part of the blood. This takes the power of the soul and communicates it to the body, and through the senses it takes the image of the bodies outside *(De amore* 6.6). This is basically the theory of the *Dolce stil novo* and of Cavalcanti in particular.

if he breaks the sacrament he becomes a perjurer, he offends the person to whom he swears and insults the one by whose name he swears.

Since Love had sworn by my lady's eyes and added that her eyes were his honor and power, my heart had to believe Love. For one could not possibly think Love wanted to deceive or provoke the enmity of those eyes in which resided his own honor and strength. Thus my heart did not err in believing him, and thus it abandoned my breast and went into those most splendid and amorous eyes.

VI

The dress, the time, the place where I at first
My eyes did fix on my sweet, gentle lady
To my mind often do return, or rather
They never do my memory abandon.

What she did look like then, O Love, you know,
For in her company you always were.
Her beauty and her gentleness, her charm
Beyond description are and our mind's power.

Like when the snowy, lofty mountain tops
Apollo bathes in his pure golden light,
So did her hair atop her white dress seem.

The time and place I need not specify,
For where this sun may be, there daylight is,
And paradise where such a beauty goes.

First impressions are very strong in men's minds, and it seems quite reasonable that it should be so, for since nature has created our minds capable of receiving diverse impressions and with a natural desire not to remain empty, our minds then act like a thirsty person who quenches his thirst with the first thing he finds apt to extinguish it, and the sweeter it is to the palate, the more willingly he does so. For this reason, according to Plato,[32] those of a tender age have a stronger memory, because those things they learn are better received in memory since they are first and new impressions.

Thus my heart having been reassured by Love and having already fled from me, nothing bothersome remained in my mind,

32. Plato, *Republic* 2.377b.

since I thought I could see sure signs of my lady's future kindness. This gave rise in me to great hope and sweetness. Since it is natural to desire what we like, when it is not present our memory and thoughts represent it to us, and more willingly those things that have been the first beginning or cause of the good the mind feels. Almost always present in my mind were the dress with which my lady was adorned and the place and the time when I first looked in her eyes, that is, when already in love with her I looked at her with the greatest pleasure, for there are two reasons only for looking fixedly, either to know well the object of your staring, or because this object gives us great pleasure. The first of these did no longer apply, since I already knew the beauty and the power of her eyes, therefore there remained only pleasure in my looking at her. Although I had seen her eyes at other times, not having yet had the boon of knowing them, I had not yet looked at them fixedly. I first looked at them fixedly after knowing this great good, after which I immediately and necessarily burned with love for them, for first comes knowledge and then love.

What she looked like to my eyes was most difficult for me to imagine or describe, for her beauty, as Dante says, surpasses our intellect "like the sun's rays on a most fragile face."[33] Therefore, what was impossible for me I delegated to Love who being always with her and residing, as we have mentioned, in her eyes could better know and describe such excellence to a higher degree. Moreover, my statement that her beauty, charm, gentleness and mercy were impossible to imagine or describe must seem amazing and almost impossible to the reader, and therefore it seems most fitting to produce an authentic witness to certify this statement, and there is no better witness than Love, especially since he was present and still merits to be believed, at least by those who have been his subjects. These, as we said in the preface, must perforce be lofty and gentle souls who have faith in such amorous wonders. Should those beyond this circle not believe them, then we can say that it is not proper for rude, vile hearts, rebels to Love, to enjoy this great sweetness.

Having spoken in general terms of this lady's excellence and how at first sight she seemed beautiful, gentle and pious, it seems we should mention the three things proposed in the beginning of the sonnet, that is, her dress, the time and the place. In regards to her dress, though it seems minor in comparison to

33. Dante, *Convivio, Canzone* 2.55–60.

her excellence, since she was dressed all in white and showed her golden hair, it seemed to me I could compare them to the sun's rays when they spread over a mountain of whitest snow, for her hair covered what was no less white than candid snow and it had no less splendor than the sun's rays. And while her hair was so bright, her eyes were much more so. As for the time, it was undoubtedly daylight, or at least it was caused by the sun of her eyes, and since this was so, the place must perforce have been paradise, for where there was so much splendor, beauty and piety can certainly be called paradise. For "paradise," if someone wants to define it correctly, means nothing else but a most beautiful garden in which abound all pleasant and delectable things: trees, fruit, flowers, running streams, songs of birds, in short, all the beautiful things a man's mind can imagine. Thus it can be affirmed that where such a beautiful woman was, there was paradise, for there abounded all the beauty and sweetness that a gentle heart can desire.

VII

Eyes of my love that are within my heart
And do the torment see that he endures
And his sincere, pure faith, do tell me why
My lady that he suffers does not care.

Go back to her and with you now take Love,
For he also has witnessed my deep sorrow.
Tell her that my last hope in you does lie
And if in vain your prayers are, I'll die.

Do take to her my wretched, sad laments.
Alas, how foolish my desire now is:
Without her lovely eyes my heart can't live.

O eyes that my harsh torment always soothe,
Oh do come back to my poor wretched heart.
Let Love go there alone and speak for me.

The image of the beauty of this woman had already descended into my heart through my eyes, and her eyes had made such an impression on it that they were always present. And Love who, we have said, resided always with them had also come with them. Because of this, my heart was surrounded by so many flames that it seemed impossible to bear the anxiety that was born of his ardent desire. Thinking what remedy would be best for this illness, nothing more effective occurred to him than to let my lady know his sorrowful condition and wretched state, for she was the only one to reprieve him from such pain since she was its only reason. It seemed necessary, then, to elect an ambassador or messenger that would meet two conditions: one, that he should be welcome to the one to whom he was sent since he had to make her favor my heart and this would be easier to gain through a person who enjoyed her favor; the second condition was that in addition to being well-informed about my heart's wretchedness, the messenger would be believed by her, so that the reality of the heart's suffering would move her to pity more easily. And so my heart decided to ask my lady's eyes that being in him saw his torment to go to her and refer this to her. And he also asked that Love accompany them, so that having more witnesses of his torment and the number of those who interceded being higher it would be easier to obtain her mercy through these gracious messengers. For no one should enjoy more favor with my lady and be more credible than Love and her own eyes.

Those eyes and Love were witnesses of my heart's suffering and also of his faithfulness, which was not exceeded by the greatness of his torment. Because of all this, the heart thought that his condition was known to her, and in this he erred as can be seen in the development of the sonnet, for my heart, unable to live without those eyes, and being alive when he was sending these messengers, showed by his own words that those eyes had never left my heart. Thus when my heart says, "Go back to her," almost assuming that they had left him at other times, it can be seen that my heart is dying because of his passion. This is also shown by his surprise that my lady does not care about his suffering, assuming that she knows of it. My heart then begs the two messengers to go and placate my lady in her harshness as his last refuge and only hope of salvation. The reader must assume that her eyes and Love were already on the way when my heart realized his error and that it was impossible to live without those eyes, and so called them back, begging them to remain with him and that Love should intercede for him by himself.

An amorous passion can be driven from the heart in two ways, that is, either forgetting the beloved or placating her. My heart tried both ways, and wanting to drive away her eyes, tried to send her into oblivion, for what we don't remember can't be in our heart. But he tried this remedy in vain, and so recurred to the second, that is, placating her. This cannot be done except by means of Love, nor could my lady feel pity if Love were not there together with the certainty of the heart's torment and faithfulness, for love, torment and faithfulness are those things that give rise to pity. The present sonnet, then, addresses my lady's eyes that were continuous witnesses of my heart.

VIII

How foolish to desire or hope for what
Beyond our power is or our own skill.
If one his eyes does fix upon the sun,
The sun he will not see, nor other things.

If true it is, as some believe today,
The harmony of the celestial spheres
Beyond the scope of human ears must be,
Desire one must not that which harmful is.

Oh foolish thoughts of mine why do you wish
Pity to add to my fair lady's beauty
And to her lovely eyes, to her sweet words?

More than celestial harmony her words
Beyond us are, more than the sun her eyes
Do burn. If pity added is, what then?

It often happens that men desire what would be very harmful to them and hope to obtain what is impossible to get, moved by presumption and ignorance, which is the mother of all evils, according to philosophers. This defect is found more often in those whose desire and passion are greater and whose afflictions and pain are so great that they will try all desperate ways to free themselves. This error can be noted in the above sonnet, which first states how great is the harm of desiring or hoping to obtain what is beyond our powers and for which our nature is not in harmony, being inferior and less worthy, and adds two examples as proof of this fact. The first is against those eyes that presume to look at the sun, which they not only can't see, but because of it lose vision for other things. The other example refers to the ears that are insufficient for hearing the music of the spheres. To make this part clear, we must understand that it was the opinion of philosophers — which Cicero reports in his book *De somnio*

Scipionis[34] — that the motion of the spheres generates various voices according to their greater or lesser speed, and all together give rise to a most sweet harmony of such great voice and sound that human ears cannot perceive, just as mortal eyes cannot look at the sun. The example given is that of men who are born near the cataracts of the Nile, that is, where that great river leaps down from high mountains. Because of the roar and noise, these men are all deaf. This opinion is not yet fully shared by me, and so it is not given as certain by saying. "If true it is, as some believe today...."

From these examples of human eyes and ears not able to see the sun or to hear the above-said harmony, I come to demonstrate the error of my eyes and ears, which have been presumptuous, the eyes by looking at the sun of my lady and the ears by listening to the most sweet harmony of her words. While this is a grave error, much greater is that of my thought, and more presumptuous, in desiring that pity be added, for that would add much greater power to my lady's beauty, which if my eyes and humble senses could not withstand before, just think how my thought acts against itself by its desire, which would add force against itself. It seems proper for the present subject to understand the reason for which we mention only my thought, my eyes and my ears, and no other force or sense, so we shall state for what reason we have done this. According to Platonists,[35] there are three types of real and laudable beauty: beauty of the soul, of body and of voice. That of the soul can only be perceived and desired by the mind, that of the body pleases only the eyes and that of the voice the ears. The pleasures of the remaining senses are rejected as being vile and not proper for a gentle soul By thought, then, we mean the mind, which has for its object the beauty of the soul, which consists in the perfection that it receives from virtues, and it is more or less beautiful and adorned with more or less beauty in accordance with the number as well as the quantity and perfection of virtues with which it is endowed.

The beauty of the body and its gracefulness consist, it seems, in being well proportioned and of graceful aspect and also in a certain charm and grace, which at times pleases not so much by the perfection and good proportions of the body, but because of a certain affinity it has with the eyes, which it pleases, and

34. Cicero, *Somnium Scipionis* 5.

35. Ficino, *De amore* 1.3.

this comes from heaven or nature. And all this is the object and realm of the eyes. The third beauty, of the voice, is when of many voices in concord there is a full agreement that is called harmony, and this may arise from various voices, as we have said, or from the sweetness and softness of words well connected and placed together, which cannot be composed in this manner without harmony. All this beauty pertains only to the ears. For this reason we have used only these three factors for learning about my lady. For when I speak of that mercy that my thought desired in her, we must understand that I mean the beauty of the virtues and talents of my lady's soul that our mind desired. For mercy is a worthy act of the soul moved by justice, for since it is a rational soul, without some merit the beauty of the body loved by my eyes would not appear in her eyes. Through her words, which outdo celestial harmony, we come to the third beauty, that of voice and harmony, to which only my ears listened intently. These three types of beauty were in this most gentle, beautiful and sweet woman who was dear to me above everything else.

IX

O eyes, I ever sigh as Love decrees
And through my suffering you joy receive.
Always I burn, but my eternal ardor
Cannot acquire what it does most desire,

But through my sorrow you well-being acquire
For you do gaze upon the noblest object
That one can have, and to your perfect weal
The grief of me, the heart, does you straight lead.

And if you cry, I am the one who gives
Relief in part to my own ills through you,
Nor does the heart by suffering harm you.

With me do now beg Love to be serene,
For if benign will be those brilliant eyes,
So will your sun more beautiful then be.

If the definition of love we gave in the preface is true, then the same may be said of the purpose and intention of the present sonnet, which is to prove through clear reasons that a heart that burns with love will never find peace and that a lover's eyes seem happiest when the heart's torment is greatest. The definition we gave of love was that it is a desire for beauty. If this is so, then one can truly say that love does not possess the beauty it desires, for if it did there would be no reason for desiring it, for one cannot desire what he possesses in plenty.[36] We shall say, therefore, that love is one thing while the purpose that moves it is another, for love is moved by and desires an end that is called "happiness" and "beatitude," which consist in union with the beauty that love desires and remaining with it inseparably. Until this end of beatitude is reached, love not only is not a good, but is unbearable pain and torment, more or less depending on its own depth. Therefore, supposing that the heart has not achieved the perfection of true beatitude and sweetness, one must admit that the heart is seriously tormented, since the heart has as its object the beatitude that is denied it. But the more beautiful what the eyes see, whose function is to see, the happier they are, and the greater the love, that is the heart's desire, the more beautiful everything seems to the eyes. For if the love is great, then beauty must perforce be or appear great to the eyes, otherwise there would not be love, that is, desire for beauty.

We can conclude, therefore, that for the same cause the more the heart is miserable, the more the eyes are happy. We must take these terms, however, in a broad sense, that is, the heart as the seat and site of passion where all desires are born, and the eyes not in so far as they are a sense, because as a sense and being exterior they cannot judge the beauty of any object. We must by eyes understand the activity of our soul that operates through the eyes and the happiness and pleasure that it feels through the instrument of the eyes, when by their report it judges an object beautiful and from this derives consolation and comfort.

In the present sonnet, therefore, my heart speaks to my eyes, showing the affliction and wretchedness of his condition, as Love wants, and the pleasure that the eyes derive from his misery, first demonstrating his affliction and then their pleasure. My heart's wretchedness consists in that he always wants what he does not have and that he never achieves that effect and end that he desires and longs for with an ancient, ingrained desire. The eyes instead not only see their own object, that is, the eyes and beauty of my lady, but see the most beautiful and excellent object they could possibly see, that is, my lady again, for the heart could desire nothing as much as her. From his desire is born the

36. This theory is found in Plato's *Symposium* (200–201) through Ficino, *De amore* 6.2 and 6.7.

greater beauty of my lady, whose beauty and perfection is in direct relation to the greater sorrow of the heart, that is, his desire for her for the reasons we have mentioned. He then answers the unspoken criticism that could be posed as a contradiction, that is, that the eyes too sometimes cry, which seems to be against the happiness he affirms is in them. He states that although the eyes may cry, this does not arise from any grief of theirs, but from the sorrow and desire of the heart, who by means of the tears gives vent to part of his grief. Then turning to them, he begs them to ask Love to make our lady feel pity, and this they should do, not only through compassion for the heart's misery, but also from the hope of greater good for the eyes, for the addition of pity in my lady would make Love tranquil, that is, the desire for beauty would be sated and would no longer disturb the heart. In this event, the sun, that is, the eyes and beauty of my lady, will be so much more beautiful to the eyes, and the more pity will increase beauty, the more beauty they will see.

It seems reasonable in order to confirm what we have said about the heart being the cause of tears to state how tears proceed naturally from the heart, rather than from the eyes, and understand what cause gives rise to the tears, as we shall show. According to physicians, all perturbations of happiness, grief, anger, hope and all other passions are born in the heart. Because of a certain connection and affinity that exists between heart and mind, all the passions that are born in the heart are immediately communicated to the brain. It then happens that when grief or happiness is communicated to the brain, it is oppressed or compressed by these passions and almost shrinks into itself, and being humid by nature and being compressed like a sponge, it distills part of that humidity through the eyes and thus generates tears, which are more or less abundant in different individuals in accordance with the greater or lesser humidity of their brains.[37] It is known that one may cry for happiness as well as for grief. But according to Aristotle there is a difference between tears of happiness and those of grief and that is that those of happiness are cold, while those of grief are warmer. And he states this as the reason: happiness and grief, being different passions, have very different effects, for happiness dilates and renders vital spirits more rare, while grief restricts them. Where there are a greater number of spirits there must perforce be a greater degree of heat, and vice versa, and so is born the difference between warm and

37. Cf. Aristotle, *Problemata* 31.23.

cold tears that are born from grief or happiness. We conclude, therefore, that tears have two causes, one is the heart's passion and the other the distillation of humidity effected by the brain, and for this reason the eyes are a path for tears rather than their cause.

X

If with my sighs that from my breast do come,
As my most cruel fate now does demand,
Love mixes some, it seems he to the others
Sweetness does bring and balm to my poor heart.

Her lovely face that with its splendor has
From Death's own grasping hands more than once rescued
My spirits and also my body's forces,
Now to preserve itself does help my soul.

Envious does Fortune see those sighs that Love
To my poor heart does send and bears with them
Thinking that my own grief they aggravate.

Thus I do her deceive and fool her more
By crying when Love vent gives to my tears,
And she knows not the sweetness tears bring me.

In the preface we promised that when we came to the present sonnet we should tell how great and pernicious was the persecution I had to bear at that time on the part of both Fortune and men.[38] Nevertheless, I am disposed to go over it very briefly to avoid seeming proud and vainglorious. For one can only with difficulty narrate his own grave perils without presumption and vainglory. I think this is due to the fact that when a ship, after the many dangers and much fear in a turbulent tempest, reaches the tranquility of the port, most times the skipper and the pilot attribute their survival to their own skill, rather than to any goodness on the part of Fortune. In order to make their endeavors seem greater than is the case, they magnify their past dangers beyond actual truth. Continuing with our example, physicians today always magnify the patient's peril beyond reality, often saying that some are in danger of death whose appearance

38. Lorenzo refers to the Pazzi Conspiracy, in which his brother was killed and he himself wounded (April 26, 1478). The theme of Fortune is characteristic of Lorenzo and the Renaissance in general.

nearly testifies to good health. In this manner if the patient dies the fault is attributed to nature rather than to the cure, and if the patient recovers, their cure and care will seem so much more effective.

We shall, therefore, say briefly that the persecution was very serious because the persecutors were most powerful men of great authority and intelligence, firm in their desire and intent to bring about my entire ruin and desolation, as shown by the fact that they tried all the ways that exist to harm someone. I, against whom all these things were aimed, was young, a private citizen without any help or counsel beyond what divine goodness and mercy gave me from day to day. Attacked at the same time spiritually with excommunication, in wealth by robbery, in government by different snares, in my family and children by new treachery and machinations, and in my life by frequent conspiracies, I was reduced to the point where death would have seemed a not slight boon, since it seemed to me a lesser evil than the others.[39] Being enveloped in darkness and the disfavor of Fortune, at times in this gloom there appeared the loving rays, at others the eyes, and still others the thought of my lady. This sweetness and respite drew my life from the hands of death as long as Fortune remained unaware of this relief, since she did not distinguish the sighs of love from those she caused in me. And so I say that when Love mixed some of his sighs with those caused by my adverse Fortune and harsh fate, the love sighs sweetened and mitigated the others and encouraged my heart. And if it happened sometime that I saw my lady's face, this defended me against the death of my soul, just as at other times it had extorted my spirits and strength from the grasping hands of Death. And "extorted" means one thing only, that is, taking something from someone against his wishes. And Death is really avaricious, because there can be no greater avarice than that of one who wants everything for himself, as Death does of all earthly things. I must add that Fortune, enemy and envious of all my good, did not recognize as amorous the sighs that Love emanated from my heart and, thinking that they were caused by my harsh fate and the above-mentioned persecution, tolerated them since she believed that they would add to my sorrows and that my pain would be that much more severe, never believing

39. Lorenzo refers to Pope Sixtus IV, who excommunicated him, and to various wars and to a second conspiracy against him that was revealed on June 2, 1481.

that they brought me relief. Being aware that Fortune was being deceived, to deceive her even better, at times I cried and lamented as Love urged, and Fortune could not understand the sweetness of my sighs and tears. In this manner, then, through the power of those beautiful eyes and of Love, at times I felt some relief and sweetness that I would never have had if Fortune had become aware.

XI

If when most close to you, my dearest lady,
At times my heart, that fortunate is, sighs
Do not for this his wrath or sorrow blame
Or scorn, or fear because of you he feels.

The happiness that Love has granted him
Makes all the spirits stray and to him go,
So that forgetful of himself the heart
Now burns without relief of cooling breath.

Love sees that to his aid he must soon come,
Or else the heart of happiness will die,
And to his aid the roving spirits calls.

To him obey they all do quickly rush
So that at times they do create some sighs
Just to relieve the heart that wants to die.

I should like either to have such a powerful style or to enjoy the trust of all men to such an extent that it would permit me to express fully the excellence of my lady and have it believed, for it would honor her and I should avoid the danger of being judged a liar. Unable to express or show her eyes and her beauty, for as commonly happens what is a virtue will perhaps be seen as a fault, I shall strive to show partially the nobility of her mind, by telling some of her *bon mots* that in my opinion are loftier and more subtle than one expects in a lady. Since we have said earlier that at times her words and questions have provided the argument for our verses, we can say that this is one of them, as we shall make clear.

I was very close to her eyes so I could see them and her other beauties from a short distance, and as I looked fixedly in them, I felt full of hope and sweetness so that at times I gave vent to deep sighs. This most gentle lady, who already knew the condition of my heart and my desire, with sweet words asked how I was and how content. I answered I could not be happier, nor could my heart be filled with more sweetness, and she then said, "What is the cause for your sighs, then?" Because of timidity and because her beauty and her words had almost made me lose my senses, I could not then answer anything. But when I had left her, I wrote the present sonnet in which I strove to express the natural causes of sighs. The present sonnet is written as an answer to that gentle lady's question so that it speaks to my lady and says that if my fortunate heart, that is happy and content — for '"fortunate" means having favorable fortune — sighs when it is closest to my lady, that is united with her beauty, it is not due to any disturbance or anything offensive like wrath, anger, pain or fear. To fully understand the truth, the cause is the sweetness he feels, which is so great that it involves all his strength and vital spirits and sways them from their natural tasks to the enjoyment of that sweetness.[40] Since the spirits are all intent on this, the natural operations that they perform must perforce cease. Among these natural operations is breathing, or shall we say respiration, which is diminished for the reason mentioned above. The result is that the heart lacks its customary relief, for since the heart is warm by nature and is even more heated by the gathering of the spirits, he would be smothered and would die were it not that it is refreshed by means of the air that is continuously renewed and refreshed through respiration.

It then happens that Love, seeing my heart in such a danger, calls on the vital spirits to help. And Love truly moves them, for nature loves to preserve life and so spurs the vital spirits at once whenever the heart is taken by passion. In obedience to nature's love then, the spirits quickly and promptly rush to his help. The result is that if the heart had need of respiration for cooling off, he will need it much more after the arrival of these spirits that are warm by nature. Thus he must perforce draw into the chest a greater quantity of air in order to restore the ordinary operation of respiration, which has been interrupted. Thus there is sighing, which refreshes the heart that had already forgotten himself and did not care if he would die, in fact, he desired such a sweet and happy death.

We can then say that sighing is caused by any mental passion or any fatigue of the body as long as the mental passions

40. This theme is common to the *Dolce stil novo* and is also found in Ficino, *De amore* 6.9.

are such that they interrupt or divert the natural operation of breathing, which among the Latins is properly said *refocillare,* or we could say "respiration." Physical labor or agitation, as in one who runs or exercises strenuously, also generates sighs because the natural heat is excited and increased, and the body could not persevere in its labor if the heart did not get relief through frequent breathing. I should have liked to express this concept of mine better, for it would have been proper in answer to such a meritorious and gentle request. I have, nevertheless, chosen to have a sonnet lacking ornament and the clearest expression of this concept, rather than be guilty of lack of prompt desire to satisfy what Love demands.

XII

Since that dire time when my "well-ventured" heart
Overcome was by his so cruel torment,
And after he did send some sighs ahead,
My sorrowful, poor breast he did abandon.

With Love he has been staying in those eyes
That lovely are and where they turn they make
Most gentle all who do upon her look
And have to him this honor also given.

My lucky heart, by them to this bliss raised,
So gentle has become through their great virtue
That he wants not, nor prizes, mortal goods.

Although by now all vulgar thoughts and vile
Those eyes from my own breast have driven out,
He won't to me return and nothing wants.

As we have related in the above sonnet, my heart had fled from me, emboldened by Love. From this derives the need to understand where he went and his condition. These things are told in the present sonnet whose argument is as follows: I say that my heart was "well-ventured" as may be seen in the conclusion of the sonnet, for "well-ventured" may be used for what is gentle and perfect as will be shown in the definition of "gentleness." Therefore "well-ventured" is not used in reference to his being overcome by the intensity of his torment, but for the good that derived from that. I say then that my heart sighed heavily, overcome by sorrow, and finally left my breast. His torment consisted in the burning desire for my lady's beauty. Having thus fled, he reached my lady's eyes and was graciously received by them. This may be interpreted as that my heart was nourished by the beauty of those eyes and by the hope of future mercy, which Love, who also dwelled in those eyes, gave him, for Love is never without mercy.

This most sweet refuge made my heart gentle through the virtue of those eyes, for if it is true that, moved by Love, those eyes instill gentleness in all they look upon, then so much more they had to make my heart worthy of such honor, that is, of gentleness since he dwelled in them always. To better express this truth and verify what has been stated, we shall say the following: If those things looked at by those eyes moved by Love become gentle, we must then suppose that those eyes have unique beauty, and that Love is merciful. Where these two qualities concur, there is born great sweetness and love in the heart of those who see, and love is never without gentleness, as we have said. The eyes moved by Love, that is, with affection, cannot look upon anyone who is not actually or potentially gentle, for affection can be felt only for those who please us, and no one can please us unless there is some affinity with us.[41] Therefore, assuming the gentleness of those eyes, it is proven that they cannot look with love upon anyone without making him gentle.

My own heart, then, not for his merits but by the generosity and graciousness of my lady, brought to this degree of gentleness, had such a high opinion of himself and believed he had already reached such perfection that he did not value anything vile and mortal. To avoid the appearance of contradiction, since we have said that without some merit no one can receive gentleness from those eyes, and yet we have stated that my heart was given this without merit of his own, we confirm what we stated above, that is, that we can deem one gentle in actuality or potentially. This means really "gentle" with all the virtues that come from "gentleness," or having the potential of becoming gentle, just as we can say that a blacksmith who holds a piece of iron without any particular shape is holding a sword, a hoe or whatever he desires to form with that iron. My heart at first was like this rough iron but had the capability of becoming what those eyes desired, and since they had the power to leave him rough or change him into other forms, the smith elected to make him gentle. In respect to this election, he was without merit, in

41. Cf. Ficino, *De amore* 2.8.

respect to having the disposition and potential of being gentle, he was not without some merit, and thus this matter becomes clear.

Seeing that my heart was so gentle, I began to love him more and wished he would return to me. And to bring him to do this, I purged my mind and breast of all vile and vulgar things through the means of those eyes, whose perfection penetrated in me through my own eyes and remained in my imagination. That most gentle form would never have remained in the midst of all my thoughts, if my thoughts had been vile and vulgar. Thus in accordance with the nature of good, my breast was first cleansed of all evil. In spite of this my heart did not want to return to me, nor did he desire any beauty other than that of the eyes where he resided. And this had to be so necessarily, since those eyes were most beautiful and my heart had become gentle, as we shall better explain in the comment on the sonnet that begins: "Delicate, beautiful and candid hand."

It seems that now it is only necessary to define once and for all what in my opinion is the meaning of "gentleness," since in our verses the words "gentleness" and "gentle" appear often. I would not have presumed to do this if the great poet Dante had not limited himself to the gentleness of men in the *canzone* where he defines that term, which he says means almost "nobility."[42] But since this term, in accordance with our language may be applied almost to all things, it does not seem improper to state what I understand by it, especially since in the connotation with which it is used, it is a new word restricted to the vernacular, which cannot derive any certain value from the use or definition of the ancients. It seems to me that the term "gentle" was born from those who were called '"Gentiles," that is, the Romans who were called "gens" and then "Gentiles" by Hebrew theologians and by the Christians, as one can show with many examples. Since the "Gentiles," that is, the Romans were deemed most excellent in those things that the world honors and values, I believe the word "Gentile" became the attribute of all things that excelled among others, almost as if it were something done by the "Gentiles" or worthy of them. Usage has then broadened its meaning so much that it is very difficult to define. For example, one will say a "gentle" ivory, and a "gentle" ebony, when one is more beautiful the more it is candid, and the other the darker it

42. Dante, *Convivio* 4. Here Dante speaks of "gentilezza" (gentleness) seen as spiritual nobility.

is the more it is valued: these are the opposite one from the other and yet expressed by the same term.

We shall say then that those things are '"gentle" that are well disposed and inclined to perform perfectly the operations proper to them, accompanied by grace, which is God's gift. For instance, we shall speak of a "gentle" race horse in reference to one that is swifter than others. But to this we should add the beauty that makes it pleasing to the eyes, for, in addition to being swift, it has to run gracefully and with no appearance of effort or panting if it is to be called "gentle." It would not be "gentle" if it were not beautiful or did not have a small, slim head, broad nostrils, lively well-proportioned eyes, small ears, slender and graceful neck, a not excessively broad, but muscular breast, well-colored strong feet, long and broad heels, short phalanxes, legs neither thick nor thin, but muscular and with both equally joining the shoulders, the rest from the point of the shoulders to the croup well-proportioned, back not very long, double loins, the body small and not leaning and longer underneath than the back, good thighs, straight rear, small tail, a coat that is pleasing to the eyes with some good marks such as, for example, a bay horse with white left rear leg and a white star on its head. If one wanted to praise in these terms a war horse he'd be mistaken for it has to serve a very different purpose.

And so "gentleness" is almost a judgmental distinction of all things. If one wants to see what my heart was like when he was "gentle," it is necessary to understand what his purpose was. Since he had as his object the eyes and beauty of my lady, it seems to me he had three functions: one to know, two to love and the third to enjoy that beauty. And if this beauty was great, as we have said, then great perfection had to be the heart's to know, love and enjoy it. At this time we shall not discuss this argument further, for in the sonnets that follow we shall better explain this subject and shall clearly show why, once the heart became gentle, he could not desire any other beauty than that of my lady.

XIII

Delicate, beautiful and candid hand.
Where Love and Nature did together put
The many wonderful and sweetest charms
That make their other works all seem in vain,

My heart you drew so slowly from my breast
Out of the wound those lovely stars had made

The time Love made them merciful and sweet,
Little by little you did follow them.

My heart with many knots you did then bind.
You made it over new, and when it was
Gentle by you remade, the bonds you cut.

If gentle he now is, there is no need
To seek new bonds with which to tie him down
Or think that something else he might desire.

We have said that those things that perfectly and gracefully perform what they are created for may be called gentle. Because of this it would seem at first sight that once anything becomes gentle, it will need nothing else for achieving its perfection. This seems to contradict what the present sonnet declares, whose conclusion is that the most gentle hand of my lady, by drawing out my heart, made him gentle, after having formed him anew, while the sonnet we have just commented that begins: "Since that dire time when my 'well-ventured' heart" states that the heart had already been made gentle by her eyes. And so, before we come to a detailed explanation of the sonnet, we shall eliminate the contradiction as follows: If gentleness is what we have said, then as many things may be gentle as are the purposes to which things tend. This may be seen by experience in a man, for in his tender early years we can call him a gentle child, then a gentle boy, a gentle youth, a gentle man and so on in accordance with the diverse purposes that age and nature assign him, for different purposes are proper for different ages. So then, when my heart fled into my lady's eyes by which he was made gentle, we can suppose that the heart then had as his object only my lady's eyes and her other pertinent beauties and enjoyed only those by means of my eyes' vision. Thus he was made gentle for the purpose of understanding, contemplating and enjoying that beauty by means of my eyes. But then when that most candid hand had entered my breast and drawn out my heart, it seems that he was raised to a more worthy office. This shows the authority that my lady exercised over my heart and makes it specifically clear that she deemed him her own, and since he was hers by her own choice, she perforce loved him. This shows more clearly that she had begun to make him gentle with her eyes, that is, she had privileged him because we love more those things that we consider our own and have begun to bestow privileges on. My heart's purpose, then, was one thing before my lady showed any signs of loving him and another after so many kind demonstrations. And so he had to be made gentle in accordance with his new status and purpose, for now his object was not only the beauty, but the love of my lady, so much more worthy in that it was more spiritual and less physical, and nevertheless no less desirable beauty for my heart than her eyes for my eyes. It was, therefore, necessary, as we said, to make him gentle again and form him for this new object, and this task was more indicated for my lady's hand than for any one else's. We must understand that this was the left hand, which came from the heart as a more certain messenger and witness of the intention of my lady's heart,[43] for it is said that in the ring finger, that is, the one that is next to the one we commonly call the little finger, there is a vein that comes directly from the heart, almost like a messenger of the heart's intention. We see then that the heart necessarily had to be formed again and made gentle in conformance with this new and more worthy purpose and that the true agent for this was the left hand for the reasons we have mentioned above.

Now we shall come to a more detailed explanation of the sonnet. Among the other most gentle beauties of my lady, her hands seemed beyond earthly standards. Although they were both beautiful, the present sonnet, as we stated above, is directed to the left hand, which is called "delicate, beautiful and candid." not that this adequately describes all the beauty of that hand, but by depicting a part, it is then possible for the reader to understand the exact perfection with which a hand can be endowed. That this is true is shown by adding that Love and Nature had contributed all their "wonderful and sweet charms," in short, all kinds of ornaments, so that all their other creations seemed like nothing in comparison with these beauties. Here we must note that all things that please do so for two reasons, either because they are perfectly beautiful or because they are much loved and desired. It often happens that one loves something that is not deemed beautiful, but when love is conjoined with natural beauty, nothing can please as much. For this reason, we say that Love and Nature had endowed that hand with all possible ornaments, which may be interpreted as that the perfection of natural beauty and the great love did not let that hand lack

43. At this point there may be a lacuna in the text, as some believe, or a syntactical error. We have opted for the second cause and with a slight correction have what seems to be a logical solution.

any part of beauty, even the most minute. This hand that was so beautiful, then, entered my breast through the opening that had been made by the eyes, which it followed immediately, entered and drew out my heart.

My eyes received the grace of first knowing the beauty of her eyes, and then, as often happens in dancing or other proper ways, I was made worthy of touching her left hand, for on the ladder of love one rises step by step. The hand that I touched had such power that it took from me all self determination and, as we said, drew my heart from my breast, that taken by this hand was at first bound very tightly and then formed anew and made gentle by that hand, for forming is a proper task of hands. Once he had been formed anew and made gentle, that hand loosened all bonds and set my heart free, for having been made gentle, he could only love gentle things and have only most gentle objects, and nothing could be found more gentle than my lady, who was gentleness personified. So there could be no fear that he would leave her, for though without bonds he remained, and one could not think that some other beauty would please him. For if one likes most what seems or is most beautiful, no one could be found more beautiful than my lady, of whom one could say truly in regard to her gentleness and beauty what Dante says. One could say of my lady:

> In woman gentleness is what in her
> Is found, and beautiful what her resembles.[44]

XIV

O lovely hand of mine that charming are,
For mine you are since Love gave you to me
As pledge for all the promises he made
On the same day he did my freedom scorn.

O most sweet hand of mine with which Love does
The arrows gild, his kingdom to enlarge,
With it the bow he stretches and takes aim
At all the gentle hearts that love do feel.

Candid and lovely hand, you then do heal
Those so sweet wounds just as Achilles' lance
In time long past once did, as some still say.

44. Dante, *Convivio* 3, *Amore che ne la mente* 48–50.

O ivory hand of mine, you ever hold
Both life and death for me and the desire
No mortal eye will see, or ever has.

As we said in the preceding sonnet, Nature and Love give all perfection and ornaments. This is confirmed by the present one that also speaks to that gentle hand and calls it lovely and charming: lovely for her natural beauty and ornaments, charming for love and desire, for were it not for love and desire, one could not say charming, even though most beautiful. In addition to these two attributes, we must note that I call it mine. Since this may seem arrogant on my part, for I was not worthy of such a beautiful and gentle object, I immediately repeat the word "mine" in the second verse, and I justify my calling it thus by showing that Love is responsible for he gave it to me as pledge for the promised mercy of my lady. It is a common and ancient usage among men that in every pact and transaction we touch with our right hand the right hand of the one with whom we are making a pact, as a more binding sign of our heart and will. It is also commonly used when peace is made after some war and injury suffered. In the same way, whenever in such or other cases we take an oath, the right hand is the instrument and agent. I believe that this usage was introduced for the reason that follows. If peace or similar pact and oath is broken and not kept, it must perforce be broken by some new injury that most times is inflicted through the action and means of the right hand, which is the one that strikes and in the majority of men is quicker and ready to attack. Thus by using the right hand in the above-mentioned circumstances as witness and confirmation of what is done, it seems that we bind what can violate the pact first and most easily.

Love, then, gave me this pledge of his promises the day I scorned my freedom, that is, the day he bound me. And we must note that this seems to be against truth, for the day her eyes bound me, I still had not touched this most gentle hand. We must understand this in one of two ways, either that the day Love bound me, he decided within himself to give this hand as pledge, although he deferred carrying it out for some time, or that I was entirely bound and without freedom the moment I touched that hand, for as we said in the preceding sonnet, it bound my heart with a thousand knots. This shows that at the time my heart was restrained by bonds and that if it had been possible, he would perhaps have freed himself, and thus he retained yet a modicum of freedom. But once he was formed anew and the bonds were removed and he remained with my lady of his own will, then one could say that he had lost all his previous freedom and that Love scorned his freedom, that is, the freedom the heart had enjoyed before he had known this new freedom that Love had provided. For "freedom" is understood to mean that one can act according to his own will, as my heart could since he was unbound and free of all restraints. We shall discuss this at greater length in the comment on the sonnet that begins "He whose sight, etc." Add to all this that this truly most sweet hand gilds Love's arrows, bends back Love's bow and wounds all gentle hearts who then fall in love and are the target of Love's arrows, as our Petrarch certified when he said:

> Love who all gentle hearts sweetly entraps
> And scorns to try his strength on other targets.[45]

We must note here that all these are acts that are performed by means of our hands. In addition to this, when we say that this hand gilds Love's arrows, we must understand that this hand prepares for Love the arrows that cause one to fall in love and are said to be golden, and not those of lead, which destroy love and give birth to hatred. Just as all these are tasks for the hands, so is also that of caring for the wounds, because surgery, the nature of which is extended to similar medical care, has no other meaning than operation of the hand. It wounds, then, and heals, that is, it causes desire to rise and then fulfills it, as it is said was the case for the spear, that is, the lance of Achilles, son of Peleus, which had two points according to poets, one of which wounded, while the other healed the wound. From this it follows that since this hand can wound and heal, it then can also kill and vivify. It is properly said, then, that those ivory fingers hold my life and death. And this is a proper function of the fingers because when the hand presses something, it does so through the means of the fingers. This hand also holds my great desire and truly so, as has been said in the previous sonnet. For since it holds my heart, in which is the seat of covetousness, that is, desire, it holds my desire, which I hide from men's eyes and is invisible to them. For if it is true, as we said, that my lady is most gentle and that my heart was made gentle by her, for otherwise he could not know and love such

45. Petrarch, *Rime* 165.5–6. The citation should read "Amor, che solo i cor leggiadri invesca."

great beauty, other men's eyes cannot see my most gentle desire since they were not made gentle by her and are incapable.

Now not to create confusion in the minds of those who read something in the preceding comment that seems at first sight contrary to this, we shall expound further on this matter. We said that this hand so praised and loved by me is the left hand, while all the examples we have given regarding the promise I received from Love, the gilding of the arrows, bending the bow and medicating more likely refer to the right hand. In order to eliminate this confusion, we must understand that the left hand is naturally worthier and stronger than the right, for it is closer to the heart, which is the giver of virtue and power. It is true that human custom has caused this natural power to degenerate like some other things, so that if the right hand has greater dignity or power, it is through custom rather than by nature. Nor must usage oppose the fact that what is willed by nature is worthier. Thus in spite of perverse usage, good minds like my lady's in this and other matters have wanted to be better than others. Since my lady had to assure my heart of the mercy and disposition of her own heart, she did so by that means that was more natural and inspired greater trust since it was closer to the heart. Furthermore, gilding arrows, bending Love's bow and medicating love wounds are tasks for the left hand, for although beauty binds us, the heart of the woman we love presses much more and thus heals better. All these manual operations, which are in reference to the heart, are much more proper for the left hand because of the vicinity mentioned above. Thus the error lies in what men do customarily rather than in what my lady elects to do in this matter.

XV

How I do envy you, my blessed heart
That her sweet hand always does press and fondle
Until all vulgar harshness has been cleansed.
And since you have most gentle now become,

That dear white finger does at times inscribe
In you the name of one Love gave you to,
Or does design that sweet angelic face,
Sweetly perturbed at times, at others gay.

At times that hand so lovely her sweet thoughts
Will one by one most lovingly depict,
Or some sweet words so proper and so pure.

What else can you wish for, my lovely heart?
Nothing but that the power have those stars
To make you be like a firm diamond firm.

We have more than once previously defined "gentleness" and come to the conclusion that we may call "gentle'" what in accordance with human perfection performs the activity for which it has been created perfectly and gracefully. And since my heart had reached this perfection by means of that most beautiful hand, the present sonnet mentions the way in which he was made gentle and also some effects of beatitude and sweetness the heart feels as a result. For memory and mention of this pleases the heart as much as it pleases sailors to tell of some dangerous storms after they have reached the safety of the harbor.

The present sonnet then speaks to my heart, showing that it envies him, not because it dislikes his well-being, but because it would want to achieve the same good. By calling him "blessed heart," it clearly shows the reason for envy, which is, as we have said, a desire for the same good. Envy is perforce greater and more apparent in proportion to the greatness of the good that others have, and there is no greater good than beatitude, which is enjoyed in fact by those who are gentle. When we speak of the heart's beatitude, therefore, we presuppose the heart's "gentleness."

The sonnet then tells the way in which that hand transformed my heart from his natural hardness and vileness to the perfection of "gentleness" by caressing and pressing him, which may be interpreted that her hand at times treated him pleasantly and sweetly and at others harshly and powerfully. This because it had to struggle against two enemies, hardness and vileness, and so had to oppose them with two contrary virtues, power against hardness and sweetness against vileness. For those who rightly think of what militates against perfection will find that there are only two things, a natural inertia, first of all, and a contrary disposition to the beatitude one seeks. This is caused by defective constitution and body organs and by natural desires and inclination to many errors, for the way to perfection has always been difficult and fatiguing. These contrary things often are such strong impediments that they will not let one reach beatitude even once, let alone permanently. This may be called "hardness." Even though at times this beatitude is known hazily and therefore desired, men have a natural vileness and diffidence that makes them despair of achieving it, and even when trying to pursue the path for achieving it, they will not reach it. And this is the second obstacle, vileness or cowardice.

It is necessary, therefore, to use power against that hardness and coddling and sweetness against cowardice, using one or the other in accordance with how powerful the enemies are, for one breaks hardness, the other gives rise to hope against cowardice. The present sonnet shows the two effects when it says "press and fondle," for with these two hardness and cowardice are eliminated from the heart, and when these are removed the heart becomes gentle, that is, it becomes capable of receiving all worthy forms and gentle imprint. From this it follows that as soon as the heart becomes "gentle matter" he can stay without "gentle form" just as long as matter can remain without form. Since love joins matter and form through a natural desire that one feels for the other, Love, who moved that hand to render my heart gentle, makes it move again to give him such gentle imprint. Finding my heart without hardness, that is, softened and capable of receiving any imprint, Love begins to write in him the name of my lady, the name I say to which Love consecrated my heart. For "consecrating" is used for dedicating a temple to God or a church to a saint, giving it that name so that it will always be known by that title. My heart, therefore, was truly consecrated, for Love made of it a temple and site for the celebration of my lady's name forever more. That candid finger also depicted the likeness of my lady's face and those passions and perturbations proper for a gentle lady, like some modest joy and sweet perturbation. Since what we are about to write may seem impossible, that is, that one may describe or depict thoughts, which are not subject to sight, one must understand that the passions that are proper for my lady are three, that is, the two we have mentioned, modest joy and sweet perturbation, with the addition of love at this time, which must necessarily include a sweet hope. Of the four perturbations we exclude only fear, for this would not be proper in so gentle a lady, although it is common to all men.[46]

Since we wanted to mention this most gentle passion, that is love, and since thoughts are the true nourishment of love, we said that her amorous thoughts were depicted in my heart, and if we wish to make this painting the object of vision, we must understand that my lady's face, which before had been painted at times joyful and at others sweetly perturbed, was also painted at

46. Cicero's *Tusculan Disputations* are the source for the discussion of the four perturbations (*Tusculanae Disputationes* 4.4).

times as expressing love. Just as we recognize joy or grief through laughter or crying or other signs, so amorous thoughts may be distinguished through many signs: in fact, they may be hidden from amorous eyes only with great difficulty. Among other signs, as is true of other emotions, they may be known best of all through words, which most times are the expression of thoughts, and so it is added that the same hand inscribes also the words of my lady as messengers of her thoughts and external witnesses of what the heart does within.

We must then assume that the painting that adorned my heart was a most worthy one, for three things in my judgment are necessary for a perfect painting. These are a good subject; a wall, wood or canvas or other material on which to extend the paint; and a painter who is a perfect master of design and color. In addition to these, the subject painted should be naturally likable and pleasing to the eye, for even if the painting were perfect, the nature of the subject it depicted could be unsuitable to the nature of those who would look at it. For some enjoy cheerful things like animals, nature, dances, festivals and such; others would like to see land or sea battles and similar martial subjects; others yet like houses, towns, foreshortenings and perspectives in proportion; and others still some other subjects. If we want a painting to be entirely liked, therefore, we must add this other condition: that what is painted is pleasant in itself. My heart was matter and subject capable of receiving any impression. No hand was ever so gentle and skilled for such painting as was my lady's, nor could any more pleasing matter be expressed in my heart than the sweet emotions and the name and face of my lady. Therefore in my heart's judgment this painting was so perfect that he wanted it to be preserved and kept as it was for eternity. This is a most natural desire and follows from the stated principles. For one goes through the way to perfection that is very difficult and laborious in order to reach beatitude. One who has been granted the grace to reach it can have no other desire than to establish himself and stop there as my heart desired. Thinking that this was the way to remain forever in such a wonderful state, he wished that my lady's eyes would have the power and virtue that one reads of Medusa's face,[47] and just as her appearance changed men into stone, my lady's eyes would change my heart so painted and so beautiful into hard diamond.

47. Medusa was one of the Gorgons. Her eyes had the power of turning to stone anyone who looked at her.

One must understand, then, that the painting of such beautiful and sweet things in my heart stands for the thoughts he had and the imagination of those things. Since those thoughts were so sweet, the heart desired them to be preserved and to last like hard diamonds and that new bothersome thoughts would not arrive to chase away those sweet ones, as often happens to lovers, who generally remain in the same condition but a short time.

XVI

O purple, fresh and lovely violets[48]
That a most candid hand just now did pluck,
What rain or what pure air did nourish you,
Much lovelier flowers, than they're wont to do?

What earth, what sunlight or perhaps what dew
So many beauties did all place in you?
Whence did the tender fragrance Nature take
Or heaven that did wish to bless you then?

O my dear violets, that lovely hand
That where you were chose you from all the others
Did you adorn with all these finest virtues.

She who my vile heart took and gentle made
And now is making you this fortune share,
She is the one to thank and no one else.

Not only was my lady more beautiful than any other and endowed with most worthy ways and decorous customs, but she was also loving and graceful. One can truly affirm of her that she excelled so in all virtues that a lady should have, that if another woman were endowed as perfectly with one only of all the virtues my lady had, it would be sufficient to make her excel among all other women. That she was most loving and graceful, as we have stated, was shown by many evident signs, but in addition to these there was one most extraordinary gift most dear to me that I mention in the present sonnet. It happened that since I had been for some time unable to see her because of some circumstances, it had become almost unbearable, and I could not have stayed without seeing her any longer, no matter how short a

48. While in the language of the time "viole" meant carnations, "violets" has been used for the sake of sound.

time, without endangering my life. She became aware of this, not through visible signs, for that would have been impossible, but because she knew the great love I had for her, and also perhaps because she also experienced how difficult and unbearable it was to deprive my eyes of her own eyes. Since she could not remedy the situation at that time, she came to the aid of my affliction in the only way she then could. She naturally enjoyed, among other gentle things, having in her home some beautiful vases with certain plants of violets, which she herself cared for with water in the excessive heat and whatever else was needed for their nourishment. She selected three violets among the many she had, either because it was Nature's will which had created them more beautiful or because Fortune made them come to her most candid hand before the others. She sent me these violets she had picked as a gift, and nothing could have soothed my grief more, except her own presence. The present sonnet, then, speaks to the above-mentioned three violets, which reasonably seemed to me much more beautiful than what nature usually produces, since they were marvelously beautiful in themselves, were a gift from my lady and had been picked by that most candid hand. And thus the present sonnet asks the reason for their great excellence, as one does in the case of all marvelous things. Since the present sonnet seems sufficiently clear in itself, we shall briefly mention that in asking for the reason, we touch upon all the means by which nature produces plants, shrubs, grass and flowers. Since all these together did not seem sufficient to explain this extraordinary beauty, the color, shape and fragrance of those fortunate violets, it seemed that there must perforce be some other reason and that some extraordinary power had produced them. And it was impossible to understand what this reason was, except for one who had experienced a similar power and virtue in other objects. Since I had experienced in myself the virtue and power of that most candid hand, which, according to the preceding sonnet, had taken my most hard and vile heart and made him gentle, I could believe and affirm that the same hand could have given those violets their excessive beauty, for it would be more difficult to make gentle something uncouth and vile, than most beautiful something that was already beautiful, as violets are by nature.

Thus we may conclude that the same hand had given the violets such quality and excellence that had changed my heart from rude to gentle, and for this reason those violets were my heart's consorts for "consorts" are called those who have shared the same fate. For their great beauty, then, those violets did not have to give thanks to the sun, the earth, the air, the dew, the sunny site or any other natural factor that could participate in such a production, but only to the virtue and power of that most candid hand. It may not be out of place to see if the beauty of these violets was just my opinion or whether it could be possible in reality. I cannot judge if it was really so, for I can refer only what seemed to me in accordance to what my senses referred to my judgment, and it is difficult for me to know whether they were reliable or whether they were depraved and corrupt, for the same judgment must assess what the senses relate and in what ways. I confess, nevertheless, that it is possible that a strong imagination may cause the senses to be corrupted, as often happens in a maniac who seems to see what is not there, for imagination has great influence over the senses, as we shall see in the exposition of the sonnet that begins "My thoughts always and only do admire."[49]

But this does not mean that this beauty was not true or that its cause was not the power of that hand, for we see that either by the grace of God or celestial influences or for natural virtue different men are endowed with different powers and virtues. We often see a most learned doctor kill many men while an ignorant one cures almost all his patients; some men have a particular virtue and cure certain illnesses with their presence and a touch of their hand, and some have profited more by their presence against those who attack them than by the sword. We read in certain books on astrology that one who is born under a certain constellation has the power with his sole presence to cure the possessed. And is that of words not a greater force since they are listened to by brute animals, by plants and herbs as it is said of serpents and other animals? And do they not have the power of making plants and herbs die? Does a charm not have such diverse and great effects as we read in Cato, in Pliny and in other trustworthy, respected ancient authors?[50] What other examples do we wish to find? Do we not see that human eyes at times have a greater force and that with a simple glance they almost kill and bring back to life, make blood recede and come back, take away strength and restore it, and what is more, they corrupt

49. This is Sonnet LXXI of the *Love Lyrics*, p. 49, which was not commented on by Lorenzo.

50. Cf. Cato, *De agricultura* 160, and Pliny, *Naturalis historia* 28.10–21.

the judgment of the human mind? Given all this, it seems quite possible for a hand to be endowed with such virtue that will give, I'll not say new qualities, but to the same qualities more beauty and excellence than Nature usually gives. And this more so by a hand that is perhaps the most beautiful Nature ever made. And if I were to be the judge of this question, I should answer that I judged the beauty of that hand before I loved it extremely, for cognition must perforce precede desire. If then that hand seemed beautiful to me so that I should love it, it must follow that I was not influenced by passion and that her hand was truly most beautiful. And if this is so, it seems more impossible that such great beauty was not endowed with some marvelous virtue and power than difficult to believe what I write of her.

XVII

Clear, sparkling waters, I do hear you murmur
And ever utter my fair lady's name
Because I think Love did you happy make
By letting you her lovely face reflect.

Her lovely image you could not retain.
Contrary to your nature it would be.
Only her charming name you may recall:.
To hear it Love permits no one but me.

How much more wise my eyes on that day were.
Perhaps more fortunate, my dear clear waters,
When first they mirrored there her lovely face;

The holy rays they did forever keep.
Look where they may, they nothing else do see.
No shade or sun can hide them now from me.

Although in the preceding comment we said we should reserve to the discussion of the sonnet beginning "My thoughts always and only do admire" the subject of the power of imagination over the senses, it nevertheless seems convenient at present to say something of the effect of this, rather than the cause. It happens many times that when one hears a continuous and inarticulate sound, our imagination will relate it to that subject it is then contemplating, and it will seem that the sound is articulated so that in our imagination we give it the sense and meaning we want. The sound of bells, of water falling steadily will commonly seem to say what he who imagines it will want. Another example is that at times we see diverse and strange forms of animals and men in the clouds above. Also when we look at certain types of stones that are streaked with veins, we often see formed in them whatever pleases our imagination.

This happened to me when, finding myself in some beautiful place with a clear and bountiful spring with water continuously falling with a sweet murmur, it seemed to me that this murmur continuously repeated my lady's name, for that was what I imagined most and most desired to hear. This most sweet deception was helped by the fact that my lady had previously been in this beautiful place and had looked in the spring, which had become her mirror, for that beautiful and most limpid water had for some time retained the most beautiful portrait of my lady. And thus it did not seem impossible to credulous lovers that the water, which had fallen in love with such a beautiful face, would from then on repeat continuously her most sweet name with its amorous murmuring. It then seemed right that if that water was in love with such a beautiful face it should forever retain it with itself and never let it leave, just as it seemed to me that it perpetually repeated my lady's name. And one can well believe that the same imagination that made me hear that name at all times, inspired by an amorous simplicity, led me to look in the water to see if my lady's face was still there. When I did not see it, I realized my mistake and at once saw that water cannot reflect such a form unless there is present the object itself, for such is the nature of water since it is a diaphanous body. But it is perfectly possible to recall her name with its murmur, as it seemed to me. Since this was born of my imagination and desire, no one but I could hear it, nor did Love permit such sweet harmony to reach other ears than my own amorous ones.

I then began to compare the happiness of the water with my own, and since it seemed that I was happier, if I had at first felt any envy, I now arrogantly thought that either my eyes had been more fortunate or they had been more prudent and wise. This because from the first time my eyes saw my lady's beautiful face, they always retained that most sweet image, and from then on they could not see anything else in shadows or darkness or in the light of the sun. Shadows and darkness may be interpreted as night and the sun as day, and this is the equivalent of saying that neither day nor night could take those eyes away from my own. Or with a broader interpretation we can say that two things corrupt human sight and weaken the eyes' power, that is, a deep darkness, which is nothing else than the shadow born of the interposition of matter between us and the sun or by excessive light as when we look at the sun. That same imagination, then, that made me hear my lady's name in the water's sound, made me see that most sweet face at all times and everywhere. This concept expressed in this manner is present in this sonnet, which speaks always to the water of the above-mentioned spring.

We must clarify further that part that states that my eyes were a mirror for my lady's face, which we have reserved for last not to interrupt the meaning of the sonnet. Since it seems that we should not omit it, we say that if we wish to verify that my eyes were a mirror for her face, we must understand naturally that the eyes see and how the potential of sight becomes operative. According to the Aristotelians,[51] the object that is seen is represented inside the eyes, with the species and form of this object being multiplied until it reaches that part of the eye that is called "crystalline," because it is transparent and diaphanous like crystal, which receives the form of the object seen as a mirror does what is placed before it. This form seen by the crystalline lens is transferred to the common sense that judges the quality of the object. According to Platonists, in our eyes there are some minute spirits that leave our eyes and go to the object seen and bring it by reflection to the eyes that almost take the form of the object, which they represent to the already-mentioned crystalline as if in a mirror, and from there to the common sense. In accordance with either of these opinions then, we have rightly said that my eyes were a mirror for my lady's face, for in the eyes is formed the image of whatever object is seen, as is the case with anything placed before a mirror.

XVIII

On that most happy day I left you here
With Love and with my lady, my dear soul,
While she with Love did walk, to him she spoke
With such sweet words that you were led astray.

In tears and sighs, I now do here return,
To the place where you first abandoned me.

---

51. Cf. Aristotle, *De sensu et sensili* 2 and *De generatione animalium* 5. Lorenzo also speaks later of the Platonists' theory, which is also treated above.

Wherever my sad eyes I turn about,
I do not you nor your companions see.

Where more in bloom the earth appears I look
And where her presence made the air more clear,
Whose eyes another site do gladden now,

And to myself I say, "From here you fled
With Love and with my lady, wicked soul,
But fate does me deny that lovely path."

If something is favorable and the desire for it great, but the enjoyment of it is impeded for some reason, most times one recurs to those remedies that represent it better and more closely to our minds, either because they are similar or because they are near. And since the beginning is the most important part in all things, our mind willingly turns its thoughts, and if possible the senses, to those things that concurred in the beginning, such as time, place, words, ways and whatever else had participated. I think enough has already been said about how great was the desire to enjoy her most sweet presence. Being deprived of it at that time, when I composed the present sonnet, I had perforce to recur to the above-mentioned remedy of seeking the most similar and nearest thing possible to the real one my heart desired. I therefore first began to recall in my mind that most happy beginning from which so many happy events have derived. From this thought was born the most ardent desire to go to that place in which my soul did first go far away from me, together with my lady and with Love. For only a short time had passed from the time her eyes bound me when I saw her most beautiful and most loving and sweet in a charming place very near our city. As Fortune willed, after this time she left, and I was deprived of her sweet sight for some time, and it was then that I wrote the present sonnet.

Finding myself in this place, then, in which I had left my soul, I tried to see if I could find it. But seeing neither my lady nor Love, I at once thought that my search was futile and that my soul had fled elsewhere together with my lady and with Love, which was obvious since I saw neither my soul nor its companions, that is, Love and my lady, whom I had left all together in that charming place. My soul was led away by Love and by the words my lady spoke with Love, for speaking with Love means nothing but speaking words that are pleasing to the soul and thus binding it more. It is certainly true that on that day she made me hear many most sweet words of love and mercy. Not only did I then return to that place, but I also recalled her words and ways, for nothing could be of greater comfort while she was absent. These thoughts and place, which continuously represented that happy day, gave rise in me to a greater desire for seeing her eyes and investigating the path by which she had left. Since it was unknown to me, there was nothing better for finding it than to look at the ground and the air. For wherever her feet had touched the ground flowers had bloomed, and the air through which her face and eyes had penetrated and her walking had parted acquired much virtue and grace, so that being more clear and splendid than the rest it showed that my lady had passed that way. This was similar to the Milky Way in the sky that, because of its great splendor due to the multitude of stars more plentiful and closer together, closely resembled the way taken by my lady made splendid by her eyes.

Thus the path through which my soul had fled with my lady and Love, leaving me behind, was very clear. But my destiny and adverse Fortune did not permit me to follow that lovely path as my soul had done, a path that had to be most lovely since it was adorned with fresh flowers and made splendid by the brilliance of those eyes. I should want these amorous moods to be expressed in this sonnet, which speaks always to my fugitive soul, and one must suppose that it was written and recited in the same place where these loving events had occurred.

XIX

Give me peace now, O ardent sighs of mine,
Thoughts on that lovely face forever fixed.
Do let a tranquil sleep to me come now
And close my tearful, my poor grieving eyes.

Their labors men and beasts have put aside
As well as their harsh thoughts and pressing cares.
Chariot and horses ready are by now
To take the sun on his long journey East.

O Love, a truce let's have. I promise you
That in my dreams that loving face I'll see
And her words only will I ever hear,

And that white hand I'll touch that holds my heart.
O Love, too envious of my happy state,
At least let me in dreams so blessed be.

In general all physical ills increase and torment the patient more with the coming of night. This happens because as the sun's force, which is beneficial to human nature, disappears, evil humors become stronger while our vital strength's opposition becomes weaker. This occurs because night is naturally given to man for resting, and since the night is more inclined to rest than the day is, it is not so intent and watchful over the body's preservation. The same is true of our soul's infirmities, which are nourished by pernicious and sad thoughts, as the physical are by malignant humors. Perhaps there are many causes for this, but at present we need consider only two. Just as we have said that physical illnesses are influenced by a greater force of malignant humors and a lesser resistance by natural forces, so do spiritual ills have two reasons for being more severe at night than during the day. The first is that naturally the humors of which we are composed circulate within our bodies at certain precise hours proportionate to the length or brevity of day and night. Night and day, whether long or brief, are divided into twelve parts, each of which is called an hour, so that towards evening our melancholic humors begin to move and last part of the night, while almost all the rest is taken by the phlegmatic. According to physicians, during the last three hours of the night and the first three of the day blood circulates, and the choleric humors are in motion during the next six hours, so that the melancholic humors circulate during the last three hours of the day and the first three of the night, and the phlegmatic for the remaining hours of the night.[52] Since melancholic and phlegmatic humors give rise to melancholic and sad thoughts, these must perforce be more powerful during the time those humors circulate. The other reason why spiritual illness is more serious during the night is that at night one cannot use the remedies against these ills that can be used during the day, for no better remedy can be found against these evil thoughts than diversions. These proceed from seeing, hearing and practicing various things that will distract our minds from bothersome thoughts, and these can hardly be exercised during the night. Thus we can conclude that thoughts are more powerful at night, and when they are pernicious they

52. Ficino, *De studiosorum sanitate tuenda* 1.7.

are much more bothersome, since they are more powerful while there is less resistance and no remedies.

It was night, then, and I was so afflicted by my amorous thoughts that I could no longer resist, being deprived of sleep altogether, that is, of the only thing that could give me some relief. The fact that I tried to put aside those thoughts clearly shows that they were bothersome. The annoyance caused by these amorous thoughts could arise from two causes. One, from a suspicious and continuous jealousy, which even without cause accompanies our minds like a shadow does the body, for as we said in the comment on the third sonnet,[53] it is the nature of the melancholic to doubt even the splendor of the sun. Or two, that in thinking of the beauty of my lady, there rose in me such a great desire that burned so that my heart could not help feeling such passion, greatly desiring that of which at the time I was deprived. Whichever of the two may have been the cause, I was moved by my suffering, and in the present sonnet I beg my ardent sighs, that is, the sighs caused by the above-mentioned desire. I also beg my thoughts that were always fixed on that beautiful face and never saw or thought of anything but her. I also beg the tears shed by my eyes, since all three things bothered me all together, to give me some peace, so that some tranquil and sweet sleep would come to my tearful eyes filled with dew. To give rise to compassion in those I begged, I show that all men and brute animals were peacefully at rest without burdens or thoughts, while I sighed and cried. And I also show that I had spent such a large part of the night with my sorrows, that it was now time for me to rest, for the sun's steeds had been hitched to the sun's chariot to bring light to the world, for the light of the sun's rays, that is, the dawn, which precedes the sun, gave signs of the approaching day to the world.

Since it may seem improper to say that melancholic and phlegmatic thoughts had such power at the time of the dawn when we have said that the blood circulates, we must understand that, as we said in the preceding sonnet, lovers for the most part either are or become melancholic by nature. Although their thoughts are always related to this nature of theirs, they multiply at the time in which the effect of the humor is added to their nature. So that even when the time that seems contrary to melancholy arrives, the same thing happens as in a furnace, which, although the fire has been extinguished, still gives off heat for some time

53. Pp. 97–99.

because of the fire's effect, for naturally one cannot go from one extremity to the other without an intermediate state. The effect of the melancholic humor is great, and the phlegmatic one that takes its place is not so opposed to the preceding humor that it can annul its force because of the way it participates with cold melancholy. So then, since these thoughts are so fortified by the humors, when the blood circulates it is necessary that the force of the humors decrease degree by degree and the thoughts take on the nature of the blood. At the hour mentioned, therefore, the strength of those pernicious thoughts had not decreased sufficiently for me to be able to sleep.

My prayers did not succeed in having my wishes granted by my sighs, my thoughts and my tears. Thus as I thought of what I could do, I realized that the true cause of my evil state, that which caused my tears, sighs and thoughts, was Love. Thus I began to address my prayers to him, and since before I had asked those others for peace in vain, I only asked Love for a truce, something that he should grant more easily, for peace is a perpetual tranquility, while a truce is temporary. To make him grant me this more easily, I promised Love that even though I slept, I should not rebel against his dominion and in my dreams I should see my lady's face, hear her sweet words, and touch her most candid hand, and while I slept my thoughts would be of love, as they had been while I was awake. The only difference would be that while awake my thoughts were bothersome and cruel because of my jealousy or my desire, but in my sleep they would be sweet and tender, for my desire of seeing, hearing and touching my lady would be fulfilled. I could surely promise this, for generally in our dreams we see those things we imagine and desire while awake. If Love did not grant that I should be happy at least while asleep, I should then be truly able to call him envious for refusing to make me happy even by a false and most brief sweetness.

XX

O sleep most peaceful, do to me come now,
To this afflicted heart that longs for you.
Shut the eternal font of my sad tears,
O sweet oblivion, that do me elude.

Do come, O only peace that can restrain
The course of my desire, and bring with you

My good and pious lady whose eyes are
With pity filled, so sweet and so serene.

Show me the happy face where at one time
The Graces chose to stay, and let a visage
So kind, a tender word my desire still.

If her to me you show, then let our sleep
Eternal be, or through your gates of ivory
May peaceful dreams and sweet no longer pass!

In the previous sonnet we have shown that at night thoughts are more intense than during the day and that when they are pernicious they are much more bothersome. Although this is generally true, yet I believe that amorous thoughts are much more persistent than the others and much more unbearable when they are bothersome. If we presuppose the absence of the loved one, these thoughts must perforce be bothersome, for all the evils to which men are subject are nothing but the desire of the good of which one is deprived. One who feels physical pain or that his body is burning wishes for the health of which he is deprived. One who is in jail wishes for freedom, one who has been deposed from some honorable office wishes to recover that status, and one who has lost his property or money wishes for wealth. From this we can conclude that if one should be without desires, he would not be subject to any circumstances and that the greater desire denotes greater affliction.[54]

If this is true, then, lovers are more wretched than anyone else, since their desire is greater, and at night they are most miserable because then desire grows since in the absence of other occupations to distract the mind, they have no recourse against the thoughts that afflict them other than those same thoughts. They are deprived of any relief for their passion, relief that might be there during the day, such as seeing the woman they love, speaking of her with some friend, seeing some person near to her or related, or a servant, or at least seeing the house in which she lives. While these things are nothing more than what rinsing one's mouth is for a feverish thirsty man, which actually makes thirst increase, yet they let one pass the time with less affliction. One can truly say that lovers live by the most sweet deceptions that they practice on themselves, and since at night they are partially deprived of these, all alone and in

---

54. See above, p. 110, n. 345. Evil defined as privation of good is also in Ficino.

thought, they find neither consolation nor sleep, as shown by the present sonnet, very similar in subject to the previous one.

The sonnet addresses sleep, begging it, after so many sorrows and worries, to come and shut the font of my tearful eyes, everlasting font, that is, eternal, flowing, almost as if saying that if sleep does not close those eyes, they will never cease crying. It then calls sleep a sweet oblivion and the only quiet able to curb desire, for my affliction had two remedies, either to interrupt my thoughts so I should forget them or to lessen desire, and since it seemed to me impossible not only to sleep but to live without imagining my lady, I beg sleep to bring her along when coming to my eyes, that is, show her to me in my dreams and make me hear her and see her most sweet smile. The same smile I say where the Graces have made their dwelling, the smile that is graceful and gentle above all others, and I say that without adulation, so graceful is my lady in this particularly and in everything else. I also wanted that she should be shown to me by sleep to be merciful and to speak appropriately, so that both these aspects could assuage my ardent desire. It was necessary, then, that both her appearance and words be amorous and full of hope. In all this sonnet, as one can see, nothing is attempted except curbing and tempering my most ardent desire. Since my thoughts believed sleep would grant their request, they went further, as happens to insatiable human appetite, and wished that this happiness would continue forever in my sleep or when awake sometime, for the sonnet says that if sleep consented and granted my request to show me my lady as beautiful and merciful, then I should want to sleep forever and never awaken, assuming the presence of my lady in accordance with the above-mentioned conditions. And if this should be impossible, at least let not these dreams be lying and false like those that pass through the ivory gate. In the ancient poets,[55] I found written fictitiously that in the underworld there are two gates, one of ivory and the other of hornwood, and that all dreams that arise in human imagination during sleep pass through these two gates. They are distinguished by the fact that true dreams pass through the wooden gate, and vain and false ones through the ivory one. So that my asking that these happy dreams not pass through the ivory gate is the same as saying that they not be false, but true and have the same happy effect that those passing though the hornwood gate usually have.

55. Homer, *Odyssey* 19.562ff.; Virgil, *Aeneid* 6.893–96.

XXI

Let those who wish great pomp and highest honors,
Great halls, the forum, sacred temples seek,
The treasures, the delights that with them bring
A thousand cares, harsh thoughts and deepest grief.

A cool green meadow full of lovely flowers,
A brook that all around the young grass bathes,
A little bird that so of love complains,
Much better to our ardent soul bring peace,

The shady forests, cliffs, the highest mountains,
Dark caverns and the beasts that from us flee,
A charming, graceful, shy and fearful nymph.

There I can see with swift and ready thoughts
Her lovely stars as if they were alive.
Here one or other care takes them from me.

In the previous two sonnets we have shown abundantly how thoughts are more forceful at night, particularly those of love. Since we have mentioned only the affliction caused by pernicious thoughts, it seems proper that they should be followed by the present sonnet, in the exposition of which we show what great sweetness amorous thoughts bring when they do not arise from bothersome causes. It is reasonable that they bring greater sweetness than other thoughts, if it is true that pernicious thoughts bring greater discomfort, for the same circumstances that cause excessive unhappiness will cause even more excessive happiness. This is just as in the case of a miser who will suffer as much grief at losing a sum of money as would be his happiness at gaining the same sum. For if it is true, as we said in the preceding sonnet, that our appetite is what makes us subject to Fortune and to events, it seems necessary that our good and our evil be measured in accordance with our desires. And since these desires are for one and the same object, it seems not only true, but necessary that the happiness and unhappiness caused by that object be equal in accordance with the degree of privation of the object or the fulfillment of desires.

Amorous thoughts, then, are most sweet and more tender than others when they are caused by sweet reasons, as shown in the present sonnet. Since we previously said that unhappiness was caused by being deprived of the object of love and by the suspicion that is usually felt by lovers, then we can say that the happiness of the said thoughts also proceeds similarly from two causes, always presupposing the certainty that lovers can have of the fidelity and love of their beloved. One is the memory of a new or recent happiness and satisfaction, with the mind going over it and willingly recalling all details, so that it seems to us that we are prolonging the past sweetness. The other is the hope of the achievement of the desired good, so strong and certain as to make it appear almost present. Just as the first cause that takes place after the fact makes a past good last longer, the second before the fact makes it begin at present, as is shown by the fact that those who expect a similar sweetness and those who have recently experienced it would all want to banish all other thoughts. I have known someone who received suddenly the unexpected news and unexpected certainty of good in the near future, who then remained almost amazed and did not hear anything that was said to him or use his senses, since that thought had alienated him.

The present sonnet, then, shows these amorous effects and by putting these loving thoughts ahead of all the things that are generally pleasing and sweet to men, it shows clearly enough how great is the sweetness of amorous mental contemplation. It says, then, to leave to those who want them pomp, high honors and public magnificence like the forum, the temples and other public buildings, and by these it denotes the ambitious and those who seek honors with great efforts. It then states to leave to whoever wants them all civil delicacies, and by this it denotes all human pleasures and lusts. To these it adds wealth, showing man's love for and eager efforts to gain money. All this because our appetites concern these three things only, that is, ambition, physical pleasure and avarice, since honors, pleasure and gain impede all other human operations. The sonnet then continues by showing what are the objects that aid amorous contemplation, that is, a small green meadow filled with beautiful flowers, a brook that bathes the grass and flowers all around where it flows and the love songs of some little birds. Here one must note that in opposition to the pomp, great buildings and other things denoted by noble and magniloquent words we have all humble things presented in diminutive terms, like small meadow, brook and little birds. This is to make it quite clear that if the above-mentioned great things are accompanied by innumerable harsh thoughts and sorrows, the humble ones on the contrary induce tranquil and peaceful thoughts.

The sonnet then continues with woods, mountains, rocks, caves, wild animals and some timid nymphs, which are all propitious to these amorous thoughts, in order to show that in reality solitude and avoiding human concourse bring peace to our mind and does not bring force to bear on our thoughts. And since these are not being forced, they turn to nature and imagine what they desire and love most. Imagination, then, has such power that it shows our eyes whatever it wants, and to me it showed the lights, that is, the eyes of my lady as if I were seeing her alive and real, but while in the city one or another care deprived me of this sweetness, which is really great. Even if this were not shown by other reasons, it would become apparent by the fact that the sweetness of imagination is similar somewhat to real beatitude, that is, what the soul, to which eternal glory is given, achieves, which is not enjoyed in any other way than by imagining and contemplating divine goodness. Although this contemplation is very different from human contemplation, for the former contemplates truth while the latter a vain imagination that is formed by mortal desire, yet they are both somewhat similar in the method. Thus this mortal one, although imperfect, is considered to be the highest earthly happiness when its object is the true perfection and goodness in so far as this is possible to achieve in mortal life.

For these reasons we can say that contemplation of something not objectionable entails great sweetness for it has some resemblance to the highest sweetness and perfect happiness. We must suppose that the present sonnet was written in the city, for when it says, "here one or other care takes it from me," in the last verse, we must perforce understand that "here" means in the city, since it is presupposed that there is some recent pleasure due to contemplation or other reasons felt in the solitary countryside. The comparison shows that the countryside is desired, while hatred is felt for the cities

XXII

"O my poor tired eyes, stop your woeful tears.
That dear angelic face you will soon see."
"We see it now." "Why do you then shed tears?
Why is your heart so frightened in your breast?"

"We are so wretched! For were she to look
And fix those happy lovely eyes on us,

Just like the basilisk to stone she would
Turn us, or else our soul would surely die."[56]

"What makes you wish then, or what fate makes you
Both fear and want what will destroy you soon?
Who urges on and who does hold you back?"

"Nature instills in us a fear of death,
But to his denizens Love sweet does render
What others have always most bitter judged."

We read in Homer, an ancient and most excellent Greek poet, that when Jove wants to give men the fate that is proper for them, he has two very large vases, of which one is filled with adverse fates and the other with happy and unhappy ones all mixed together. When he wishes to give someone an adverse fate, he takes it from the one that contains only the evil ones. When he wants to make someone happy, he takes his fate from the other vase in which prosperous and adverse fates are mixed together.[57] This signifies that men can easily be unhappy without any joys at all, but they cannot be happy without a share of adversity. If the authority of a poet so excellent that he was called "divine" should not be sufficient to confirm such an excellent affirmation, then it would be abundantly shown to be true by human experience.

We also embrace this truth in the present sonnet, and having in the three preceding ones shown two truths, that is, the happiness and unhappiness of amorous thoughts, it seems that not without reason we can now show that often happiness and unhappiness in love are present together and mixed. In fact, they are almost always together, although one or the other will at times have greater force. This is true not only in love matters, but also in natural ones and commonly in all human events. In so far as natural ones are concerned, we see that all things that live in this world are composed of opposites and live by the opposition of humors, with components that individually are very offensive to the object itself.[58] Were it not for the mutual repression of these opposing humors, nothing would live in

56. It was thought that the basilisk was a monster capable of killing merely by looking. See Pliny, *Naturalis historia* 8.77–78 and 29.166.
57. Homer, *Iliad* 24.527–33.
58. Lorenzo presents this theory of contraries also in *Devotional Poems* 1.23–38, pp. 413–14 and in *Sylva I*, 9, p. 224.

the lower world. Thus we can say that all living mortal things, vegetative, sensitive and rational, live not because of benefits received from these humors of which they are composed, but in spite of them and against their will. This because each humor naturally wishes to vanquish its opposite, and as soon as this natural appetite is fulfilled in any of them, so that one defeats the others, death must necessarily follow, while life is preserved while their powers remain equal and war among them proceeds. We shall then say that our life consists of opposition, enmity and diverse evils and that our death results from peace. This proves, then, that life, which mortals value among the highest goods, is always accompanied by this conflict of the elements.

As for worldly events and what happens to men, for the most part it is quite clear that they are either pure evil without any beneficial aspects or good mixed with much evil. Although it does not seem to me that this fact needs any confirmation, nevertheless, dividing human operations into mental and physical, I believe it is easy to understand that our minds and intellect always have the senses and physical passions as opponents and enemies. This is necessarily so since intellect and body are very contrary by nature, and physical passions and appetites are always opposed by the pangs of conscience, which originate in the intellect. Moreover, often, or rather almost always, one passion is contrary to another and one desire to the other, and this is necessarily so because human passions are mostly due to the humors of which we are composed that are, as we have said, in direct opposition to each other.

In civil and domestic operations we see that the difficulty of arriving at decisions is due to the fact that in any course of action there is always some drawback and that not once in a thousand times is there a true plan that may not be contradicted. For this reason, those who are more prudent take longer to arrive at a decision and because of this delay they are known as "serious" men. And time is called "most wise" because true wisdom consists in waiting and seizing the opportunity when it arrives.[59] This would not be necessary if it weren't for the many difficulties entailed in the necessary deliberations. We see then that all human actions are not entirely good or sweet and always

59. This passage on "civil and domestic operations" reflects Lorenzo's experience in government and, to us, points to certain aspects of the following century found in Machiavelli's theories on fortune and "occasion," and Francesco Guicciardini's pessimism.

have their share of misery. And this is seen much more in those matters that are governed by passions and appetites, as is the case for love matters, for love is nothing else but a gentle passion, as we said in the sonnet that begins: "where shall I go, etc."

The present sonnet, which is in the form of a dialogue, confirms the above statement. In the first quatrain the sonnet addresses my tearful eyes. In the second that begins, "We are so wretched," the eyes answer. Then in the first tercet ("What makes you wish then..."), the sonnet speaks to the eyes, and in the second that begins "Nature instills in us," the eyes answer once more. Going back to the beginning, one must presuppose that my eyes were filled with continuous and heavy tears. This seemed strange since they were very close to the angelic face of my lady that was almost present, and their happiness seemed to consist in this vision, as we said in the sonnet that begins "O eyes I ever sigh...." Thus it seemed reasonable to encourage first the eyes to stop their tears since they would soon see my lady who one could say was almost there. Since the eyes persevere in their crying, one reasonably asks why they cry and why the heart is fearful and suspicious in my breast. The eyes answer this question by showing that their crying is due to the fear they have of the power of the eyes of my lady, whom they call "basilisk," a creature who is said to have the power of killing with its sight. Thus, since it kills merely with its eyes, my eyes were afraid they could not withstand my lady's glance, for if she looked at them fixedly, she would either turn them into stone as well as the rest of the body, or the soul would depart and life would come to an end. These two doubts my eyes had may be seen to be based on the experience of things that had happened, for in so far as being turned into stone is concerned, we read that of Medusa, as we said, and as for death we have the example of the basilisk.

Having cleared the first doubt and shown that there was just cause for the tears, a second doubt arises. This is that since this fear is justified, my eyes should have fled from my lady's sight as a mortal danger, and since they proceeded on their way to seeing her, they had to make clear what desire or fate guided them, since they desired and feared the same thing. In this desire and fear is shown the above-mentioned mixture of bitterness and sweetness, for fear presupposes bitterness and desire sweetness. We say "desire or fate" for men at times are moved by their own natural desire, but at other times they are almost compelled by destiny, for one reads: "Fata volentem ducunt, nolentem trahunt."[60] Experience shows that often men do many things against their own will. What desire or what fate, then, urges you on or holds you back? These two terms show the simultaneous desire and fear of proceeding. If there were desire without fear, they would proceed quickly and with determination, and if there were fear without desire, there would be no movement towards the object of fear. The nature of fear is such that it leads one to flee, since we should hate what we fear, and what is hated we flee. To this point the eyes answer by showing that the reason for fearing is most natural, since by nature everyone fears death. The reason for their advancing is Love, who through no natural reasons miraculously makes lovers see as sweet what to everyone else is bitter and most harsh. "Miraculously" is truly well said, for all things that are against natural order are miraculous, and nothing could be more opposed to natural order than the desire for death, for tears, for sighs and for other amorous passions.

We shall conclude, therefore, that lovers are the most wretched of all men, not only for a common fate that we have said is true of all human matters that must perforce have a share of evil, but for a particular reason. This reason is that lovers never have any good, either for its own nature, like other things, or by participation, for it seems that the greatest amorous sweetness consists in what other men call "highest evil." Yet it suffices for lovers to enjoy a happiness that seems to them to be their own, for human happiness consists rather in seeming than being. And if it seems to them that they are happy, then they are, but never without the mixture of happiness and amorous cares. For this reason I judge that the happiness of lovers is a rare one, and at times very great, but their unhappiness is almost continuous and their grief incomparably greater, for grief is often without sweetness, while their sweetness is never without grief. And thus it must be where there is infinite passion and insatiable appetite.

XXIII

So sweetly does my lady call for death
As she for love does evermore keep sighing
That soon among the harsh desires of mine
She made a sweet one grow that longs for death.

My heart so much does love this gentle wish
That he drives off and snuffs all other sorrows.

60. Seneca, *Epistulae morales ad Lucilium* 107.2.

From this my weary soul does gather strength
And seems to gain her breath against her wish.

With such sweet words invoked by my sad lady,
Death does not listen but instead feels pity
And so will not her lovely eyes then close.

My beautiful sun thus on earth remains.
For me retained is my sad tearful life
By a contrary wish that death excludes.

Since in the preceding sonnet we said something about the miracles of love, I should like to have the ability to make them credible to others as they are to the most gentle minds of lovers. In truth, just as one can consider it a great defect to believe easily those things that seem impossible at first sight, so does it seem to me that one cannot approve the opinion of those who will not believe anything that in some ways goes beyond common use or natural order. At times great difficulties have arisen because of presupposing false something that seemed almost impossible, but that nevertheless proved to be true. Moreover, just as believing easily seems to be the way of superficial minds, not to believe absolutely seems to be most presumptuous. One who says "this cannot be" presumes to know all the things that are possible and what nature's power is. And yet one sees many diverse natural effects that would seem almost impossible, if they were not known well to almost everyone. Who would ever believe that a small grape without definite color, odor or taste could generate a vine with so many worthy qualities? The same is true of other seeds, which have their own diverse species, but do not seem miraculous because they are commonly seen. To me these natural effects that are seen at all times seem more miraculous than some other things that seem so because they are very rare and not well known to us. This is true of some types of animals that we believe cannot exist because they are unknown to us, and yet in those lands that produce them they are as common as dogs, horses and other similar animals are to us. Those six marvels that our poet Petrarch puts in his *canzone* that begins: "What more diverse and new," may be found in the works of ancient and truthful authors."[61] If we consider well those and other things that are seen as miraculous, we shall see that Nature, if one may-use these terms, expends much more labor in producing these

61. Petrarch, *Rime* 135.

common things that are always before our eyes than it does for those others that seem miraculous to us because they are rare rather than impossible.

We must then, if not fully believe in the miracles of love, at least believe in their possibility. It seemed to me that I had to prepare the way in this manner to the explanation of the present sonnet, since I had to relate something that may perhaps seem impossible, but is nevertheless true, for this sonnet intends to prove nothing else but that the desire for death is the immediate cause of life. To come to the point, we must understand that my lady had the habit of often mentioning death and showing with her words that she yearned for it. It seems to me that seeing that she was so gentle, this life seemed tedious and unworthy of such a wonderful person. Since I had at times been present when she sweetly invoked death, I felt such bitterness and grief as one may feel if in fear of being deprived of all that is good to him. For it seemed to me that she called death so sweetly and with such effective terms that she could not be denied, and my grief was made greater by the reason for which she invoked death, which was love, and she invoked death in her amorous sighs. Thus the reason for this desire had to be necessarily either great bitterness and passion or a sublime sweetness. Both these conditions give rise to similar desires in men, for one yearns for death either to put an end to sorrow or to avoid future bitterness that would contaminate a great sweetness and happiness, as in the sentence, "Tunc pulchrum esse mori."[62] Whichever of these two was the cause, I was in great grief, especially since I could be blamed, for love was the cause of this desire. Struggling with this passion, I finally resolved on the only remedy, that is, to accompany my lady in this most harsh desire for death. This desire became so strong in me that it began to seem sweet and sweetened all my other passions. Since naturally one desires and pursues what he likes most, my heart abandoned all other thoughts and put aside all other desires and cares in order to pursue this most sweet and gentle desire for death. Although all thought on a subject, being intense and forceful, will usually banish all other cares, yet thought on death will do this more effectively. This is because all other thoughts drive out all lesser thoughts, not permanently, but only for a period of time, because as life continues they may return, in fact, they must return perforce, at least those that life

62. Lorenzo is citing from memory; the correct citation from Virgil, *Aeneid* 2.317 is "...pulchrumque mori succurrit in armis."

necessitates. But thoughts of death must free the mind of all other matters, for after death in so far as the body and the world are concerned there is nothing to think.

For this reason we say that all other desires and passions and all cares and suffering one feels were gone from the heart, driven away by this sweet desire for death. Since all these passions were gone and only the sweet thought of death remained, life drew strength and a breathing spell. This had to be necessarily, since all its enemies were gone, and there remained only that sweet desire, that is, a desire he liked, and since he liked it, it gave strength to the soul and prolonged life against his will, that is, not against his natural will, but against the desire for death. Although this should have bothered him somewhat, being against the sweetness of his desire, yet since my lady was alive, as we shall see, and kept on being alive, it did not disturb him, in fact, it made him happy since the true desire of my heart was my lady's life.

It is shown, then, that the desire for death that my lady often invoked preserved my life. This same desire preserved her own life, for her desire made her invoke death with her most sweet words, and death, hearing herself called, did not, however, close my lady's beautiful eyes but through pity prolonged her life, and thus life was preserved for her and for me. And this preservation of life was caused by a desire contrary to life, that is, a desire for death that excluded death, that is, it kept death away as we have shown. These and many more miracles of Love we have seen and believe will be credible for all gentle hearts who will bear witness and should be believed by others.

XXIV

When I do think of lodging some complaints
With you for my sad tears and sighs, O Love,
I look with pity at my grieving heart
And of that holy face the image see.[63]

So beautiful she seems and ever sweet
That then my previous thought of shame does die.

63. Cf. Ficino, *Sopra lo amore* 2.8: "L'amante scolpisce la figura dell'amato nel suo animo. Diventa dunque l'animo dell'Amante un certo specchio, nel quale riluce la imagine dell'amato." (The lover sculpts the beloved's image in his soul. The lover's soul, therefore, becomes a sort of mirror in which the beloved's image shines.)

Full of desire to thank her then another
Its place does take, and I her praise do sing.

The lovely image hears herself being praised
In my thought's paean that only her admires
And so more lovely grows and full of mercy.

Hence in my mind a new desire then grows
To see the one who hears, speaks, breathes and lives,
And I to you return, most bright, sweet stars.

I was all alone without any company except for my thoughts of love, and since they were disturbing me as they do most times, I began to think I should complain to Love as the cause of my tears, sighs and other sorrows of love. Since I intended to speak of these one by one to him, it was necessary to begin with my heart as the part that had been hurt first and more vehemently. Since I wished to speak of my heart's affliction, it seemed necessary to look within my heart, and as I looked consider his condition so that I could narrate it. Although there were many passions and torments depicted in my heart, yet the greatest impression had been made by the image of my lady's face, which was most beautiful and like the original, very splendid and bright, and so because of that beauty and splendor it drew my eyes and made them look at that image and obliterated the vision of the heart's sorrows. It seemed very natural that something very beautiful would eliminate the sight of all others, as happens when there is excessive light, and would draw my eyes to itself as beauty always does.

As my eyes looked at this image instead of at the sorrows, it seemed very beautiful and sweet to them, that is, very merciful. At first my eyes had intended to look at my heart's sorrows in order to complain of something bothersome and without grace, but when they saw my lady's beautiful and merciful face, which was the exact opposite of those afflictions, an effect contrary to complaining had to arise necessarily. For this reason the early thought of complaining was ashamed, died and was completely extinguished, and an opposite one was born that wished to thank and honor my lady, who was so beautiful and so gentle that I should have no cause to complain, but to thank her even if I could only look at such a wonderful woman and she had no mercy whatsoever. Passion that blinds one and darkens the intellect with shadowy ignorance had given rise to the thought of complaining. But the light of truth had appeared and driven away the darkness so that one looks at his past error, not without shame, and the first thought dies in shame, and in its place another is born, more true and more praiseworthy, that wants to thank my lady, praise and exalt her. These praises, reaching her image that is in my heart, make her seem more beautiful and more merciful, for thus she seems to my thoughts that see nothing but this image.

Above we have said that the eyes see the heart and what is in it, yet these things are invisible, and we now say that thought, which has no power of seeing, looks at the image of my lady. To resolve both these problems, we must understand that "eyes" and "seeing" stand for "thought" and "imagining," for when we attribute to the heart eyes, ears, tongue and all other senses, we do not mean anything but thought by means of which the heart, that is, our mind, imagines and operates, as the body does by means of the senses. Thus all bodily functions like speaking and feeling that the image performs must be taken as imaginations. If we understand all this, then we see that it confirms what we said, that is, that the image on hearing us praise it becomes more beautiful and merciful. For the stronger the imagination, the more it seems to see what it imagines, and imagining my lady as merciful and beautiful, it seems necessary that the more it imagines her, the more beautiful and merciful she must become in my thoughts. From the imagination of such beauty and sweetness, there is born a new and most ardent desire in the mind to see my lady alive and in the flesh. It does not say "new" desire because this is the first desire I ever had to see my lady, but it says new in regards to those other thoughts, as if reborn right at that instant. This new desire, then, moves me to see my lady alive and in the flesh because speaking, hearing and breathing are functions of a live being and not of something imagined.

With this desire, then, I once again see the brilliant and sweet rays of my lady's eyes. And I say "once again," which shows that the desire is not new, that is, the first I ever had to see her, for "once again" presupposes that I went to see her at other times. By saying "most bright, sweet stars," we show the beauty and mercy that was in that image, which through its affinity to reality moved me to see that beautiful woman of whom it was a most sweet model. In the present sonnet we note three thoughts and one consequence. First there is the thought of complaining, which dies in shame; then there is born one to thank and praise my lady, imagining her as beautiful and merciful; the third that arises is to go and see the real lady because of the resemblance with the imagined model. After these three thoughts there comes as a consequence the operation of putting into effect what the last thought had proposed.

XXV

O lady mine, in your most lovely eyes
I can now see an amorous desire
That Love from everyone always will hide,
But generous and kind to me does show.

To speak does this desire so gentle seem
And promises my heart sweet peace and rest.
A warm and pitying sigh does this confirm
That as a pledge of faith to her Love gave.

This sigh that pity from your breast does send
As your heart's messenger now comes to me
And of your most sweet kindness brings me news.

When to those lovely lips that sigh arrives,
It forms some words of such a sweet effect
That all and Love himself do stunned remain.

Of all our senses, sight is unquestionably the worthiest and most valued. This is not a human judgment only, but one shared by nature in that it placed the eyes higher than any other sense and nearest to the place where the intellect is. It is clearly known that sight is more necessary to human life than any other sense, for it seems that through the knowledge of visible objects the function of the other senses is facilitated. Through the eyes we can know the most beautiful object that the senses can know, that is, light, for neither odor, taste or any sound or sensitive thing can be compared to light. The eyes are also privileged and are more excellent than the other senses in that the heart does not reveal itself through any of the other senses and keeps its thoughts almost hidden from them and reveals them only through the eyes. For the eyes often give clear indications of happiness, grief, wrath, love and all the other passions of the heart. The sense of sight is so close to our soul's qualities that according to Pliny when one kisses someone's eyes, it seems almost as if he were kissing that person's soul.[64] Although this applies to all passions, it is particularly true of amorous matters in which the eyes have a major role. This is true because the eyes provide the way through which Love enters and departs, and they are in themselves the most beautiful part of the human body and have beauty as their object. Therefore, since they are the most beautiful part of a beautiful woman, I believe that most times they are the first thing that is loved by the lover's eyes. If Love from the eyes of the loved one enters the heart through the lover's eyes — and this proves that the eyes actively and passively are the beginning of love — and thus Love makes the first impression in the eyes and through them opens the way to the heart, then the heart must communicate its love passion to the eyes much more easily than the others. Love has provided this remedy for the affliction of lovers who, being denied speech and all other ways of revealing their heart to each other, often will understand each other through the eyes and amorous glances.[65]

My lady was more beautiful than any other, as we have said, and so we can imagine how beautiful were her eyes, since we have said that the eyes exceed all other physical beauty. Since our desires always seek what seems best, although I loved my lady entirely, my eyes nevertheless were drawn to look at hers as her greatest beauty. I looked fixedly at her lovely eyes, and it seemed that I saw in them an amorous desire full of pity and sweetness, that was what her most gentle heart wanted me to understand through them. And Love did not show this most sweet desire to any but my eyes, hiding it from other eyes that did not look so fixedly, nor was the path from my lady and them made so direct by Love as the one from her heart to mine, as we said above. Moreover, since Love who was between her and me was the one who showed me my lady's desire, others could not see this since Love did not stand between them and my lady to show them.

It seemed to me that her gentle desire spoke to my heart and promised him, after so many afflictions and amorous persecutions, peace and rest, thus presupposing the past war for the future peace, and past suffering and amorous toils for future rest and quiet. Those eyes showed all these most sweet thoughts. Since my lady suspected that because of past history I perhaps did not entirely believe the words her eyes expressed, she accompanied these amorous expressions with a sigh. This sigh that was sent as

64. Pliny, *Naturalis historia* 11.146.
65. See above, p. 82, n. 5.

a messenger to my heart left the white breast of my lady as proof of the pity she felt, which had caused that amorous sigh to enter my heart. Since I have spoken of the natural causes of sighs in the exposition of the sonnet that begins: "If when most close to you,..."[66] it does not seem necessary to discuss this matter further. But we must understand that this sigh arose in the heart that drew to himself, by means of his breath, the air necessary for cooling himself, and before it was expelled it formed on my lady's lips certain most sweet and loving words, so that the words and the sigh seemed to exit simultaneously from her beautiful mouth. Since it seemed to my lady that neither the eyes' message nor the sigh's testimony were sufficient to express her pity and love, she added the message of her words, which were much more effective than the others, so that my heart would have greater certainty because of the efficacy of the testimony and its number that being three was sufficient.

My lady's words were so kind and beautiful and of such sweet effect that Love was stupefied. From this fact we can imagine the effect they had on me. Those who believe me must not be surprised that I do not relate her words verbatim, for I was overcome by the same amazement that struck Love, so that I not only forgot her words, but almost forgot myself. According to my judgment, the present sonnet proceeds most naturally and according to truth, for one who loves first gives some sign of it through the eyes, then a sigh rises necessarily because of the pleasure of seeing the object of one's love, and the firm intention of looking venerates sighs for the reasons given in the cited sonnet, and sighing shows the power of love more than looking. The sigh is followed by words that are so much more effective as they express the certainty of the matter. This is because looks and sighs could be ascribed to other reasons than what appears, but words show the truth more clearly and are caused by a greater force of love. And thus nature brings about its effects step by step.

XXVI

Love in my heart the lovely image put
Whose grace and virtue so extreme were that
If for whatever else desire there was,
It snuffed and banished was for evermore.

---

66. P. 116.

When now, alas, with eyes so full of tears,
In vain I seek the lights that I have lost.
I from my eyes do to my thoughts then flee
And seek my love that never hid from them.

Alone and in the midst of my desires
My most dear lady my kind thoughts did show
Right in the center of my troubled heart.

My poor sad heart then with new fire did burn
And would in ashes now already be,
Were it not for the power sighs do have.

In the previous sonnet we have shown how excellent sight is among the other senses and the dignity that Love has awarded the eyes by making them the gateway for his entrance and often making them ministers and messengers of the heart's thoughts. We must therefore confess that lovers receive great sweetness from the eyes. Given that this is so, it is almost an unbearable torment on the contrary for lovers to be deprived of them, or rather it would be absolutely unbearable if Love had not provided an only remedy, that of helping the heart in this case through thoughts. This remedy, however, is not different from the other aids of love that spur one on and add fuel to the amorous fire rather than providing any relief to the heart.

The present sonnet denotes this fact and at first shows Love's providence in that, having foreseen this particular lover's grief like all the others, he begged the help of thoughts against this evil, after having placed the image of the beloved in the heart that represents her to the thoughts when the eyes are deprived. Love, then, in accordance with his custom, placed the beautiful image of my lady within my heart, either because of his graciousness or because of my heart's virtue, that is, either through Love's favor that made my heart worthy of such a worthy image or my heart's own virtue since he had become gentle. When the image came into my heart, it destroyed and drove away all other impressions that may have been there as a result of my heart's desires, and my lady's lovely image remained there alone.

On the day I composed the present sonnet, I had tried with many steps and much time to see the eyes of my lady, all in vain, for I never did receive the grace of seeing them on that day. With my tearful eyes, I sought then the lights I had lost, that is, my lady's eyes that I could not find, and because of this I felt an intolerable torment. Since there was nothing else I could do, I recurred to the only remedy Love had conceded me. Having stopped seeking my lady with my eyes, I fell back to seeking her with my thoughts, of which I asked for my salvation, that is, that they at least show me my lady since it was in their power to do so since she never hid herself from them, and she was always with them My request was kindly granted by my thoughts, and they immediately showed me my lady all alone, for in the center of my heart there were no other thoughts, as we said above. There could not have been any others since the center of my heart was the foundation of thought, the center of the earth and the universe, and thus there could be no thought unless based on my lady. Any others, if my heart could have produced them, would have been like all things that lack a foundation. My lady, then, was in the center of my heart surrounded by all my desires, thus showing that the thoughts did not refer to anyone else, nor did the heart's desires wish for anything else. Naturally, the font of desire and site of the passionate soul is the heart, and it is the virtue and power of the heart.

Love helped the heart with thoughts to make up for the eyes' defect, and from this nothing came but the accumulation of sorrows. For as we said in the sonnet that begins: "When I do think of lodging some complaints,"[67] the image of the beloved multiplies the desire for the real woman, as happened then, for from seeing my lady within my heart a new and greater flame of desire for my lady broke out. Since it seems impossible that my heart could resist such a fire without burning and becoming ashes, in order to show the credibility of these marvels, we mention the remedy that did not let the heart be consumed, that is, the sighs that as we said are generated by the heart for its relief and exhalation against suffocation that threatens it because of the gathering of the vital spirits.

XXVII

No sweeter sleep nor more untroubled rest
Did ever eyes so lovely close to light
Than that which then obscured the sacred rays
Of her so proud and loving happy stars.

And while they were so hidden and obscured,
Of your great strength, O Love, you did much lose.

---

67. P. 153.

The power that you wield and your own rule
Those eyes can give you or can to you deny.

O tall and leafy oak that with your leaves
From the sun's rays defend those lovely eyes
And with your shade protect that charming sleep,

No longer fear if Jove in anger thunders,
No longer fear that he may strike you down,
For sacred have those eyes to Love made you.

XXVIII

O charming flowers, O green fragrant grass
That do the fields adorn like stars the sky,
Amidst the glory of your lovely tints
Those lovely limbs so sweetly tired you saw.

My lady's lofty thought in silence speaks
And all those honors who its subject are.
How fortunate I was to be of them,
As Love, who all our hearts does hold, told me.

How sweet you are, O breeze that give or take
Away of Phoebus sight in all his glory,
The branches moving and with them the shade.

On this tall oak do all your trophies hang,
O sweet sleep. Let Love never angry be
If you the splendor of those eyes did conquer.

If I could narrate one by one all the acts and events of my lady, this love story of ours would be much more ornate, and my lady would receive much more praise. Every act of her life, even minimal, has been worthy of being celebrated by me, and since I have omitted a great part of them, I blame only their great abundance. For I have been like one in the midst of a most beautiful meadow that produces flowers of diverse colors, who wants to pick the most beautiful, but cannot decide which to pick first, for the quality of beauty makes the selection more difficult, since our desire is drawn more to those things we like most. Since I cannot pick all the flowers of the excellent meadow of my lady, nor list all her praises, and I do not know how to select those that deserve to be picked first and celebrated, I have picked those flowers that chance decreed by guiding my wandering hand, thus letting fortune be the judge, rather than my choice.

As we said in the preceding sonnet, my lady was elsewhere, as shown by the fact that I had sought her a great deal with my eyes, but only found her in my thoughts. She was in a villa not very far from the city, but in a position from which she could not see it. She thus stepped out and climbed a tall and wooded mountain and came to a part from which she could easily see the city where I was because, I believe, she thought she could give some present or future relief to the affliction I suffered for her absence. This place was rural, as we said: the soil was covered by grass and flowers in the shade of an old oak tree. Since my lady was somewhat tired because of the steep and difficult path, when she saw that beautiful place she decided to honor that grass and those flowers by letting them be bed and cover for her most gracious body.

Thus, lying down for some time, she contemplated the city and place where I was and had some sweet and lovely thoughts, moved by pity for my affliction. Finally she was overcome by sleep, a slumber aided by the oak's shade and a sweet summer breeze that moved the branches of the oak and other near-by trees, causing a murmur that induced that most sweet sleep. I learned of this loving gesture and judged it worthy of the two sonnets above. The first tells that since nature granted sleep to human eyes, no sweeter sleep or more peaceful repose closed mortal eyes, nor did sleep ever close eyes more beautiful than my lady's. What made her sleep sweeter than any other was the shade, the softness of the place where she lay, the sweetness of the light breeze, the murmur of the trees, which of necessity was born of it. and the fatigue that had preceded sleep, all things that favor sleep. That her eyes were so beautiful I cannot prove by any other means than my opinion, which was based on the effect they had on me. And if they were so beautiful, it followed by necessity that Love acquired great strength from them. Thus since they were closed in sleep and their amorous light hidden from the world, Love's valor and power were necessarily lessened since those eyes gave and withdrew power as is the case for some types of flowers that open up when the sun is there and at sunset close up, so that the meadows bloom during the day and at night are deprived of the flowers' ornament. Thus we can say that gentle hearts open up to receive amorous influence in the presence of the sun of their beloved's eyes and would close when these are not present.

In order for the heart not to close up ever, Love's power makes such an impression by means of those eyes, that we can say they are never without sun. Love then, who makes his power felt by means of those eyes, would lose it if they were to disappear.

Going back to my lady's sleep, one can easily understand that it would much please my lady since it was so sweet, as we have said. Since she was most gentle in all things, being grateful she showed her gratitude to all those things that had contributed to her pleasure. Thus to the grass and flowers, which without hardness had softly received her limbs and provided such a delicate bed and ornate cover, she made the most pleasing gift of being touched and pressed by such lovely limbs. The breeze that had moved the branches and cooled the air similarly touched her most lovely body. The shade wandered over that most lovely face and her limbs as it pleased. There was left only the oak tree, which had not been the least cause for this sweetness, for it had caused the shade, which had encouraged that beautiful sleep. So that the oak would not remain without receiving its share of the reward, my lady's eyes consecrated it to Love, thus freeing it of the blows and force of lightning and tempestuous arrows. Since the oak tree is Jove's, it is struck by his arrows more often than others. Instead of that, from the time it came in view of those beautiful eyes, it is the recipient of Love's arrows since those grateful eyes consecrated it to Love.

In the first sonnet there is no mention of the meadow where my lady slept, nor of the pleasant air, which, as we have said, were very effective in encouraging that most lovely sleep. This is because it is very difficult to put many things within the conciseness of the sonnet. Thus we mention them in the second, which begins: "O charming flowers, etc.," where it is seen that my thoughts remembered all those amorous particulars with great pleasure. Nor was the fact that the grass and flowers received my lady, so sweetly tired, recalled without envy on my part. By referring to the grass as fragrant and making the variety of flowers reflect the effect of the stars in the serene sky, we effect the qualities that the meadow can have, that is, the fragrance and beauty.

We have said that my lady, as she lay there, had amorous thoughts about me. Now this is impossible to know except for the fact that where there are thoughts, Love introduces himself as witness of the hidden vision and as one who heard my lady speak cautiously of me, who could call myself most happy of being worthy of being in such high and sweet thoughts. This because thinking is nothing but a silent speech, for one who thinks imagines those things, calls them within oneself by their own names, so that we can truly say that thinking is nothing but silent speech.

My thoughts then go to all the other circumstances such as the air, or better say light breeze, and by almost attributing grace to it we show the effect it had. By moving the branches that caused the shade by their interposition between the sun and her eyes, the shade must have perforce moved also, and thus those eyes could see the sun at times, and at others not. Since these eyes were of such perfection and beauty that they commanded Love, as we have said above, Sleep achieved a glorious victory when he overcame such lovely eyes. To make it eternal and memorable, Sleep had to hang the trophies on the tall oak with the spoils of the eyes by him defeated, as the ancient Romans did, who when they defeated some powerful or famous enemy used to take his spoils and cover a tree trunk with them in memory of the victory gained. We must see what were the spoils of those eyes in order to see what Sleep had with which to cover the oak tree. Nor can one say that my lady's eyes were dressed with anything but beautiful amorous looks and with an amorous light that can be seen only by lovers' eyes. These looks and amorous light, therefore, had to remain like stigmata in the trunk of the oak, and these Sleep took from my lady as soon as she closed her lovely eyes, and I believe that oak tree is still adorned with those spoils. Nor does Love have reason to be angry at the triumph of Sleep, if what we have said is true, that is, that her eyes commanded Love and gave him and withdrew power, since Sleep had then overcome those beautiful eyes.

XXIX

So many are the charms and such the beauty
That in my lady's face together are
That every new expression it assumes
From it new worth and beauty does derive.

If welcome pity it does show at times,
Then never pity was so sweet and pious.
If it does burn with anger, so fierce 'tis
That Love in her sweet face to tremble seems.

Sadness always does charming there become,
And if the tracks of tears her face do mark,
Love cries and then says: "This my kingdom is!"

But when this world so blind deserving is
Of seeing a lovely smile in that dear face,
It will at last find out what true bliss is.

When in things that are varied and opposed to each other some power operates forcefully and at times achieves effects that are almost beyond the natural order of things, I believe it is clear proof of its extraordinary might. Since this often happens in the lives of lovers, we have previously called them "love miracles." The present sonnet intends to prove that the power of my lady's beauty was extraordinary by citing the diverse and extraordinary effects it had on me. For when I contemplated the beauty of her face in various moods and emotions, it seemed to me that all the emotions that appeared or were reflected on her face gained beauty and power from it. It seemed that they induced more powerfully in others fear or pity, sorrow or joy, and that they not only moved one forcefully, in accordance with the nature of the emotions, as we said, but did so always maintaining beauty and grace, which in some passions like fear and sorrow seems almost impossible, for one who fears must necessarily hate the cause of his fear. The same is true of those who grieve, for if possible they would flee from its cause, and those things from which we flee, we do not love. It was an extraordinary power of this beauty, therefore, that while inducing fear and sorrow it was still desired and loved in spite of these passions.

The present sonnet, then, introduces only four passions, that is, pity, wrath, sorrow and joy. which draw more beauty and force from my lady's face. Beginning with pity, when it is expressed in that beautiful face, it shows that it never found a place or dwelling where it seemed more truly pity or where it seemed more sweet and pious. Since pity is beautiful in itself, it suffices to mention only the power it acquired, presupposing beauty. Coming to wrath, her face should properly have been afire with ire and scorn, for wrath is nothing else but the burning of ire around the heart, and the effects of anger are generally similar to those of fire that soon makes itself apparent, so that those who are wrathful and warm by nature are more disposed towards ire. When that lovely face burns with wrath, it becomes more beautiful and severe and is to be feared more as the following example shows. When Love trembles in her face, it is a clear sign of the fear that power instills and the fact that notwithstanding his trembling, a sign of how great his fear is, he does not flee, clearly shows that its beauty is what holds him back, for were it not so, fear would make Love flee. The same happens in the sadness and sorrow of my lady, who shows the same power and beauty in sorrow that she had shown before when in wrath, for she moves Love himself to tears, and by crying he affirms that her face is his reign and empire.

The conclusion of the sonnet is born of these premises very well, for if the beauty of that face had the power of appearing more beautiful in those circumstances that generally obscure and diminish beauty and of strengthening these emotions that are opposed to beauty, then she can more easily grow in beauty in circumstances that naturally enhance beauty and also strengthen these emotions, as is the case when my lady is happy. My lady was most beautiful in her own right, and so is happiness in any person at all. If she is beautiful in her own right, then, and the emotion itself is beautiful, when such beautiful nature was combined with such beautiful emotion, the result was an extraordinary beauty, if we presuppose that each was enhanced by such a union. As we previously said in regards to other emotions, we must also presuppose that the emotion was very strong and almost at its pitch as is the case for laughter, which is the clearest sign of joy in men, as crying is of grief, which we cited above as a sign of excessive sorrow.

Imagining this great beauty and sweetness together, one can say that such beauty is not only extraordinary in this world, but perhaps never before seen, so that the world can be esteemed to be blind. This beauty must produce what we may call true happiness and beatitude in those who see it.

XXX

What do I feel, alas, in my breast move?
My heart it cannot be for he left me.
If he has gone, why then these many sighs?
Whom do they succor, whom do they now please?

If lost my heart now is. who then can move
The sweet and lofty thoughts that feed my mind?
Love, who made him so daring as to flee,
With his own lips all this has now told me:

"When those most lovely eyes the way had opened,
Her white hand entered and your heart did take
And in exchange a nobler one gave you.

That one in you does live, and yours so proud
In a more candid breast did will to live.
One of my miracles this is." said Love.

Although my lady in many diverse ways gave proof of her love and caring for me, as we have shown in many places, she never gave, nor could ever give, a more effective one than what is in the present sonnet. Nor could I receive a greater gift from her, for there is no greater gift than when one gives what is hers and is also most dear to the giver at the same time. According to Epictetus, we can call nothing our own in this world except our opinion, for everything else belongs either to Nature or to Fortune. That this statement is true is shown by the fact that often against our will we are deprived of these things by Nature or Fortune. So then without further discussion since these things are well-known and proved, we shall admit that our opinion is the only thing we can call our own, as we said. This opinion is always free and cannot be forced in any case. It is my judgment that if one speaks of opinion he must perforce presuppose our will, which is nothing else than the desire for the good that seems good in our opinion. For this reason, although opinion and will are not the same thing, we can say they are so similar and close and necessarily united one with the other that as far as I am concerned it is not improper to speak of them as one, since I am not defining matters, but speaking in broad terms.

If then only opinion and will are ours, one who makes a gift of them is giving all that he possesses, and one who donates all that he has does perforce donate what is most dear to him and therefore cannot make a greater gift. Broadly speaking, in these love verses the heart stands for our opinion and will, so that when my lady exchanged her heart for mine, that is, took mine for her own and gave me hers as the present sonnet shows, she could not have given me a greater gift, nor given a clearer sign that I enjoyed her grace. Since it would seem very arrogant on my part to believe that this is so and to say and believe that I am worthy of such a gift without my lady's testimony, I must speak truthfully of these love proceedings both to avoid being arrogant and for the pleasure the most sweet memory of that act of love gives my heart.

I was very close to my lady's face, and I was looking at it fixedly, and as I felt almost faint and weak because of the sweetness her eyes conveyed, I supported my head with my right arm. Thinking she would comfort me, she came closer to me in a gentle way and placed her candid hand over the left side of my chest. As she kept it still there for some time, I asked very timidly what she intended to do. With a proper boldness she answered that she was listening to the motion of her heart, and I said to her: "In truth this and everything else that lives in me is yours." She then added: "I say in truth that this is the heart that once lived in me and now lives in you, and the one that once was yours I keep within my breast." What such sweet words seemed to me and what effect they had on me, I shall let those who know Love's flame and power judge, for as Dante says in one of his *canzoni:*

> A boorish heart does not such genius have
> To make him see of this the slightest part.[68]

When I left her I considered which was greater, the gentleness of those words or the love shown through them, and I decided to compose the present sonnet and the following two with the same theme, although they come to different conclusions. I did so in spite of the fact that those words of love and that most gentle act were worthy of another pen than mine to make them endure. Although the facts are as given above, I pretend that I myself feel a new motion in my breast and in some surprise ask myself what the cause may be, particularly since my own heart had fled from me, as we said in several places above, and so could not be the cause of that motion. The motion then, and the many sighs of mine, which are naturally caused in order to give relief to the heart, showed that a heart must have been there moving in my breast. This was also shown by the lofty and sweet thoughts that my mind conceived, which must also have been moved by the heart, not as the locus of thought, but as its cause, for since the heart is what desires, those thoughts came from the heart since they were a desire for my lady. And since the thoughts were lofty and sweet, that is nobler than what was normal, I began to think that they were moved by a worthier cause than my own heart.

In the midst of these doubts, Love came to my aid, since he had been the one who had given my heart courage to flee,

---

68. Lorenzo is citing by heart with a slight change verses 35–36 of Dante's *canzone* in the *Vita nova,* "Li occhi dolente...."

as shown in the sonnet that begins: "Alas, poor me, when in the presence of, . . ."[69] and thus knew that my heart had indeed fled. And so he showed me this truth in his own words. If we interpret this in accordance with the truth, as we said, then Love was my lady, who in her own words showed me this miracle of love, which was as follows: When Love first opened the way to my lady's eyes through which they entered and came into my heart, that most gentle hand followed the eyes into my breast and took away my heart, as shown in the sonnet that begins: '"Delicate, beautiful and candid hand, . . ."[70] and in my heart's place put my lady's. Since this seems unheard of and marvelous, Love added that this was a marvelous example of his power. When we consider the facts, Love is nothing else but the transformation of the lover into the beloved.[71] When this is reciprocal, it necessarily follows that there is the same transformation into the one who first loves, who then becomes beloved, so that miraculously lovers live in each other, and this is what this exchange of hearts signifies.

XXXI

That noble heart that Love as pledge gave me
In a miraculous exchange for mine —
To greater heights then raised — now wants to leave.
Of such a heart my breast unworthy is.

Mine now so worthy is that when I beg
Him to come back, his ancient home he scorns.
"If her proud heart," I say, "my breast does scorn,
Her breast will then scorn you, poor heart of mine.

Poor thing, what will you do?" His answer is:
"In those sweet eyes I shall in exile stay,
If I should be expelled without regard.

69. P. 103.

70. P. 121.

71. See Ficino, *Sopra lo amore* 2.8: ". . . dove lo amato nell'Amore risponde, l'amatore . . . nello amante vive. Qui cosa meravigliosa avviene, quando duo insieme si amano: costui in colui e colui in costui vive. Costoro fanno a cambio insieme, e ciascuno da sè ad altri, per altri ricevere." (When the beloved responds to Love, the lover lives in the loving one. Here something marvelous happens when two love each other: this one lives in the other and the other lives in this one. These exchange each other, and each gives himself to another in order to receive another.)

From me these can't be taken, nor can Love
Them hide. Of me at times you will have news
Through the sweet rays of those most lovely eyes."

Those things that because of their excellence and worth seem to exceed the merits of the one who receives them usually seem to be short lived, for this is true of all excesses. We see at times, therefore, that those who from a low point have reached exalted positions have greater fear. Moreover, given the course of human events, those who enjoy greater happiness have more to fear than others since human happiness most times is brief and unstable.

These conditions applied to me, as shown in the comment on the preceding sonnet. That my breast had become the dwelling place for my lady's heart and my own, too proud and noble, had gone to dwell in my lady's candid breast seemed to be something much above my own merits, so much more so since I from a humble place had been exalted to such heights, and so I saw myself as the happiest of men. For all these reasons then I had to fear and think it almost impossible to remain in such happiness for a long time. And although my lady's fidelity and constancy gave me no reason to doubt, it yet seemed to me at all times that my lady's heart, which dwelled in me for Love had given him to me in exchange for my own, wanted to leave and abandon my breast. This doubt made me think of recalling my own, begging him to return to me. But he, having been elected to a greater good, that is, staying in my lady's candid breast, had become so arrogant and proud that he scorned my breast, where he previously had stayed, and refused to come back to me. Since I thought the cause of this was that he thought he could remain in my lady's breast, to make him return to me I explained that when my lady's heart no longer deigned to remain in my breast, her breast would no longer deign to shelter my heart. The consequence of this could be that at the same time he would be deprived of my breast by election and of my lady's by necessity, when he would be driven out. His answer to this fear was that even if he would be driven out by her, he would stay in a place from which he could not be driven, that is, in my lady's eyes. And this because she and Love have made those eyes common to all and in them there are no sighs, no words, no other sign that originates in the heart. There are only the glances of my lady, which will often give news of my heart, because her eyes will often be seen by mine.

It is necessary to understand the natural proceeding of this sonnet with which these amorous tales must be in accord. Love is born in the lover and goes into the beloved, and thus first of all the lover's heart flees to the beloved. Love then is born and reciprocated in the beloved, and then occurs the exchange of hearts, as we have stated. Then jealousy is born, the true wretchedness of lovers for it is an endless torment. The fear is born, then, that the beloved's heart will return to her, and from this arises the thought of withdrawing one's love from the beloved, and this takes the form of recalling one's heart to himself. But since a lively love grows in the midst of afflictions, the lover cannot withdraw his love but must necessarily continue with it. Although he is sure within himself that he cannot have any sweetness from it, but only afflictions and tribulations, since he is not loved by his beloved and is never free from jealousy, he is finally brought by necessity to take what he may more easily receive from the beloved. Though he cannot have the lady's heart, his own does not leave the beloved but stays in her eyes, that is, he enjoys the exterior beauty and is content with that since he cannot dispose of the beloved's heart, that is, of her love. And then the eyes of the beloved give signs of love that is in her, for at times pity and love and scorn and wrath can be understood from signs that the eyes give. And one often gets news of this since the beloved can hardly be hidden from one's eyes or become invisible, and love urges and incites the lover to see the beloved often, especially when the other things that used to console the mind are lacking. I wish that all these effects were expressed better in the sonnet in order to remove all difficulties from those minds that will deem my verses worthy of their recognition.

XXXII

"O loving sighs that now do come to me
From the white breast of my sweet, lovely lady,
Do let me have some news of my lost heart
That you always in her so kindly nourish."

"In her your heart is happy, quiet and mild.
Always he does give rise to thoughts so sweet,
And often he does speak with them and Love
Of lofty matters, but hear them you can't."

"Kind sighs is what I hear from you the truth?"
"It is just so." "At least now tell me still
If where he is my heart will long remain."

The wind takes them away while I still speak.
Love then did swear by all that sacred is
That never would my heart to me return.

In literature one finds two statements that are contrary to each other, which nevertheless have been often proven true in human action. It is said that the wretched easily believe what they would like and in opposition to this there is the statement: "A wretched man does not in hope believe."[72] I believe that the diversity of opinion is born more from the character of those who hope for or desire something, than from reason, presupposing that the two opinions have equal causes, which do not tend in one or the other direction. And I believe that those who are melancholic by nature are less likely to hope than others, especially if in life Fortune has been so inimical that they have accomplished few things in accordance with their desire.

At the beginning we said that every strong love is born of strong imagination and that such lovers are melancholic by nature. I confess that I am one of those who have loved fervently, and as a lover I should reasonably have doubted rather than hoped. To this we should add that although I have acquired greater honors and position than I should have, yet in my life I have had rare joys and few other things in accordance with my desires. I am referring to those things that our soul desires as relief from dangers and public and private duties, although I live happily and satisfied with my fate. For the reasons given in the preceding commentary and in the present, therefore, I should reasonably have doubted. Once suspicion was born in my breast, and it is a great and intolerable passion, nature taught me everything possible to drive it away. I was afraid my heart would be expelled from my lady's breast, as shown amply by the previous sonnet, and I did not know whether he was there or elsewhere. So then it seemed to me that I should get some news from those who came from that same place, and since sighs are born in the very place where their heart is, they could tell me the truth.

The present sonnet, then, composed in the form of a dialogue, turns to and addresses those sighs that came from my lady's breast, which of course would be coming from my own heart if he dwelled in that breast. To avoid confusion we must understand that in the first quatrain I speak to the said sighs; in

72. Petrarch, *Rime* 150.14.

the second the sighs answer me. In the ninth verse beginning with the words "kind sighs" I again speak to the sighs. With the words "It is just so," the sighs answer me. For the rest of the sonnet it is I who speaks partly to the sighs and partly for narration. Returning to the beginning, we must note that as I speak to the sighs of my lady I call them "loving," that is, moved by Love, and so there was, or I wished to show, some hope mixed with doubt. This is also shown by the fact that I asked them for news of my heart, which they sweetly nourished in her breast, thus taking for granted that my heart was there and was well treated by her. It is truly said that her sighs nourished my heart for he was in that breast where Love also was, without whom my heart could not have stayed. Thus what gave rise to the sighs really nourished my heart and maintained him in that breast, for the sighs were moved by Love. The sighs answer me that my heart is happy, quiet and full of humility and sweetness and is the cause of many sweet and loving thoughts in my lady, and he speaks often with these and with Love, and discusses many lofty amorous mysteries and most gentle matters. By this we show that not only was my heart in that breast, but that he dwelled there familiarly, for he heard all the thoughts of his lady, which others cannot, that is, all those who have not been made gentle and worthy by Love, as my heart had been.

The sweetness of this desired news was so much the greater to me than great had been my fears, as always happens with some hoped-for joy. Almost unable to believe possible what had been intimated by those amorous spirits, I ask again if their news is true. They confirm this with a very brief answer: "It is just so." They could not have given a longer answer, as the rest of the sonnet shows, for when I asked another question, the air for those sighs was not sufficient to let them answer. Here we must note that all that is said by the above sighs in this sonnet are the words that one could have naturally said in comfort in one breath, that is, without having to draw breath again. Thus when the air that the sighs had was exhausted, they could not reasonably utter other words. Although I say "sighs" in the plural, that is, more than one, we must imagine that my lady's sighs were many, but only one gave answer.

It is natural for one who has acquired a great gift to do everything possible to conserve it and make it endless. Thus I, who had heard what I wished about my heart, wished further to know how long this beatitude of his would last. I therefore asked the spirits how long my heart would dwell in that breast. And since, as we have said, the sighs' breath had been exhausted and the sighs dissolved in the wind, they could not answer. Love then, who was in the place from which came the sighs as we have said above, answered in their place and swore by his breast that my heart would always remain with my lady and would never return to me. And he assured me by swearing as he had first assured my heart when he first left me, as shown in the sonnet that begins: "Alas, poor me, when in the presence of...."[73]

XXXIII

There where her splendid eyes my lady turns,
Like a new Flora[74] and a new bright sun,
The earth she makes with new spring blossoms bloom
And into color burst with many flowers.

Hearing her sing, the birds in love then fall
And harmonize with her in songs of love.
The forests hear her speak in her sweet voice
And the bare branches all dress up in green.

If sigh she does or smile with lovely lips,
Love then some sweet and tender thoughts instills
In the chaste breast of timid, charming nymphs.

To render clear the grace that so abounds,
There where with her white hand she bends to touch,
No tongue will ever and no mind suffice.

It was the month of April when in accordance with the common usage of our city, men willingly go with their families to stay in the pleasant countryside for their enjoyment, for at that time the year is so much more beautiful, just as first youth is more beautiful than any other age of man. Moreover, our city has many beautiful and pleasant places nearby that, in addition to custom, induce one to leave civic and private duties in order to enjoy rural idleness. At this time then, it happened that my lady went, like many other times, to stay in a most pleasant villa of hers where she remained several days, depriving me of her desired presence. At this time a very good friend, who knew

---

73. P. 103.

74. Flora was the goddess that made flowers bloom and, together with Zephyr, brought spring. See *Sylva II*, 19–38, pp. 231–32.

of my great love for her, said to me: "Now one should be in that villa to see your beautiful lady, for now the birds sing, the meadows are renewed with new grass and flowers, the trees are covered with new leaves. Nymphs, men and all animals at present feel the power of love more, and so it would now be the right time to see your most dear lady in the midst of all these natural ornaments.'" I answered him that my desire to see her could neither grow nor diminish at any time, and that I too believed the entire world was most beautiful and adorned at this time more than at any other and that the village where my lady was must be more beautiful than any other. All this because where she was there was no need of sun, new season nor any other power than her own to make the earth bloom with flowers and the trees renew their leaves, the birds sing, and cause all the other effects of springtime.

Our talk ended with similar words. When I left the said friend with my mind all full of these thoughts, I composed the present sonnet in which I strive to express the effect of my lady's power that took place in those rural places where she was at that time. I first show that her eyes have the same power as the sun, for wherever she turned them she made the earth produce diverse colors of new flowers, and I call her beautiful Flora in that she made flowers bloom, that is, the goddess of flowers. She also made birds sing amorously, for when they heard her sing most sweetly they fell in love with her singing. The withered branches of the trees that in winter lose their leaves regained their greenery when they heard her speak sweetly. Here we must note that in my lady's singing and speaking are included the three parts that according to Plato are in music,[75] which are speaking, harmony and rhythm, which I believe is what we call *rima* in the vernacular, that is, a composition in rhymed verse. Rhythm is nothing else but speaking marked by a certain measure like verses and rhyme in the vernacular. Speaking is called musical, although not measured by feet, when it is composed in such a way as to please the ear, as can be seen in those who are called "eloquent."' Harmony is a consonance of human voices or of sounds, as is well known. We have already said what rhythm is.

The first type of music, that is, speaking, is expressed in the verse that says: "The forests hear her speak in her sweet voice." The other two, that is, harmony and rhythm, are included in my lady's song, and we must presuppose that she sweetly sang

75. Plato, *Republic* 3.398c.

certain verses and rhymes of love, which pleased her exceedingly. I heard her sing some of mine and of others many times with great sweetness and gentleness, which afterwards sung by others could not please me. Therefore, when she sang similar verses and rhymes with a most tender melody, we have all three forms of music mentioned, and since this was so, part of the marvel at the effects achieved by my lady must vanish. For since music is common to all things that in fact could not exist without a certain consonance, it is reasonable that they should move because of music. We see that tuning two string instruments to the same pitch, when we put one next to the other if one resounds, the strings of the other vibrate on their own without being touched by others simply because of the affinity of tone and pitch that exists between them.

Having spoken of two powers of my lady, that is, of her eyes and harmony, etc., and since we have to tell of a more marvelous operation of hers, we must attribute it to a more powerful cause. Although having the earth bloom, the birds sing and the trees regain their leaves are great effects, yet these are all natural things. But it is a greater thing to cause an effect that is contrary to one's nature to grow in one, such as having timid and chaste nymphs admit some tender and sweet thoughts of love in their stony hearts, since love is completely contrary to timidity and chastity. A more powerful cause has this greater effect, such as my lady's smiling and sighing, that when they appear on her lips give rise to amorous thoughts, as we said of the nymphs. That this is a more powerful cause is shown in my opinion by the fact that it is capable of giving rise to emotions, and so her smile and her sighs have greater effect than singing or speaking as we shall see, and the greatest effect of all is caused by her touch. Thus the sonnet concludes that this has a greater effect than the others by showing that where her candid hand touches there is such grace and virtue that one can neither tell nor imagine.

Thus we proceed from the less great effects by steps until the most great. For if we presuppose that Love moves all my lady's actions as we have said, that is, seeing, singing, speaking, smiling, sighing and finally touching, we see that seeing shows a lesser effect than singing, singing than speaking and so on, until touching. For if we presuppose that a lover is enamored of the woman, I believe that if she looks at him lovingly, he will be very pleased; if he hears her sing love songs, it will seem a greater sign of love to him; if he hears her talk to him, he will deem this an even greater sign of her love; if he sees her smile or sigh because of love, it will seem to him to be an increase of her favor towards him; and the greatest of all would be if she touched him. Thus all these things will have a greater or lesser effect on him according to the quality of the causes. In the present sonnet, then, are included those steps or levels of love that the most ingenious poet Ovid puts in his book in which he gives his precepts of love.[76]

XXXIV

My poor sad heart in my afflicted breast
The wandering thoughts calls and draws them in
Around himself, and he first loudly sighs.
And then with sweet and piteous words he says:

"Although you all of Love now subjects are,
Yet I who now do look at you and speak
Created you. Why then this eternal war
Against me wage and never give me rest?"

"When at the sun's first rays," one answered him,
"When Flora's lovely reign does then appear,
Of many flowers honey make the bees,

So we from her sweet words and charming looks,
Her ways, her beauty do a potion make
That bitter-sweet always will nourish you.

Although in the sonnet that begins: "O my poor tired eyes, . . ."[77] we said a great deal about how wretched is the human condition, particularly the lover's, we happen to mention it again in the present exposition, since one cannot equal in words the entity of this wretchedness and also to prove the truth of this statement. I know of no better argument than to consider in what human happiness consists, speaking in broad terms and in accordance with the depraved habits of men, putting aside at this time true happiness, which I do not think we can find in this life of ours.[78] We shall say, then, that happiness is greater that is preceded by a greater desire and ardor. Since the greater is every appetite,

76. Ovid, *Ars amatoria.*
77. P. 146.
78. Cf. Ficino, *Theologia Platonica* 14.1, and Lorenzo's *Disputation* II.79–81, IV.49–57, V.154–62.

the greater is the passion, we must confess that the basis of this happiness is great wretchedness. And it is clear that appetite is its true foundation because if the appetite is not there, the will is also lacking. For example, one who has a great appetite for food enjoys more the taste of what he eats, and this enjoyment lasts as long as hunger lasts and dies together with hunger. In fact, what is a pleasure while it is desired becomes unpleasant and bothersome when that desire is spent.[79] Thus we can say that happiness consists more in the elimination of what bothers us than in anything that brings some good with it, and that it is a medicine that only relieves the patient of his illness without then fortifying nature in order to give him some other benefits, as Horace says in one of his *Epistles,* where he says: "Nocet empta dolore voluptas."[80] And since this happens in all human things, in honor, in utility and in pleasure, it is necessary to admit that human life that depends upon these things is nothing but suffering and that happiness is always mixed with it, for suffering is its only immediate cause and accompanies it as the shadow does the body.

Since this effect was present in me, and I was continuously and gravely bothered by my thoughts, and since it seemed impossible to be able to live without these thoughts, I composed the present sonnet to express the condition of my heart. Since he was placed in the center of my breast, full of sorrow and tired by the bothersome thoughts, he called to him these thoughts which, as we have said, naturally stay around the heart that gives rise to them. From this it happens that the heart sighs, for diverse passions concur at the same time and give rise to sighs for the reasons we have given. After sighing, the heart turned to the thoughts and with sweet and pitiful words begged them to stop molesting him and put an end to the long and continuous war they wage on him and come to a peace. He tells them that they should satisfy him in this for they are his children created and generated by him. Although they are thoughts of love and speak of nothing else but love, yet it was the heart that made them amorous, and so they should not acknowledge any other father but him and as his children stop giving him so much bother. One of the above-mentioned thoughts answers this sorrowful request, saying in effect that they are the cause for the heart's being alive

---

79. Cf. *Disputation* III.54, p. 393.

80. Horace, *Epistularum liber primus* 2.55: "Sperne voluptates: nocet empta dolore voluptas" (Pleasure bought with grief is of no use to us).

and making a comparison between themselves and the bees: In the spring when Flora adorns the world with flowers, the bees from many flowers produce one sweetness, that is, honey. Like the bees, the thoughts from the diverse beauties of my lady generate a certain sweetness mixed with some bitterness with which the heart nourishes himself and lives. Placing in my lady her glances, her words, her ways and her other beauties as if flowers in a meadow, my thoughts, feeding variously, produce this bitter sweetness for the above-mentioned reasons, that is, that there is no joy on earth that is not mixed with suffering. In amorous thoughts one sees the bitter more distinctly than the sweet in spite of the fact that they are mixed together and that it is a great sweetness to contemplate and imagine the many marvelous beauties of my lady, but yet it is a great torment and bitterness to desire them and be deprived of them. The heart is drawn by the above-said sweetness and thus cannot help but think of his lady, and the thoughts necessarily bring with them the desire, that is, the privation of that good. It is truly said that the heart nourishes himself with these sweet and most bitter thoughts.

XXXV

If my tired eyes now here or there I turn
And do not see the blessed one I love,
In misery they stay and find no peace.
The same is true of thoughts, of words, of steps,

So that most times in tears I do them keep,
And lower them, and my poor tongue keeps still,
And my tired foot in its first track does lie,
And all my thoughts around my heart retreat.

I then see her so beautiful and gentle
Within my heart, where her did Love engrave
That other blessings I don't seek or peace.

I then my heart, alone and silent, cherish,
And all at once he does with my life flee.
Alive I don't remain, nor dead, but worse.

Since it has not been determined whether it is a greater unhappiness to be most unhappy or not to be at all, I shall leave the truth of the matter to greater minds than mine. I shall say, however, because of many experiences, that many times things happen to men that make them choose to give up life rather than support them. Although this desire is reprehensible, in these cases it overcomes all better resolve. We also see many times men deprive themselves of the function of their senses for a short time, rather than support their being offended. An example is one who blocks his ears against a great or fearful noise; another will shut his eyes not to see something ugly or something else that would cause pity or grief; another will block his nose against some stink, and one must believe that all these would keep their senses blocked forever if forever lasted what gave offense. This being so, there may be many cases where we would consider the privation of being a lesser evil than what offends it.

Since it was a great offense to my senses when they were deprived of their true object, that is, my lady, the present sonnet verifies the above-mentioned facts, for in such cases I elected to be deprived of all external operations rather than suffer such an offense. I judged that being deprived of my lady was a greater offense than my life being deprived of the above-said functions. Although it may seem that this is not a complete privation since I had deprived myself only of the act and not of the potential,[81] presupposing what has been said, that is, that the offense could be lasting forever, we can affirm the privation of the act as well as the potential.

The sonnet, then, says that when I sought my lady with my eyes or walking, with words or with thoughts, and did not find her, the result was great wretchedness for all these that were seeking her. For there is no greater wretchedness than never achieving peace or quiet or the end of passions, particularly when the object of which we are deprived is greatly desired. Nothing could be more desired or dear than my lady, presupposing that she was the only good that pleased me, which means that everything else but she displeased and disturbed me. Therefore, since the number of other things was infinite, so much the greater was my displeasure as was the number of things that offered themselves to me, and thus my annoyance was almost infinite, and all these things were very serious because they represented my being deprived of my lady. It is the case with our soul that it has no peace until it finds that object it likes more than others, and although it may like many things, the desire that fixes on what it likes most puts aside all else if it can achieve its first desire. For example, one may take

81. Cf. *Disputation* VI 49–54, p. 407.

pleasure in various things like dogs, birds, horses, and with these things he is miserly by nature and intent on accumulating them more than anything else. So that putting aside other pleasures that he naturally still desires, his appetite is only quieted by what he desires first and above all other things, and everything else bothers him.

My annoyance was much greater for I only desired my lady and nothing else could satisfy me, since my desire for her was not only the first and greatest of my desires, but the only one, without the company of anything else that could please me, so that my annoyance was most great both for the number of what bothered me and for its quality. I could find no better remedy for these things than the above-mentioned privation, so that I closed my eyes filled with tears and kept them fixed on the ground. I stopped my feet in their tracks, that is, in the impression in which they stood; my tongue kept silent and my thoughts closely surrounded my heart. Here we must note that these thoughts were about my industrious search for my lady, thinking of the way in which I might find her sooner. They were different from those I shall mention later, which were seeking her in another way and in another place, and when she was found there, the more the distraction of the senses was missing, the more force my interior thoughts and imagination derived from this cessation of operations.

And so, almost through necessity, my thoughts gathered around the heart contemplated my lady sculpted by Love in my heart, and they saw her there most beautiful and gentle as she really was. And so then, with my thoughts' eyes I cherished my heart who was really beautiful since in him was sculpted my beautiful lady. And my imagination was so strong that within myself I felt the same pleasure as if my eyes had seen the real woman. Since a strong imagination can only last a short while except in very few exceptional people, I would become aware of that most sweet deception almost as if I were awakening from sleep, and finding myself without my lady I suffered a great deal. Because of this, my heart would depart and leave me almost senseless, silent and alone, for the beauty of my lady who showed herself to my thoughts in my heart would give rise to desire for the real woman, as we said in the comment on the sonnet that begins: "When I do think of lodging some complaints."[82] That desire would make, not only my thoughts, but almost all

82. P. 153.

my spirits leave that imaginary form and go to the real one, for my thoughts could stay only where my lady was.[83] They therefore stayed in me for as long as they saw her, and as that image departed, they too would abandon me.

I then remained neither dead nor alive because since my heart, the seat of life, was leaving me, I could deem myself dead. But since some vital force did yet remain, I could call myself neither dead nor entirely alive. If those things we said in explaining the three sonnets on the transference of hearts are true,[84] one who lives in another as lovers do cannot call himself alive, nor dead if he lives in some place. The condition in which I remained could not be interpreted in any way as being anything but the first shown in this sonnet, that is, the suffering of seeking my lady with my eyes, my words, my footsteps and so on, without finding her. And therefore what we proposed at the beginning of this comment is verified, that is, that the privation of being may at times seem a lesser evil than a most bothersome annoyance, for I remained in a worse state than if I had been all alive or all dead. And since death includes the privation of both the action and the potential for action, it seemed to me a lesser evil than the misery of the most unhappy condition.

XXXVI

"What is, alas, my lovely lady doing?
Where does she sit? What does she think or say?
Whom do those eyes and hands now happy make?
O Love do tell me now," but there's no answer.

My eyes then sad and desperate warm tears
Let overflow to learn about their fate.
Some reach the breast, and others further go
And wet the ground and there remain and stop.

My heart then does send out so many sighs.
These with the wind are gone, so that the heart
The thoughts does spur to undertake the journey.

They go to her and fall in love with her,
So that no one does come to bring me news.
My heart then follows. I my fate bewail.

83. Cf. Ficino, *Sopra lo amore* 6.9.

84. Sonnets XXX, XXXI, and XXXII, pp. 166–74.

Although lovers' torments are many and varied, yet if we consider this matter well, we see that they are all brought about by two causes: jealousy and privation due to the absence of the beloved. It must necessarily be so, for their happiness also consists in two things, that is, in two qualities of the beloved, the first being the external and apparent beauty and the second the love, that is, the heart of the beloved. For there are two things in the lover that must be nourished and fulfilled, that is, the senses through which one knows apparent beauty as well as sweetness of words and other perceivable ornaments, whether natural or acquired. The other is the heart that nourishes himself with the reciprocal transmigration of the loved heart into the beloved and likes the above qualities so much that he transforms himself in others, as we have said. If these then form the happiness of lovers, their unhappiness consists in being deprived of them, which can occur only by means of jealousy and absence, as we have said. That the lamenting of the beloved's absence is found in our verses quite often is not surprising, for since passion dictates the verse,[85] a greater passion forms a greater number of verses. Since my passion at my beloved's absence was very great, the more often I was away from my beloved at my sorrow, the more often did my heart recur to the remedy of verses.

Finding myself away from my lady's eyes for some time and divided by great distance, I began to think to myself, and not without much suffering, about what she may have been doing at that moment, where she may have been sitting and thinking, and who may have been so favored by Fortune or worthy of being seen by those eyes or touched by that hand, so that he must have been made most happy. Since I could not find out what I wished from anyone except Love, I asked him about it, and since he refused to give an answer, I began to think who might be able to give me some news. No speedier messenger appeared to my tearful eyes than the tears themselves that came from them. But since they could not reach the place where my lady was since their path ended on my breast when they fell or at most reached the ground wet with my tears, my heart, seeing that the plan for the eyes and tears was useless and that my tears could not reach my lady, decided to send her many sighs to gather some news. And here is verified what we said above, using the eyes as an example of all the sensitive means that have as object the external beauty and the heart whose object is my lady's heart.

85. Juvenal, *Satires* 1.80.

The eyes are the first to move, and the heart follows them, for once the external beauty has been approved, there immediately follows the heart's desire, not only for that beauty, but for that of the beloved's heart. My heart then sent many sighs after my eyes' tears whose voyage did not endure much longer than that of the tears since they dissolved into air and wind, just as they were before they became sighs

Since the heart was deprived of this hope, he recurred to thoughts, encouraging them to go to visit my lady, for even if the journey was long, they could quickly get there, being so swift and eager. The thoughts immediately went to find her, and they found her so beautiful and so sweet that they fell in love with her and could not leave her. Forgetting how wretched they had left me, they sent back no answer or any news at all. Because of this, my heart that nourished himself only on these thoughts, as we have seen elsewhere, left and went to my lady also, abandoning me in tears, wretched and disconsolate, and I in my tears complained only that my adverse fate had not made me agile and swift so that I might have gone to my lady together with my thoughts and my heart.

Since we have often mentioned this flight and departure of my heart and his transformation and the flight of life, it seems necessary to see how this can be, showing especially how at times my heart and my life depart and yet I remain alive, as shown by the preceding sonnet in the last verse. We shall say then that our soul has three powers, or we can say three types of life. The first through which we only exist, nourish ourselves, and grow without any feeling, just as trees and grass live, is called vegetative. The second allows us to see, smell and use the other senses like brute animals and for this reason is called sensitive. The third, through which we understand beyond the senses and through reason decide that one thing is better than another and seek the cause of things, is called rational. This last we share with the angels, and it is this part of us that is said to be immortal, for the first two we see that they come to an end and die.[86] Therefore the lover transfers two of these three powers to the beloved, that is, the sensitive and the rational, for all the powers of our intellect and what is known through the senses are given into the power of the beloved, and the beloved governs and disposes of them. It must necessarily be so, for since we voluntarily submit our free will, which is the source in us of every operation, it

86. A concept originating in Aristotle, *De generatione animalium* 1.18–19.

must necessarily be that all operations follow the source without which they would not be made. In one who loves, then, there remains only that part of life through which we only exist like plants, as we have said. And thus is verified the departure of life and the heart, that is, of rational and sensitive powers, without life coming to an end since the vegetative power remain in the lover.

XXXVII

I can no longer see those saintly eyes,
Of my own peace and only true sweet object,
And since all else I see I do but scorn.
Kind Love always with tears my eyes does fill.

The flowing tears that out in front fall down
My breast do bathe and do my heart awaken.
The heart then asks of Love what harsh event
So wet the eyes does make and the tears flow.

When Love explains, the heart much pity feels
For my poor eyes, and my wet face he covers
With the dense fog of his most doleful sighs.

O my sweet sun, my only true, sweet good,
Do show yourself and chase this fog away.
My eyes have no more tears, my heart no sighs.

It does not seem necessary to say much in the exposition of this sonnet since its theme is very similar to the two preceding ones and does not denote anything else but the wretchedness of a lover's condition when he is deprived because of the beloved's absence. Since the sufferings of love that are caused by absence are relieved in three ways, that is, by tears, sighs and thoughts, I believe with reason that these are repeated many times, although in various ways, for if this suffering is often experienced by lovers and there are no other remedies, it is necessary to repeat the same things.

The present sonnet, then, shows that since my eyes were deprived of my lady's most sweet eyes, which were their only object and locus of peace, they scorned everything else they saw. Love, moved by pity for my eyes' misery, filled them with tears, so that covered by tears they would at least be free of the vision of other things, which they scorned, for when the eyes are filled with tears they can see only with difficulty. Since these tears fell over my breast on the part beneath which the heart is located, they awakened the heart that sensed that my breast outside was being assaulted by falling tears. In this way we show the abundance of the tears by which the heart had been awakened, that is, removed by the tears' new assault from a sweet thought that had held his attention. Like one who is awakened by a strange and horrible noise, he asked Love, who was present, why the eyes were crying so much. Love told him the reason for the tears and had to tell him that he had been moved by pity for my wretched eyes and so had provided the tears so that, since the eyes were deprived of their lady and scorned everything else, he could at least help them avoid what they scorned, although he could not give them the particular sight they wanted. For there are two remedies for wretchedness, that is, make one who is miserable happy, and this is the most perfect, or to remove his wretchedness, that is, take away the evil without giving him happiness. For example, in the case of a beggar in need of everything, if one took away the need of these things with which he cannot live and gave him just a sufficient amount of them, he would remove this beggar from misery and a terrible evil, which is the necessity for everything. But if one made him very rich and gave him an abundance of everything, he not only would remove him from misery, but would give him well-being by making him very rich.

Love then did this for the eyes, giving them the lowest degree of well-being by taking away that which offended them, that is, the sight of all other things. For them there were two causes for grief, that is the desire to see my lady as their greatest happiness and ultimate good and the fear of the hurt coming from the sight of all other things. Hearing the reason for the tears, my heart was moved by the same compassion that Love had felt and so helped to occlude my eyes, as tears had been doing, by emitting a great number of sighs, and veiled the eyes with their fog so that added to the tears they would be able to defend the eyes from the sight of all other things. It is natural to say "fog" of sighs that rises and goes up to the face, for sighs bring with them a certain air more vaporous and thick, almost like smoke or fog, and they naturally ascend to the eyes where they are sent by the impetus that rises from the lower chest.

But all these remedies were not sufficient for such misery, for the loss of sight of all other things was not the sole and true beatitude for my eyes, and so I began with all the desire in my heart to beg my lady's eyes to show themselves somewhat and let themselves be seen by mine. Since my tears were like rain and the sighs like fog, no better remedy could be found for removing tears and sighs than the light of my lady's eyes, just as for dissipating fog and rain there is no better force than the sun's. We therefore begged my lady's eyes to show themselves, recurring to them as the only remedy, as we said, for if they delayed or hid their light and power for some time, my eyes would fall back into the greatest misery. And this would happen because, not only would they be deprived of this sun that was their true beatitude, but would be forced to see the other things, which we said they scorn immensely. This would be so since tears and sighs could not block their sight as it seemed impossible that the source of tears would not dry up or that the site of sighs had so many of them that they would not at some time be lacking for their merciful ministrations.

XXXVIII

To you I do return, bright lovely stars,
To your sweet light, to infinite true beauty
Whence every gentle heart derives its life
As from the sun, light other stars derive.

I come with heavy steps to see them now
With whirling thoughts of which some lead to hope.
Others much fear do in my soul instill
So that she fears she'll hear ill news of them.

"Look in your heart," Love now does say to me,
"Her sweet last words that you did hear with me
Inscribed you'll find, for I did write them there."

All thoughts of scorn or wrath from her I took,
And in her lovely breast there only burn
The flames that I for you did then put there.

It is a great wretchedness for someone who suffers because of his desire for something, and when it seems he will now obtain it, he still suffers as before since he fears that once he has obtained what he wants, he will still remain miserable. Since this happens often in the course of love, one can say that a lover's life is wretched above all others, for whether he obtains what he wants or not, his unhappiness never changes, although the cause of his misery may. The present sonnet expresses this concept, for it shows that I had been away from my lady for some time with much suffering, as we stated above, and was now on the way to return to her so-desired presence and near the sight of her beautiful eyes. And as if I were quite present, I speak to them saying that I am returning to see the sweetness of their light and their infinite beauty from which every gentle heart must acknowledge he receives life, just as the stars in the sky acknowledge that the source of their light is the sun's splendor. To prove the truth of the fact that the life of gentle hearts is derived from this infinite beauty, one must presuppose this beauty to be without end so that it would then be not only the greatest beauty, but all the beauty there can be, for such is the nature of all infinite things. And since, according to Plato,[87] highest beauty and highest goodness and highest truth are one and the same, goodness and truth are necessarily in true beauty related in such a way that each converts into the other. If we understand that by gentle hearts we mean lofty and perfect spirits, as we have said, it must then be true that every gentle heart lives on infinite beauty, for beauty, goodness and truth are the object and the end of every rational desire and give life to those who desire them. One who abandons beauty, goodness and truth may be said not to live, for outside of these absolutes one cannot say there is anything at all.

Therefore, just as the sun with its rays makes the stars shine without losing any of its own light, thus this highest beauty instills in gentle hearts the rays of its grace, that is, a spiritual light through which they live and spiritually reflect the light. Although the subject of which our verses speak is not of such perfection, errors caused by love make us think that there can be in others what we have in ourselves. Since I lived of the light of those beautiful eyes, their beauty seemed so marvelous that I thought it must have been as pleasing to everyone as it was to me, and so I ascribed to all the others what I felt

Coming back to the infinite beauty without which I judged myself to be wretched, I was full of various thoughts and the more confused the closer I came to her, so that mine must be deemed a great unhappiness since in the good I sought I suspected evil. The variety and confusion of thoughts consisted in that some told me that I should find my lady full of love, kindness and sweetness, while the others frightened me by telling me the opposite. Within myself I was afraid of hearing true news of my lady because of the suffering my heart would

87. Plato through Ficino, *Sopra lo amore* 2.1–3.

endure if I learned that I had completely lost my lady's favor. This made me slow down my steps, and it was a most potent force, for although I desired to see my lady's eyes above everything else, I yet slowed my pace on the way to see her. Love came to my aid in that most difficult perplexity of mine, for he reminded me of some words that my lady had told me as I left her, which were all full of hope, and said that in whatever place and time I should always enjoy her grace and assured me of her fidelity and loyalty. Love had inscribed these words in my heart with his own hand, and this sweet memory made me put faith in what Love added, saying that he had taken all other thoughts, indignation or wrath from my lady's heart and that there remained no other desires or ardor than what Love had instilled for my satisfaction and happiness. One can assume, therefore, that I, filled with this hope, quickened my steps, although the sonnet does not mention it, since the fear that had slowed my pace was no longer there.

XXXIX

That sudden amorous and candid pallor
That in that lovely face presumed to come,
For all the other beauties it then did
What young green grass to flowers does in spring,

Or a serene light sky with color makes
More brilliant and more beautiful the stars.
That face in beauty then was equal to
In meadow flowers and to stars on high.

In that angelic face I then did see
That Love stood there rejoicing and amazed
For his creation did too lovely seem.

As by that pallor my own eyes were struck,
And of her lovely eyes the light appeared,
My powers did leave me and are still gone.

Plato, a most excellent philosopher, speaks of two extremes, science and ignorance.[88] Science is almost a light that shows us truly and perfectly what is, and ignorance a deep darkness that deprives us of the knowledge of the things that really are and wanders only in what is not. Since there must always be a mean between extremes, he places opinion between science

88. Plato, *Republic* 5.478c–d.

and ignorance, which at times is true and at times not, so that it seems that in some ways at times it participates in science and at times in ignorance. Not that it can ever be a science even when the opinion is true and of real things, but it can certainly be ignorance when it is about what is not real. Science includes those things that are certain and clear; ignorance includes nothing, and opinion what at times is and at times is not and that may be or may not be. For this reason opinion is always filled with anxiety and disquiet since our spirit is satisfied only by that which is true, and since opinion cannot be certain, it causes disquiet and judges things in relation to others and by comparison more than according to truth. For example, I shall say that this fellow is tall because he exceeds the height of five feet ten, which is the normal stature, but if normally men were over six and a half feet tall those who are five feet ten and more would be deemed short. Among Ethiopians, who are black by nature, one who is less black than the others will be called white, and among westerners one will be called black who would be judged very white among the Ethiopians. You will say that a fellow is good, while according to the prophet David, "non est usque ad unum,"[89] but you call him good in comparison to the malice of others. Some are very rich in Venice, Florence and elsewhere today who with the same wealth would have been beggars in comparison to many wealthy men in Rome at the time of the monarchy.

We shall then say that in human opinion there can be no real knowledge of anything, but that one judges best what approaches good the most, and that true is what is most distant from its contrary. For example, if one thought that a pearl would be the more beautiful the more white and candid it was, that is, the more it approached true and perfect whiteness, he would like to see it on a black background or with dark colors so that the comparison with its contrary would show the pearl approaching real whiteness more. Although the primary intention is this whiteness, he mixes it with the color black, which is its opposite, and deceives himself by thinking that this would strengthen its whiteness, while in fact that pearl is no whiter on black than on white. Thus beauty is born, which comes from the variety and diversity of things, so that one draws power from another and seems to approach perfection more. For if opinion understood reality, we should select only those things that are more beautiful

89. Cf. Psalms 14.1 "Non est qui faciat bonum, non est usque ad unum" (There is no one who does good; there isn't even one).

without admitting others that are less beautiful, and whereas in human life we generally seek variety as the highest beauty, we should avoid it more than anything else, if we had perfect understanding.

This discourse has seemed necessary since in this sonnet we deal with the highest beauty that appeared in my lady's face through an event that in others most times hides and undoes beauty, while in her it enhanced it. I was going through a very solitary path alone, but full of amorous thoughts, and while I had no expectation of being able to see my lady in such a place, I suddenly met her, and she was already very near when I saw her. This unexpected vision and sudden assault by her eyes on mine made me at once lose almost all my strength and the color of my face, and as I looked at her face, it seemed to me that it was similarly adorned by an amorous and beautiful paleness, not of lifeless color, but one that tended towards whiteness. At first it seemed to me that the pale color had been most presumptuous to fill such a beautiful face. But thinking about it better afterward, I saw that it had enhanced the other beauties, just as green grass makes flowers more beautiful, and the sky with its color and serenity makes the stars brighter and more distinct. Although flowers are more beautiful than grass and stars than the sky as background, grass makes the flowers seem more beautiful than if the entire meadow were of flowers and they did not have the green of the grass as background. The same is true for the sky as background for the stars, not only for the sake of variety, but because opposites are enhanced and show themselves to advantage when they are near. And the beauties of my lady were no less in number for me than those of flowers in meadows and stars in the sky. Those beauties, then, in the midst of the pale color were like the flowers in the midst of grass and stars in the midst of the sky's color

Among all these flowers in the midst of that face, there was Love, a most beautiful flower, and among so many stars, there was also the star of Love. Love was happy and marveled at the same time for having created such a gentle and beautiful work. He was happy for she was most beautiful and marveled because what he had done was a great thing and most unusual, having added such ornaments by means of that pale color that, as we have said, usually makes others ugly. If Love, who was the author of this beautiful work, was amazed, you can imagine how I was thunderstruck and full of wonder and how my strength left me for some time since I was overcome by the excessive new beauty. I believe the same would have happened to anyone who had been favored by seeing her, contemplating her and loving her.

XL

Alas, I do not know what I should do
When I am where my lovely lady is;.
If I at a bright star or other look,
Flashing in them my very death I see.

If I do flee and then call out for help
To one of these great beauties or another,
To her sweet idiom or her graceful ways,
I do not find a place where safe I'd be.

I could her hand now touch, but it holds tight
My willing heart and thoughts that now rejoice
And so has me of my poor life deprived.

From numerous sweet enemies of mine,
Many sweet blows I get and do await
So sweet a death that live its thought lets me.

All human affections without controversy are passions, and the causes that give rise to human affections are two, wrath and covetousness. Since these two are very different passions, according to some they have different sites and seats in our bodies, for wrath is generated in the heart and covetousness in the liver.[90] But according to some others they are both in the heart. That they are different forces is shown by the effects of these causes, of which a part that comes from wrath most times disturbs our spirit. Those that come from covetousness more often are pleasant and sweet. Since all these affections are passions, as we have said, it follows necessarily that every desire, even for something sweet and pleasant, is also a passion. In fact, as we have said at the beginning in the definition of Love and in the comment on the sonnet that begins: "O my poor tired eyes,"[91] every appetite shows that the privation of what is desired is a great unhappiness, for he who cannot satisfy his appetite

90. Cf. Ficino, *In Platonis Timaeum commentarius* LXVI; Plato, *Republic* 4.440c–442b.

91. The comment to Sonnet XXII and also II and XIX, pp. 146–50, 95–97, and 138–41.

and curb it lives in continuous affliction. Thus the same thing is sought and avoided at the same time, for he who much desires to quiet a great appetite has great desire, and one who does not wish to quiet it similarly has much desire. But the greater error is made by one who tries to quiet his appetite for something by remedies and ways apt to increase it and enhance anxiety, as happened to me who had great desire for my lady when I thought of her, and thinking of quieting it, I would go to see her.

As I would begin to see her eyes, they seemed so beautiful that my desire grew, which was the opposite of what I wanted. Not finding peace in her eyes, but seeing in them shine and flash my death, that is, Love, I used to avoid them and think that I should find in some other of her many beauties the peace I had not found in them. Thus at times I asked her gentle ways for help, that is, for the above-mentioned peace, considering them with great attention. At other times I sought this help when I heard her most sweet speech, and in other ways in accordance with the manifold diversity of so many charms of hers, both natural and ornamental. But in effect in all of them I found Love armed and ready to cause my death, for the true function of infinite beauty is to give rise to infinite desire, as we can say proportionately of all beauty and desire.

Despairing of finding peace in the beauty and ornaments that I continuously saw with my eyes, I thought I should restore my quiet if I could touch her most candid hand. But then I remembered that it was this hand that had deprived me of life and held my heart and all my thoughts within herself, and so I despaired of this also, for if my thoughts were happy in that hand, it would be impossible for them to leave that happiness that all things seek. And I without my thoughts could not find peace, for thoughts are at the root of all human action, and since they precede action, one cannot do anything without thinking first, and thus if thoughts are lacking, there will be no action.

Thus I could not obtain my health, that is, the quieting of my desire, for since it grew more and more, necessity showed that I had to endure these most sweet offenses and had to love these sweet enemies, her eyes, her words, her ways, her hand and my lady's other charms. And these were really sweet, for it was a great sweetness to watch such beauty, but they were also real enemies for they were the cause of the increase of desire, that is, of passion. I believed then that I was close, not only to that beauty, but to the fulfillment of my hope for a much sweeter death, which I awaited with great desire at the hands of the above-mentioned enemies by means of their amorous offenses. The stronger were these offenses, that is, the desire for such great beauty, the sweeter death became. Thus the hope for this death filled my heart with such sweetness that the heart already nourished himself in it and lived. By this death we mean death in the form we have said, that is, the death of lovers when they transform themselves entirely into the beloved, when nothing matters but the fulfillment of desire, which occurs when the lover is transformed into the beloved. And so this death not only is sweet, but is the sweetness that human covetousness can have. Therefore, as the only remedy for my health, it was awaited by me with great sweetness and desire, as the true end of all my yearnings.

XLI

Alone my lovely lady never is
So far away from my sad grieving eyes.
Love. Faith and Hope are always there with her,
And all my thoughts also are there with them.

With these so sweetly she laments and speaks
That Love does pity her beyond all measure,
And in those lovely eyes that grief keeps low
He cries and both bright stars he thus does darken.

A faithful thought of mine does tell me this,
And if I should not him believe, he brings
Proof of her sweet and lovely company.

And were it not that I always do hope
To see those eyes that my own heart does see
And always present are, of joy I'd die.

When I composed the present sonnet. I was very far from my lady, as had happened many times, as we have said. Among many painful thoughts that made this absence most bothersome, one in particular hurt my heart terribly. This was that as I considered the many passions that arose in me because of being deprived of her presence, the thought came to me that the same thing likewise hurt her. Thus to the grief I felt for my own condition was added this, as my heart felt pity for her sorrow at being alone and without me. Since nature and every good doctor that imitates nature find a remedy first of all for what is the principal ailment that threatens life, my amorous thoughts that were the only medicine for this most sweet ailment first thought of the remedy for what hurt me most of all, that is, pity for my lady's loneliness. They showed me in effect that she was not alone, although away from my grieving and tearful eyes, for in her company there were Love, Hope and Faith, together with all my thoughts. She was not alone, therefore, although no persons were there, and she was deprived of conversation with others, as shown in Cato, who said he never was less alone than when alone.[92] Jeremiah called Jerusalem "alone,"[93] although full of people, for real solitude is to be deprived of the things we like. And it is said that one is alone in the midst of many enemies because when the real purpose for which an object is ordained is lacking, then necessarily that object is no longer the same, as for example we call a man "rational" because he is ordained to have reason as his end, but when this is lacking he cannot be called a man. The society and company of men is ordained by nature so that all the commodities necessary to human life that cannot be found in one alone, can be had from many. And if this is the end of association, every time there is a great number of people to hurt one, we have not "association" but "enmity."

So then, if the association of others was bothersome to my lady, and she only liked Love, Hope, Faith and my thoughts, without these she would have been in great solitude even though in the midst of many, while even in the sand-filled deserts of Libya she would have had company if with them. That she was not alone is also shown by the fact that she spoke and complained with this company. She complained so sweetly that Love marvelously felt pity for her and, moved by compassion, he cried while in her eyes. Since we said that the seat of Love was in my lady's beautiful eyes, he necessarily cried in those eyes. Because of these tears and because they themselves were overcome by grief and so looked down, some of their splendor was lost. Not that those eyes became less beautiful because of this darkening, but they shined to other eyes as the sun does when some cloud is interposed; I mean as it appears to our eyes, not that the sun loses part of its light. Since what has been said seemed marvelous and almost incredible, it was necessary to show that the author of these statements had been present, as one of my thoughts had been, for since all my thoughts were there, he

92. Cicero, *De officiis* 3.1.17.

93. Lamentations 1.1.

necessarily must have been there. For as we said at the beginning, this remedy came from my amorous thoughts. In confirmation of this truth, he brought the attestation of the other thoughts that she was in the company of Love, Faith and Hope, a truly sweet and beautiful company, for there is no other good in human life or a greater sweetness. And if Love and Faith were really with my lady, there must perforce have been compassion for my not being there, and since my thought had these witnesses, he had to be believed. This faithful messenger filled my heart with sweetness at the thought that my lady, not only was not alone, but was in such beautiful company. On the other hand, hearing that my lady complained and cried, my heart was filled with great pity, so much so that between that sweetness and compassion I should have died, if I had not been helped by the hope of seeing her eyes soon, which my heart always saw, and since the heart's eyes are thoughts, it is confirmed that my thoughts were always with my lady.

Eclogues

Corinth

The moon among so many lesser stars
In the serene quiet sky did brightly shine
And of the others did the splendor hide.

Sleep had all men and animals on earth
From their diurnal labors then delivered,
And the world silent and in shadow was.

In the thick woods alone among beech trees,
The shepherd Corinth of his love did sing
For Galatea, but not a soul did hear,

Nor had his ever-tearful eyes a rest
Or quiet been given. All alone instead
With these sweet verses he of love complained:

"O Galatea, why do you scorn so much
The shepherd Corinth who does love you so?
Why do you wish that he, poor man, should die?

My doleful sighs and my sad tears are known
To all the woods, and you, O night, hear them,
For I beneath your starry mantle am."

The calm and well-fed herds without suspicion
In the deep stillness of the night do stay,
And keep on chewing the pale grass they love.

The tender sheep still safe within their fold,
So well protected by the watchful hound,
Stay in the light cool breeze asleep and happy.

Unheard, I do lament my harsh affliction
With words, with tears and prayers in the dark,
But if unheard they are, what good are they?

Oh how she flees before our very eyes,
But does not flee before our thoughts so swift,
And more than when she's there my heart she gnaws.

Oh come, don't let your heart so hard now be!
The harsh commands you have now of Diana[1]
For fifteen years of your chaste life obeyed.

Isn't that enough? Now do give me some help!
O nymph, there is no pity in your heart.
But woe is me, my voice still goes unheard.

If only it were heard one time at least!
I know that verses can, if they are heard,
From the sky make the moon to earth come down.[2]

The men from Ithaca into wild beasts
Verses did change. In meadows fresh and green,
Verses can break the sly and frigid snake.

So then my own rough verses, unadorned,
To the wind give we shall, and now I've seen
How my laments will soon to her be brought.

The breeze does move of trees the tall green tops,
Which when they move give voice to soft low murmurs
That with her name the air and woods do fill.

If they bring this to me, it shouldn't be hard
To this hard woman my laments to bring
Through the tall mountains and in narrow vales

Where Echo dwells and doubles my laments.
Let him on the fresh wind bring them to her.
I know that tears in stone are never planted.

In some deep cave she may hear me right now.
I do not know if you are near. I know
Wherever you do flee, I'm there with you.

If you less cruel were and showed more pity,
If I should see you here, if your white hand,
Your sweet face I could only touch, O God!

---

1. Diana, the Greek Artemis, is seen as a goddess of women who lived in forests, and whose cult traditionally seems to have required chastity.
2. Cf.Virgil, *Eclogues* 8.69–71.Verses are seen as magic formulas capable of miracles.

If you on the green grass would rest with me,
The bark I would then take of slender willows
And make a flute, and I'd want you to dance.

I'd see your floating hair by vine shoots tied.
I'd see you dancing move your candid feet
On the green grass and leap and kick the wind.

Then tired, you would beneath an oak lie down.
In the fresh meadow I'd some flowers pick
And on your face I would let them rain down,

Of colors and of fragrances so many.
You would make others grow soon with your smile
Where the first ones I had for you then picked.[3]

So many garlands for those golden locks
I would then make of flowers mixed with leaves.
Their beauty would by yours be overcome.

The murmur of a fresh, clear little brook
Our sweet companion in our bliss would be
With the love songs of amorous young birds.

Drive out, O nymph, this cruelty of yours.
From your heart now drive out such bitter thoughts.
Oh do not lethal your great beauty make!

If you do wish the tracks of beasts to follow,
There is no shepherd more robust or skilled
In following and hunting fleeing beasts.

Silent, without a word, you'll stay well hidden
With bow in hand, and I with strong sharp steel
The fierce wild boar where it will come await.

How terrible the pain, alas, I've felt
When you barefoot before my eyes did flee!
With what deep sighs I have always so feared

That thorns, or poisonous snakes, or sharp rocks
Would your feet harm. How angry I then was!
Your feet I tried to lift to protect you,

Like one who with sharp eyes shoots at the target,
And when the arrow from the bow has sped,
He turns his head as if to guide it home.

---

3. Cf. Petrarch, *Rime* 165.

But you're so light that I of you believe
That you so agile are that you could run
Over deep water and your feet keep dry.[4]

But what great fear within my heart did grow
That you would do what once Narcissus did
Whose own great beauty he did too much like,[5]

When you did wash your face at that cool font,
When still became the waves you had then stirred,
You did at yourself stare in the quiet glass.

How foolish can we lovers ever be!
When you had left I did run there at once
And did not think the image wouldn't be there.

In the font I did look but didn't see you,
But I did see myself, and the thought came
That I couldn't be condemned for wanting you.

If I'm not pale, do the sun blame, and yet
I think it does become a man like me:
What good can a man be who dark is not?

If full of hair my chest and shoulders are
Displease this should you not in any way,
If taste and mind you have to match your beauty.

Perhaps you do not know how strong I am.
If a fierce bull by its sharp horns I hold,
In spite of its great strength I'll make it fall.

In a cave dark and deep the other day,
I went to get a pair of young bear cubs,
And groping in the dark was going ahead.

I reached the den and took the young bear cubs,
But then the mother bear so fierce and raging
Heard me, and all at once did rush at me.

I then a strong branch grasped and just right there
I killed the bear and with the prey I left.
And if you do so wish, it shall be yours.

---

4. Cf. Virgil, *Aeneid* 7.810–11.

5. Narcissus admired his image in water, fell in love with it and drowned in his attempt to embrace it. See Ovid, *Metamorphoses* 3.407–510.

As for strong arms, none can with me compare.
During the feast of Pan[6] the other day,
I won a cow together with its calf.

Diana I can challenge with the bow.
As prize I won a ram with four great horns,
With long white fleece that to the ground did reach.

It shall be yours, though Neifil hurt will be,
To whom for love of you I am ungrateful,
While she adorns herself to please poor me.

Whether I'm rich you know, for on all sides
The valley does resound with my sheep's bleating,
And heard is the loud lowing of my cattle.

Fresh milk I have, and nice strawberries, too,
Red in the meadow that is all in bloom,
But pale they do become next to your cheeks.

Ripe fruit in every season does abound.
Many a thousand bees in hives I keep,
So you would think no more on earth could be.

So sweet their honey is that it resembles
The sweet ambrosia that they say Jove ate:
Sweeter it is than Etna's sugar canes.

O nymph, if my sad song does not move you,
Be moved at least by that of these sweet birds
That with such sorrow and new voices sing.

Do you not hear sad Philomel[7] of love
With me lament? In such sweet verses she
For her love cries, as I do cry for you.

On sleepless nights, just she is there with me.[8]
To pity I did think I could move you,
But if my tears the ground do bathe, you laugh.

Where cruelty joined is to such great beauty,
There is live death. Yet something comforts me:
Eternally your beauty does not last.

---

6. Pan was the god of woods and shepherds.
7. Philomel was raped by her brother-in-law, Tereus, who then cut off her tongue. Turned into a nightingale, she sings to lament her fate.
8. Cf. Petrarch, *Rime* 311.

To a small garden on the way I was[9]
The other morning, when the sun did rise
With its bright rays, but I aware was not.

Within the garden some rose bushes are.
My craving eyes I did then turn on them
For that which I had never seen before:

The roses were all candid and bright red.
Some did their petals to the sun wide spread
That first were tight, but then wide open burst.

Some younger ones there were that hardly did
Peek from the bud, and others still refused
Their tight, closed petals to the air reveal.

Still others as they fell the earth made bloom.
Thus I saw them as they were born and died
And saw their beauty fade in one sole hour.

When pale and languishing I saw their petals
Fall to the earth, the thought then came to me:
The flowering of youth a vain thing is.

All trees their flowers have and later on
Their tender leaves spread open to the sun,
When the air seems itself to be reborn.

To form themselves the little fruits begin,
And so much then they slowly seem to grow
That the strong branches by their weight are bent.

Nor can they then without great peril bear
Their own full weight, and as they still do grow,
Too great for their own strength almost become.

Autumn then comes, the ripe sweet fruit is picked,
And as the fine good weather goes away,
The trees of flowers, fruit and leaves are shorn.

O nymph, do pick the rose while spring is here.

---

9. For verses 163–93 cf. Poliziano, *Stanze per la giostra* 1.78 and *Canzoni a ballo* 3 ("I' mi trovai, fanciulle, un bel mattino…").

Apollo and Pan

In Thessaly a mountain tall there is,
Pindus by name, by sacred bards more sung
Than all there are from Atlas to great Indus.[10]

Luxuriant grass and flowers at its foot
By a cold spring are bathed of fresh clear waters,
Which then trace paths through beautiful green meadows.

Not satisfied with their restricting banks,
They spread through such a place of which the sun
A lovelier one didn't see or we did read.

Peneus the river is and all around
The fertile land is Tempe called and is
Into two parts divided by the river.

Shady, not dark, a forest girds the land
And full it is of beasts that though wild are,
Inimical are not to our own nature.

Flowers of various colors may be seen
So lovely that new pleasures they give us,
So to restrain our steps obliged we are.

Nights here are never languid or too long,
Cold winters do not long the greenery hide,
Or can the birth of tender leaves delay.

The cloudy air the frigid North Wind here
Does not congeal. The flowing waters ice
Does not to a halt bring or hide the fish.

Of the dog days the rage is never felt,
Nor does the arid hot and thirsty sand
The languishing poor flowers down constrain.

Crack open the earth won't to let its prayers
Rise and reach Juno's ears at once to beg[11]
That she grant men the water so desired.

Eternal spring its only season is
Present always in this so lovely place,
Nor can a planet's path a change bring here.

10. From West to East.
11. Juno as the goddess of storms and other cataclysms.

The leaves green always are, the flowers new,
As in springtime the earth is wont to boast,
And of spring do the birds so sweetly sing.

Phoebus[12] this place does love and here he still
His laurel does adore. Why marvel then
If mild the winter is and so the sun?

Both of her father's banks Daphne does hold.
At times the father cries and the waves grow
So that he can then touch his own beloved.[13]

And in the sacred laurel's deep cool shade,
Sing candid swans, and their sweet song the river
Always does hear and murmuring responds.

Because the evergreen leaves Phoebus loves,
The swans the font of Pegasus[14] have left,
And only in this place their song is heard.

Above all lands on earth the god Apollo
This place did love from where the spring comes forth
To where the name Peneus lost becomes.

Even more so when Phaeton had been killed.
And to avenge his dearest son the god
Forced Steropes the Acheron to cross.[15]

Angry, the lord of the great council then,
This grave mistake to punish, as was just,
From heaven did him banish for some time.

Himself a shepherd's clothes he then assumed,
But hardly any difference one saw
In the new form from the primeval god.

Only the bow that from his shoulder hangs,
That at one time of solid gold was made,
No longer shines, for now it is of yew.

---

12. Phoebus still loves the laurel into which his beloved Daphne was turned.

13. The laurel into which Daphne was transformed is on the banks of the river Peneus. Peneus was her father.

14. The spring Hippocrene on Mount Helicon to which the winged horse Pegasus gave life by stamping the earth with his hoof.

15. Steropes, the cyclops who had forged the bolt with which Jove killed Phaeton. Apollo killed Steropes to avenge his son.

The ivory plectrum too of wood is now.
His eyes still are with divine flame all lit:
This he who gave it take away can't now.

His blond mane does its wonted look retain,
But where a crown of gems did it once press,
A laurel garland now the god does wear.

A shepherd now become, he sings or plays
Or the sweet arts together entertains.
With Daphne and Pencils at times he speaks.

Pan heard him sing by chance and said to him:
"One who so well does sing no shepherd is
Who ever watched a herd or did cows milk.

I should much like some day to challenge you,
But I'm a god and can not vie for shame
With one who watches of the herd the steps."

The shepherd said to him: "There is no need
To worry for this reason, for my lyre
As sacred fully is as your sweet pipes.

If you do not the song now recognize.
Look at my eyes." Their splendor then made Pan,
The one whom Delos loved, soon recognize.

"With much more ardent zeal I shall now sing,"
Said the great one, who now in all Arcadia
Is held above all those who are in heaven.

"I am content. Much pleasure this gives me,"
Apollo said, and then the gods did sit
On the green tender grass with flowers sprinkled.

Pan chose to sit there in the shade of Syrinx,[16]
For he did not forget his ancient love.
She moved and seemed to smile upon his song.

Of his own sacred laurel in the shade,
Apollo of his lyre did tune the strings,
While Pan his pipes did harmonize together.

---

16. Pan, the native god of Arcadia, loved the nymph Syrinx, who fled from him and was saved by being turned into reeds. From these reeds, then, Pan made his melodious pipes.

O lovely nymph whom I so often called,[17]
Beneath that old beech tree in shady vale,
And you then didn't refuse our song to hear,

O, don't your lovely face from me now hide,
If my desire so daring mad is not
In wanting to relate such lofty matters.

I do beg you in the green hills' name now,
And of the pleasing shade, and the surging springs
That did your candid feet so often bathe,

And of tall mountains high and lofty passes,
Of your chaste charming beauty and your eyes
With which at times you dare the sun defy,

And of the candid tunic that does cover
Your limbs of ivory, and hair so fair,
The happy grass that by your foot was pressed,

The shady caverns where at times you hide,
Your lovely bow, which if of gold it were
Diana you would seem amidst the green.

O nymph, help me recall the song the gods
Once sang when all the nymphs to listen came
To these two gods from near and from afar.

Peneus held back his swiftly flowing waters,
The herds forgot they were supposed to graze,
All the birds in their flight the song did stop.

To honor their own god all the fauns came,
The satyrs for the concert did arrive.
The murmur of the leaves at once was stilled.
Pan's sweet song then did rise into the wind[18]:

"O goddess,[19] who were born in restless seas,
Were you, or was it your own impious son,
The cause of the Sicilian shepherd's death?[20]

---

17. The poet invokes the aid of his "nymph," probably Lucrezia Donato.

18. The original is written in tercets yet contains this one quatrain.

19. Venus.

20. The shepherd Daphnis, who offended Venus by resisting love, was punished by the goddess who made him fall violently in love. But he refused to give in and died of unsatisfied desire.

You were the one, or rather your son Cupid,
Or rather impious you gave him vain hope,
While he, most fierce, blind ardor did give him.

And from which Fury did you poison take,
O Cupid? Did you then the arrow dip
In Cerberus's most foul and foaming mouth?

How could a god immortal be so cruel?
How could you look upon such evil death,
So wicked and so bitter, without tears?

If Venus did to this give her consent,
I will then say a goddess she is not,
And so then you are not a goddess's son.

Of Caucasus the strange and snowy peaks
Did give you birth, and there amidst hard rocks,
By the milk of fierce tigers you were fed.

They were harsh nurses, yet in pity you
Those savage nurses let surpass yourself.
Your heart of stone must be, but they did cry.

The crying then did on those furry cheeks
Deep furrows draw with tears that were so new
From eyes that never had till then shed tears.

But you, O lovely nymphs, where were you then
When Daphnis did his last laments there breathe,
Invoking all the cruel stars above?

Of the green shady woods, O Daphnis, lover,
Of my reign honor who did please me more
Than any one who ever flock did tend.

O Daphnis. Daphnis. how well you the herd
Did tend, but not yourself, but then who can
From his relentless fate find an escape?

Who can oppose of Fortune the set course,
Or bend the will of those so evil sisters[21]
With prayers or with tears that bathe the cheeks?

Can ever one your fury, Cupid, flee?
You know. O Syrinx, how my feet were light
To follow you, but fear yours lighter made.

21. The Parcae, or the three Fates.

Since Cupid's harsh will bend pity could not
For Daphnis' death, let lovers then know that
No mercy will they ever find in him."

The fierce lions' dens did with their roars resound,
And all around through the green meadows then
The air was filled with tears from plants and rocks.

Never had Lycaon before this cried,
But he shed tears this time, and those whose form
Frigid Callisto with her son did take.[22]

---

22. Lycaon, known for his cruelty, was turned into a wolf by Jove. Callisto, loved by Jove, and her son were turned into bears by Juno, and later Jove changed the constellation of Arctophylax and her into the Great Bear.

Ambra

Fled is the season that had then transformed
Flowers to fruit, by now already picked.
No longer can the leaves hang on the branches,
But through the woods less thick are now spread out
And let themselves be heard if hunters do
Through the woods go. Though few they many seem.
Although its own vague tracks does hide the beast
The leaves don't keep its secret in the least.

Happy the laurel is among bare trees.
Of Venus fragrant green the myrtle is.
In the white Alps the green fir tree stands out
And bends its branches now weighed down by snow.
The cypress still docs hide some secret bird,
Against the winds the strongest do resist.
The humble juniper with sharp leaves thick
Does not the hands now prick that wisely pick.

In some sweet sunny hill the olive trees
Green or white seem depending on the wind.
In these does Nature nourish and maintain
The green that lacking is in other leaves.
The migrant birds beyond the sea have led
Their families so tired with so much effort,
They showed them Nereids all along the way
With Tritons and with monsters all astray.[1]

The night has fought and has the battle won
And in dire bondage she now holds the sun.
In the serene dark sky by flames encircled,
The starry chariot on its way she leads
And as it rises, the sun's golden one
In the deep painted ocean then does sink.
His knife does Orion[2] then threaten to throw
If the sun dares his lovely face to show.

Night's glowing chariot is then followed by
Vigils and wakes and by all pressing cares

---

1. The Nereids were sea divinities daughters of the god Nereus; Tritons were also sea divinities, often shown playing on conches.
2. Orion was a mythical hunter turned into the constellation that bears his name.

And sleep (that though most powerful, so often
By all the others overcome can be),
And such sweet dreams that can our minds deceive
When harsh and fierce does Fortune them oppress.
Rejoice do some for state and for their wealth
Who then wake up still poor and in ill health.

Wretched are they on dark and long nights, who
Do not find sleep and for daylight they pray,
If day holds out to them the promise of
Something so sweet that they have long desired.
Though both their eyelids they do press together
And all sad thoughts exclude and sweet ones welcome,
When sleeping or awake time to deceive,
A century the night they do perceive.

Wretched is he who on so long a night
Far from shore is among tempestuous waves.
The blind prow is by howling winds opposed,
And the sea rages with the fiercest roar.
With many prayers and felt vows invoked.
Aurora with her husband[3] does remain.
Fearful and wishful the lone sailor numbers
The night's slow steps and those of time that lumbers.

How different, how opposite the fate
Of happy lovers is in wintry fog,
For whom the nights are all too short and clear
And the days dark and slow that never pass.
In this cold season dark and long and harsh,
The little birds, now in new plumage dressed,
Have put aside for all this season long
I don't know whether tears or happy song.

On high and shrieking loud the cranes are seen
That with their lovely forms do stamp the sky.
The one behind with neck outstretched does touch
The empty tracks the one ahead has left.
Then when their new and sunny site they reach,
One stays awake on watch, the others sleep.
The lakes and meadows now are all well covered
By many birds so beautiful and colored.

---

3. Aurora, the goddess of dawn, was married to Tithonus, who was given the gift of immortality, but not of remaining young.

The eagle often with majestic flight
Over the ponds does fly and threatens all.
Together they all rise and drive it off
With their wings' wind, and if one all alone
Too far away remains from all its friends,
The sharp-eyed eagle swiftly does it seize,
And if it thinks to Jove it will be taken
Like Ganymede,[4] it surely is mistaken.

By now to Cyprus Zephyrus[5] has fled.
Over the grass with flowers he cavorts.
No longer limpid and serene, but dark
By the north winds the air perturbed now is.
Ice does the running stream to crystal turn
That tired now rests and does no longer murmur.
The fish remain in clear and hardened wave
Like a fly buried deep in amber cave.

The mountain that fierce Caurus does oppose
To shelter and defend the noble flower,
That there did grow in honor, wealth and rule,[6]
His hoary head in thick cold fog does hide.
From his proud head the long white hair comes down
His back to cover, and the rigid beard
His hairy chest. A fountain do create
His nose and eyes that hard by ice is made.

The foggy garland that the temples girds
The wet south wind has laid on his old head.
The north wind then does soon it chase away
And bare and white the ancient head remains.
The south wind then on his wet evil wings
The fog does bring and dresses him once more.
Angry Morello, now in fog, now clear,
The plain does threaten ice or rain to bear.

The warm and dark south wind comes from Ethiopia.
Over the salty, deep Tyrrhenian waves
His thirsty sponges dips until they're soaked.

---

4. Ganymede, because of his exceptional beauty, was seized by an eagle and brought up to Zeus, who made him his cup bearer.

5. Zephyrus was the god of the West wind, bearer of spring.

6. Mount Morello that protects the "gentle flower," that is, Florence, from the northwest wind.

When once the destined site he does then reach
With water heavy, tired, and with clouds dark,
The sponges with both hands he tight does squeeze.
Happy the rivers from old caverns come
To meet all friendly streams away from home.

Their heads adorned with fluvial leaves and algae,
The river gods old father Ocean thank.
Happy they blow their raucous twisted horns,
Their swollen bellies are already filled.
The wrath against the timid banks they felt
For many days now satisfied all is.
Their enemies, the banks, they break and foam
Nor can the old beds hold them as they roam.

Not through uncertain ways or crooked paths
Like snakes, the great dark flood straight on does rush
And hurries to rejoin old father Ocean.
The waves together join far distant streams,
They to each other talk like long lost friends,
And of their customs and their country chat.
Speaking together thus in a strange voice,
To seek the river mouth is now their choice.

High in a mountain, swollen and broad they
Come to a narrow pass into the valley.
Held back, they roar and turbulent and evil,
With earth they mix and yellow they all turn.
In anger with the rocks and with the pass,
Stone after stone they push along their path,
The wild and foaming waves do whirl and tear.
Though safe on high, the shepherd still feels fear.

Within its hollow ancient belly deep
The earth a like rage feels with smoke and flames
That mixed with water roar and rage as they
(So horrible and fierce to eyes and ears)
Through a thin narrow mouth a way out find.[7]
Nearby Volterra high and strong does fear
The thunder and the muddy geysers' smoke
And hopes for rain if higher they do poke.

7. The effect of the rivers through the narrow pass is compared to that of the fumaroles near Volterra.

The fierce proud torrent angrily does rage
And the opposing banks it now erodes,
But when the plain does broaden it expands
Almost so happy that it can't be heard.
Uncertain whether to above return
Or to descend, its banks the mountains are.
Triumphant it proceeds to the quiet lake
Dragging along its prey as if by rake.

The fearful peasant woman just in time
To save the herd the stable doors did open.
The cradle with her crying son she holds.
Her daughter carries all their poor old clothes
Of wool and linen and does follow her.
The other old effects go floating by.
The pigs do swim, the bulls are by fear torn,
The tender sheep no longer will be shorn.

From the rooftop where refuge they have sought,
Some members of the family look on.
All their poor wealth they see by water swallowed,
With all their hopes and labors, but in fear
They don't complain and silent they look on.
The fear of death their poor sad breasts does fill.
They do not seem for their dear things to care
For greater worries hold them still in fear.

The green familiar banks do not restrain
The fish now happy for their broader space.
Desire both old and just for them to see
New shores now satisfied in part has been.
Not sated, they pursue their new desire
And rush to see of buildings the remains
And other ruins and under water walls,
Still doubtful but with many happy calls.

Ombrone then, the fierce proud lover, does
Ambra embrace that now an islet is.[8]
Lauro loves her no less and jealous is

8. The river Ombrone bathes the islet Ambra where Lorenzo had a villa by that name. Here after a long introduction begins the myth of the river god Ombrone's (Umbro's) love for the dryad Ambra that will result in Ambra's transformation into an islet. Ombrone's rival in love, Lauro, is Lorenzo himself.

If touch and hold her tight his rival does.
The dryad Ambra to Diana dear
As much as any who an arrow shoots,
So swift and agile more than one can say,
Her grace and beauty did her then betray.

Lauro. a gentle mountain shepherd, then
With a chaste love had loved her many years,
A chaste nymph who of love the flame had not
Ever as yet burn felt in her chaste breast.
Because of heat, she did one day all naked
In the cold waves go wading of Ombrone,
Who of his father proud and brother streams
In customs and appearance proud he seems.

Ombrone felt the maiden's limbs the dark
And gelid waters enter and at once,
Moved by the beauty of her lovely body,
The proud god did from his dark cavern come.
In his left hand he held the twisted horn,[9]
His body bare and burning with desire,
A garland of fir leaves the sun's hot ray
From his tousled dark head did keep away.

Straight toward the place then where the nymph was staying,
Well hidden by the leaves he slowly went.
He was not seen nor could his steps be heard
For they were covered by the river's murmur.
So close does he come to the lovely nymph
That he can reach, he thinks, her golden hair
And the beautiful nymph in his arms fold
And naked then the naked body hold.

Like a poor fish that careless fishermen
Do cover with a net of too broad mesh
Escapes the net it feels above it fall
And to flee leaves behind one or two scales,
Thus when aware did the poor nymph become,
She from the god did flee who leaped at her.
So fast the god himself at her did hurl
That fleeing in his hands she left a curl.

9. The horn was the symbol of the river gods.

She runs away from the cold water leaping,
Barefoot and naked she flees full of fear.
Her clothes, her quiver and her arrows leaves,
She pays no heed to all sharp thorns and stones.
The god afflicted is and does much grieve.
In grief his hands he wrings, looks at the sky,
He curses his too cruel and slow hands,
When to the shorn blond hair his eyes he bends.

Pursuing her, he says: "O hands of mine,
Savage and quick in ripping her blond hair,
But slow to hold that body so divine
That could forever more content make me."
Over the first mistake in vain thus crying.
If his slow steps cannot to her arrive,
He thinks that with his voice he'll make her turn,
And shouts: "I am a river, yet I burn.

A burning blind desire in my poor breast
Of these cold waters in the midst you lit.
Just as your body in these waves did lie,
Why not with me now lie? It would be better.
If my cool waters and the shade you like,
My cavern better shade and water has.
My things you like, but I do not please you,
A god I am, so why not like me too?"

The nymph does flee and deaf is to his prayers.
Fear wings does lend to her swift, white bare feet.
The god his feet on urges in pursuit,
Swift by love made as he pursues her still:
He sees that thorns and cutting stones do wound
Her beautiful white feet and feels much grief.
His desire grows that him so ill makes fare,
Seeing her flee so beautiful and bare.

Shy and ashamed, on running Ambra keeps,
More swift she is than the most swift of winds.
Her light feet could run over stalks of grain
That surely would support her gentle weight.
Ombrone sees the distance slowly grow,
At every step the nymph on further seems.
In the broad plain he sees less he can cope,
So that to reach her he does lose all hope.

Before through mountains that were steep and high,
He did come down with speed among the rocks,
While her steps were less swift, and she was hindered.
This gave him hope he would succeed at last,
But when, alas, they reached the flat broad plain,
Ombrone was held back as if by reins.
Since on foot he can now no longer follow,
He with his eyes pursues her full of sorrow.

What must the god now do who burns with love,
When he can't reach at all the lovely nymph?
The more denied she is, the more his heart
With love does burn, and he the more will strive.
The nymph the place had reached where my own Arno
Receives Ombrone, and their waves are joined.
Ombrone is encouraged by the sight.
Hope grows and he will now go on to light.

He from afar, "O Arno," shouts, "in whom
Most Tuscan rivers refuge seek and find,
That lovely nymph that like a bird does flee,
Through woods and mountains high I have pursued,
But merciless she now my poor heart breaks
And does not seem to know what real love is.
Give her to me and so my own repose.
Her course do interdict and do oppose.

I am Ombrone who for you does gather
My azure waves and keeps them all for you.
Once they are yours, they do become so deep,
You tall and proud can bridges scorn and banks.
This is my prey, and now this golden curl
That I in my hand hold, for which I grieve,
Does show it's so. In you is all my hope.
Do help me now. Alone I cannot cope."

By pity moved as he Ombrone sees,
To answer him does Arno not take time,
But back the waters holds, then grown and swollen
Poor Ambra's course opposes from afar.
As she draws nearer, greater grows her fear.
By new sharp fear the virgin breast is seized.
Behind Ombrone, before her a lake.
What can she do? Her heart with fear does quake.

Like a beast that from dogs itself does save,
Swiftly from fierce and eager jaws escaping,
When out of danger suddenly a net
Before its eyes it sees, so filled with fear
That it will soon be caught almost sure is.
Ahead it cannot flee, back it dares not,
The net it does not trust, the dogs it fears,
With fear it howls, and terror its heart tears.

The beautiful nymph's fate like this one was,
On every side by new fears oppressed.
She knows not what to do, but wish for death.
She sees the two approach her from both sides
And in despair she then cried out aloud:
"My goddess, to whom once I was entrusted
by my dear parents, do me now support,
For my last wish you are my last resort.

Lovely Diana, this chaste breast of mine
Was never stained by any mad desires.
Protect it now, for I poor nymph cannot
With two such enemies and gods them both.
Within my heart with the desire for death
There is the most chaste love of Lauro mine.
O winds the sound of my last voice now bear
To Lauro mine who'll hear and his heart tear."

These words had hardly by her lips been uttered
When her so lovely candid feet began
To be there seized by new and most strange feelings.
They then did grow and like a stone became.
Her limbs, her body did then color change,
But still you see she had a woman been.
Her limbs like those of figures there appeared
Sculpted in stone that incomplete remained.

Weary and tired Ombrone from the race,
With hope renewed that his dear prey he'll reach,
New vigor does acquire and speeds the pace.
He seems to think she is already his.
He sees the stone that grows before his eyes,
But does not realize what it must be.
But when he sees that his desires are vain,
He stops full of surprise and in sheer pain.

Like a poor deer that by fierce dogs pursued
In a park by a tall stone wall enclosed,
Or other fence, no longer hopes to live
When the wall it does see, but by fear driven
Leaps and before the dogs does lightly rise.
The dogs inside remain disillusioned.
Unable to go on where the deer went,
They only stop and stare with their hopes spent.

Thus did the god his rapid feet then stop.
He looked with pity at the growing stone,
The stone that some resemblance still then held
To that most lovely nymph who still could hear,
And as both love and pity him commanded
With bitter tears he did the stone then bathe.
"The waters in which once to bathe you came,
Ambra," he said, "these are the very same.

I never would have thought in so much grief
That pity for myself could be outdone
By that for my own nymph, or would recede
Before the greater pity for my Ambra,
For whom I now do cry, not for myself.
Yet my sad worthless life eternal is,
And so to me it is more an offense
Than turn to stone for her and lose all sense.

My father's mountainous domain, alas,
Is home for many nymphs who live in safety.
Among a thousand beauties, the most fair
I chose, I don't know how, and her I loved.
As a first sign of love, her hair I tore
And from the shade and water I drove her,
Tender and bare, and then to flee the flood
Sharp thorns and stones she tinted with her blood.

And in the end into a rock transformed
Because of my own cruel, fierce desire.
I lost her, but I don't know how for never
Was she my own, yet I my life can't lose.
Thus more inimical my own fate is
Since I am both immortal and so wretched,
For if in death I could ever find peace
This just eternal sorrow would then cease.

I have now learned how one should try to please
A woman one does love and her love gain.
For the one you love most you most do harm.
O boreal wind that do to ice all turn
The flowing waters, to hard ice turn mine
Like stone to keep fit company with her.
Let not the sun with rays both warm and yellow
This rigid crystal make again to flow.

THE LOVES OF VENUS AND MARS

Come nymphs, the glorious mountain now adorn
With songs and dances and the lyre's sweet sound.
Garlands of flowers make for your own hair,

For I do think I hear my friend Mars coming,
And in the sky in its white Milky Way
I have just seen his happy star appear.

Your hair by veils now covered to the wind
Then spread and happy Acis's font[1] now visit
And there do wash your charming face and hair.

The sacred Muses at Castalia's font[2]
With their sweet poems to come you will invite.
Hang out the drapes, the sky do well adorn.

Bacchus and my Silenus do you welcome,
And if no longer angry Ceres is
For Proserpine, you will invite her, too.

Clymene, my nymph so dear, go to Aurora,
Tell her the lovely morning to delay
And happily with her Tithonus[3] stay.

You, Clytie, will to Mount Pachynus go,
You to Pelorias, you to Lilybaeum.[4]
Do watch now all of Sicily's long borders

So that from fiery Etna my own Vulcan[5]
Mars[6] in adultery with me won't find
And then make all the gods about me gossip.

---

1. Acis, loved by Galatea, was turned into a river when he was killed by his rival Polyphemus.

2. Fountain on Parnassus sacred to Apollo and the Muses.

3. Bacchus was the god of wine who loosened cares and inspired poets and musicians. Silenus was his tutor and constant attendant. Ceres was the goddess of agriculture and mother of Proserpine; the latter was carried away to the infernal regions by Pluto. Aurora was the goddess of dawn, and Tithonus was her husband, who was granted the gift of immortality, but not of eternal youth.

4. Pachynus, Pelorius and Lilybaeum are promontories in Sicily that here become guard posts for the observation of Mount Etna from all directions.

5. Vulcan, god of fire, was Venus's husband, who resided on Mount Etna where he had his forge.

6. Mars, god of war, was Venus's lover.

O Moon, do hide the lucid hemisphere,
And you, O dogs, do not in woods now bark.
Let not of infamy the truth be known!

Come happy night and you O gods of Ades
Do darkness bring, and you, my dear child Cupid,
I give myself to you. I'm in your hands.

With your sweet flames I'm burning and I smile.
The way do light for Mars, my lord and lover,
You did wound me. O Cupid, you I trust.

O Mars, if dark the day to you does seem,
Come to my sweet refuge. I wait for you.
Vulcan isn't here, he can't our love disturb.

Come, I invite you naked in my bed.
Do not delay for time does pass and flee.
With crimson flowers I my breast have covered.

Come Mars mine, come, come now for I'm alone.
Take out the lamps. I never mine put out.
Let no one dare just now to speak to me.

Mars arrives and speaks as follows:

Not as an enemy to you I come,
My lovely Venus, but unarmed I am
For I no arms do have against your blows.

It's different to see in someone's glance
The light of love, no matter where one goes,
Than banners or standards, sharp sword or lance.

"Love reigns in his empire without a sword,[7]
Without a cover bare the body wants,
Happy to follow what does one well please.

Listen to him, he never ruthless is
Nor cruel, but always so truly sweet.
Let this the weapon be, the lance, the shield.

Do let a tress descend around her neck,
A sturdy chain for those who with love burn,
A soft strong cord that never comes undone.

7. Cf. Petrarch, *Rime* 105.11 ("Amor regge suo impero sanza spada").

Oh to kiss her lips and her serene calm face,
The two celestial stars and her white breast,
The long white hand that Beauty has so formed.

One thing it is in golden beds to lie
With your sweet friend and there sing songs of love,
Another to get tired with helm and shield,

To taste the fruit that happy can make me.
The highest scope of this, a trembling pleasure.
A time there is for love, for war another.

THE SUN DISCOVERS THEM TOGETHER.

A great offense it is to breach one's bed.
It's no excuse to say. "who'll ever know?"
The sun, the stars, the sky and moon do see.

And you who happy with your Mars do stay
Do not believe that heaven will judge you,
But often to great grief great joy will turn.

Every long secret its own limits has:
That one who keeps on tempting Fortune long
Should strike a reef should not surprising be.

Do run, O nymphs, to see the shameless Venus,
Of adultery goddess, who is there
With that betrayer Mars! O stars! O Moon!

If it is not, O Jove, too much to ask,
Come to the crime with your so-jealous Juno.
If you don't want it known, then do not sin.

O Mercury, come, come look at the chains
And then relate in heaven what you see,
For never did a crime unpunished go.

Pluto, if you by now have heard the news,
With Proserpine the netherworld do leave
And to the brilliant air do now come up.

O souls, who the Elysian fields adorn
That are eternal, come to the great crime.
Eternal secrets now must all be aired.

Glaucus and Dores, Neptune, Alpheus run
To this adultery, and Ino, too,
And Melicesta and the Dryads all,

So that on land, at sea, in heaven, too,
The infamy of a most wicked goddess
To all known be, as well as her sheer lechery.[8]

O Vulcan, come and see your dearest Venus,
Come and see how so happily with Mars
She lies and how she broke the faith due you.

A wife's fidelity to you she owed
And to no other. O how hard it is
A woman's lust for long to keep in bounds,

For if she wants, all guardians she'll avoid.
Asleep you may be, but if noise you heard,
A wicked woman's crime do come and see.

Your Sicily now leave, let your state be.
Such injury to bear does you dishonor
Revenue does god demand for a heart's wound.

VULCAN SPEAKS:

To hurl me down from heaven should suffice,
And then keep me away from their lush banquets,
A smith make me and of hot fire a god,

But to increase my grief, to injure me,
All gods do try and show how great they are,
But such an injury I won't condone.

I labor so to make for Jove his arrows,
Sweating around this ancient forge of mine,
And Mars does elsewhere labor in my stead.

Venus, O Venus mine, of waves the foam,
And you adulterer, you Mars, will pay:
A crime so great, great punishment deserves.

8. All these are gods of heaven and of the depths, nymphs and semi-gods, who are called to witness Venus's crime.

Sylva I

O servitude so sweet, my heart you freed
From slavery so low, abject and vile.
When you to happy service did bind me,
You freed my heart from many humble cares.
O lovely hand, when you today tied me,
You did make me so gentle[1] and so free.
May now, O Love, the first knots blessed be
With which in many ways you did bind me.

In you, O sweet and lovely lady, are
Beauty and gentleness that do exceed
That of all others and that then do vie
One with the other so to rank supreme.
How sweet and blessed Fortune really is
That made me such a gentle lady serve.
In serving I more worthy am and free,
For to serve her a king does make of me.

If by both banks the river held back is,
It yet in its slow course does happy flow.
A pleasure to the eye, the clear wave moves
And does the fish maintain in the quiet bed.
With lovely flowers the green bank it bathes,
And free it flows and so does happy serve.
Tranquil the waves within the dark banks stay,
Murmuring they press and all around they spray.

But if the sun its light to us denies
And in a fierce storm, rain the clouds do bring,
The river more and more you will see rise
Until no more it can itself restrain.
Of the tired ox the labors it destroys,
Trees it uproots and drags them on with rocks.
Over the font a turgid lake lies wide
And in its midst the banks and bridge do hide.

When a soft wind so tenderly does blow,
With sweet restraint, the flowers it may bend,
Around it will then whirl and play with them,
Together it does tie them, then unties.
The wheat it does inflate. in waves the grass,

---

1. "Gentile," noble in the *Stil novo* sense.

Ready to cut, as if in anger moves.
Softly the young and tender leaves resound,
No fallen flowers here are to be found.

But if sometime from his deep cavern Aeolus
Freedom does give to fierce tempestuous winds,
Not only mere green branches broken are,
But entire old pine trees to earth are blown.
The wretched ships with their sharp curved prow
Threatened are by the angry, furious sea.
The air by fog is covered with a veil,
Thus the earth, the sea and the sky bewail.

A little spark that from the flint is struck,
Nourished by leaves and by dry little sticks,
Will give off warmth, but then if by wind struck,
The brush it burns at first, and then small bushes.
It then the thick deep forest does approach
And will to the ground burn the tall old oak.
An enemy most cruel sates its rage,
Strange noises and the smoke the air engage.

The shady houses and the sweet nests go
In smoke and flames, and also rural stables.
No animals will dare to cross the woods,
But frightened by the fire away run fast.
By shrieks and bellows is the air soon filled.
By these sounds struck, the valley echoes all.
The careless shepherd, who let fire wide spread,
Looks on in wonder, cries and grieves in dread.

A law benign has boundaries imposed
To keep the earth from being by water covered;
The universe the earth has at its center,[2]
That is opposed to fire that upward tends;
A whole together various matter makes,
And though opposed, together work in peace.
Together they are moved by law benign,
And thus a sweet chain holds it all in line.

The sweetest, loveliest chain around my neck
That happy day her tender hand did put.

---

2. In accordance with the Ptolomaic system. See *Devotional Poems* 1.25–36, p. 414.

My breast it opened wide and in my heart
That name did write and carved her lovely face.
From that day on, my sight was ever fixed
On those so tender eyes and all else scorned[3]:
Only this beauty can my sight content
That once on many things had been intent.

On sunny valleys with green trees adorned,
On clearest streams that bathe the tender grass,
With colors dotted, white and red and yellow,
On the most proud of manors or great city,
On fiercest jousts, soft dances or strange games,
On ships at sea that Zephyr urges on,
On lovely birds, on monsters or strange beasts,
On stones or gems my eyes no longer feast.

In a disordered way in all these things
My eyes did search and ever looked for peace
That hidden was in one they did not know,
But once they found her they did like her so.
In secret my good Fortune did then lead
My sole desire that in the heart does lie.
Without his knowing it, led was my heart
To see one once seen in another part.

On that dear day when that so loving hand
The lovely image in my heart did paint,
Restrained the eyes were then by willing rein
And only looked at her, not this or that,
A thousand thoughts were into one condensed;
Since then my tongue of nothing else does speak,
Nor do my loving steps another seek,
My heart always with her stays bound and meek.

In Janus's great temple tightly bound
With many cords and knots proud fury[4] is.
He tries to free one and the other hand.
With blood all stained, he rages, awful sight.
In the dark netherworld, the poor sad spirits
Are terrified by Cerberus[5] who barks.

---

3. These concepts have been expressed at length in many of Lorenzo's sonnets, particularly in the *Commentary* XI–XV.

4. Cf. Virgil, *Aeneid* 1.294–96.

5. Cf. Dante, *Inferno* 6.13–18; and Virgil, *Aeneid* 6.417–23.

He seems so full of wrath, held by a chain.
At the mouth foaming, he does rage in vain.

Not like those others is my lovely chain
That binds my gentle heart of sweetness full.
With its three knots he happily is led
By her own hand: the first Beauty did tie,
The other Pity did for such sweet sorrow,
Love did the third, and time cannot them break.
Together she did press them with her hand,
And bound my heart is now with Love's own band.

On that so blessed day Love did show me
Her most serene bright eyes more lovely yet.
The Graces did my lady all surround.
To hold me other chains she did not use.
Why marvel if I now myself don't free?
Who can from his beloved wish to flee?
Beauty supreme, Love and sweet tenderness
The heart submit do make with willingness.

When this most lovely golden chain was forged,
The air, the earth, the heavens all concurred:
Never the air did so serene appear,
Nor did the sun a brighter light give ever.
With tender leaves and all bright tinted flowers,
Where a clear brook did flow, the earth rejoiced.
With her dear father Venus[6] stayed that day.
Down at the earth she looked and smiled all gay.

From her divine and golden hair and breast
With both her hands she many roses took
And let them float in the serene quiet sky,
And with them all she did my lady cover.
Such happiness did kindly Jove then feel
That human ears that day he did will open
To listen to celestial melodies
That came to earth with lovely harmonies.

Beautiful ladies to the music danced
With a most gentle love in their warm hearts.
Next to his lady did the lover stand,

6. Venus sat in Jove's lap to make him be in a good mood and assure a serene sky.

Together twined the so desired hands were,
Looks, nods and sighs and other lovers' guiles,
Brief words that only lovers understood.
A rose to the ground fallen from its place
He kisses and does on her breast replace.

Among such charming and most lovely things
My gentle lady, beautiful and sweet,
Outshone the others and did honor them.
An elegant and candid dress she wore.
In her new silent idiom she did speak
To my own heart, not with her lips but eyes:
"Do come to me," she said, "dear heart of mine,
The peace you have desired is now all thine."

This lovely voice my breast did open wide[7]
And then did force my happy heart to leave.
Her charming hand halfway did then him meet.
So sweetly did she press it that the heart
That once had been so rude she gentle made.
Her lovely name and face she painted there.
Thus with beautiful things all ornamented
In my lady's sweet breast he was soon led.

There he now stays, from there he cannot leave.
He cannot leave for leave he does not want.
His high desire no sweeter object has,
Nor can he have, and so he does not want;
A law unto himself, he wants to serve
This gentle lady that his own choice is.
With his two hands he did make a true bond,
And does not want of others to be fond.

Let those who want at diverse things then look[8]
And objects seek to proffer to the eyes.
If first to one and then another drawn,
In neither can he have true beauty found.
Just like an avid bee that turns and wanders,
New flowers ever seeking for its food,
It wouldn't to many fly of diverse kind,
If what in many is, in one could find.

---

7. See above, p. 226, n. 3.

8. From stanza 23 to 29 Lorenzo presents the topic of the uniqueness of female beauty, which is compared to divine beauty.

At the time when first Love my eyes did open,
This beauty he before my eyes did put.
After he had this beauty offered me,
Laughing, alas, he did her hide from me.
With what tears I diverse beauties did seek
And for how long and in so many things!
At times I saw with my poor eyes in tears
What to this beauty a resemblance bears.

Like at the hunt the eager hound does search
To find the hidden prey in all the bushes.
If it the print does see on the soft ground,
It knows the beast had then through there just passed.
Thus I, since a resemblance seems to give
Of the true beauty's presence certain proof,
Did this and that search, here and everywhere,
Until Love did show me that she was there.

My happy eyes then to my heart did say:
"This is the one that Love did show at first,
For whom we have so yearned and so long searched.
First she was taken, now she is restored."
Her true sweet soul does clearly show me now
How much true grace and virtue in her are.
In many we could never this one find,
Her beauty's such that she's one of a kind.

Rather she may be found in every part,
For to my eyes from her all beauty springs.
Beauty so varied in so many things
The source of all that's good to the world gives.
What in part only other things do show
Entire in him is found in perfect state.
If pleasing is the likeness to the eye,
So much more perfect peace in Him does lie.

Contrary voices a sweet sound can make,[9]
And diverse colors a new beauty give,
High tones do please when to the low opposed,
With black in contrast white its beauty finds.
The highest beauty admirably wrought
That one contrary supplements the other:

9. Cf. *Commentary* XXIX, pp. 164–66.

The highest beauty for which all do pine
I only see in this fair lady mine.

Only for her I yearn. In other things
My wishful eyes do never respite find.
Just as the blessed spirits watch intently
The holy face and only that always,
Nor can the pure celestial minds admire
Other things ever for all lesser are,
Thus that first time and that so lovely face
On my own neck the sweetest yoke did place.

Of my fair lady in the loving breast[10]
I hear my heart that now does wish to sing.
As his wont is, my lady's lovely lips
To praise that blessed time he now does use,
For songs and words an instrument so sweet,
With a most pleasing wonderful effect.
Himself restrain the heart cannot and stays
Thus singing through her lips and so then says:

"O sacred, blessed day,
The first day when before our eyes you came,
That with your true light did
Expel all shadows and show what they are!
A shadow black and dark
That to our eyes always so present was,
And yet this they had seen
And the high light serene

They could not see: O poor sad eyes of mine!
How fortunate for me
The time was when I such a sun did see!
Ungrateful I may seem,
O sweetest time, since all
From you my good does come,
If the heart you made happy in the past
Now wishes beyond time all this to last.

10. Ibid., XXX, XXXI, XXXII, pp. 166–74.

Sylva II

After such sorrow and so many sighs,
That lovely face, O Love, I do not see.
After so many tears and so much grief,
Those sparkling eyes, alas, do not return.
Oh my poor thoughts, oh my so foolish hopes,
For such a long time held from day to day!
The day I'll see those eyes does me await?
Whenever it will be, it will be late.

O beautiful eyes, O sweet timid words,
I can no longer hear or see you now.
How long the hours are now that were so short,
To my bliss hostile then and now, always.
O destiny of mine, O cursed fate,
For my long torment do have pity now.
Those eyes do give to these sad eyes of mine,
For without them I until death shall pine.

Living this isn't, and yet I cannot die;
Away, alas, from those bright sacred lights
I do not live. My life with her must be.
Only my body, sighs and tears here rest.
My deepest sorrow a blind hope does nourish,
And this thin thread does not allow to part.
To serve for so long Love has been my fate,
And he, O wonders, keeps me in this state.

My poor tired eyes, why more content than you
Are beasts and mountains, woods and rivers, too?
Why ever happier should those stones all be?
From time to time the lovely eyes they see!
Away from them my life cannot continue,
It must be that the rest in tears be spent.
Let it end soon, if I remain must long
Without the face to whom I do belong.

If on that lovely mountain where she now[11]
Without me all alone for long has been,
Her lovely eyes with their amazing power
Had into those hard rocks at least changed me!
Perhaps at times with pity in her eyes

11. *Commentary* XXVII and XXVIII, pp. 160–64.

She'd look at me, or with light step touch me.
If it I'd feel, my wish would sated be,
No longer otherwise it grieve would me.

If those divine eyes changed had me at least[12]
Into the leaves so green whose name I bear,
Perhaps on passing there close to that tree,
A branch with pity she would then have taken,
And while she sweetly spoke or sang with Love,
Her hands, perhaps, which I so much do love,
Would have a garland made for her sweet head.
Would that new grass I were for her to tread!

If with her steady kindly gaze at least,
There on that mountain where my heaven is,
She had into a fountain then changed me!
Her candid hand at times in it perhaps
She would have dipped, and in those waters clear
Mirrored her face that is so far away.
If changed she had into a wild beast me,
I think I should not flee if her I'd see.[13]

And yet I sigh. My sighs away do fly.
Your lovely name I call, but none does answer.
I cry in vain, and grieve, and do lament.
No longer a sweet sleep my tearful eyes
Can close, and such a fire inside I feel
That always burns and does my thoughts confuse.
O my foolish hopes! I'm tired to the core.
'Tis her I want or death, I ask no more.

O most sweet nights, O joyful, blissful days,
O amorous sighs, O sweet lovers' tears,
O mighty Love who witness happy secrets,
Long nights of love, O such sweet words, O songs!
O wicked fate, why this deny me now?
Why of sad lovers all their dreams deny?
So much you did give me, now you deprive
To magnify my grief while I'm alive.

---

12. Cf. Petrarch, *Rime* 23.
13. A reminiscence of the myth of Actaeon, who was turned into a stag for having seen Venus bathing, and then was killed by his hounds as he fled.

If I no longer can her bright eyes see,
Then shut let mine now be and see no more,
For anything I see, except for them,
A greater sorrow to my life does bring.
O Love that of my woes with me do speak
And in these sorrows are my lord and guide,
Together with those eyes give me my peace,
Or if you wish let my sad life now cease.

I do well know, O sweet dear lady mine,
The grief you feel because of what I suffer,
And that kind face from here I can well see
All wet with tears, and your laments I hear.
Your words, your pity and your sweet desire,
Your loving thoughts are present here with me,
And many signs of a most strong desire,
And so my grief does grow, and so my ire.

Habit and love at times do still lead me
To where we saw each other that last time,
An end to my well-being, a start to grief.
Wherever I do look, I do not see
Those lovely eyes. Then grieving and so sad,
Barely alive, and with slow steps I leave,
I go where from afar I may see well
At least where my beloved does still dwell.

With Love and with myself I do here speak,
"Alas," I will a thousand times then say,
My beautiful dear lady in the shade
Of leafy trees or some hillock now is.
Some boorish peasant does with her now speak,
Who does not care or show respect for her.
And I for sight of her always do sigh
And all I can do now is call and cry.

I do not know if I should speak, or think
At least, without a flood of endless tears,
For someone else may love those charming eyes
And in them gazes steadily and near.
That beautiful hand he does touch and move.
To make me suffer more than I then did,
The prey of others in the end Love shows
Her beauty is, and so our sorrow grows.

Alas, how I do suffer when I think
In peace someone that beauty now enjoys,
And her sweet candid limbs does touch and see
As he desires, and yet he does not cherish
Them, while for so long I away am kept
From her so lovely face and such great sweetness.
Nothing I wish or value more on earth
Than those dear limbs. of news there's yet a dearth.

Even if news should then to me arrive,
This only does my mind always show me,
And with a thousand fears will torture me.
Desire and jealousy torment me now,
Yearnings and scorn, and envy and sad worries,
And Fortune ever to my harm intent
Persecutes me always, while Love still kills
And then is cheered and laughs at all my ills.

While my poor heart in torment is and moans
And of great woes with me does still complain,
When he most yearns and when most he does fear,
And to tears is a prey and death calls him,
A sweet and so desired hope does arise
That comforts me so much with its sweet words:
"You will once more that beautiful face see
Sweet and in bliss as ever one can be.

Happy and loving those most charming eyes
And a few words from her, sweet and appropriate,
Will all your worries calm and your desires
And your afflicted soul that justly grieves.
Those eyes that now from you so hidden are
Will do for you what sun to fog soon does.
All signs of sorrow, fear and tears and sighs
Will flee before those loving ardent eyes.

As soon as at your black and blind horizon[14]
Appears the light that in the heart does shine
And from the top of that most sacred mountain
That loving ray will to the eyes descend,
No need to cover with your hand your eyes,
For this sweet light the eyes does not offend."

---

14. From line 145 to line 304 we have a description of summer through the effects of his lady's beauty, a more or less traditional theme.

What a bright dawn, Tithonus, O old man,
Your Aurora's love now enjoy you can.[15]

One will the bare dark slopes with colors see
Cover themselves as in springtime they do.
The earth no longer of the cold complains,
But decks itself with violets and roses.
The stars in heaven to the spring adverse
The new sun will soon sweet and kind them make.
The endless snowy and most frigid season
Will then soon be transformed beyond all reason.

Happy and marveling the earth will see
Bare branches dress themselves in new green leaves,
And the dry twigs turn into lovely flowers,
Progne and Philomel[16] to us return,
The bees abandon all their old cold hives
And from one flower to another fly,
And the wise ants take up their work anew
With little steps as is proper and due.

The good, kind shepherd in the sweet springtime
Will the flock lead from its old winter quarters.
Happy and bleating all together do
To the mountain return and to fresh water.
The little lamb trots in its mother's steps,
One that was born that day the loving shepherd
With care and tenderness in his arms bears.
The faithful dog on watch does not have fears

Another shepherd on his shoulder bears
A poor hurt sheep that on the way was lamed.
Another on the pregnant mare does carry
The rolled up net and all that needed is
The sheep to shut in when the sun goes down,
So that in the wolf's way they will not stray.
Into cheese and ricotta they then bite,
Happy and tired they sleep and snore all night.

15. Tithonus was loved by the goddess Aurora, who obtained immortality for him, but not eternal youth.
16. The swallow and the nightingale that here are given their mythological names.

As the sweet birds in the green trees now sing,
The silence of the shorter night they break.
Some their old nest try to repair once more
With bits of straw they pluck and little twigs.
In the green meadow the mushrooms stand out
And cheerful women this or that will choose;.
Its den the dormouse leaves and its deep sleep,
The owl's loud wail at night the land will sweep.

In her old realm will Flora[17] reappear
After a while together with her nymphs.
She has till now been in her lover's arms,
But she and Zephyr now cavort around.
Its hoary head will winter with leaves crown,
Inspired by new fresh vigor in the air.
Fierce tigers, bears and lions will become meek,
The ice will turn to water in the creek.

Her ancient lover Clytie[18] will then leave
And her so pale tired face elsewhere will turn.
Towards this new rising sun so full of love
All other flowers will then also turn
At that most radiant light to firmly gaze
That in her eyes does shine and her adore.
On all the leaves and on the grass the dew
Will bid the sun and all its rays adieu.

Through the green shady valleys you will hear
Sweet flutes and pipes from bark of willows made
And chestnut trees. Beneath tall elms in shade
You will see dancing when the sun high is,
And in the liquid crystal all the fish
Of those so charming eyes the force will feel,
For the god Nereus[19] calm will be the sea,
The world will smile and happy it will be.

Just like a tree that will be grafted well
Will be amazed when later it will see
Itself seeds nourish that are not its own
And new strange leaves and flowers grow and thrive,
So will the cold frost feel a like surprise

---

17. Flora the goddess of flowers loved by Zephyrus, the wind of spring.
18. Clytie, the sun flower, will abandon the sun.
19. Nereus was a sea god and father of the Nereids.

When the earth will so beautiful become,
In its new gay and festive clothes all dressed,
And to itself will ask, "Am I possessed?"

At these strange things its wonder will then last
Until the light of those so lovely eyes
Itself will show to winter's gelid face.
When it will see those sweet and brilliant lights,
Into its daughter it must change itself.
Or else its way then make to the antipodes.
One who admire will this so gentle face
Gentle becomes or must leave in disgrace.

If the frost then this gentle face will see,
If it will see the lovely face come near,
Its earlier marvel will soon disappear
That the new day so longed for had brought.
In silence then it will say to itself:
"A greater marvel is that no more than
Of the sun's rays their force she does deprive,
But no greater effects does she contrive."

The light of those so charming eyes will make
The frost then fall in love as it departs.
By many flowers is the path now filled,
Happy and waiting to be touched by her.
The air she parts so blessed and limpid is.
A rain of petals from a loving cloud
To honor her floats down from up on high
And of Love spirits for sheer joy do cry.

With garlands on their heads arrive the satyrs,
Leaping and agile just my sun to honor.
Playing his pipes, Pan[20] comes with all his fauns,
All in their hand do bear the branch of love.
Pale violets and candid roses nymphs
In their hands and in baskets all do bring.
The river gods arrive that weeds adorn,
With leaves and flowers they have filled their horn.

Happy my dear blue Arno with a crown
Of poplar leaves so green on his own head,

20. Pan, an amorous god born in Arcadia, is seen as having the power of making flocks fertile.

Abandon did his mother Falterona[21]
And all the caverns of the ancient mountain.
He murmurs to himself and so does speak,
And of his lovely bridge he will complain,[22]
Arno that labors and does strive to claim
Just like the Tiber great eternal fame.

We now do see of those sweet eyes the light
At the forlorn, sad city walls appear.
Vile hearts do tremble and are terrified
That close to them this gentle fire might come.
In those of lofty and more gentle nature
Now love and gentleness the heart do fill.
Ladies and damsels do run up to see,
Envy they don't and lovelier seem to be.

When within of the walls the charming circle
Entered she'll have, what sweetness will those feel
When they at last the source of peace will see,
For whom they have so long with yearning waited.
O country mine so dear, you must no more
Envy the old primeval age of gold,
The Fortunate Isles out there in the west,
Or where the first parent sinned while a guest.[23]

They all applaud and they do all her greet;
They point her out so happy to each other.
All gentle hearts do welcome her and say
Our life she is, our peace and only sweetness.
Silent vile souls will keep in deepest sorrow
And will not care to joust with those keen eyes.
My gentle lady has at home just come,
Though humble, it now is a happy home.

No marble columns are there to support
The building's small and short walls all around;
No great hard stones in all the lightest colors
Add beauty to the building, nor the sculptures

---

21. The Arno is the river that crosses Florence; the river god of the Arno leaves its mother Falterona, which is the mountain where the Arno has its source.

22. Because the bridge slows it down.

23. The Fortunate Islands is the ancient name for the Canaries. The other reference is to the Garden of Eden.

That to the vulgar herd do so appeal.
Mosaics there aren't, paintings do not appear,
No gold or silver or what gems there be,
But nobler works are there for one to see.

Beauty and charm are there in both the doors,
Sweet glances from those amorous bright eyes;
Within does Pity show itself and seems
To sweetly sing with Mercy and Hope, too.
(Oh what a wonderful, sweet, sacred melody!)
Beautiful customs, pious, honest ways,
Bright sayings on the stairs and words of sweetness,
In the small hall with her. Faith, Love, and gentleness.

A pale old woman[24] sat in a dark comer
And to avoid all sunlight strove, alone.
She sighed in silence and a cloak she wore
Of an uncertain color that did change.
A hundred tearful eyes and many more
Ears in her head the evil goddess has.
What is or isn't she sadly sees and hears,
Sleepless, for only her beliefs she cares.

In the same far-away primeval time
When the dear son of Chaos, Love, was born,[25]
This vicious goddess saw the light of day:
Delivered they both were in one child birth.
Jove, to the world a friendly, loving father,
Did then her banish to the nether depths.
With Pluto and the Furies she remained
During the age of gold when Saturn reigned.

Since Cupid later the immortal gods
Did often catch in one or other net,
And this did deeply all of them offend,
The gods in anger by divine decree
Did bring this woman from the netherworld
To stay with Love and ever be with him.
Over the world thus looms this evil fiend
Trying always Love's labors to rescind.

---

24. From line 305 to 440 Lorenzo deals with Jealousy, drawing in particular from Ovid, *Metamorphoses* 2.760–70, and from various other sources including Boccaccio's *Filocolo.*
25. Cf. Ficino, *De amore* 1.2.

The sublime father Jove was quite afraid
That beautiful sweet Cupid, son of Chaos,
With his strange powers would his place usurp,
Of the great council only ruler be,
And for himself the scepter take and reign.
This fiend he thus recalled from her exile,
And then the oath he took by holy Styx
That she her steps always with his would mix.

By this expedient did great Jove then think
He would the arrows' force from Cupid take,
Undo the knots and all the snares remove,
For if immortal gods could only see
The grief of those who all did fall in love,
The tears, the sighs, and many other ills,
No longer would they dare give Love a thought,
Whose power then would be reduced to naught.

Thus taken was the oath, the law enacted,
And by the holy senate then approved,
But soon thereafter Jove indeed was sorry.
In vain did he repent the oath he'd taken,
And to an inner torment soon fell prey.
Before Love safe had been all gay and blessed.
Were it not for the oath he had then given,
Again to Hades would she then be driven.

Of Chaos born and on the Furies' milk —
Malignant goddess — by Pluto then raised,
She makes all mortals feel while still alive
The torments of the reign that has no light.
Her wounds do not know healing ever more.
A sword she bears dipped in the evil foam
Of Cerberus in the depth where he lives.
Good evil is, and she the worst believes.

She feeds on all sad thoughts and all vain shadows.
Her vicious mouth the heart always does gnaw,
And when it is consumed, reborn it is —
Woe is he who by such a fate is marked
From his own cradle and from early years.
In her breast hate and envy always dwell,
Always she follows where my sun will be
And like a living death is always she.

How often has my sweetest sun then tried
To drive away from her this monstrous being,
At times with threats, at others with sweet words.
Love and Faith say: "Our enemy this is,"
And they both cry and they in vain do suffer.
In vain can earthly will so weak oppose
What was by Jove in heaven sanctified.
She leaves one place and elsewhere is espied.

O venomous pest by all so abhorred,
O fertile source of all that man torments,
Of love a mortal enemy and pleasure,
Of hope and faith and all that man enjoys,
You make our breast with fury ever burn.
O Jove, do break your oath — unjust it was —
The wretch drive back into eternal flame,
But hell perhaps will not want her to claim.

All men and gods with joined hands do beg you
To quench her fire and her exterminate.
Let your breast pity feel for everyone,
For the laments of gods and human tears.
O, don't let these just prayers unheard go,
No longer keep the oath that you then took.
Harmful to all it was to take that course,
To do it wrong was, to persist is worse.

So justly persuaded you were once
To free that most wise son of Iapetus,[26]
Who in the Caucasus by chains was held,
To him reward for giving good advice.
Why then, O father, scruples you now have
To send her back into exile again?
Now her condition does exile require,
You can, for just is what Jove might desire.

Just like an ancient oak up there on high,
When struck by the fierce fury of the winds,
Attacked first on one side and then the other,
Its leaves does lose, and then its hanging branches

26. Prometheus, according to one version, was condemned by Zeus for giving man fire. Lorenzo follows a version in which Zeus himself freed Prometheus from his punishment as a reward for warning Zeus that he would lose his throne to his child if he had one by Thetis.

Bend so that the ground some almost do touch,
But the trunk steady is and unafraid,
Scorns Aeolus's fury and will not then squirm,
For in the earth its roots deep are and firm.

Thus you are moved, most good and most just father
If to your sacred ears our dire sad tears
Almost eternal do up there arrive.
You'd like to show us pity, but can't err,
So when you think of your most sacred oath,
Proper it is to let your pity wither,
For divine will cannot corrected be,
Thus this hard law aborted cannot be.

Where, my blind hope, have you led my desires,
Escorting them, so sweetly luring them
From one sweet thought to ever sweeter ones?
While you give comfort with so many falsehoods,
With colors, lovely flowers, fresh green leaves,
You offer unripe fruit so hard and bitter.
In vain you do show me my lady's face,
I Jealousy and Love see in her place.

Alas, when once you in my thoughts did enter
I saw such real and beautiful bright splendor.
With flowers all adorned Love's path I saw,
Satyrs and nymphs, Pan, river gods all running,
Just like one does who what is real does see.
O my false hopes, how you destroy me now.
The real now flees, sweet hope is dry as bone,
Jealousy and Love do remain alone.

Love as a joke all my dire ills does take.
At his deceit he without pity laughs.
If Hope herself a glimmer does present,
All my vain thoughts with her at once do go.
Love's fire, however, always present is,
And these deceits do make it burn much more.
Jealousy looks with eyes so fierce and dire,
The heart does suffer, grieves and shows his ire

In that sublime site now my lady stays
Where first was born my beautiful desire,
When from my heart Love other thoughts erased,
And there did plant what ever green then grew.

Among all women Love my lady chose
And did give her to me — no other site
Could ever please me so — now I'm away
And without me alone she's night and day.

My lady here her tearful, lovely eyes
Does always in this place all around turn.
Of Love the mysteries in grief she sees,
And all our first sweet moments does remember.
At every step she sighs and calls for me —
(And when I from afar call her, she answers —
She cries and crying then her grief does grow,
This to herself she says as I do know:

"Here I did wait for him and him I saw,
From here I heard him coming on light feet,
Here timidly my hand I did hold out,
Here I did say with trembling voice, 'do sit.'
Here all alone he sat right next to me;
Entirely I did here give myself.
The two of us were here by Love then bound
With such a knot that could not be unwound.

When in the shadows I heard him and then
Saw him, with fear my heart did tremble so,
Doubtful was my desire, and I perplexed,
Both fearful happiness and happy fear
At the same time did come to fill my heart.
I do not know what I should then have done.
By Love encouraged, with fear under stress,
I was then filled with timid happiness.

Here, to him I said, now do content stay,
Do let your heart joy feel, its wish fulfilled!
O words of love, o sweet embraces, kisses,
Sweet sighs that from both breasts did then arise.
Oh fleeting time, brief hours that fly away,
That with you took away so great a lover,
He then left me, desire was in my heart
When near the dawn, alas, he did depart.

Alas, daybreak already was so near,
Phoebus almost at the horizon was.
So sweet had been that lovely night then that
It did seem like a mere heartbeat in time.

'Alive or dead, to you return I shall,'
He said, and left, and was from me then severed.
This hand that guided him on his blind way
He held and kissed and my heart took away.

With my face turned towards him and tearful eyes,
From here the best I could I followed him.
With sweet fire burning, all alone he went
With backward steps and face all turned to me.
This last sad sweetness did not long endure,
The night's dark shadows soon took him from me.
No further power my poor eyes possessed,
But in my heart his image was impressed."

Thus speaks my lady, but those near don't hear,
But I, yes, I do hear her from afar!
That moment when the sacred bond was made
The memory alive does keep for me,
And I reject reality so that,
I do almost relive the time and way
That by that lovely hand I was then bound,
But pleasure does a short time last like sound.

O memory so stubborn and so hostile
That keeps that lovely time before my eyes,
Oh hope more cruel still and more deluding
That promises my heart all this and more,
But I don't see what I alone do like,
Nor do those sacred lights return to me.
One eye looks back, the other forward spies
And my sad angry heart always still sighs.

O foolish thoughts, so often so deceived,
Why persevere on following her still?
Even more foolish I to follow you!
O, do cease now, O sad tired thoughts of mine,
With tearful eyes I rather should remain
And shout my grief a thousand times a day,
In grief, in fire, the time that does remain,
And to my end then come, than hope in vain.

If memory does spur desire, at least
Before my heart the truth does represent,
But in short time vain hope away does flee —
More distant she becomes if you pursue.

She's ever running but nowhere arrives.
Hope and desire the heart do so torment.
Love who does her compel always to follow
In this way does depict this sweet sorrow:

She is a woman of immense, strong build,[27]
Her hair does seem to reach up to the sky,
Formed of dense fog she is and so is dressed,
Of highest mountains on the peak she dwells.
When at the clouds we look high in the sky,
We see new and strange forms of fleeing beasts
That the wind changes and then soon reforms:
Love's depiction of Hope with this conforms.

Lovely she seems from far away and large,
Her shadow nearly covers the whole globe,
If one does happen to approach her close,
Little by little she does fade away,
Just like when sharply the North Wind does blow
You see the clouds just vanish from your view.
Thus you will not find her where you believe,
Ahead you will, however, her perceive.

Just like a dog that thinks it soon will bathe
Its ravenous mouth in a poor beast's hot blood
That it pursues and nearly overtakes,
But cannot reach it, though it still does hope,
Thus its desire so ravenous and foolish
It does not sate and hungry does remain.
The swifter beast does flee and gains ahead,
And the hound rages, seeing its prey has fled.[28]

Or when the sun on our warm backs does burn,
If one the shade he casts to reach does wish
And with it even draw by walking fast,
The shadow must by equal space advance.
Even if he does run as a deer runs,
He'll still behind the same as earlier be.
He thinks he's pressing or thinks he does gain.
The same remains the distance. All is vain.

---

27. In line 529 to 664 Lorenzo treats Hope as he had treated Jealousy earlier.

28. Cf. Virgil, *Aeneid* 12.749–55.

The wheels that swiftly move can't ever reach
The ox or horse that pulls the cart ahead.
Just like this, Hope our touch cannot reach.
Her fraudulent face mortal eyes can't see.
An eye she has with which ahead she looks
At distant lofty things, but never back.
Only Minerva[29] her face has espied
And us poor mortals did so then deride.

On nebulous shoulders do there grow
Beyond imagining two huge plumed wings.
She does to great heights fly from which will fall
Those who believe she'll still afloat keep them.
This beast on wind does feed and on vain shadows
And other food she only rarely takes.
By night she flies and always quickly flees
When with the dawn the sun's bright light there is.

She's kept from heaven and from Pluto's reign,
She through the intermediate region flies,
Where into ice the moisture Juno changes
And into rain she does the clouds dissolve,
And there does Vulcan forge his many bolts;
Aeolus there the South and North Winds does move,
Where lightning is and comets, falling vapors
And Iris bright with her so many colors.[30]

This so unhappy one always is followed
By many falsehoods, auguries and dreams,
All other lying arts and chiromancers,
And all soothsayers, fate and all false prophecies —
Both oral and in foolish cards all written
That what will be foretell when it has happened —
Alchemy and those who the sky consult
And to one's wish do tailor the result.

In the most dark shade of her great wings
All that is vain on earth does shelter find.

---

29. The goddess Minerva symbolizes Wisdom and thus can see that Hope is but an illusion to which weak mortals are subject.

30. Pluto's reign is the underworld. Juno is the goddess responsible for atmospheric storms produced in the intermediate region, that is, between heaven and earth. Vulcan forges his bolts on the volcano Etna. Aeolus is the ruler of the winds, and Iris the rainbow.

Oh how you wretched mortals all blind are,
What ignorance there is, great, vain and poor!
To count all our own ills the same would be
As the stars count above and fish below,
Or in the fall the birds that cross the sea,
Or the leaves that from the bare branches flee.

Is there an ill that mortal man does suffer
That from you doesn't, accursed one, proceed?
Or a great sorrow that you nourish don't?
How many victims have you offered Love?
And if a poor wretch should in you believe
Would he not dare to face the greatest dangers?
From heaven to us mortals you were given,
And you give life to ills by which we are driven.

O you most foolish, poor son of Iapetus,[31]
In vain did your wise brother then warn you
Not to look at Pandora's lovely face,
Or any gift accept that from her came.
O Prometheus give back what you did steal,
That to the world so many ills has brought.
It's hard to tell who was the more inept,
He who fire stole, or he who'd gifts accept.

Prudence most foolish, wisdom most blind yours
Were, and your brother was so madly foolish.
Do give back what you stole, so Jove may please
To rid the world of all those ills and malice.
You did not yet know then that at all times
Regret must follow what was badly started.
You thought you'd Jove deceive, oh great mistake!
Those who wise are, the greatest errors make.

Had it not been for you, Jove never would
Have ordered Vulcan to Pandora make.
All the fine arts and exercises Pallas
Would not have added to make her more lovely —

31. Epimetheus, foolish brother of Prometheus and husband of Pandora. To avenge the theft of fire by Prometheus, Zeus had Vulcan make the beautiful Pandora, whom he then sent to earth with a box that contained all the evils possible. In spite of Prometheus's warning, Epimetheus married Pandora and opened the box, thus scattering all the evils on earth.

Vice in her mouth, all beauty in her face —
And Venus would not grace have given her
And sweet glances and lovely human face.
Nor would just Jove our death in her hands place.

So beautiful and charming she would not
The box have offered to the madman then.
Although before warned, as you do know, he
The box then took and opened it at once,
And from the box at once sprang out and fled
Throughout the world all ills and diverse passions.
Of the divinely forged box then inside
Only Hope all alone did there abide.

Too dearly paid and much too harmful was
The fire you stole and in the reed did hide.
Since then the world has known all greed and cruelty,
The mind became desirous and so peevish,
Wars did then come, fires, wrongs and bitter tears,
From then on ships on the green waves did sail.
All ills on this vain hope do ever feed,
From it deceit, lies, broken faith proceed.

All alone you remained perched on the bed
Because Hope never can to earth fall down.
Born from desire, she promises fulfillment.
From one vague thought another seems to grow:
From bad good she expects, from good much better,
And like a bird she flies from branch to branch.
Not certain, neither in nor out she stayed,
Alone she in Pandora's box remained.

Of mortals the sworn enemy Hope is,
Too arrogant and humans does coerce.
She wants to extend her vast and hidden power
As far as the blind kingdom with no light.
A worthy noble custom to some seemed
To now abandon our sweet present life.
Life they scorn, and death they do acclaim,
Hoping to live forever through their fame.

Before of the dire theft the harmful thought
In the mind of Iapetus's son did come,

Saturn did rule then in the age of gold[32]
All the quiet world with justice under law.
Happier and longer human life was then,
Truth seemed and was the same for everyone,
Wishes were sated and did not persist,
The words for "yours" and "mine" did not exist.

The earth most liberal all life in common
Did at that beautiful time well support.
Wounded not yet by plow or by sharp hoe,
All grains and fruit the earth did then produce.
Sweet herbs and flowers did it all well cover,
And neither sun nor frost did them destroy.
The clear sweet water as it ran did prate,
And the then frugal thirst for all did sate.

Through the green fields so happy and all free
The flocks without dire dread did then yet go,
And the so timid shepherd did not fear
That bears or wolves would ever kill his sheep.
Untamed the bulls were at that time so many,
Not yet deprived of genital drive then
By heavy labor from first dawn to dark
With on their necks deep of the yoke the mark.

In the same field one could together see
The wolf and the dear happy little lamb
Without a trace of fear one of the other:
The wolf was not then fierce, the lamb not timid.
The fox was not deceitful or malicious,
And the farm maiden did not need a dog
To keep the fox away far from her home,
In fact, if it did come, it was welcome.

The hare and dog in the same bush did stay,
The dog did not then bark nor the hare moan.
Between the hound and deer peace did then reign,
Swiftness of foot caused neither hope nor fear.
They played together and each one the other
Did like to tease. If they did run together,

32. From lines 665 to 856 Lorenzo describes the Golden Age, drawing from traditional accounts, but emphasizing in an original way the lack of fretfulness that is born of desire and hope.

They did not run to flee from fierce sharp teeth,
But they did race as in a friendly meet.

Simple, without a blemish and so white
The dove its nest did make where it did please,
Happy, without fear that its envious mate
Or its companion would the eggs destroy.
It did not fear the falcon in the field
Nor of the hawk the snare in the green tree.
Happy the heron shrieking did then go
And did not fear the falcon's beak or claw.

The pheasant did not fear that savage hawks
Would grasp it tight as pliers do to iron.
The quail when fat, about to start its flight,
Was not afraid of falcons' sharpest claws.
To hear the lark sing, glad the blackbird was
And from the ground see it the heavens climb.
There was no need for serpents then to fear
When of the crane the chick was so near.

Barefoot throughout the meadow you could walk
And the snake's wrath not fear as you stepped down.
Serpents did not rattles or poison have
That make the blood rush to the heart in fear.
The basilisk[33] if you did stare didn't kill
Nor was one hurt by its most deadly glare.
At the spring animals didn't wait to drink
For unicorns to do what some do think.[34]

The savage tiger, the fierce lion and panther
Like rabbits were so indolent and tame,
And every animal fearful and gentle
Like lions and tigers did ferocious seem.
The human form all animals didn't flee.
Birds of all colors, white, red, black and yellow,
Deep in the woods where trees were thick didn't hide,
But on a man's shoulder would then abide.

33. The basilisk was a mythical monster with the power to kill by sight. See Pliny, *Naturalis historia* 8.77–78 and 29.166.

34. The unicorn was a mythical animal that was said to make water safe by touching it with his horn.

The fierce desire to feed themselves on flesh
Was not yet present in the breast of men.
This nourishment does make us like all beasts
For human nature it negates in man.
Thus war there is between all men and beasts,
The bird in fear does flee from branch to branch,
Cries and laments in sorrow with no rest
When missing is its offspring from the nest.

The doleful bleating never was there heard
Of mothers that their dearest lamb had lost.
The cow its lowing did not raise to heaven
When it returned without its slaughtered calf.
No animals were slaughtered for their fur
To keep warm human limbs in wintertime.
To animals the woods were not denied
For no one then for food or sport had died.

Singing the birds flew from branch to branch
Without the fear of nets or other traps.
The partridge found its offspring at its call,
If it did look them over or them count.
Under the bait well hidden the hook then
The fish had not yet found or nets or traps.
Mollusks felt quite safe for they had no foes
Nor was their blood then used to dye rich clothes.

Quite safe and with no fear the octopus
With many tails near the moray did stay,
Nor did it squeeze the lobster's two mouths tight,
And then the lobster did not the back bite
Of the moray that can't itself defend:
Neither had to avenge the other's blow.
Today one does the other cruelly slay
And thus in turn it will become the prey.

Just as the day that brings fatigue and light
The pale and rosy dawn does drive away,
And dawn the night, so then it must so be
That in its turn the day of night prey be,
And while the hunter sounds in triumph the horn,
He, too, does lose in this eternal hunt.
Thus do all these sea creatures ever fare,
If one can them to others well compare.

The earth did keep well hidden in its tomb
The sad and dismal veins of all the metals,
Nor did desire for gold, that yellow is,
But not for fear, the human heart then seize.
Iron for warlike deeds could not be found.
The steed did not resound with hoof or rein.
Bronze statues did not yet preserve the name
Nor did men thirst at all for mortal fame.

Quiet Nereus and his daughter in the sea
Yet in their kingdom had not been surprised
Of the first ship, the Argus,[35] by the sight,
Or by ships moved by oars or by the wind,
Nor seen the sea and shore being measured yet,
And other strange and harmful processes.
No one had yet then heard that strange word "island"
For the world seemed to end where did the land.

In plants there were the flowers, leaf and fruit,
Nor did the order, time or place confuse.
In every place did Nature then produce
All animals on land, in air or sea.
All things were then a certain name assigned
According to their natural condition.
Nothing at that time was new or old,
No strange things there were to be seen or told.

The human body was so well disposed,
So balanced, well divided were the humors[36]
That controlled, and composed desire was then.
No hope, no wrath, no envy or dire pain.
Neither did nature so ordain all matters
That a birthmark, warts or excessive hair
One would then get, or would his weight increase
Through food too sweet or that does too much please.

Robust and beautiful, and healthy, clean,
They felt no heat or cold for there was none.

---

35. The sea god Nereus and his daughters had never been surprised by a ship until the Argo sailed with Jason and the Argonauts on their quest for the golden fleece. Cf. Dante, *Paradiso* 33.95–96.

36. The proper balance of the humors was believed to be necessary to insure good health. A lengthy explanation is given in the comment on Sonnet XXII of the *Commentary*, pp. 147–50.

They didn't flee frost or rain beneath a roof,
Nor did Jove's bolts in terror make them quake.
Time for sweet sleep on soft fresh beds of grass
For them was when our sky without sun is.
When the fog is dispersed by the sunrise
With animals and flowers did they rise.

With love then filled, but with no lust or passion,
With them did not go jealousy or hope.
Always one love as heaven did dispose
And also nature that without fault is.
Such was their character and disposition
As through the fields they went alone and happy.
Never too few or too many a year.
Flowers for garlands and leaves they did wear.

Can a Tyrean purple match those colors?
What red, what crimson in soft silk or wool?
What gold, what silver does the flower equal?
Thus did they lead their lives always so happy.
O sweetest time of old, most sweet of loves,
O life so quiet and strong desire of living!
No torment was then caused by hot desire,
No one did pine because love did expire.

With nature in accordance desire was:
What he did have he wanted and did like.
No plaints there were for having or not having.
Desire did never fail or grow excessive.
What he then liked he would always so like,
Sated he never was or have regrets.
Himself desire does call or in does rein
And does for neither ever suffer pain.

Desire that others harms then there was none.
Kingdoms were then not lost to sheer ambition.
In total harmony then nature was
With happy humans and celestial signs.
The eyes did see, the mind did also see
These properties and those exalted forms.
There was no doubt at all, the mind was free
Without confusion it the truth did see.

The mind was then appropriate for desire,
For understanding desire the same was.

They then content were all to know of God
The part that human beings can comprehend,
Nor did our vain and evil intellect
Presume to rise beyond what is its limit,
Nor with such useless labor and much prose
The causes seek that nature won't disclose.

The mind of mortals does presume today
A hidden good there is for which they yearn.
Human desire does spur weak intellect,
But no firm ground they find and angered are,
And say the mind does see what is not there
When it presumes a secret good there is,
At seeing little grieves, sees it doesn't see,
Perfect or blind he now would want to be.

He cannot grasp the infinite, too little
The finite seems. He thinks there must be more,
Just like green wood does not a clear light give
But with its smoke it soon does make us cry.
Nocturnal birds of others prey they are
If they the sun do seek; the strange new feathers
Icarus lost when he too high did press,
A wingless bird on high and in distress.

A migratory bird that for the cold
To cross the sea its dearest shore does leave,
When tired in flight it all around does look
And only water sees, and so despairs.
No reef or branches can rest offer it,
And if a ship it sees cutting the waves,
Afraid of man and of the stormy seas
In doubt remains and no way out it sees.

Thus if the human mind its native shores
Does leave, it will confound itself, and if
An unknown shore to seek it takes to flight,
Tired and afraid will in the waves remain.
Instead the quick mind at that time did see
Truth in relation only to its power.
Presumption didn't from this blessing entice.
What was within its power did suffice.

What nature or the heavens did then show,
They understood at once and had no doubts,

Nor did too subtle, vain or useless cares
Nourished by burning humors bile provoke.
The naked truth so pure does not require
Long and cold vigils and long hours of study.
So beautiful the mind this sweet truth found
That it then felt no need to go beyond.

Prometheus,[37] who had wished to know too much,
The world of this so happy time deprived,
And did from man beatitude then take;
From too much knowledge restlessness arises.
Knowing too little, his vain brother then
A multitude of plagues and death let loose.
Too much or too little knowledge life demean
For both are distant from the golden mean.

Foolish presumption and mad prescience then
And of vain intellects most foolish cares
Fire took away from what was its own sphere.
Its powers then did spread beyond its reign.
From this was born the war that still endures
Among the elements that umbrage took:
Trembles the earth, the heavens with bolts glow,
Evil excesses all from this do grow.

This evil fire the elements made burn
With the desire each other to defeat.
This evil wish did lower then descend
Into men's bodies and in human minds.
From hope did this desire its strength receive
That with its winds revives the evil fire,
Thus the world suffers and all mortal life
Because of fierce wars that are still so rife.

Like a ship that on the high seas is struck
By strong opposing winds will be distressed,
But nothing will it budge from its site
If the opposing winds both equal are.
But if one harder blows and stronger is,
Tired, overcome the loser it will follow.
Oh wretched world, fools only it can please
Who think amidst war they will soon find peace.

---

37. See p. 247, n. 31 above.

Let this fire burn, let it so burn at least
Till other evil humors are consumed,
Then to its sacred place let it return.
Never again do let it stolen be.
Sweet idleness bring back, no hope or tears.
Let the oak honey give us, grief do ban,
With milk and nectar let the rivers run
And with sweet love let blissful hearts then burn.

In these sweet places, Love, in these sweet times,
Let me be with my beautiful sweet lady,
In my green youth and my innocent years,
And drive out jealousy, do banish hope,
And let time not on us mature years bring,
But let our sweetest love eternal be.
No more beauty for her, no other fire,
Only that time and place I so admire.

That sweetest place and earthly paradise,
That lovely age had only one defect:
It lacked the presence of my lady's beauty.
If it could then have had her words and smile,
It would have been just perfect and most sweet,
Above what is divine true love and joy.
The bright gold of that age almost divine
My lady's sweetest fire would now refine.

And if the law above this does deny
At least drive far away, O Love, this Hope,
An enemy both intimate and secret
That with its poison sweet the heart destroys.
The loving happy light give back to me,
And with those sweet, serene, angelic eyes,
Make sweet the glance of this most cruel Hope,
A basilisk with which we can not cope.

If you give back to me my lovely lady,
Gentle and lovely as I did leave her,
I will not ask you evermore, O Love,
For golden ages, whether false or real,
Nor other paradise or other marvels.
Where is my lady, as you do well know,
There sweetness and true virtue really are,
And there is beauty true and without par.

Now in that high and sylvan place, alas,
Where she in such great sorrow and sad is,
The age of gold now is, our sweetest Eden,
And the primeval era is renewed.
If sad and woeful in that alpine place
Of grace and sweetness she the center is,
If she's so lovely now, what will she be
When she'll be happy once again with me?

What she will be, when sad of it I think,
Makes this poor heart of mine burn with desire,
That wounded by immense and cruel sorrow
Only with effort death he does escape.
And if Love promises or does permit
To think of other things, this wounds him more.
Of love without thoughts he can't stay alive,
But the same thoughts to death do him then drive.

O Love, you do now see her wretched state,
And for her grief I think you must be sorry.
Fly then so swiftly to her lovely side.
Do bring to me my lady, or on me
Your wings do put so that like you I fly
And go to her. You must my rival be,
I think, by beautiful bright eyes so smitten.
Do not touch her, by jealousy I'm bitten.

If into a love bird you do turn me,
I shall burn like the phoenix always does
In the sun's rays and will become more lovely
By the great splendor of my sun renewed.
If your wings burn in that so gentle fire,
It is your fault and you cannot complain.
It is not just that you do feel offended
For that so gentle fire by you was tended.

This fire my lady's eyes from you did steal
And my poor heart with it she made to burn.
You were offended, for it I did suffer
And with a new most strange desire I burned
Between my heart so swift and heavy body.
The fire and thought to her place draw me.
My body here, with her does go my thought,
I neither stay nor go, not whole nor naught.

Of a most gentle nature this fire is.
At the peak always of the heart it stays.
The hard and most rude matter it found there
It first consumed, and not without some pain.
The fire pure light did finally become
That in the heart does clearly show itself.
Not that the heart its light does generate,
The light of two bright eyes does it permeate.

In my breast I do keep it with great effort,
Lest it should flee together with my life
If the way is not ever blocked by force.
This gentle fire can so stay down below,
Just like a stone can in mid air there stop,
For the earth draws the stone, the sky the fire.
Never does nature give him time to rest,
But to the lovely thief he must run fast.

Thus like a net I am that is unfurled
That the cork keeps afloat above the waves.
The heavy lead that weighs it down below
Always does pull it down towards deepest bottom.
In the end each of them does lose the fight:
The cork is wet, the lead does not go down,
Thus neither purpose can be carried out.
The net is torn for it can't be so stout.

The lovely image that the white hand does
In my heart print as if it were alive[38]
The loving flame deceives in such a way
That there it does remain and saves my life.
That sweet deception does my life preserve,
For without it both fire and life would go.
Its thief it sees so lovely in my heart
That it believes she's there and won't depart.

Just like the hunter that from the fierce tiger
Its dearest cub has just so slyly stolen,
And though at first he has some distance gained,
The tiger that by nature swifter is
Almost has reached him and its claws has bloodied,
When seeing its own clear image in the mirror

38. Cf. Sonnet XXXV of the *Commentary,* p. 179.

That it finds in the vast expanse of sand,
Thinks that it is its son and comes to a stand.[39]

Of my own heart within the mirror thus
This amorous fire does now quiet itself,
But when it will its error realize,
This savage tiger will in fury rise,
And if the thieving hunter it can't reach,
It won't find any rest in its wild fury.
O Love, you see the peril and my pain,
To help or counsel me do not disdain.

If you do not give me my lovely lady,
At least let a quiet sleep my moist eyes close.
If as I sleep I her do see, my life
With wandering and maddest thoughts defend.
O sleep that at all times with tears contend
My poor eyes to possess, flatten the hills,
The woods, steep road, rivers and rocks do clear
And do bring me to those bright lights now near.[40]

In the dark shadows something I do see,
A fire that from the heavens falls to earth,
Almost a vapor[41] and its purest light
Reaches the earth and seems to be reborn.
Up to the heavens does the flame return
And lasts without its then being further fed.
To our eyes do propitious gods then show
That soon I'll see my lady, this I know.

A breeze so sweet I feel that is now blowing
From where the red and brilliant dawn appears.
All animals can now to swift flight take
If they are dazzled when the light they see.
The lover does his kisses now redouble
For now night's shadows are about to go.
With effort great and with greater desire
From his sweet friend's embrace he does retire.

Already some of the more eager birds
With their sweet verses to the sun now call,

39. Cf. Claudian, *De raptu Proserpinae* 3.263–68.
40. Cf. Sonnet XX of *Commentary,* pp. 141–42.
41. "Vapor" is a falling star.

And then their song intone, and the sweet choir
Of many and diverse birds does them follow.
The flowers, that without the sun their beauty
Lose, eager did seem from their buds to burst,
Dull at first till the sun rose in the sky
All painted then, and art with them can't vie.

Chased is the dawn and then away it flees,
The air removes its varicolored dress
And cloaks itself in light that it does gild,
While black become all things not in the sun.
Here is my sun who from the mountains comes
And leaves that path sad and in shadow now.
I feel the great warmth and the light does glow,
The light of beauty and the warmth of love.

This light does not at all the eyes offend,
It is a comfort that the thirst does sate
Other things to see, and the fire burns not,
But gives a warmth that gentle is and loving.
My lady these two now holds by the hand:
The blind god on her left she does now lead
And Beauty she does hold by the right hand.
Between the two more lovely she does stand.

Love that is steadily fixed on her bright eyes
The fire with which himself does burn redoubles.
Beauty herself mirrors in her soft face
And to herself she then becomes more true.
With a sweet smile my lady's face is etched
From which the world its beauty all derives.
Only this beauty does the world adore
Though that the source this is it may ignore.

Together they do come and happy sing,
But the sweet melody not all do hear;
My heart does hear it, but doesn't want it known.
The nature of this lovely melody
Is like that of the music of the spheres
That mute in these parts of the world does seem.
With it does not the common ear accord,
And thus that song by people is not heard.

My heart just me in confidence does tell
That of this song the beautiful sweet words

Beauty composed, and that then he does hear
Love that most courteously the song intones,
And though the mind does hold it as a secret,
All gentle persons he does not exclude.
To tell it then to those it is not wrong
And as he remembers this is the song.[42]

O charming, loving eyes
When you do fix your gaze
On one or other face
A thousand diverse beauties you will see.

While hidden from you are
These two so lovely lights,
Let no fool now presume
That what real beauty is, he could have seen.

Here real beauty is
All gathered in one face.
The model this has been
For all the forms of beauty you can see.

If you this beauty see,
Of sweet eternal love you'll ever sigh.

42. The sylva ends with a repetition of a favorite theme of Lorenzo, the beauty of the beloved compared to divine beauty. See *Sylva I,* 27–29, p. 224.

II. COMIC WORKS

Nencia da Barberino I

Aflame am I with love and I must sing[1]
About a lady who consumes my heart.
With its mere sound her name does every time
Enflame me so, my heart leaps out of bounds.[2]
Beauty like hers no one can ever match,
Her flashing eyes do burn with Love's own torch.
In towns and city I have often been
But such a flaming beauty I haven't seen.

To Prato I have been to sell my goods,[3]
To Empoli and San Casciano, too,
To Monticegli, Colle San Donato,
To Greve, Decomano high up there,
To Borgo and San Piero I've been, too,
To Fegghine, Mangone and Gagliano,
But fairest in the world is Barberin,
For it is there my Nencia[4] lives within.

A girl more lovely I have never seen,
Nor one brought up in such a careful way.
A head like hers can never have been about,
So shining and well-squared and so bright, too.
Beneath her lashes when she looks at me,
Her eyes do cheer me and do sparkle so.
Right in the middle is a nose so small,
It seems it was cut out with a sharp awl.

---

1. For a study of the three texts of this work, see M. Fubini, "I tre testi della 'Nencia da Barberino' e la questione della paternità del poemetto," in *Studi sulla letteratura del Rinascimento* (Florence: Sansoni, 1947), pp. 62–125. The conclusion is that the *Nencia* printed here is definitely the complete one by Lorenzo, while the other version, given here as *Nencia da Barberino II* represents additions by others, particularly Pulci, without much regard for unity of tone and story.
2. Images and metaphors are exaggerated and given more realistic tones and forms in a parody of the poetry of courtly love.
3. Prato, Empoli, etc., are all locations a short distance from Florence that form a circle with Florence at its center.
4. Nencia is the diminutive of the names Vincenza and Lorenza.

The redness of her lips like coral burns,
And there within are two long rows of teeth,
Twenty or more in either of two files
More white and shiny than a horse can boast.
Her cheeks do look like crystal, they're so white —
She never uses ointments or foul creams —
Yet spots they have all red just like a rose,
More fair than any flower that here grows.

Her thieving eyes have stolen many hearts,
So keen they are that even stone they'd pierce.
Before her glance all must give in to love,
But in her breast her heart is like a stone.
A thousand would-be lovers follow her,
All captured by those two bewitching eyes.
To look at one or other she does turn,
While I to see her strain and slowly burn.

She has so fixed and overpowered me
That I no longer can my own field till.
She has so blocked and twisted me inside
That even a small bite I cannot swallow,
And I am now no thicker than a rail.
All this because with passion I am so filled
That for her I would suffer anything,
For she has me tied to her apron string.

If we did her compare to lovely ladies,
She would then overcome the entire city.
She stands out well among a thousand more
With her sweet words and also with her grace.
Her eyes are dark, more black than coal itself
Beneath those tresses that do seem of gold.
Her hair on top does form so many curls
And rings her head and all around it swirls.

When she does dance she shows the greatest skill,
She leaps so agile that she'd beat a goat.
She whirls like a mill's sails turn in the wind
And with her hand she strikes her little shoe.
When at the end she does come to a stop,
She first does bow, then in the air she leaps
And she performs a reverence with grace
With which no one in Florence could keep pace.

Nothing at all does my dear Nencia lack:
She's white and rosy and of proper measure,
And there right in the middle of her chin,
There is a hole that beautifies her face.
With graceful feelings of all sorts she's filled.
Creating her, her power Nature showed
And did such grace give her and lovely parts
That many men to her have lost their hearts.

No greater fortune can one ever have
than such a woman have as his own wife.
A favored child of all the stars above
Is he who will enjoy this thornless rose.
Greater will be his joy than any saint's
For she can gratify all his desires.
Oh to look at her face and hold her hard,
So white and soft just like a leaf of lard.

If you could know the love I feel for you[5]
And for your shining eyes, O Nencia mine,
And all my torment and the pain I feel,
As if my teeth were one by one pulled out.
If you could see, it would then break your heart,
Nor would then others interest you still.
No other in your heart could find a place,
Vallera's love is such that leaves no space.

O Nencia mine, you cause me to despair
And seem so pleased that I am brought so low.
But for the pain, I would now split my chest,
So you could look and see and touch my heart,
So you would know that there your home now is.
I'd place it in your hand and let you look.
If you were then to cut it with a knife,
It would loud shout: "O Nencia, you're my life."

If with a group of friends I do see you,
I stick around and on you keep my eyes,
And if another turns to look at you,

5. The herdsman Vallera here begins to address Nencia directly. Also, from here to the end, the tone changes, with parody being less evident, while there is a certain sympathy for the lover, which indicates understanding of the basic situation. This is no longer so comic since it is the basic situation of any love, rustic or courtly.

It's like a knife that sinks into my heart.
I am so taken by my love for you
That every day a thousand sighs I cast,
Broken by such sobs that would your heart rend,
And all with tears so wet to you I send.

Last night I could not sleep, not the whole night.
A thousand years it seemed to wait for dawn
In order to go out and lead the herd,
But really you to see, your lovely face.
I could not wait and had to leave my bed
And all alone I stood beneath the shed,
And there I stayed and waited for daylight
Until the moon then did call it a night.

When finally I did see you come out,
Leading the tender sheep and with your dog,
My heart so large did grow it seemed to burst
And tears of joy appeared in both my eyes.
Holding my crook, I then pushed on behind
My herd of steers and the young calves with them,
And drove them on ahead till here within
To wait for you, but then you went back in.

Next to the rill, down I myself then threw,
With the wet grass that did my face rub down.
There I remained for more than a half hour
Till all your rams and ewes did pass me by.
Why do you stay in there and not come out?
Come out now then! Do come here to these hills.
Let me my herd into your own push, do!
And we'll appear as one, though we are two.

O Nencia mine, on Saturday I'll go
To Florence where I want to sell a load
Of firewood that I have just now cut down,
While in that pasture there my herd did graze.
Think hard, decide, what can I bring you now?
What can I buy, what can you really want?
Powder and rouge is what I can bring you?
Or a supply of pins and needles, too?

If you should want around your neck to wear
A necklace all made up of bright red beads
And with a pendant, I'll get it for you.

But tell me how you want them, large or small?
I swear to you I will find them or else
I will make them for you out of my bones.
I swear to you I'll put them in your hands
Though to buy them I'll have to sell my pants.

Why don't you ask me now for some nice things
Like those I know you use of various kinds?
Why not a little something for your dress,
Perhaps some hooks or buttons or some clasps?
Why not for your nice dress a little purse,
Or a nice ribbon to restrain your hair?
Perhaps what would now be perfect for you
And for your nice gown is a belt in blue.

O Nencia mine, farewell, do go with God,
Now close to home my steers and my calves are.
I hope they are all here. Did I lose some
While I did dream of you, my dearest Nencia?
Across the stream they are, there near their home,
And mistress Masa now is calling me.
With God do go, be happy, Nencia mine,
I sing to tell you that my heart is thine.

Nencia da Barberino II

Aflame am I with love and I must sing
About a lady who consumes my heart.
With its mere sound her name does every time
Enflame me so, my heart leaps out of bounds.
Beauty like hers no one can ever match,
Her flashing eyes do burn with Love's own torch.
In towns and city I have often been,
But such a flaming beauty I haven't seen.

To Prato I have been to sell my goods,
To Empoli and San Casciano, too,
To Monticegli, Colle San Donato,
Up there so high way up to Dicomano,
To Borgo and San Piero I've been, too,
To Fegghine, Mangone and Gagliano,
But fairest in the world is Barberin,
For it is there my Nencia lives within.

A girl more lovely I have never seen,
Nor one brought up in such a careful way.
A head like hers can never have been about,
So shining and well-squared and so bright, too.
When she her eyes does raise to look at you,
They always sparkle like a real feast day.
Right in the middle is a nose so small,
It seems it was cut out with a sharp awl.

The redness of her lips like coral burns,
And there within are two long rows of teeth,
Twenty or more in either of two files,
More white and shiny than a horse can boast.
Her cheeks do look like crystal, they're so white —
She never uses ointments or foul creams —
Yet spots they have all red just like a rose,
Fairer by far than any here that grows.

No greater fortune can one ever have
Than such a woman have as his own wife.
A favored child of all the stars above
Is he who will enjoy this thornless rose.
He surely can himself most happy deem
For she can gratify all his desires.

To have fair Nencia and hold her so hard,
So white and soft just like a leaf of lard.

In you I have seen the powers of Morgana,[6]
By all the nobles followed at all times,
To me you seem to be the star Diana
When she above my hut does bright appear.
Brighter you are than the most bright of springs,
Sweeter you are than the most sweet of wines.
The whitest flower isn't like you so white,
When I do look at you morning or night.

Her thieving eyes have stolen many hearts,
So keen they are that even stone they'd pierce.
Before her glance all must give in to love,
But in her breast her heart is like a stone.
A thousand would-be lovers follow her,
All captured by those two bewitching eyes.
To look at one or other she does turn,
While I to see her strain and slowly burn.

Just like a pearl my dearest Nencia is,
And every morning she to church does go.
A blouse she wears that is of purest damask,
Her lovely gown of fiery colors is,
A belt she wears that is of finest gold.
When she does kneel she spreads her skirt right out,
So that no one her ornaments can miss,
And to her home she'll go all full of bliss.

No one for hardest work can equal her
When to the fields she'll go to harvest grain.
She earns good money at the spinning wheel —
How well she weaves God only can describe.
Whatever she does see she wants to learn,
And she is fond of governing her home.
Tender and sweet she is and will all please,
Just like the softest and most tender cheese.

She has so fixed and overpowered me
That I no longer can my own field till.
She has so blocked and twisted me inside

---

6. Morgana was the beautiful friend or sister of King Arthur. In the Arthurian cycle she was credited with forceful magic power.

That even a small bite I cannot swallow
And I am now no thicker than a rail.
All this because with passion I am so filled
That I for her would suffer anything,
For she has me tied to her apron-string.

Such passion I always do feel for you
That I do spend all night for you lamenting.
Friends and relations all of me do talk,
They all do say: "You surely will her get."
The neighbors all do make much fun of me
For I the night will spend around your fields,
And if I do you serenade all night,
You stay in bed and laugh with all your might.

Last night I could not sleep, not the whole night.
A thousand years it seemed to wait for dawn
In order to go out and lead the herd,
But really you to see, your lovely face.
I could not wait and had to leave my bed
And all alone I stood beneath the shed,
And there I stayed and waited for daylight
Until the moon then did call it a night.

Nothing at all does my dear Nencia lack.
She is quite tall and large and of good measure,
And there right in the middle of her chin
There is a hole that beautifies her face.
With graceful feelings of all sorts she's filled.
Creating her, her power Nature showed,
And did such grace give her and lovely parts,
That many men to her have lost their hearts.

Berries and mistletoe I've brought for you
That I for you did in the fields just pick.
To you I'd give them, but you put on airs
And ne'er for good or ill a sign do give.
They all do say that you do scorn me so,
But loyally I don't to this pay heed.
I do go by and see you all the time,
And all do know how I wish you were mine.

For you I waited at the mill all day
To see if you would pass near there by chance.
The flock has gone up there on that small hill.

Come on up here for you do seem so tired.
We'll stay right here where it is now so warm
Now that I feel my luck is looking up.
We'll go up there together if you please,
And all our animals we'll both there tease.

When finally I did see you come out,
Leading the tender sheep and with your dog,
My heart so large did grow it seemed to burst,
And tears of joy appeared in both my eyes.
Holding my crook, I then pushed on behind
My herd of steers and the young calves with them.
In a ravine I stayed hoping you'd come,
But while I waited you did go on home.

When you do go for water with your pail,
Would that for once you came to my deep well,
We could then have much pleasure for some time.
I'm sure we would do justice to our labor.
A thousand times I would embrace you then
When you and I would both together be.
If you must come, do now make up your mind.
The time is ripe just now for joy to find.

April it was when I did fall in love,
When I saw you pick lettuce in a field.
For some I did ask you, but you scorned me,
So that then all these facts become known.
I then did follow you so well and close
That out of sight you never more could be.
From that time on you've had me to possess
With the result that I am now a mess.

O Nencia mine, now that the sheep must drink,
I cannot wait but wish to go up there
To that fresh spring where I will wait for you.
Once there I will sit down on the cool grass
Until I see you come there on the hill.
There on the grass I'll roll a while for pleasure.
I'll wait for your arrival nice and fair,
But please do not for long make me despair.

O Nencia mine, on Saturday I'll go
To Florence where I want to sell a load
Of firewood that I have just now cut down,

While in that pasture there my herd did graze.
Think hard, decide, what can I bring you now?
What can I buy, what can you really want?
Powder or rouge is what I can bring you?
Or a supply of pins and needles, too?

When she does dance she shows the greatest skill,
She leaps so agile that she'd beat a goat,
She whirls like a mill's sails turn in the wind
And with her hand she strikes her little shoe.
When at the end she does come to a stop,
She first does bow, then in the air she leaps
And she performs a reverence with grace
With which no one in Florence could keep pace.

Why don't you ask me now for some nice things
Like those I know you use of various kinds?
Why not a little something for your dress,
Perhaps some hooks or buttons or some clasps?
Why not for your nice dress a little purse,
Or a nice ribbon to restrain your hair?
Perhaps what would now be perfect for you
And for your nice gown is a belt in blue.

If you should want around your neck to wear
A necklace all made up of bright red beads
And with a pendant, I'll get it for you.
But tell me how you want them, large or small?
I swear to you I will find them or else
I will make them for you out of my bones.
I swear to you I'll put them in your hands,
Though to buy them I'll have to sell my pants.

Even in flood I'd jump into the Sieve,[7]
If you did say: "Go on, do jump in now."
My head I'd bang into a wall for you,
Even if I should die of such a blow.
Do order me to do what I can do
And do not worry for what may ensue.
I know that many promise what they choose,
But just try me, ask for a pair of shoes.

7. The Sieve is a Tuscan river that flows into the Arno.

O my dear Nencia, I have just found out
That someone else scorns me by courting you.
What if I should right now cut out his guts
And scatter them around from the rooftop?
You know that at my side a knife I wear
That cuts and pierces that's a joy to see.
If ever I should find him in my hut,
Up to the hilt I'd stick it in his gut.

Nothing more beautiful, nothing more sweet
Than my sweet Nencia ever can exist.
She is somewhat stout, well stacked and full of life,
So fresh, so tender, just like butter soft.
It is quite true, astray an eye will go,
But if one does not stare, it won' be seen.
In dancing she's quite far from being the least
And when she sings she livens any feast.

I can do everything my dearest Nencia,
As long as I do set my heart on it.
I know how to dress well and to undress,
And how to purchase pigs I know quite well.
I know full well how to strap on my purse.
Above all things I am a good strong worker
And know how one must handle spade and hoe,
And I can blow a horn or an oboe.

More beautiful you are than lady Lapa,
More white you are than where we store the flour.
I like you more than flies do sweet molasses
And more than birds do like the sweetest figs.
More beautiful you are than turnip flowers,
More sweet you are than what the bees produce.
I would so like to kiss your lovely eyes
That sweeter are than all the sweetest pies.

Next to the rill I did myself throw down
And did kiss your face down on the wet grass.
There I remained for more than a half hour
Until the rams had then all passed me by.
How come you don't come out, O Nencia mine?
Come out now here, these hills do climb right now.
Let me my herd into your own push, do!
And we'll appear as one, though we are two.

My dearest Nencia, I now wish to go
And bring my calves back home all safe and sound.
God be with you, I can no longer stay,
For mistress Masa now is calling me.
My heart I leave with you, don't hurt it now.
Good luck to you, may Fortune smile on you.
Go now with God, may nothing you regret,
And never do your Vallera forget.

"O Nencia mine, what say we play a while
Throwing snow balls there in that clump of willows?"
"I'll gladly play with you, but you must not
Make it too hard or else you will hurt me."
"O Nencia mine, you must not ever fear.
The love I bear for you would not let me.
Should you be hurt and something should go wrong,
Be sure that I would cure you with my tongue."

There isn't much snow up here, let's go down there
In that small valley where there is no sun.
If someone should call us from town up there,
Do answer for I have no voice right now.
Take off your veil and now do play with me,
Let me look at your face that is so lovely,
As are all other parts that go with it,
So that I think for heaven you'd be fit.

O Nencia mine, I have this minute heard
A little lamb that bleating was so loud.
Come on down now, I'm sure the wolf is there
And with its teeth does now tear it apart.
Come down into the valley now at once
And with your spindle tear its heart apart,
So that both loud and clear all will then say,
"Brave Nencia did right here the fierce wolf slay."

While in the woods down there in a green thicket
I found a nest all full with little birds.
I'm keeping them for you, they are so many,
More beautiful than any you have seen.
Tomorrow I'll bring you a tasty pie,
But to prevent the neighbors from suspecting,
As an excuse when I come by your way
I'll make believe I came the pipes to play.

O Nencia mine, you would not think me low
If I did wear a doublet of silk made.
And if I had and wore the proper hose,
I'm sure you'd think a lord I really was.
I do not let the barber wave my hair
For I do not pay him more than a penny,
But if I should get an abundant harvest,
I will let him on me try out his best.

Farewell my lily of the lovely face,
For I do see the steer that can do harm.
I'll bring you some strawberries later on,
If I do find some there out in the woods.
When you will hear me with the pipes sound out,
Come out where you have come this year so often,
Right where the bushes are, you do know where,
And to bring you some rouge I will come there.

I've had your father asked to give consent,
But Beco has so long let words drag on
And with your mother he remained alone,
Who also seems to now refuse consent.
But down there I'll come with such strong forces
That you I'll take with me in spite of all.
I've told them both and not for just one time
That I've decided that you will be mine.

If with a group of friends I do see you,
I stick around and on you keep my eyes,
And if another turns to look at you,
It's like a knife that sinks into my heart.
I am so taken by my love for you
That every day a thousand sighs I cast,
Broken by such sobs that would your heart rend
And all with tears so wet to you I send.

O Nencia mine, come have a snack with me.
Oh how I wish that we prepare a salad.
But do your promise keep and so your word
So that no one will ever come to know.
No weapons have I brought to defend you
Against that wicked Beca,[8] a true wretch —

8. Beca is the heroine of Luigi Pulci's *Beca di Dicomano,* a parody of Lorenzo's *Nencia.*

I know she is the one behind these woes —
The devil take her soon by her long nose!

When for a feast my Nencia does get ready,
She does adorn herself like a real gem;
Powder and rouge she uses and makes up
And on her fingers seven rings she puts.
She has so many jewels in a box,
And with them she adorns her lovely self.
Valuable pearls she wears on all feast days.
When I see her it's like the sun's bright rays.

If you could know the love I feel for you
And for your shining eyes, O Nencia mine,
And all my torment and the pain I feel,
As if my teeth were one by one pulled out,
If you could see, it would then break your heart,
Nor would then others interest you still.
You for Vallera then would really care.
You are the one that makes my heart despair.

O Nencia mine, from church I saw you come,
So beautiful you were that I was dazzled.
You tried to leap into that field right there
And so did stumble just a little bit.
I tried to hide right then just in a corner,
And slowly then you did begin to sneer.
I then came out and thought it would be best,
Your back you turned on me just like a pest.

O Nencia mine, you make me lose my senses
When I do see the colors of your face.
I would give up all food for a whole year
Just to see you so beautiful forever.
If I could then just speak to you a while,
I would be happy then for my whole life.
If for a bit I then did touch your hand,
No man would happier be in all the land.

O Nencia mine, why don't you now wake up
And at the window show yourself sometime?
You hear quite well the ringing of the bell,
But you just laugh and make me suffer so.
You're not accustomed to being shut inside,
And you're so fond of ever singing out.

I have not seen you here I know not why,
And I've been wanting to give you a pie.

Can it be possible to be so cruel
As not to turn all sweet like sweetest honey
If one a lover has as great as me?
And yet you make me grieve and suffer so.
You know quite well that I so faithful am
That I should be bedecked with laurel wreaths.
You could a bit more pleasant try to be:
Like honey draws a bear, so you draw me.

Of hats no one can such a master be
as my own Nencia who does make the best.
She does make them bedecked with ornaments
better than which no one has ever seen.
On all feast days her neighbors come to see
And stay around my Nencia all the time.
Everyone will in justice recognize
In basket-making she must get the prize.

To you I'm drawn in love, O Nencia mine,
More than the moth is to the lantern drawn,
And everywhere I go to look for you
More than the drunkard for the tavern looks.
I always would have, next to me, want you
More than at night I'd want a shining lantern.
If love you have for me, do make it clear,
The time for wine and chestnuts is now here.

How wretched I now am and full of grief!
I have my efforts and my time all wasted.
Her love my Nencia gave me at one time,
But now for me she feels but scorn and hate.
I now go shouting my despair to all
And my great grief I must to all make plain.
To such a pass I've come that when she's near
I shake and tremble and I'm filled with fear.

O Nencia mine, you cause me to despair
And seem so pleased that I am brought so low.
But for the pain, I would now split my chest,
So you could look and see and touch my heart,
So you would know that there your home now is.
I'd place it in your hand and let you look.

If you should then to touch it see your way,
"O Nencia, lovely Nencia," it would say.

O Nencia mine, farewell do go with God,
Now close to home my steers and my calves are.
I hope they are all here. Did I lose some
While I did dream of you, my dear Nencia?
Across the stream they are, there near their home.
And mistress Masa now is calling me.
Farewell with God do go, O Nencia mine,
I must help Nanni to now make his wine.

The Hunt with Falcons

All red the eastern sky already was
And topped with purest gold the mountains seemed,
The sparrow loudly did its joy proclaim,
And to his plow the farmer was returning.
By now the stars had fled, chased by the presence
Of the bright god who had the laurel loved.[1]
The owl and many others thought it best
In the deep woods to hide and get some rest.

The fox did to its lair with speed return,
And the wild wolf its lone domain did seek,
For come and gone already had Diana[2]
And in the new-born light they might be seen.
Already sheep and pigs had been let out
By the farm maiden who for them did care.
Crisp was the air then in the light's first ray,
And for our hunt it augured a bright day.

It was just then that I came wide awake
At the most happy sound of dogs and bells:
"Hunters come now, it's late, there is no time.
Do move on now, the grounds are far away.
Do let the pack and master go ahead,
Do not crowd them and watch your horses' hooves.
O Cappellaio,[3] go, do move on fair,
We do not want of dogs to lose a pair."

And Cappellaio swiftly moves ahead
While calling out of his dear dogs the name:
"Do come Tamburo, and you O Martello,
Move on Castgagna, Foglia and Guerrina,
And you Fagian, Capello, Fagianin,
Ghiotto, Pestello, Torta and Viola,
Serchio, Fusé and my Buontempo of old
Do move ahead and do what you are told."

1. Apollo who loved Daphne, whom he chased without success. When he was about to reach her, her cries for help were heard by her father, Peneus, who saved her by turning her into a tree, hence the "laurel." Apollo here stands for the sun.
2. Diana here is the moon.
3. The master of the pack.

When the dogs had already moved ahead.
Four hunters with their falcons did advance:
To this his art Guglielmo has been born
And always has with pleasure practiced it.
Giovanni Franco then comes next, and last
Rides Dionigi with Amieri in front,[4]
But since it was so early at the dawn
Dionigi then does nod and widely yawn,

But Lady Fortune, who is ever pleased
All things to change from one to other forms,
Made Dionigi fall as he slept on
And made him fall just right on his left side,
So that on his poor falcon he crashed down,
Breaking its wing and squashing its side, too.
The consequences of the fall and clout
Do please him now for of the hunt he's out.

It is not just a fall, down he does tumble,
He barely touched the ground, believe me do,
When like a stone he down this steep slope rolled,
And like a stone the bottom he did reach.
"Why did I leave my bed," he did then say,
"I should have stayed in bed just like Gismondo,[5]
Barefoot in his night shirt on breasts so cool.
Never again will I be such a fool."

"How was it I could be so great a fool
As to go out at such an early hour.
I should have stayed at home and in my bed
For my own sake and for the hunters' too.
I could have set some flowers on the table
And a complete good dinner then prepared.
Better to use our beds and sheets for sport
Than horse and servants only to get hurt."

He then did try to put the bird in place,
But it no longer could on the glove stand.
With his bare hand Dionigi hold it dared,

---

4. Guglielmo de' Pazzi was Lorenzo's brother-in-law; Giovanni Franco (or Francesco), son of Roberto da San Severino, was a friend of the poet Luigi Pulci and of Lorenzo; Dionigi is Dionigi Pucci, also a friend of both Pulci and Lorenzo.

5. Gismondo della Stufa, a friend of Lorenzo.

But it still falls, and this does show his master
That there is need for a much stronger cure.
As he to make it stand did try, the bird
Bare flesh did claw. Dionigi then struck out,
He squashed the bird that then did lose the bout.

"Where is Corona and Giovan Simone?"
I did ask Braccio, "Where is the big nose?"[6]
He then did answer me, "For various reasons
Each one of them did choose to stay behind.
As you well know, Corona never did
A partridge take if not by a mischance
If we left him behind we're not to blame.
If he had come we would have found no game."

"Where is this Pulci? I don't hear him now."
"He went into the woods some time ago
To conjure up some new bizarre idea.
Perchance he now is writing some new sonnet.
Let Corona beware for just this morning
I heard him mutter while he was in bed.
Among some other things I heard your name,
So beware, O Corona, you're fair game.

Giovan Simone has gone on his own way
Without a by-your-leave or a farewell.
He to the tavern went without a word,
A place he loves for there his thirst he quenches.
As for Luigi, when his nose he moves,
He makes both dogs and horses shy away.
We are glad, then, he chose to stay behind,
If they see him, he frightens deer and hind."

Three hunters with their falcons now remain,
Followed by many, each for his own reason:
Some for sheer pleasure, some just to observe.
Braccio I see and Bartolo, Parente,
Who never had a partridge seen in flight.
With Ulivier I stayed and Alamanni
And Portinai who then did surely scowl
Like in daylight a poor disturbed owl.

6. Probably Giovan Simone Tornabuoni and Braccio Martello, friends of Lorenzo. "The big nose" is the poet Luigi Pulci, author of the *Morgante.*

Behind all these came Strozzo by himself
For then he was the master of the hunt
And bore himself as one with special skills,
Who many times the game has practiced well.
Through the green countryside we did ride on
Until the appointed site we all did reach,
So lovely made by Nature's own design,
Of perfect hunting it gave every sign.

A valley one could see so fair and gentle
With dotted here and there green growths of trees,
Untouched it seemed and beautiful and clean.
Inviting shade was offered by the trees.
On every side a gentle slope there was,
An invitation to the hunt for all,
Even for those who happened to be blind.
In all the world its equal we can't find.

The mountain slopes were warmed then by the sun,
But still in deepest shade the valley was,
As all the hunters did arrive and stood
There to admire and for the hunt make plans.
They all then went to where they were assigned
To ready what is needed for the hunt.
As of the hunt the master then decrees
They all go here, there and among the trees.

A hunter with a falcon on each side
Fairly on high, for launching a good place.
A third the pack does follow and is ready
To launch his falcon when a flock will rise.
Bartolo and Ulivier were further on
Where they could watch, and someone else besides.
The master of the pack, at the right place,
Turns the dogs loose, so eager for the chase.

Just like the Arab steed when at the races
Waits for the moment when the trumpet sounds
And then it gallops off, nay flies away,
Thus went the dogs then when they were released.
To follow them would have been hard, indeed,
Had not the master to some loudly called,
His stick on others used and not in vain,
For words and stick did then the dogs restrain.

"Go on my good swift dog, walk on! Do go!
Come now, let us go on, and you come back!
Oh what a wretch. Tamburo and Guerrin
Take care of Serchio that now wants to rest.
Oh you big liar, you have become so lazy.
Look my good dog, look what a pretty flock.
My good Fagiano, that was quite a flight,"
And the pack master bubbled with delight.

"Be careful all of you, search on, search on!
And Scaccio you, my love, what will you raise,
But I don't see you raise a thing right now
In spite of your desire and eagerness.
Just look at Torta out there that seems at play.
Oh what a noise they'll make, of it I'm sure.
Of all these dogs that one will be the best
That runs and jumps and gives the birds no rest.

"I see Buontempo has the scent now found;
I see he's after them to make them rise.
Pay heed my Buontempo, he sees them.
I, too, can almost see and hear them fly.
I know he's old, but do not be surprised,
For I have seen and know what he can do.
My good Buontempo is the best by far.
Look, Uliviero, look! There they all are.

"There is one on the slope, one in the dale.
Didn't I tell you I could them almost hear?
There is one on the vines and yet another,
Two there near me, a flock they seem to be."
Giovan Francesco was the first to launch
His falcon towards the flock with many a shout
To give it courage and spur it to move.
In his hurry the hood he didn't remove.

"Guglielmo, there's one right there near you,
Take off the hood and raise your fist to launch.
No longer wait. That's it, you'll do so well."
Guglielmo shouts and does the falcon launch.
The falcon rose so quickly in the air,
Followed the partridge and then all at once
Swooped down and seized the bird with its sharp claws,
Came down to earth, then, and the partridge gnaws.

"Call back that dog right now," Guglielmo shouted,
"It wants to grab the partridge from my falcon."
Too short the sticks were then, and so Guglielmo
A stone did take, aimed and Guerrino struck.
He then ran down alone and with no help.
Near he did come, but could not see the bird.
Not seeing the bird, but knowing it was near,
He did stand still and tried the bell to hear.

While he so stood, he saw it all at once.
"Quick, mount up," he shouted, "there, it got it."
They follow him for he is skilled and able,
Like one who is well-practiced in this art.
He takes the thongs and with them holds the falcon,
Then strikes it on the head and none too gently.
He pulls the prey away and holds on tight,
Puts on the hood and waits for one more flight.

Giovan Francesco with his falcon then
Stood in a better place for the next launch.
He thought he saw then come with open wings
A real great partridge, and when it near came
Opened his fist and, with his fingers stretched,
The falcon launched in a most skilled way.
But wily was the bird and also old
And did with the poor falcon then make bold.

In truth it was a real poor sort of falcon,
It was so small, like a poor crow it looked.
I do not think it could a sparrow seize.
If in brief flight it did not then succeed,
It would give up and would no longer try.
Only a game its flight would then turn out.
How could a falcon lose in that contention?
The reason is it did not pay attention.

Meanwhile a new large partridge did appear.
Foglia did see and a good launch then made.
Over the open slope the falcon rose
And then the partridge seized in a short time.
A perfect falcon Foglia did possess
And so he's sure and towards the prey does run.
Down came the falcon straight down on clear earth,
Of blood and feathers then there was no dearth.

A perfect catch if ever there was one.
And Ulivier was shouting then aloud:
"Fetch Cappellaio, call these others, too.
Look now, there is one here," so did he speak.
"The dogs keep on the leash for our own Rocca
All by itself will make the birds all rise.
Guglielmo, come down here, don't try to rest,
You here and Foglia there, so would be best."

This they did do and when in place they were
The master of the pack began to shout:
"There Rocca, there, that's where it did come down.
Go find it now! Find it and it's all yours.
And you, are you both looking over there?"
The partridge at that moment did arise.
"There Foglia. Launch your falcon, do not wait."
Guglielmo also did not resist the bait.

The falcon then the partridge let fly on
And tried to flee from the pursuing one.
"You got it Foglia," then Guglielmo said.
Happy the other is, but shows it not.
"You, Ulivier, run there, you are so close,"
Foglia did say while still Guglielmo stayed.
Ulivier runs the prey from claws to ease,
But finds one falcon did the other seize.

There Foglia's falcon had Guglielmo's seized,
But Foglia thinks his own the victim is,
And so with angry words he spoke to him:
"You have been rude and so discourteous, too.
I do not think your falcon can distinguish
Partridge from falcon. Rash it is indeed
To hunt with children who should really stay
At home with their own toys. Here we don't play."

Guglielmo quiet remains, but finds it hard
His happiness to hide with a sad mien.
Then he does keep with humble words on saying:
"Your bird I did not see, God's truth this is."
Time and again he keeps on saying just this.
Meantime did Foglia down the slope then go.
When close he is and sees the falcons well
He sees his own as sound is as a bell.

His lure he then threw down without delay,
The falcon just as quickly stepped on it.
Tender things Foglia says and pets his falcon
As to the winner in that war was due.
Guglielmo meanwhile sees his own mistake:
His falcon is a mess, and to poor Foglia
"You, sir," he says, "are rude and have sunk low,"
And he does raise his hand to strike a blow.

But Foglia, having his intention seen,
Away did move and so the blow struck air,
And so Guglielmo thus did speak to Foglia:
"Do not think you will not for this slight suffer.
Vengeance I'll have, or else I'll hang myself.
If Rannuccino or Michel Di Giorgio
Were here, you old deluded, stupid fool,
You'd change your mind and soon would lose your cool."

Before this fury Foglia moved away.
He did keep quiet and also patience showed.
In looks and in his speech Guglielmo was
Like one who sure had been of being acquitted
And then heard all the judges find him guilty.
In the end, "Prudent I shall be," he said.
"I will keep it in mind until my death,
Until then you had better hold your breath."

The sun the zenith seemed to slowly reach:
Shadows were lessened and were shorter, too.
Proportions were distorted by the sun,
Foreshortened as one in some paintings sees.
The cricket's song became both loud and strong.
Under the sun's rays everything did burn.
So still the air was, and the leaves stirred not,
The season was most tiring and so hot.

Then Dionigi, in the face all red,
Covered with sweat and like a fish all wet,
"No longer can I here remain," he said.
"Giovan Francesco, will you leave with me?
Why don't you all away come as a group?
To keep on with the hunt would foolish be.
Now that the sun burns us with its hot rays,
We can't stay here all greedy for more preys."

He did not even wait for his Francesco.
He had his say, then turned the horse around.
But since the sun was burning one and all,
Soon every one did follow him behind.
With all the dogs did Cappellaio come last.
The dogs were gasping with their tongues far out.
As they go on, the heat does still increase,
It burns like fire, indeed it does not please

Some sad, some happy as they all return.
Some have their bags well-laden with their prey,
Others do not, and so they silent go.
They must now elsewhere look for different game.
Guglielmo follows full of ire and wrath,
Still burning with desire for vengeance dire.
Giovan Francesco does no longer mind
For he for pleasure hunts and is so kind.

Once home the master to the pack must tend:
Dogs in the stable, in its place the rig.
The hunters then around the barrel meet.
To keep their glasses filled they all do know
Another hunt is now well under way,
Where no one fails to bring a partridge down.
The wine is not the best, but with their thirst
The quality from poor changes to first.

Without a word they all the food attacked,
All pay attention only to their jaws.
But when the fury of the assault did wane,
Of this and that they all began to boast.
The prowess of his falcon each did praise,
For every mishap an excuse there was.
All those whose falcons little did in flying
Now did for it make up with words and lying.

Guglielmo's ire and wrath against poor Foglia
Our spirits dampened and our joy curtailed.
Dionigi then stood up — he did mean well —
And with these words did to Guglielmo speak:
"Do you wish this our festive day to spoil?
Although the event does seem to you most strange,
Accept it as I do, for I am wise.
You shall my falcon have, is not that nice?"

His words Guglielmo liked and his dry humor,
For Dionigi in truth a good friend was,
And since he was of a most gentle nature,
With Foglia to seek peace he did decide,
And so to him he spoke these humble words:
"I do not wish to be at odds with you.
I shall now bear in peace this sad event."
When this was spoken, they all to bed went.

How lovely it would be if we could tell
What everyone did dream in bed that time.
I know they will make up for time they lost,
In bed they will remain till very late.
We then shall go all to the river bank
Where we, I'm sure, will always some fish find.
Just so we did, my friend, all pass the time
With friends, with music and with sweetest rhyme.

Symposium

Chapter I[1]

When in the season that their green leaves lose
And still another color they assume,
And all the trees white are and lose their leaves,

The farmer so uncouth in all his ways
For the reward of all his labors waits,
And of his efforts sees at last the fruit.

Summing up then, he sees if the past year
Did in some way his hopes well justify,
Or whether for the future ill it bodes.

In every street and town does Bacchus[2] reign,
And I beg him as he around does go
To succor me as I begin my story.

As usual I had my city left
For a few days in search of rest and sport
And was returning whence I had begun.

To make my trip both shorter and more swift,
For highly prudent I have always thought
To go on straight, avoid a crooked road,

I took the road to the Faenza gate,
There to return to my beloved Florence
And see once more the city that I love.

I then saw that the roads were jammed with people.
So many people were there in the streets
I could not even try to guess their number.

Of some of them the name I mention could,
For I knew them and had some news of them,
But I knew not what drove them all on so.

1. The poem is a parody of didactic and allegorical works, aiming particularly at Dante's *Commedia* and Petrarch's *Trionfi (Triumphs)*. The references and the allusions are too numerous to list.
2. Bacchus was the god of the grape harvest and wine, whom Lorenzo invokes, instead of the Muses, for obvious reasons.

I there saw someone who my friend had been,
My friend he had for such a long time been,
From the time when I still a small child was.

To him I turned and said: "What is the cause,
O Bartolino, that on this road now
So swiftly spurs you on and all the others?

What desires drive you on, may it be known?
Stop here a while and see that I do learn."
My words he heard and so he did then stop.

Not otherwise than a dear tiny bird,
Hearing the most sweet song of other birds,
Though on its way, does stop to listen in,

Thus did he then though he could hardly wait.
With effort only he restrained himself
For steps once lost aren't easily regained.

"What you desire to know, I must tell you,
Although with greatest speed I must move on,
For this the reason I'll to you reveal.

Towards Ponte a Rifredi[3] we are going
For a wine barrel tapped Giannesse[4] has.
'Tis that our feet does turn from slow to fast.

We are all speeding to go drink that wine.
'Tis that that so speeds us on our quick way,
A bird on wings with us cannot now vie.

It is now quite a while that Delia Spada
With furious speed got there, and Basso,too.
I must tell you, idle they have not been.

No greater wrong was ever done to me.
Their word they gave that I could go along,
That is the reason rage devours me so.

They pay no heed to what the wine may be,[5]
But soon they drink it all, I don't know how.
As for their food, 'tis better not to speak.

---

3. Rifredi was a short distance above Florence.

4. A tavern keeper.

5. The original gives the names of two wines, Trebbiano and Greco, to express this idea.

Let them continue on their path of old.
I know I'll be avenged, I am quite sure:
Already one of them the gout has now."

"O Bartolino, whom do I see there,"
Said I then, "there right next to Romitazzi?"
And he to me: "A man who looks for joy.

If you to see do wish how wine he hates,
With greatest ease I can show it to you,
Suffice to say they baptized him 'the grape".

Parched lips and his constrained throat always do
Make it impossible for him to speak.
That is what wine to him has done till now."

"Who is that one whose cheeks are flaming red,
And with him there those two with such long cloaks?"
And he to me: "Priests they are all three.

The fat one is the pastor of Antella,[6]
Though he may so distracted seem to be,
Know that without the cup he never is.

The other one with such a tender smile
And with a long and thin and most strange nose
Has found his paradise in the wine cup.

He holds high rank, of Fiesole the bishop.
He most devout is now to a strange relic:
A cup that his Anton, the chaplain, bears.

In every season and in every place
The trusted cup along with him does go.
What can I say? It's taken in processions!

I know it will always be there with him,
Wherever he may go, in towns or courts,
At Peter's Gate he will with that cup knock.

With him it shall be too when he is dead,
It shall be put with him there in the grave.
Still in the grave it will some comfort give.

Instructions in his will he so will leave.
Have you not seen how in processions then
He makes from time to time everyone stop?

6. A small locality near Florence.

He calls his brother priests to come to him;
They stand around and do protect him then,
Blocking all prying eyes with their long cloaks,

While with his mouth the cup a lid he gives."

Chapter II

I did stand there just like a man who dreams,
In part with shame so filled at what I saw,
But at so strange a sight I also laughed.

Just then to me did come right by my side
A man whose strength by drinking had all faded.
I did know him at once for he was lame.

I turned and said to him: "Stop, stay a while,
O you who like a greyhound swiftly go.
Stop here with me a while, now in this place."

His step he slowed and then to a stop he came,
Nervous just like a steed that rears to go,
And I to him, "O Adovardo, welcome."

"Not Adovardo now," he said to me,
"But very thirst I am, the strangest gift
Among all those that God did give to man,

The dearest, choicest, worthiest and most precious,
But here a problem most abstruse we have,[7]
And what I have just said to doubts gives rise:

If drinking does chase thirst away, and thirst
A sweet thing is, always to drink then must
An evil be, but this resolved can be.

An innate thirst like mine cannot quenched be,
The more I drink, the more the thirst does grow
Just as if I salt water always drank.

Like Antaeus[8] who they say his strength regained
Whenever he would tumble down to earth,
My thirst from drinking ever gains more thirst.

---

7. A parody of neo-Platonism as found in Ficino, the same subject Lorenzo discusses in a serious vein in his *Disputation*, for example below, p. 386ff.

8. Antaeus was a giant, son of Neptune and Earth. He compelled everyone he met to wrestle with him and killed those he defeated. When thrown, he regained strength by contact with his mother the Earth.

Since water that the woman drank, I say,
Does quench all thirst,[9] I will not drink it ever
And so without this water there's no risk.

Let this suffice. In this I find my pleasure,
It does make me so happy, cheerful, gay,
It is my sole, my highest perfect good.

If that which has enabled me to live
Should ever from our world then disappear,
You with a club may strike me dead at once."

So low he whispered one could hardly hear,
Whose voice so strong and fierce at one time was,
And Bartolino, then, began to speak:

"Alas, tell me where did you lose your voice?"
And with great effort he to him then said:
"Being San Giovanni's[10] vicar did me in.

Its wine is such that no one can refrain,
And I do tell you that of what I've done,
Though it does hurt me, I do not repent.

Weak was my voice then, feeble it now is,
And if of it I die I don't repent:
I don't repent, I do say it again.

To die as I have lived I am content,
For a good death does honor one's whole life."
No more said he and like the wind he left.

He was then followed by one more I knew,
Who seemed from him that art to have well learned,
For if the other drank, this one devoured.

Freckled he was and had white hair, but few.
To him I turned and said: "O Grassellin,
Who do so honor all the Alimari,[11]

Is it the love of God that spurs you on?"
And he to me: "Do not show such surprise,
For this I would so much more distance cover,

9. John 4.6. The water here symbolizes divine grace, while Adovardo's parody gives it a literal meaning.
10. Probably San Giovanni Valdarno, a town not far from Florence.
11. An ancient Florentine family.

A hundred miles a single step would seem.
Whatever effort would for this fine be."
No more said he and did regain the others.

And I, "O Bartolino, look! Be quick!
Tell me who that one is, who are his parents,
Who now so hard the going seems to find."

He answered me: "To me he is related.
Do you not Papi know? Look at him smile.
Just look how gay he is as on he comes.

He can now drink not for just one, but two.
The one behind, who follows him so near
And is so fast the wind his cloak makes fly,

Has been by us so justly recognized
As the true master of this art of ours.
'Tis only fitting for a knight he is.

He did once joust and honored was for it.
Your Pandolfin he is, a worthy knight.[12]
In drinking bouts his courage he now shows."

His knightly ensign I did then so honor,
I bared my head and then to him did bow,
And like the swiftest vessel he slid by.

In a great hurry now another comes.
So warm is he that bare he keeps his head
And neither hat nor hood does he now wear.

"Who is this one who with such fury comes,
So fast that he does seem with steeds to vie?"
And he to me: "He is Anton Martelli.

His cheeks are red, his lips are dry and burned,
His nose is red and like a sponge also.
The same to him wine is in flask or cask.

Don't you recall the clamor he did make
That time in Prato, there just at the fair,
When he was robbed of partridges a brace?

---

12. A knight mentioned by Pulci in his *Giostra* (32) as having participated in the joust of 1469 when Lorenzo was the victor.

If one did steal his standing or his money
Rather than what I said he lost above,
Know that not half as much he would complain."

"Who is this one so like a drunken monkey
With little eyes whose lids seem to be stuck?"
And he to me, "A fit description this.

This is of Banco our dear Simoncino,
Who started to imbibe just to be funny,
But now his glass he raises night and day.

So much he likes to drink all sorts of wine
And to take part in banquets and in orgies,
That his skilled trade he has by now let go."

"Who is that one who comes with peach in hand,
Who smelling it does seem to so enjoy,
Though he scents can't detect without a nose?"

"The one you mean Zuta the tailor is,
A whole year's vintage through his nose he'd take,
No matter what, for he cannot refuse.

The thirst he ever feels by day and night
Has great renown achieved in all our town.
Though for the wine we drink we are all known.

When he is loaded he will speak so long,
To hatred he gives rise in one and all,
So beautiful and flowing are his words.

If he the bridge does ever reach today,
He will take on of wine the greatest load,
But he'll no duty pay on his return.

Let with the others go this dirty pig.
Tegghia Candiotto now is there with him.
So much does he love him that he holds on,

And will drink all he has during the night."

Chapter III

As soon as Bartolin had told me this,
He turned to me and said: "I must now go,
For time goes by and for no one will wait."

And I to him, "Don't be in such a hurry.
Stay and tell me who all these people are
So that I shall of this tribe know the rest.

Who is that one who does a hat now wear
And on his back a hood he also has?"
And he to me, "His looks should now tell you.

Look at what happiness in wine he finds.
He is Corsin Bertoldo, him I love.
Of glasses to the sound he dances well.

When he has drunk, he urinates a flood
That would allow a mill to operate.
Look at his son, who does with him now come.

Some signs he gave already when quite young
He would to drink then take and all delights
And did so prove them true in later life.

I can't tell you how proud the father is
When he says that with wine his son is best,
And does all that he can to spur him on."

"Who's that who one chin has beneath the other?
Illness does not seem to waste him away."
He answered, "He's Scassino at your service.

At the time diabetic he became,
He did begin to feel such a great thirst
That has not left him since, and never will."

"Who is this man borne by the crowd along
Like a tree trunk by raging waters swept,
And must by day and night ever drunk be.

I say it for he falls from side to side.
I'm sure he whets his whistle all the time."
And he to me: "You will soon be enlightened.

Like one who at the target's center aims,
This one has firmly set his aim on drink,
If he should fall, the cause that would be.

Wine has enfeebled him and worn him down.
Of old Filippo you have now just heard;
Junior is here, but has not yet arrived."

I listened to his words with full attention,
And he went on to say he could then see
I was about to ask for something more.

"I know what you do wish before you speak
And I shall fully prove all this to you.
No room for doubt my words will leave in you.

"I know you're looking now at those six men,
Who swiftly come as if they're after game.
I tell you that related they all are.

In their midst is Niccolo of Schiatta.
Wine into vinegar he won't let turn,
And with great ease his share within he carries.

To the right is from Diaceto Bobi.
When like a camel he takes on a load.
To keep him quiet is difficult, indeed.

Then from the left Spinelli Checco comes.
At every meal I'm sure he must devour
Of two capacious barrows the full load.

Giulian Ginori comes right next to him;.
He may seem small and thin to you, indeed,
But when he eats and drinks a giant he is.

To his small stature do not pay attention,
For in the past he has most surely proven
A barrel can compare with him in vain.

The other is, if you do not know him,
Giovan Giuntini who one seems to be,
But when he sits to drink he does for three.

Little he knows of wine, but has his fill."
"On the left side, who is that one right there?"
"Your Marsuppini Jacopo is he.

The lesser of the clan by size and age,
But greatest does his thirst make him by far.
This war he wages well and with great valor.

Do you see one who comes to all these close,
Though he comes slowly and his time does take?
He's fat Spinelli. Yes that's who it is.

So fat and so unwieldy he now is,
That he proceed then must at his own pace.
I'll not tell you how much noise he can make.

Have you heard tell about his strange night cap?
He put one on of finest linen made,
And the next day he could not it remove.

So wonderful drink always seems to him
That all day long to stimulate his thirst
His nails he does all bite. Oh what a brain!

A bee can never to a flower go
As quickly as he answers Bacchus's call.
If dinner you prepare, he'll make it vanish.

No difference is there before or after.
Just like a pig he will all things devour,
All fruit and greens and cheese, meat, eggs and fish.

The other sinking in the mud on foot
Is not less fat and does imbibe as much.
For him bread is good only dunked in wine.

Grasso the druggist he's, calm and serene.
No one can him of his own share deprive.
He does not drink, unless his glass is full.

The one who does stand there apart from others,
And on him weighs the voyage, for he's fat,
Of our own art the greatest master is.

He is known as Steccuto, the thin one.
The quantities he drinks do frighten me,
He drinks more wine than all of us combined.

When he has drunk his fill, asleep he falls,
But as he sleeps so loudly does he snore,
That the noise must perforce awaken him.

He always sweats and always also stinks."

Chapter IV

My eyes were firmly fixed on this Steccuto,
When my guide said, "If I do tarry here,
I'll get there like dessert at dinner's end."

I did beg him to stay yet some more time,
And my entreaties so convincing were
That to refuse he did not have the heart.

He said: "I couldn't against your wishes go;.
The sooner you do me give leave to go,
So much more ever bound to you I'll be."

"The more," I said, "your tarrying bothers you,
So much the more I'll be obliged to you.
Come now, do tell me who this one can be."

And I did point to one who near me came.
So handsome he did look and also big,
So dignified and mounted on a mule.

At first I was amazed on seeing him,
For Peter on his cross he surely seemed,[13]
But Belfradello I then saw he was,

And said: "O Bartolin, the truth tell me,
Why does he travel riding on a mule?
Does he do so more swiftly to proceed?"

"It may be for his sense of dignity
As shown by his long cloak," he answered me.
"On foot he could not wear it in the crowd.

Perhaps his purse by now is all well filled,
Or nature has perhaps made him too lazy,
Or for the worse the pox a turn has taken.

Although so dignified he does appear,
Do not pay heed to what is false veneer,
A silly ass beneath that he remains.

This fellow is by birth a true imbiber,
But he does drink — O my! — with such finesse
As he did learn at court, not here in Florence.

Let him go on together with the crowd,
For if you knew how little wise he is,
As friend or kin you never would have him.

13. Saint Peter was crucified upside down.

You see that one who on his way does go,
Greasy and dirty just like some old tramp?
He is the courier's master and earns well.

All taverns he does visit all day long;.
During the year on drink he spends so much
That at the end what he has earned is gone.

Bertucce, Fico, Buco, all these taverns
Do know him well. And he Candiotto bothers
For he the wine he wants does never have.

When he receives of letters a whole packet
And to deliver them does happy go,
Both he and them of wine do strongly smell.

The one behind him that you now see coming,
Stumbling as if in stormy seas he sailed,
Is drunk, but not on vinegar, you're right.

Stefan Sensal he is, who the knack has
Of getting soaked in just an instant's time
More than a fish that in the sea does swim.

Just as the sun there rising in the East
Will with its brilliant rays at once light up
The entire world and all its creatures, too,

So this one here does hardly see it rise
Before he all tanked up already is,
So great a perfect souse he has become.

Not very far behind do you now see
Three men whom we should for twelve hundred count,
Running like pigs that to their feed are called?

Brothers they are of the same father born,
And brothers are when it does come to drink.
Two twins could be and the third could join them.

When at the table all three seated are,
There is no need to ask or to insist.
Being courteous, they don't wait, but just dive in.

The less fat one Matteo Stiattese is.
The one who seems with effort to go on,
If put on trial is quicker than he seems.

I did the second see, who Fat Paul is,
Through a minute and tiny doorway go,
Just like a camel through a needle's eye.

If water they did like as much as now
They do it hate just like a mortal foe,
The world would soon dry up and desert be.

The third one you now see so near to us
A knowledge of theology has gained,
And in the taverns did become a doctor,

Where he did learn that of the torments all
Our Lord did suffer here, the greatest was
When on the cross he did then say 'I thirst.'

And when he comes to preach on that event,
It seems his heart will burst with so much grief
For he in such a pass does see himself.

If he were learned as much as he is fat,
Or as much as he drinks, he would surpass
Augustine, or he who bloodied the rock.[14]

So versed is he in Latin and in Greek
That he has learned that the fat of calves
The chest expands and so drinks it like wine.

Though they do sweat as with the crowd they move,
They know full well the art of drying themselves,
But practice it cannot with a sole glass.

From this long voyage tired and parched they are,
But they well know how this disease to cure
By raising high their elbows and with glasses.

Let them on their way go in God's own hands."

Chapter V

Just like a falcon for the launch raised high
The dogs does see that run and search for game
And anxious is to start on its own flight,

So did my guide then fidget at his fate
As he did wait for me to give him leave,
For he did think too large the crowd then was.

14. Saint Jerome, who was represented scourging himself with a rock.

To me he said: "Time flies and fleets away
And one is not in any dire trap caught
Unless thirst overtakes and seizes him.

If all this crowd I am to show you now,
Overcome you and I must be perforce,
Nor would one day for this sufficient be.

But Sir Nastagio[15] far away I see.
With those who are still here he can guide you.
So slowly does he move to spite me now.

Come now, come now do hurry, Sir Nastagio!"
He heard and understood and looked and laughed,
And said: "O Bartol, what does all this mean?"

"To wait here, Sir Nastagio, will kill me.
Do tell this gentleman who these men are,"
And off he flew when near the other was.

My patience I perforce did exercise
and said: "Nastagio, I all lost am here.
Without you now I cannot cope at all."

And he to me: "There nothing is I know
More natural to my own disposition
Than trying to be of use to fellow men.

Before I did depart from our dear city,
Proper precautions and supplies I took,
So I can tarry here as you may wish."

I thought I saw two towers as he spoke,
But they were moving so it could not be.
Obvious it was that I mistaken was.

All filled with wonder to my guide I turned:
"I think the city gates are coming here.
Can they be men or animals you think?"

My guide to me then said: "Do not have fear,
Though they are huge, they are to be feared not,
For they are not of intellect so keen.

15. Nastagio Vespucci, father of Amerigo, who is mentioned elsewhere for drinking.

The pock-marked one by name is Ulivier,
Baldovin Apollon the other one.
They differ for their size but not for thirst."

When one of them to us did close arrive,
My guide did speak: "O Apollon, my friend,
Do here now stop, the trip has tired you so.

For once to my opinion do pay heed."
He answered, but with such outlandish sounds
That neither he nor I could understand.

While I did feast my eyes on them, the first
All at once did his throat clear with such noise,
I can still hear the sound, and spat a flood.

My guide to me then said: "See what he did
Now that he thirsty is. What he will do
Once he has had a drink you can imagine.

An everyday thing what he did is not.
In words or laughter he does not waste time,
And in the past I have had proof of it."

Pay heed, O reader, do not be surprised
If what did happen I with fear relate.
Perhaps it would be wiser not to tell.

As the abundant and quite fiery liquid
He spat the parched and arid earth did reach,
The liquid and the heat became as one.

The virtue, then, which from on high descends,
Did give it life and so a frog was born.
Before our eyes it then began to leap.

As Ulivier on it his eye did cast,
"I must be full of them," he said. "Their noise
I hear." O Lord, whereto did his brains go?

A short time only those two hulks remained.
Their journey they resumed with their huge steps
And in an instant disappeared from sight.

My guide did then point out one who came on.
I saw, as he came near, he had an inkwell
And so I said, "A notary he is."

And he to me, "A notary he is.
If I did bet he would a poor meal eat
If sober, I would soon my money lose.

He certified the will that Rosso had
For Ciprian made and later had him sign,
Though then his mind was anything but clear."

He then called out to him, gave him a kiss,
And said: "Domenico, my handsome friend,
Dearer to me than to a mouse is cheese,

I shall no longer keep you, for I know
That the desire that drives you on so fast
Burns within you while I to you do speak."

When he heard this, he left without a word.
A group of five then came on all together;
One of them speaks always, the others not.

Just as the pigs when they return from pasture
Run to the trough for their abundant mash,
So do these rush to their appointed place.[16]

When near the group did come and us approached,
The one who spoke then said: "'God keep you well,"
And my guide then a warm embrace gave him.

The others also had come up to us.
To speak they would have wanted, but could not
For he who first had greeted us didn't stop.

And as he laughed my guide was doubled over,
And in my ear he said: "This Strozzo is.
He chattered in the womb, before being born.

If he beheaded were, I am quite sure
The head without its bust would keep on talking.
He does so tire all men, so I keep off.

However, as he speaks he still feels thirst,
And so his words he dunks in much good wine.
And I to you confess that this is true.

16. Giannesse's tavern.

Watch out, watch out as you do flow Terzolla,[17]
With drinking and with talking this old fellow
Will dry you out as in July the sun.

The one you see right there just next to him
Does not drink wine like you, you must know this.
He lets it flow down into his dark depths.

To all they are now known as Bellondino,
Citto and Tornaquinci and Zanchina.
Giovan Giustino they are now to meet.

These five like large flasks in a tavern are,
For always filled with much good wine they are,
But they do claim the doctor this prescribed.

They often quarrel and do furious get,
So that no one will dare to intervene.
Once they cool off, the quarrel they forget.

That you should laugh at this, I'm not surprised,"
He said to me, and then, "'Farewell, farewell."
The one who spoke and their guide was did say,

And as he spoke he left. We just stood there,
I and my guide, by all his noise turned deaf
Like those who dwell in that most evil place[18]

There where the river Nile down does cascade.

Chapter VI

Like when a bell does toll a long, long time,
One hears when it does stop. If it is good,
The echo of its sound reverberate.

Thus Strozzo's chatter does remain, indeed,
In one's now deafened ears and frightens him.
We were both deaf and could not hear a thing.

This notwithstanding, we were both awakened
By two old fools who came with dry, parched lips,
And with their valet like three drunken birds.

---

17. River that flows at Rifredi where they are all rushing.

18. Deafened like those who live at Catadupa near the falls of the river Nile. This is a comparison used often since Cicero made it *(De re publica* 6.5). See also Petrarch, *Rime* 48.9–10. Lorenzo used it also in *Sylva I,* 18, p. 224, and elsewhere.

"Aeneas's friend was not to him as loyal,"[19]
My guide did say, "as Pecoraccia is
And has always to his Vettori been.

No dog the hare does always hunt so gladly,
As he does pheasants, partridges and all
To make quite sure his master has his fill.

Vettori can bear witness to all this.
His lips are moist and his mouth waters, too.
This to him food and talk of good food does.

If Lady Fortune plays a dirty trick
And from these two will Pecoraccia take,
Like helpless fools these two will then remain.

Of drink what can I say that you don't know.
The more one eats the more one's thirst will grow,
And so this one is often in a daze.

Who his companion is, I shall not say,
For I am sure you know him well, indeed.
Too bad for him, if you did meet him now.

No point so subtle is there in our art
That they do both not know as well as any.
Through long experience they have reached that stage.

I do remember that in disputation
Bartol and Belfradello[20] they did best.
That's when we did make them in drinking doctors.

Look at Agnol Bardin so sweet and dear,
Who is so fat but moves as if he's driven;
With him there come one and the other Tier."[21]

"That one whose brow so heavy is with cares,
Whose face is wet and tinted all deep red,"
I did then say, "do tell me who it is."

Courteously then my guide did answer me:
"He has no cares nor what you see is tint.
I can't let you remain in such great error.

---

19. Achates was the faithful companion of the hero in the *Aeneid*.
20. Bartolo is Lorenzo's first instructor or guide in this work; Belfradello is the drunkard on a mule in IV.13–16, p. 299.
21. Tier is the diminutive of the name Gualtieri, so that the reference is to two drunkards by that name.

Just as to go with bread has cheese been made,
So was Arrigo made to go with wine.
Just like his face he'll soon turn all wine red."

"Who is that one who's not so far behind,
With such great jaws and a hoot owl's eyes,
Who seems by idiocy to have been struck?"

"That one is Mistress Betta's own dear Baccio.
If you saw him at a well-laden table,
A master you would see, not one who's struck.

Of parasites the champion he now is,
The truest and most natural we have.
To eat he would to the asylum go.

More skilled he is in this one special art
Than any I know or have until now met,
With all respect for him who follows close:

I do mean Botticel, whose fame is bright,
Yes Botticel, the hungriest one around,
Hungrier and more persistent than a fly.

How many of his tricks I do remember.
If one does him invite to lunch or supper
He will not speak in vain or to deaf ears.

Barely can one pronounce the word invite
That he is dreaming how his mouth he'll fill.
Empty he goes but then returns well filled.

No sense of shame remains to him these days,
His only plaint is that his neck is short.
Long as a crane's he would want it to be.

Never so satisfied or full he is
That no room does remain for other tenants.
Supper not over is when he re-starts.

If you the amount did see that he devours,
You would see how his body is capacious,
A greater load a galleon does not bear.

Enough of him. Let us of these two speak:
Where these two are there then they harvest grapes.
Tell me if that is not the greatest gift.

Know they will bring about of wine a dearth,
And one of these two gluttons does complain
That no reward there is for living well.

Drunk they become of wine just at first sight.
But blind I must now be for I'd not seen
That my good friend Ridolfo Lotti 'tis.

Our own good friend, who may be somewhat foolish,
Twenty-eight pounds put on at a sole sitting.
Like Bacchus he did drink and kept on going.

Is it a wonder, then, he is put out
That no reward there is? I do regret
He hasn't yet been crowned of clowns the king.

The other one I did see in my dreams.
A dream I had right at the break of dawn.
Not a drop[22] he was losing, but a barrel.

If they are mortal enemies of wine,
Their mortal nemesis wine always is
And to their heads in all its fury goes.

Cherries and figs have been all swept away
And everything that thirst does not enhance.
Of age they're young, indeed, in drinking old."

Then I did turn to look at my good guide
And said: "Tell me who can they be, the pair
Who have sat down right here, so near to us?"

My guide then said: "The people seem to double.
The one with open belt is Pippo Giugni.
He now does rest, the journey tired him so.

The other, whose great wish is to compete
With all in this great joust, is Pandolfin.
Now towards his knightly uncle he does rush.

The wine he drinks he does in liters measure.
He led the charge in Bacchanalian wars
And in a worthy manner did his duty.

A temporary thing their thirst is not,
Nor like Bertoldo's falsely induced,
But natural and does forever grow.

22. A play on words. "Goccia" (drop) also meant apoplexy.

Pippo with wine a rascal really is,
So much of it he loads and so fills up
That it does reach his brain and him befuddles,

Its fumes a halo form around his head.

Chapter VII

On reaching us, one at my guide does look
And with an eye half shut at him then sneers.
My guide then said: "Welcome the company.

Much better it would be to be up there
Where you before the harvest filled yourselves,
Pouring good wine into yourselves at will."

The one who sneered then said: "You said it now!"
It seemed that he some other words did swallow,
But he tongue-tied was and just said, "Enough."

Since he did wish my guide then to embrace
He started out but, by his feet betrayed,
One of his own he did, indeed, embrace.

Just like a dog he was crossing a river
That thinks it is in a true straight line going,
But is by the strong current drawn downstream.

"O sir, the name of these do tell me now
So my account will not in this be amiss,"
I did ask him, and he my wish did grant.

"The one you see, the one who winked at me,
Know that he is my Lupicin Tedaldi,
The one whose hair does like a fennel look.

His eyes do burn, his feet are not well planted,
His face is red, and he can hardly move,
But what they did do hear in this hot weather.

When the earth did burn and crickets sang,
Seated they were to cool off in the baths.
The water at their weight a foot did rise.

More than one glass was floating all around.
A sad fate did await those they could catch
For empty they remained and of no weight.

But then discord arose among themselves,
And they great difficulties had to face
For one of them did so uncouthly fart.

With that the waters did their calm then lose.
A storm arose and certain glasses were
Lost in the waves in which they then did toss.

Lightly and quickly Lupicin did rise
And to the one who next to him then sat,
'You aren't,' he said, 'a man to have close by.

If such a deed, a scandal, had occurred
In ancient times when our forefathers lived,
What price would have been paid for this misdeed?'

And he to him: 'At your expense you learn,
For you did us regale with beans at dinner.
Air must then be let out. Now no more talk.

Let us our thirst well soothe with these full glasses.'
But Benedetto Alberti[23] then did say:
'Of the same father we all children are.

Wine is our father, and he does demand
That we retain our calm and noise not make,
With logic I'll convince you, Lionardo.

If you inside are all with good wine wet,
Then with spilled wine on the outside we bathe,
For water brings on thirst in its pure form.'

These words did calm their boiling spirits well.
'You have consoled us,' Lupicin did say.
'And I do love you,' Benedetto said.

With this exchange one to the other turned:
'You must from my hand drink and I from yours,
For peace cannot without wine be restored.'

Thus once again peace between them wine brought.
You must know that in drinking Lupicin
Hercules was, and like Antaeus[24] the other.

---

23. The Alberti were a famous and wealthy Florentine family that opposed the Medici and were forced into exile. Lionardo belonged to this family. The way these characters speak seems to be a parody of the well-reasoned discourses of the Alberti in Leon Battista Alberti's *Della famiglia*. *See* Leon Battista Alberti, *The Albertis of Florence: Leon Battista Alberti's* Della Famiglia, ed. and trans G.A. Guarino (Lewisburg, PA: Bucknell University Press, 1971).
24. See p. 292, n. 8 above.

If Benedetto's eyes seem to squint so
And he looks like a hawk eyeing its prey
It is because they twitch and he can't see.

To whet their appetite one does not need
Fennels and other roots, roast lima beans,
Fried crabs, frog's legs or other gluttonies.

Come now, let us no longer speak of these,"
He said, and then to them. "God be with you."
Together they did leave without delay.

My eyes were both then fixed on one who was
Coming towards us, away an arrow's flight,
And when he did us reach, I pitied him.

This new and strange corkscrew indeed did want
With my poor guide then to exchange embraces,
But far apart their bellies did them keep.

Three times he did attempt this strange embrace,
Three times his arms for that he did then open,
Three times he failed and had to lower them.[25]

My guide then said: "Like neighbors let us act
Who at the window to each other speak,
Or from across the street, if so we must.

To Stia's vicar I do welcome bid.
Did you perchance from Casentino come
In order not to cause a dearth of wine?"

And he then said, "In part your words are true,
But I did leave for to the baths I go
To take the cure and to regain my thirst.

Although with ease I still can drink for two,
What I once was I'm not, and drink now does
Too quickly fill me up like a balloon.

Already I have tried in Casentino
So many ways to just regain my thirst,
But up to now in vain it has all been.

This is the reason why this trip I take.
With fever to come down I now would want
Just to try then to bring it down with wine.

25. Cf. Dante, *Purgatorio* 2.80–87.

If I should not succeed in this my quest,
Then to give up my life glad I would be."
"Go on your way," my guide then did tell him,

"May God bless you and your lost thirst renew."

Chapter VIII

Like in a pail full of half-curdled milk
Carried by one who does not watch his step,
The milk does tremble, shake and plop around,

Just so the vicar's buttocks, big and fat,
All over the rough path tremble and shake,
Since he his feet did place now high, now low.

Just like a boy a glass of wine does carry,
Who shakes it so that he his finger wets
That o'er the edge was hooked to hold it firm,

Thus his the vicar over the belt had.
His stockings pulled all were around his knees,
As he did hurry his lost thirst to find.

Then when he turned his back before our eyes,
Soon his derriere made him look like a deer
Because of sweat that had then gathered there.

I will not say he carried in a sack
A herring and a bit of well-dried marrow,
Some sausages and a good wedge of cheese,

And four anchovies all tied on a string,
And in a broth of sweat they all did cook.
I do not know how better to draw him.

Thus with great honor did the vicar go,
With his behind all shaking and some farts,
Which loudly sounded and a stink gave off.

There then arrived one who worm-eaten seemed,
With such a queer expression on his face
That made him look just like and old woodcock.

So aptly named, he is Vicar Arlotto.[26]
No one did ever put him out to dry,
Since he has never known what water is.

26. "Arlotto" means glutton or fool.

Before the sacrament he does not kneel
If when the host is raised good wine there isn't,
For then he doesn't think that God is there.

Just as by miracle once Joshua did
The sun make stop against all nature's laws,[27]
So did he once together with a neighbor

The dark and moonless dreary night then stop.
They lost one day, and if I am not wrong
The next night, too. Oh, what a great mishap!

On the first day they did a wardrobe open
And thought they had a window opened then.
They soon returned to bed for it was dark.

The landlord did get up as God did will.
He did get up and did the sun show them,
For otherwise they might both there have died.

Thus the third day they resurrected were.
Although they had awakened on the second,
They had asleep for fully three days been.

Thus did the vicar on his way then go
While we did these events right there discuss.
Then did our eyes move on to see another.

And then I said: "Bracciata,[28] who is that
Who is surrounded by so many others
Who do so circle him like satellites?

Why does he move in such a weird strange way?
Tell me, Sir Dirty, why does he walk so
Like a child who his drawers dirtied has?"...

Chapter IX

The sun had risen to its midday point
So that all shadows fully shortened were.
The Chariot and the Horn were almost meeting,[29]

---

27. Joshua 10.12.
28. Bracciata: Sir Nastagio is called Bracciata in a playful allusion to his size.
29. The constellation of the Bear and Capricorn is a parody of Dante's *Commedia*, see *Purgatorio* 2.55–57.

And yet the crowd did keep on growing so.
Grass on a lawn does not so thickly grow
As did the crowd that to the bridge was going.

Among them some there were both lame and twisted,
Some with distorted eyes, some with huge legs,
And others who did bear signs of a stroke.

Others there were like cherubs red of cheek,
Some did have hernias hanging like big bags,
And others had huge noses and split brows.

One would at times there see fifteen or more
Well-filled like glasses just set down to cool
And all together would the others bump.

I do know these who have now close approached.
If you did squeeze all these you would spill wine;.
Just listen now to what I saw them do.

At times they wished to speak one with another,
But like the tide the crowd was as it moved
And did one from the other keep away....

Ballads for Festive Occasions

I

O Love you well do know all thoughts of mine,
You know that I've been faithful in your service,
Do make me happy then, else let me die.

To have a life so bitter and such pain,
In sighs and tears to find the only comfort
Is certainly, my Lord, more dire than death.

O Love, you have your quiver and your bow,
Why do you not her gelid heart then pierce?
A mortal woman must not gods defy.

To honor do pay heed and my desire.
Do put an end to my eternal torment.
For I have reached the point of my last sigh.

II

O lady mine, how vain it is to think
That never will old age arrive for us,
And that our fleeting youth
Its freshness will maintain forever more.

Time does so swiftly fly.
The flower of our life will soon be gone.
A gentle heart remember must always
That time with it will sweep all things away.

A gentle lady merciful must be,
And pride must not along with beauty go,
For mad it is to hope
That youth and beauty all our life remain.[1]

III

Though I laugh and sing and dance
And do seem to be so gay,

---

1. One of the fundamental themes of fifteenth-century poetry in Italy: the flight of time that destroys youth and life, with the invitation to enjoy life while you can. Among other poems of Lorenzo, see the *Corinth* 163–93, p. 202.

My poor soul is sad and bitter,
Pain and tears are my sole part.

For so long I have obeyed
This so gentle lady mine,
For so long I have hers been,
As my lord told me to be.
All my heart I did give her,
Her true subject I have been,
But unhappy I am now
Through no fault of my own doing.

I do not her ever blame,
For my sole true good she is,
Just my fate that is so bitter
Is the cause of so much pain.
All my ills from it do come.
Let it do all that it wants,
I to it will not give in.
Hard and true I'll ever be.

IV

Complain I don't of you nor of myself
For I do know you'd help me if you could.

But of my fortune, yes, I do complain
For your desire and mine it does impede.
Of jealousy and envy I complain
For of such sweetness they deprive me now.
Of my misfortune, too, I do complain
For sorrow and despair it does give me.

I of suspicion always shall complain
That interrupts the sweetest thoughts of mine.
I suffer for you do dislike it, too,
For I do know you'd want what I do want.
Never should I have thought what I now know
That so much sorrow jealousy can cause.

Cursed be he who my good takes from me,
And he who wages war without a cause,
And all that to such evil does give rise,
And he who of discretion such lack has.
Cursed be he who with us interferes,
And he who'd want to free me of my pain.

So constant and so firm my true love is —
And so is yours, O my most lovely lady —
That sorrow, pain or jealousy will not
The power have from my own heart to take
The love I've felt for you, my brightest star,
Yours I shall be, for you my lady are.

O lady mine, I beg you do be firm,
Let them all talk and their worst do. Just wait
For once again with your true love you'll be,
As Love decrees, with me alone and happy.
For grief and pain avenged you'll surely be,
Unless Death will with my plans interfere.

V

In happiness I live and in sweet peace
For this is what my lady now does please.

My lady, who my gentle ruler is
Wants me to be the happiest of all lovers.
All sorrows she away has from me driven,
And grief and tears she does not want with me.
My heart she has with such great sweetness filled
That I do fear it can't resist for long.

Never did Love with happiness endow
And with great joy as much as he did me.
If I did keep it secret in my heart,
It could not bear such great and sweetest joy.
The heavens never were gay and serene
As in a heart that its great love has found.

Let sighs and tears from me forever go,
All sadness from my heart do leave at once.
Among all lovers let me happy be
For this is what my lovely lady wants.
Since such great mercy she has shown to me,
To serve her all my life let my aim be.

If I feared not that evil Fortune might,
Of my excessive happiness so envious,
Her colors change and all in black turn out,
My joy would then without bounds surely be,
Since the one source of all that gentle is
So happy does make me and so serene.

VI[2]

With promises and with so much hypocrisy,
With such false smiles and with such pretty looks
You did your faithful lover, Lady, fool.
I do regret all this, and my heart aches.

I have so much time lost and such great efforts
Because of your great beauty and the hope
Your gentleness did cause to rise in me,
Together with your beauty that rare is.
My trust I put in you and my own fealty,
But until now all I did get were words.

From time to time you have held me tight bound,
So long a time that I can count in years.
I thought for all my sorrows and my woes,
You would want to reward at long last me,
And now I know you scorn me and deceive.
From you my trust does not require just words.

If you do love me as you once did say,
Let me of it see some concrete firm sign.
Do not keep me in such suspense much longer.
Perhaps my patience will not long endure.
If you do wish to be gentle with me,
Do not delay and don't give me more words.

To keep me waiting as you have been doing,
For me means death, you can be sure of that.
Just do reflect that waiting means time lost,
Since you do know what my desire sure is.
O Lady show yourself more kind and gentle,
An end to my woes put, don't give me words.

O my sweet song, do go and beg my lady
Not to keep me of so much doubt the prey.
Tell her for once to show me her true heart,
And if the time I've spent is time I've lost.
Once I will know what she really does think
I will know what to do, no more just words.

---

2. An example of the type of composition in which the lover betrays a sensual love and a lack of patience towards its object.

VII

Have pity all of you for my deep sorrow
Whoever you may be, O my young ladies.

Always have I with purest faith served one
Whom I did think would always mercy show
And would towards me much kindness ever have,
And proud she would not be as she now is.
I have my time now lost and efforts, too,
For she does turn like in the wind a leaf.

Alas, how could I ever have believed
That her so gay and bright and lovely eyes
For me would be the cause of so much grief,
Of such sad tears and my so woeful plaints.
O cruel Love, how can you this permit?
Of such cruelty do you cleanse her heart.

Alas, such a reward I didn't expect
For my full loyalty and truest faith.
What I was offered then, this now is not.
Our bargain then, O Love, didn't this include.
A fool is he who does believe your promise
And in that hope, in grief and tears does live.

In part I have told you of my great grief.
To pity me I'm sure it has moved you.
How my life is afflicted I've told you
So that compassion you would have for me.
I do beg Love to give you much more joy
And to grant you all that you may desire.

VIII

You with others play at love,
While for me you have no time.
Don't you know my lovely girl
You are wrong to turn me down?

You are certainly all wrong
My true heart to so refuse.
If at least you gave me hope.
Do not scorn my love for you.
You enjoy another's love
And this is like death for me

That you should so angry be
And as useless you hold me.

If you should maybe try me,
You would soon agree with me
That no one can take my place.
Of my love you would glad be
And the best I'd be for you.
My dear girl do not scorn me.
I would know how to love you
And your favorite I'd be.

Not to listen is a fault.
It's the least one ought to do.
You don't know what I would say
And two better than one are.
I am sorry to persist.
If you would just now try me,
I do know what I can do,
And you would not make me wait.

For your good I'll tell you now
If you wish to be esteemed,
You must others too respect.
To be loved you must love, too.
If you do refuse to listen,
You are fierce and cruel, too.
Here I am, your true admirer.
Wrong you are if you scorn me.

IX

Those who await the morrow will repent:
Time does not wait. The day does fly away.[3]

Sweet youth will not to us again return,
Nor can time lost in future be regained.
If time is on your side and you delay,
On earth you will not ever happy be,
But gentle souls with keen discerning minds
The best of time will make while fast it flees.

How many things in youth we justly value!
How beautiful in springtime flowers are!

3. See above, p. 315, n. 1.

But when old age so useless does arrive,
And nothing but more ills we can expect,
We see the day we've lost when night is near,
And for time lost we can now but repent.

No greater sorrow is there than to know
That precious time was lost through our own fault.
This brings on sorrow that will torture us,
This brings on sorrow that just tears does cause,
This is the spur that should make us desire
To use time well for it does fly away.

So then you gentle ladies, handsome youths,
Who do together sing in this place here,
Spend all your days in happiness and cheer,
For step by step your youth does pass away,
I do beg you in that sweet fire's name now
That in all gentle hearts[4] brings warmth and burns.

X

Sorrows and tears I pray that God will bring
To all those who of others evil speak.

And I beg you, O gentle lovely ladies,
Do not pay heed to all that you may hear,
For one who does pay heed to evil tales
Will only banish pleasure from her life.
Honestly one must live and in good cheer,
With joy and songs and with all pleasures, too.

Let all who wish their evil tongues then wag,
And let us not pay heed to their foul words.
We all must happy live and so die, too,
While youth does still hold us in its domain,
And as for those who do of us tell tales
May their hearts burst with jealousy and envy.

O my sweet song, go find all lovers now
And gentle and most charming ladies, too.
Remind them always brave of heart to be
And to their lovers faithful be and true,

4. Combined with sensual notes that are present in these ballads, there are also reminiscences of the *Stil novo* and its theories of love and "gentle hearts."

For to fear words a vile thing is, indeed,
To which true lovers never did succumb.

XI

O cruel Fortune,[5] where have you led me?
You could not treat me worse than you now do.

Happy and lovely you once showed yourself.
A tranquil and serene face you did show.
You told me that you wanted to be such
That my desires you would all soon fulfill.
You then did all at once entirely change
And did with sorrow fill me and with pain.

You once did promise that a kindly sun
Would ever shine for me and bring me joy.
At first her words so sweet and tender acts
Filled me with hope and gave my soul real peace.
But then you did show me that I had loved
A heart of stone and that you me did scorn.

I had no faith in your deceitful looks,
For I knew you too well in other ways,
But the most lovely light of those bright eyes
And of her looks the beauty and the charm
Made me in your false promises put faith,[6]
And in so doing my death I did acquire.

In my poor heart you made a hope so burn
That made me see what really was not there.
Alas, I did believe that loyalty
Ruled in your heart. How mad it is to hope,
For later I did see in what cruel way
You did scorn me and how you did deceive.[7]

Do go my dearest song and beg the one
That in her hands holds both my life and death

---

5. The theme of Fortune, most times malignant, is found throughout Lorenzo's works, as in *Lyrics* XVIII, pp. 9–11 for example. It was one of Petrarch's favorite themes, which became widespread in the fifteenth century.

6. See p. 15, n. 17 to *Lyrics.*

7. An example of unrequited love that leads to accusations and eventually, in some poems, to a rejection of the woman and love.

To listen at long last to my entreaties.
Tell her to let me know what she does wish,
And if she should to all my prayers listen,
Fortune no longer cruel would then be.

XII

Since I did leave, O Love, your kind domain,
My life has all been filled with wrath and scorn.

After my lady in her cruel way
Showed that she scorned being served in love by me,
And of her beauty was my life bereft,
True life it has not been, but cruel death.
My freedom Love gave me and let me go,
And since that time I've held my life in scorn.

One cannot love someone who knows not love.
Untouched by love one can't a lover have,
And if I Love at one time wished to serve,
I did not yet then know how wrong I was,
But when my heart of it became aware
It did not wish towards Love to show its scorn.

Against my wishes I did leave the one
That I then loved more than sweet life itself.
From that time on my life has known no joy,
Nor will it any know in future time.
Of evil Fortune I complain and Love
For both of them hold me in such great scorn.

My heart would want so to return once more
To that most ardent fire, Love's own sweet flame,
For it cannot abide its present state.
If there a lady be who mercy feels
And would accept this tearful life of mine,
I'll give myself to her, all else I scorn.

XIII

Is there anyone among you ladies now
Who has my heart, or knows where he may be?[8]

8. For the theme of the heart's flight from lover to beloved, see p. 59, n. 63 to the *Lyrics*. Here the theme acquires a lighter, almost humorous note.

He left a lovely lady whom he loved
Because of her sheer cruelty and harshness.
As he returned, a new bright flame was lit
That once again took him away from me.
Love was returning him free of all bonds,
But caught he was again as back he came.

A gentle lady's beautiful bright eyes
Adorned with pity did him steal from me,
Nor do I think he ever will come back,
For her charms are strong bonds that hold him tight.
I've called him back to me so many times,
But he for her does burn and wants to stay.

If one of you does hold him, gentle ladies,
Be merciful and pity show for him,
And since he comes to you of his own will
His faith with pity should rewarded be.
Never will he leave you or forsake you,
If a companion good to him you'll be.

XIV

O Love, if in my heart you'd wish to be,
Then pity let again my lady show.

You know why I from you did then depart.
No other cause was there but her own harshness.
Since I always had served a lady who
My faith and my attentions both did scorn,
If you wish me to love her once again
Then make her know the weight of your displeasure

Do make her love my heart that loves her so,
Of my true faith do now make her aware.
Make her respond at once to my own call.
Have mercy in her heart and pity grow,
Have her feel pity when she does see me,
Her faithful servant, who is dying for her.

If she a sign of pity would give me,
If only melt away her hardness would,
Though I cannot be worthy of such grace,
Constant and strong I'd be more than I've been.

There never was a lover in this world
In serving Love more loyal and more faithful.

I do beg you, O Love, what now must come
Let come at once for time does ever flee.
To wait too long is bothersome and painful,
And time will make all pity be in vain.
I have always and shall love her alone,
If pity she does show for my distress.

XV

The only paradise I can foresee
Is where all jealousy[9] will banished be.

If Love could then without suspicion flourish,
Happy would be the life of all who love.
Such joy and sweetness would our hearts then fill
That all the saints above one would not envy.
Alas, poor me, what sighs and what sad tears
Have been and are for jealousy all shed.

Since Love grants me all that I do desire,
Too happy and too gay my heart would be,
Did I not think that someone followed me,
Ready to seize my joy and make her his.

O wicked Jealousy, this thought destroys
All joy and sweetness and my heart leaves bare

But I do have such faith, sweet lady mine,
In your great gentleness, O faithful heart,
That driven far away are evil thoughts,
And I do know our love eternal is.
Of it you make me worthy, my dear lady,
So there can be of jealousy no thoughts.

Your love you didn't grant me to see me die.
Your heart so gentle is that you cannot
Ever betray one who does serve you well.
I know you would not want him to despair.
Your beautiful eyes do seem to tell me
To banish jealousy and happy be.

---

9. Jealousy is personified as a malignant goddess in *Sylva II,* 39–55, p. 232.

XVI

Lovely ladies a long time
Have I sought this heart of mine.
I have found it in the end
Thanks to Love omnipotent.[10]

Maybe here where all are dancing
Is she who stole it away.
She now has it and shall have
While I live this life of mine.
She is kind and ever loving,
She shall have it ever more.
I have found it in the end
Thanks to Love omnipotent.

To you ladies I shall tell
How I did find it again:
When I felt it run away
I did then look up and down,
Then I saw two lovely eyes,
And there hiding was my heart.
I have found it in the end
Thanks to Love omnipotent.

How shall we the thief now punish
For my heart away so stealing?
She's so charming and so lovely,
She has love in her two eyes.
Let her heart be ever bound,
Let it burn along with mine.
I have found it in the end
Thanks to Love omnipotent.

Love I beg you bind this thief,
Let her burn as her prey does,
Pay no heed if she begs you,
Don't you look at her bright eyes.
Take your bow and take your darts
And avenge this heart of mine.
I have found it in the end
Thanks to Love omnipotent.

---

10. See *Ballad* XIII, where the heart was lost, and n. 8, pp. 323–24.

XVII

I do not know of anything more vexing
Than have to wait for what the heart desires.[11]

To him who waits, an hour does seem a year,
And even a brief time is far too long.
All those who have so waited know it well.
I'm one of those who will say, "Now it's coming,"
But even if as fast as mushrooms grow,
It came around it would too late yet seem.

What I am waiting for I seem to see.
What I would like I think I can now hear.
If I do think of what at once I'd like,
I see you happy rushing to see me,
But then I think I will in sorrow die,

For I do see how all my hopes are vain.
My heart does bit by bit destroy itself,
And as I want I burn and am consumed,
And I beg time that now so swiftly flees
To be more slow in passing and not rush,
And while I do look back at all my past,
I see the present that on its way goes.

O lady, comfort me for all my sorrows.
Perhaps you do not see, my poor young lady,
That deadly harm you do to your own self,
So much more so in that you're very young.
Have pity for one who now waiting is,
And for the charms and beauty you have now.

XVIII

If one is not in love,
Let him away now go.
It would be wrong in such a place to stay.

If one is here who does now not know Love,
Let him away now go,

11. Combines various important themes: that of hope (see p. 15, n. 17 to *Lyrics),* of time, particularly in verses 25–26 (also see p. 315, n. 1 above), and impatience at not obtaining what the lover desires (see p. 318, n. 2 above).

For he a gentle heart[12] could never have
And not now feel that fire.
If he does feel it some,
Let him its flame revive
So all will know and won't drive him away.

Let Love now here preside at this our dance
With all who serve him well.
If one of jealousy the sting does feel,
Let him not tarry here,
Or else he scorned will be.
Let all here fall in love,
Or let them now this lovely place forsake.

If a young lady should from love hold back
Because ashamed she is,
Let her then see that the shame now would be
To Love's dictate refuse.
To love a shame it isn't
One who to serve so wants.
To be ungrateful cause for shame would be.

If one there is so timid and so shy
As to leave here in fear,
Let her think that a gentle noble heart
To fears does pay no heed.
Nature did not give you
Beauty so wonderful
For you to waste it and let time go by.

XIX

How can I then with cheerful heart now sing
If in my lady's graces I am not?

To happier lovers who feel joy and cheer
I wish to leave all songs now and all feasts,
For with much grief so taken is my heart
That only tears and pain are for it meet.
Let those who happy are seek cheer and song,
I wish for only tears all night and day.

I, too, was happy once as Love decreed,
For ardently my lady did love me,

12. Some of the usual *Stil novo* notes are introduced here and in verses 25–28. There is the invitation to enjoy life while still young.

But envious Fortune later did decide
To turn my happy fate into sad tears.
Alas, poor me, to die would better be
Than not to have Love's favor any more.

In such dire straits one thought does only comfort
My fearful heart and my dejected soul:
Always have I my lady truly served
With loyalty, pure faith and no defect,
So then if I must suffer a wrong death
I know that once I'm dead she will then grieve.

XX

My heart is filled with bitter sweetness now
And with a poison sweet, as Love decrees.[13]

None more than me is happy and content,
None can deserve compassion more than me.
The sweetness I feel and all the sorrow
Do give me cause for both deep sighs and smiles.
No one can understand so sweet a passion,
If in his breast such gentle fire is not.

The more my heart what it desires does have,
And the more kindness my true lady shows,
So much more fiercely my desire does burn,
For ever more my lady does please me.
As love increases, so my sorrow does,
Nor ever what I feel can time suppress.

So sweet a pleasure there has never been
As the great grief that now my heart does feel,
Nor suffering so bitter ever was
As my own pleasure that to death leads me,
But full of sweetness death must prove to be
Since so much sweetness sorrow does give me.

XXI

To follow Love excuses I don't need
For of all gentle hearts the way it is.

---

13. Antitheses in the style of Petrarch, around which the entire composition is formed.

With those who feel the fire that I do feel
No need there is at all to make excuses,
For their heart must so gentle and pure be
That I do know they will all pity me.
To those who such sweet passion do not feel
Nothing is due for gentle they can't be.[14]

Love, gentleness and truest honesty
But one to those who well consider are.
Wasted is beauty, it does seem to me,
That in a proud and scornful woman is.
Who can blame me if merciful I am
As honesty permits and gentle heart?

Those whose heart is so hard they can't enjoy
The warmth of Love's own rays reproach me will.
I do beg Love that those who feel it not
Unworthy evermore of it deemed be,
But with his fire to those who loyal are[15]
He give his warmth and let their true hearts burn.

Let those who will reproach me as they please,
I do not fear a heart that gentle isn't.
My ever constant love no heed at all
Pays to vain words that envy does inspire.
I've gentle Love decided to obey
For as long as on earth here I will stay.

XXII

O Love hold me forever close and tight
Since in so sweet a way you did bind me.[15]

Let loving women all well understand
And others who have hearts all warm and firm:
Love has me tied to one of his own pillars
Of alabaster, smooth, that firm is so.
All naked he has left poor me, alas,
Just like a rogue alone without companions.

---

14. The presence of the *Stil novo* is quite apparent in this composition. For the explanation of the lack of need for excuses, see the introduction to the *Commentary,* pp. 83–85.

15. Beginning with this ballad, the poems move more and more towards a sensual love.

Around my neck there is a diamond chain
By which this love of mine does hold me tight
So that I barely manage just to sigh.
My breast and my poor heart the pillar press,
My own two hands, alas, myself I tie.
To be so chained, indeed, so painful is.

He keeps my legs and both my feet so bound
With two great chains that are so very large —
Of smooth and candid ivory they're made —
They are so tight that I can never move.
What must ensue of this, O Love, you know
For all this time you have with me been here.

XXIII

A little wood there is amidst a valley
With a sweet spring that only joy does give.[16]

So sweet the waters are this spring bestows
That once of it we taste we want no other.
Given a taste I was and liked it so
That by my faith of nothing else I think.
All other sweets this sweetness does exceed,
If one selected is for such a gift.

I do not wish to mention where it is
So that no brutish beast can e'er there go,
But glad I am the way to show you then
So if you wish to go you can head there.
Two ways there are to go to this sweet spring,
Unless a certain road you wish to take.

Over a gentle mount you must then travel
That is so white, of snow it seems to be.
As towards the spring straight on you do proceed
A lovely hill you'll find on either side;
Between the two a lovely valley is
In the sweet shade of both these charming hills.

As on the way you slowly will proceed
Over a lovely mount you then must go,
A slope so sweet that it a plain will seem.
The mount is well defined and truly neat.

16. This composition is obviously an allegory of the female body.

Two lovely valleys at the foot you'll see.
The place I have told you in their midst is.

XXIV

Now I must the truth tell you,
Yes I must, O lady mine.
It may be a foolish thing
But you'll know what I do think.

You cannot just once decide
You would want and then you don't,
Then you want it once again,
You'd love me and then you wouldn't.
As you know it is a while
That this game has been going on.

Not to stick to your decision
Not a virtue, but vice is.

You do send sweet words to me
That console can for a while,
Then so suddenly you change
And you sadden me once more.
You are not at all discreet.
Yes do this knot now untie,
Put an end to all our troubles.
It is time to end this game.

You have now so long been waiting
That it's plain to one and all.
If you had sent me away
It would secret have remained.
Don't be angry if I speak
For I do so for your good:
Not to stick to your decision
Does much harm to me and you.

I believe you do well know
If you can but don't want to.
You will lose the time that's ripe,
When you'll want, too late 'tis then.[17]
Let's have deeds, I'm tired of words.
As good teachers always do,

17. See p. 315, n. 1 above.

Spend less time to look about
And in truth, make up your mind.

XXV

A young woman did desire
With a young man to converse.[18]
She knew well to play the game
And three lire[19] he paid her.

The first time he did pay her
On the corner of a bench,
But there was an argument,
So she hurried this to say:
"Only in part have you paid me,
In the end you didn't do much.
You cannot from here depart
If the rest you don't pay me.

Since a miser she was then,
This was not enough for her.
She was not well satisfied
Till the youth, who able was,
Gave her all that was her due.
In her pocket it he put.
Feeling better like a fish,
She was letting him go away.

She remembered all at once
That some interest was due.
With her hand she did untie
For the youth his own purse strings.
"What a pity," she then said,
"Straight and true it does not stay.
We must now, indeed, decide
Once again the hill to climb."

The young man was well content
For provided he was well.
The full interest he paid.
All in cash he did her pay.
To depart he then did want,

18. To converse is obviously a euphemism for love making. From this point, the ballads become erotic.
19. The currency of Italy at different periods of its history.

But the woman said: "Do wait."
She gave him twelve eggs to drink
Ere she let him get away.

XXVI

In a serious argument
Was a husband with his wife.
"If you do not change your face,
I shall not my method change."

His wife strongly did complain
That he played a certain game
That she could not ever see.
She would say: "Do change location,"
But the husband said few words:
"I will follow my own way,
I will not do it elsewhere
If I don't hear better reasons."

"You have been brought up so badly,
You have learned an evil art
So to stray it is not right
And abandon the right way."
Then the husband did so say:
"You're the cause that this is so.
If you had a better face
I would not do as I do."

To her family she wailed,
But she had been hurt before.
With her neighbors she complained,
And she asked morning and night:
"Does your husband use this way?
When to me for this he comes,
I at once begin to cry.
This is what I get for pleasure."

Said her husband, "Do be patient,
And you'll soon get used to it.
Have some patience and you will
Get to like this way of mine.
For caresses you will ask,
You will like this game of mine.
You will say what I do say:
This is surely the just way."

XXVII

Daughter mine, do all you can
To act properly and well,
So you'll seem to one and all
Gentle, wise and modest, too.

When you are with other people,
At a gathering perhaps,
Of good cheer do be and happy,
For you are not at a wake.
If you have nice things to say,
Do not use improper terms.
Let your mind control your tongue,
So you'll speak proper and well.

If someone looks at your face,
Look back true and straight at him,
Look with care and give a smile
To cheer one and lessen care.
If a hand or foot they touch,
Do not take it with ill grace,
For to spoil what is a party
Would be foolish and uncouth.

If someone who's not a miser
Wants to give a gift to you,
Show you hold it very dear
With sweet words and with signs, too,
For a villain's act it is
To refuse another's gift.
If for something you are asked,
Don't refuse. Your promise give.

This is how, O daughter mine.
You can do me such great honor.
Keep in mind and don't forget,
Let it sink into your heart.
Seize the right moment and time
To your promises fulfill.
Feasts do not forever last,
Time goes on and never stops.[20]

20. A forceful assertion of the favorite theme of time that flees and the necessity to enjoy life while you can. The advice is given in a sad tone that is in contrast with the rest of the ballad.

XXVIII

"I've received so much good counsel[21]
And so well, O mother mine,
That I think I can well say
I'm the happiest girl around.

Yesterday a gentle youth
Did appear in front of me,
With a sweet and humble mien
He kept looking straight at me.
With a sign or with a smile,
Without words he spoke to me:
"I love you more than myself,"
And I soon in love did fall.

With great skill and by the hand
Did he take me with great care,
So no one became aware,
Whether near or far away.
When my hand his own did feel,
I took his and firmly pressed.
All was done in such a way
that no one could ever see.

He his foot on mine did put
And so doing did stain my dress,
Then he told me he did want
All alone to speak to me
In the dark at a late hour.
I at first didn't understand,
Then his signs cleared it for me,
And I answered him quite well.

Speak to me he did then want
Of things I would hold so dear.
As I did listen to him
I no longer could say no.
Thus to him I clearly spoke:
"I don't want that you should suffer,
I don't want you dying for me;.
Here I am and ready, too.

---

21. The daughter answers her mother who had advised her in the previous ballad.

To me come he did last night
Through a place that was most strange,
Even if he could have flown,
He could not uninjured be.
Softly, softly he did come
Where I lay in my own bed.
If I told you of our joy,
You would surely envy me.

In that way we stayed so long
That at last he sated was,
Yet to me the time seemed brief.
While I tell this I rejoice.
Mother mine, I do thank you
For the good advice you gave.
Never have you something done
That to me more joy did bring.

You young women to me listen
Do as she for she was wise,
For if true I rightly see,
One who can must not delay.
To delay at times reveals
What we would in secret keep.
While you can, do go and live
Do not let go pleasure by.

XXIX

There can be no game so lovely,
Or that everyone likes more,
Than for two to seem just one.
Those in doubt should try it once.

If you don't know how to play,
Come to me and I'll teach you.
A great brain it does not take
Just to learn how it to play.
All it takes is just what nature
Give us, that which donkeys have,
For they never are so small
That they can't do it a bit.

I did see a woman who
Little skill did have at first.

By the second night she could
Teach us all how it to do.
The first time I did her teach
With the stalk of a broom plant.
A great labor it was not
To teach her a game so sweet.

One must ready always be
To have done what must be done,
And one's mind must open be,
If to learn at once one wants.
No one can so foolish be,
If a while the game does last,

As to not from nature learn,
For one learns as one does play.

It at first does seem fatiguing
Till the man accustomed is.
There's no one who will not say
That she's happy in the end.
Those who do for a while play,
Till there comes what others want,
Feel no pain at any time
And would play no other game.

A great master here there is,
Who does teach this game to play.
If a daughter one does have,
Who to learn wants really well,
If she has a healthy back,
She will soon play very well.
Once she has the knack acquired,
She will shake and dance a storm.

There's another way, indeed,
But more dangerous it is.
I will not it therefore praise
For it is so highly tiring.
Yet if one should now be willing,
I am here ready to teach.
I shall make him so proficient
That he'll never spoil the game.

XXX[22]

To Pisa on the way, at night I strayed
Right in the caves that on the way there are.

There in Pontolmo I thought I would tarry,
But I could not because the rain came down.
So dark it was that I did tumble down
To Empoli instead on that dark night.

At my mistake I can't at all now marvel,
It is a question of a mere half mile.
Many a time that same mistake I've made
Just as it happened on that so dark night.

At Empoli my horse did will to stop.
Now you shall hear how well he was received.
The hostess where we lodged, excuse me please,
Her arse did turn to me on that dark night.

No other supper did we have that night
Than chops and loins and a fine calf's backside.
Her finger she had cut and for her pain
She sucked an egg all through that most dark night.

Then certain apples she did offer us
That one must not forget to bake full well.

She then took out the best to honor us
And only that we drank that whole dark night.

So then when I shall undertake this trip,
I won't make the mistake to go elsewhere,
So well the hostess did here honor us
That never did I spend a better night.

XXXI[23]

Ladies and girls, I do my faults all heed
And do confess and penance wish to make.

---

22. One of the most licentious of these ballads, full of double meanings, with the names of cities (Empoli, Pontolmo, etc.) corresponding to parts of the body.
23. A parody of religious confessions, replete with double meanings and ending with the often-seen invitation not to let time slip by.

I do confess to you now first of all
That pleasures I've neglected many times,
And many things I've left just hanging there.
This first of all I must confess and heed.

For such a long time then I had desired
To speak with a most fine and gentle lady,
Then in her presence I did mute become
This also I must now confess and heed.

When elsewhere I myself did find one day,
For fear I did then lose a great occasion,
And such occasions never did return.
This also I must now confess and heed.

Oh how I have repented many times!
A mad decision I did make one time:
I did pay first and then I was not served.
This also I must now confess and heed.

I still remember other sins of mine,
For to the words of friars I paid heed,
And so did many pleasures let slip by.
This also I must now confess and heed.

I do regret also that I didn't use
My youth and of my life the sweet good time.
I know that now too late, for it has gone.
This also I must now confess and heed.

I say *mea culpa* and do so much grieve
For fears and negligence and all my errors,
Those I remember now and those forgotten.
To Love I all of them confess and heed.

And I beg all of you to now beware
Lest you do make the same mistakes I've made.
And when you're old you'll have them to regret,
And when too late you will your errors heed.

XXXII

The Seven Pleasures of Love

Ladies and maidens please do listen well
And with devotion to what I will tell,
For all these seven pleasures are so sweet

That Love will offer those who serve him well.
I say to all of you and most of all
To those who gentle are and in bloom now,
These holy pleasures do enjoy full well.
With all of them may Love give you much joy.

The first of these that Love may wish to grant
Is that of looking in two kindly eyes
Filled with a vague and sweet and lovely splendor.
To see sweet lips form a most charming smile,
And hands and neck and ways that gentle are,
A stride that does seem fit for paradise,
All motions and all acts that one may do
And thus a gentle heart does bound become.

The second pleasure Love may wish to grant
Is that of touching a beloved hand
With greatest care while dancing to sweet music,
Or softly press it on diverse occasions.
And while one plays or while one does converse,
Let certain words slip out and not in vain,
And a beloved's dress to touch and press
In such a way no one will ever know.

The third of all these pleasures that Love grants
Is when a letter she accepts from you
And deigns to answer it in her own hand,
And makes it clear she does accept Love's yoke.
He must be hard as stone who when he sees
So sweet a token will not shed a tear,
Read it a hundred times and still want more,
And with sweet sighs for his grace Love does thank.

The fourth of these of greater sweetness is,
For to exchange a word it does permit
While all alone and let your heart then speak,
And with your lips tell her of your deep sorrow.
If Love conducts the affairs as proper is
You will hear words that could the sun make stop,
Sweet tears and sighs and wrath against all windows
And doors also if access they impede.

One who comes this fifth pleasure to enjoy
Can say that Love his services accepts,
If he with tenderness will dare to kiss

A beautiful and loving gentle face,
Her lips and there within where sweetness is,
Her throat, her breast and both her candid arms
And all the other sweet and lovely parts,
Leaving behind at times of love the marks.

Of Love's sixth pleasure I now wish to speak,
Which is to get almost to a conclusion,
And to that end for which one falls in love,
And willing is to bear both pain and sorrow.
Those with experience and those gaining it
Know how it is so comforting and sweet
To hold in your arms tight and with no fear
The one you so much love and do hold dear.

The last of these Love's pleasures is the next,
For happiness does Love grant in the end.
Never can words tell with what gentleness,
With what sweet sighs, with what sweet words of love
One to the last will come of all these pleasures:
How one will sweetly cry with sweetest sorrow.
Then certain things are done without pretense
That with his brush no painter can record.

My dearest ladies these the pleasures are
That to his faithful servants Love does grant.
Let those who gentleness and beauty have
Enjoy them all while blooming in their youth,
For to let time slip by the wise will grieve.
These pleasures all of which I have just spoken
To those who speak and feel with great devotions
Will open Peter's Gates[24] and let them in.

This poor blind man who spoke to you of pleasures
Would like to recommend himself to you.
In fact, he would so like to have some alms,
At least he'd like to be in your good grace.
Love has so badly fixed this poor blind fellow,
As you can see, and blind sends him around.
Take care of him, O you most loving women,
Let him enjoy those things you all do have.

In such condition is this fellow now,
That no one does he have to share this feast.

24. Cf. Dante, *Purgatorio* 3.78.

Carnevale Songs[1]

I

The Cookie Song[2]

Look here you women, biscuits, cookies, too.
If you the finest want, then do take ours!

There is no need to show how they are made —
A waste of time it'd be and a real pity —
For those who do it waste, like some of you,
Must then content themselves with home-made fare.

When on your side time is, you must then act.
Impediments or messes do discount.
If you do lack the means, then borrow them:
Good neighbors help each other in this way

This art is to be practiced by young men.
That good our biscuits are, enough it is.
Do not for others wait to give them free,
You must now play and spend your own good money.

We don't use cards, we do use cups and peas.
One must it raise, the other does it put,
And here and there then one must it well mix.
Do pull it towards you now, see if you guess.

Look here, my woman, tell me what you need;
From head down to your toes you do then tremble
Until it comes and then you'll surely see
Strange looks and then like cats you'll hear them purr.

The one beneath quite angry will then be,
All over twists and makes strange faces, too.
The eyes wide open are and there are sighs,
And the poor wretches do cry out aloud.

---

1. Most of these songs for Carnevale are of an erotic nature. They were composed to be recited at a festival that included masques and allegorical floats in a period when all rules were relaxed in accordance with people's ideas of enjoyment.

2. The original has "confortini," which together with "berricuocole" were types of pastry, which were the prizes for winning at cards at stands that displayed them.

The one who wins does seem to melt with joy,
Does smile and laugh and joyful shakes all over.
In Fortune to believe is a mad thing.
Just wait to see if she will bend and bow.

This type of game is very fast, indeed.
It's played while standing up in any place.
Its short duration quite a drawback is,
But often drinks one who a small glass has.

Then there's the "Flood," a most accursed game,
But if one wants to play and come out clean,
Let him bet little and be tight on call.
Today low peasants, too, know how to play.

If one his all does put in a sole call,
When "Flood" does come then in sad shape he'll be.
To look at him you'd think he had been stabbed.
Cursed be those who dare so far to go.

There are some games that are still played today,
Of these some harmful are, while others aren't.
The one who holds the cards can please himself,
If with sound golden coins he is provided.

If you do wish to play as we have shown,
Our all we'll gladly put in a sole pot.
Each one of us will take on two of you
And bet the biscuits and their boxes, too.

II

Song of the Perfumes

Of Valencia we are youths
On our journey passing through.
We've been taken and then bound
By the women of fair Florence.

In our city there are many
Gentle and so lovely, too.
You do best by much all these
As your faces clearly show.

This great beauty that you have
Do accompany with love.

If you don't wish to love
Of what use your beauty is?

Our dispensers of perfume
Are at least a foot in length.
If you think we you deceive,
In your hands we can put them.
We can stand them up in place.
At their tip there burns a fire,
A sweet odor it will spread,
Oh so lovely, but so strong.

Of our oil we wish to tell,
It has such a strong perfume,
One and all it will make tremble
From the head down to the toes.
Our oil is a sacred thing,
If it's poured from a good cup,
It comes slowly, drop by drop,
If it strains, more strong it is.

Our oil heals all sorts of pain
And hard cases does dissolve.
To itself it draws the humor,
From the vessel warmth it draws,
Penetrate its sweetness does,
The more so as you caress.
For both tremors and for whims
Use our oil and you'll be healed.

A good soap we also have
That does foam up such a storm:
Rub it well where it is needed,
The more so, the more it foams.
Did you ever, my dear ladies,
Have a ring that was too tight?
Use our soap that gives and takes.
If it burns you must be patient.

Ladies, what we have yours is.
If you do with love now burn,
We will furnish our great oil,
We will rub it all for free.
From our city we have oil,
Orange, mulberry and spices.

If you like, let's try it here.
Try it, try it, try it here.

III

Song of the Pancakes

We are young, but as you'll hear, we are masters
Of our art and do all know of pancakes.

This Mardi Gras our shop we did all leave,
If the truth you must now know, we were chased
For we are gluttons all and we did eat
Our own pancakes when barely done they were.

We all now would our art to practice like
While on this carnival we all do feast,
But we cannot unless by women joined.
We'll gladly show you how the best are made.

Water and flour you do put in a dish,
As much as it can take and then you shake.
It does come like an ointment when you shake,
Just like the water used to boil spaghetti.

If as you shake you don't wish to get tired,
Mix well with your right arm, not with your left.
You then throw in the sweetest, whitest sugar
And without letting up you keep on shaking.

While you do shake you must good care then take
That you do not fall out through too much force.
When ready go and taste it with your finger,
If good, the mold then do put on the fire.

Do warm it well and if the mold is new,
Then hasten you must not. Do oil it well,
Do not a lot put in, do try it out,
See how it comes and if it warms quite well.

But if old is the mold and has been used,
You can it fill with all that you may want,
For even a full pail it can then take,
And a good ladle from Bologna use.

When you have put the mixture in the mold
And sizzle you it hear, do hold on tight.

Do shake the mold and let it settle down,
Do turn it upside down and let it cook.

Often the mixture will, if too much, spill,
Through holes it will escape, but that is normal.
When you do think it all is done quite well,
Open the mold and the pancakes take out.

If kept too long, it will fall down, not rise.
If greased quite well, it will come out itself.
While warm it then to fold is so much easier,
And then in a white cloth put it you can.

Do take a hard brush then or a rough cloth
And every little corner do clean well.
The soft mold is like of a fish the mouth,
In all the cracks it holds what you put in.

A certain size a good pancake should be
And in proportion all of its parts have.
To make them well there must at least be two:
Let one hold tight and in the other push.

If cooked quite well, all colored and bright red,
They're good to eat as much as one may want,
For even if quite large and so much raised
When they are squeezed they will small bites become.

You do hold on, dear ladies, in we'll push.
If we should push too hard or too soft be
Do take the ladle in your own two hands
And you can put it in, so good it'll be.

IV

Song of the Grafters

Of grafting we are masters, my good ladies.
We know in every way how it is done.

If you too now would like our art to learn,
We will instruct you gladly in detail.
There is no need for study or for books,
What natural does come we can all do.

To graft the tree, it should quite young then be,
Tender and long without knots and quite straight,

Most beautiful and with a tender bark,
Just at the time it to awaken starts.

Then you must cut it and a hole must make
A third in size the branch is to insert.
It must go in as tight as tight can be,
But do take care lest then the bark should burst.

You must then push it in as much you can,
Then with a twig you must tie it so well
And press one bark against the other close,
And thus the lymph can well together mix.

All this can surely be without cuts done.
Gently and with your hands the bark you pull
Without it tearing and the branch put in,
Together draw the barks and then let go.

Against the rain well bandaged it must be,
And thus for a few days it will be left.
If then disturbed, there is no way at all
The graft can take and a success turn out.

To have good oil, the olive tree do graft.
Apples and figs will quickly grow and large.
I see you'd like to know how it is done.
But you do know and still you make me talk.

This method is by all so well regarded:
A roundel take that is pierced at the top
And a thin rod, and first of all the bark
Where the bud does appear with care do cut.

I take that bud and quickly it do move
To where a hole was previously prepared,
Small as a coin, and I the bark will open
And in the bud does go — the bark will close.

In putting it inside care must be used,
All things by haste can often then spoiled be.
Better results achieves he who does wait
For when it is well moist and oh so sweet.

We now believe you do well know the art
Of grafting with a branch and that of monks

Who do it all year round, winter and summer;
All plants can grafted be, the peach tree, too.

The tree that strange and wild so at first is,
Once grafted slowly will to change begin,
More lovely and more gentle, not in vain,
For you will see what fruit it then will bear.

To graft we do invite you all, dear ladies,
If rain is lacking and all things are dry,
If you want peaches or some other fruit,
We ready are your wishes to fulfill.

V

Song of the Civet

This animal, my ladies, perfect is,
Civet by name, it many things can do.

It comes from far away from a strange country
And lives in swamps or watery low places.
At times if one should touch it with his hand,
A marvel it would be not to be stained.

Boneless meat only does to it seem good,
But in great mouthfuls wants it and so often.
As you will hear, the civet may be found
Two fingers' width down under the rear end.

A tentacle one must have fairly long,
Not sharp so that the civet won't be hurt.
In it is pushed and one must grease it well,
And it to you so sweet will seem, dear ladies.

This is how one draws out that sweetest liquor.
But there are some who do dislike the odor,
But yet it is so good, though foul at times,
If one does not always keep it too clean.

Care you must take when you do put it in
That you do not the civet's own place miss,
For it with other matter stained might be,
And grievous harm then do to that poor thing.

If you don't have the tentacle, you must
Use other means. At least your finger use,

And then do let the husband smell it well
If his is the defect and this great lack.

At times one should not pay the civet visits.
A proper time there is for one must rest
Three or four days, but some too willing are
And only a strange broth they then draw out.

The civet's liquor a true virtue has:
If it you smell, it will then clear your head.
It cures all ills a woman's body has,
Nothing is better when this is the case.

If hard your kidneys are it best is then
To of the tentacle the tip grease well.
Do put it where it hurts and soon you'll see
Out come its balm that respite will give you.

It has the power to make you conceive,
And many others that we shall not list.
Perhaps, we have too much already said.
Now see if true is what we said, dear ladies.

If some you should now want, we're here to sell.
You must now spend the dearest coin you have.
Do not be stubborn, we do wish to make
Of it you want a little flask at least.

VI

Song of the Farmer Wives

In this carnival, alas,
All six husbands we have lost,
All we had, you dearest ladies,
And we suffer without them.

From Arcetri we all are,
All of us are farmer girls.
We do gather certain fruits
That our town does grow so well.
If so gentle one there is,
Let her point our husbands out.
We shall give you all our fruit,
Which is sweet and does no harm.

We do have large cucumbers,
Rough and strange on the outside.
You may think they are worm-eaten,
But they're tasty and good, too.
You do take them with both hands,
Of the skin you some remove,
Open well your mouth and suck,
Once you know it does no harm.

We have melons that are large,
Like a pumpkin big in size.
For their seed we do keep these
So that many may be born.
A red tongue they all will have,
Winged feet and dragons seem.
When you look fiery they seem.
They will scare you but not harm.

We do have our own string beans,
Long and tender and most tasty.
We have others also here —
Large and hard and good when cooked —
They do make a tasty soup.
You do hold them by the tail,
Up and down the shell do shake.
Do not fear, it does no harm.

It is general today
To eat fruit at supper's end.
We do think it is most foolish.
To digest it then is hard
When we sated are and full.
Enough said, do as you like,
Use them first or use them last,
But before they do no harm.

If our husbands you show us,
This our fruit that you do see
Will be yours, a gift from us —
We are still in early bloom.
If ungrateful they will be,
We shall find some other way
For well tilled our fields must be.
We do want the feast to join.

VII

THE SONG OF BACCHUS[3]

Oh how beautiful is youth
That from us so swift does flee.
To live happy, do not wait
For tomorrow may be late.

Here is Bacchus[4] and Ariadne,
Both are lovely and in love.
Since time flees and us deceives,
They together always are.
These nymphs here and all the others
Happy live in spite of all.
To live happy, do not wait
For tomorrow may be late.

These young satyrs happy are
And in love with all these nymphs.
Through the woods and in all caverns
They besiege them day and night.
By their Bacchus filled with ardor,
They now dance in spite of all.
To live happy, do not wait
For tomorrow may be late.

And these nymphs do hold it dear
By their satyrs to be trapped.
Only rude and most vile people
Can oppose now Love's appeal.
Now together nymphs and satyrs
Sing and dance in spite of all.
To live happy, do not wait
For tomorrow may be late

3. This is Lorenzo's most effective presentation of the fundamental theme of time that slips by (see p. 315, n. 1 to *Ballads for Festive Occasions*). The invitation to enjoy life is tinged by a melancholy that is characteristic of Lorenzo and also other poets of the fifteenth century. The general theme, but with different tonality, appears in Ovid, *Ars amatoria* 1.525ff.

4. Bacchus is the god of wine, among other things, and Ariadne, who had been abandoned by Theseus, became his wife. Nymphs (Bacchae) and satyrs are their retinue.

On a donkey there behind
Comes Silenus[5] so old now,
But he's always drunk and happy,
Though he's ancient and fat, too.
It may be that he can't rise,
But he's gay in spite of all.
To live happy, do not wait
For tomorrow may be late.

After these there Midas[6] comes.
What he touches turns to gold.
Of what use is all this gold
If it does joy not give us?
How can happiness there be
If you thirst in spite of all?
To live happy, do not wait
For tomorrow may be late.

Everyone should listen well:
For tomorrow do not wait.
Let today make us all gay,
Men and women, young and old.
From our minds do sadness ban,
Let us feast in spite of all.
To live happy, do not wait
For tomorrow may be late.

Loving maidens and young men,
Long live Bacchus! Long live Love!
All of you play, dance and sing,
Let your hearts with sweet fire burn.
What must be will always be.
To live happy, do not wait
For tomorrow may be late.

---

5. Silenus was the tutor of the god Bacchus and is usually portrayed as old and drunk, but also wise; at times he is compared to Socrates.
6. Midas is the king who received the gift from Bacchus of turning all things to gold. The gift, which proved to be anything but beneficial, was as recompense for having rescued Silenus who had become lost.

VIII

SONG OF THE SEVEN PLANETS

From our abode we planets do here come
To all inform of what the truth there is.

From us depends all that good is and evil,
What does grieve you poor mortals and joy give.
What happens to all animals and plants,
To stones and men also from us depends.
All those who try to fight us we do strike,
But do treat well all those who honor us.

The sad and the mistrustful and the misers,
The rich, the honest and the good wise prelates,
The wrathful and impatient, brave and virile,
All pompous kings and great and wise musicians,
Shrewd orators, all liars and men of evil,
All earthly things from us derive their fate.

So splendid and so lovely, graceful Venus
All gentleness and love in you instills.
He who is touched by the sweet star's bright fire
Will always burn of beauty at the sight.
Animals, birds and fish her sweetness feel,
Because of her the world itself renews.

Come now, let's follow this auspicious star,
You handsome youths and you most lovely ladies,
The queen of love does now call out to you
To spend your days with happiness and joy.
Do not now wait for this sweet time's return
For once it has flown by it won't come back.

Of youth the sweetest time does us invite
To leave behind sad thoughts and all vain sorrows.
While this brief span of life does still endure
Let all be happy, let in love all be.[7]
With your own lot now satisfied do be[8];
Honor and wealth in vain will others seek.

---

7. Verses 21–30 repeat the ever-present invitation to love and enjoy life while it is still possible.

8. Another exhortation that occurs in Lorenzo's work is to be satisfied with your lot and the simple things of life. To desire great things is to make oneself miserable. See *Commentary* XXI, pp. 144–46.

IX

Song of the Cicadas[9]

The young women begin:

We are women as you see,
We are lovely, happy, young.

We are having a good time
As one does on Mardi Gras.
All the envious, evil tongues
Look askance if one has fun,
Then the evil tongues you see
Vent their rage by telling lies.

Most unfortunate we are
For the cicadas do prey,
They sing not just in the summer,
But they tattle the whole year.
The most evil will those speak
Who in fact most evil are.

The cicadas answer:

What we do, you lovely women,
In accord with nature is.
Many times the fault yours is
For you speak of your affairs.
Do whatever you do want,
But do please keep it a secret.

If you would just quickly act
All loose gossip you'd avoid.
Why should you make someone suffer
Just to keep him on a string?
If offend you gossip does,
Do then act while you still can.

The young women answer:

Of what worth our beauty is,
If your words can it destroy?

---

9. The "cicadas" are all the evil tongues who condemn lovers. See *Ballad* X, pp. 321–22.

Long live Love and gentleness,
Death to all who envious are.
Let the evil tongues then chatter,
We shall act while you just talk.

X

SONG OF THE BACKWARD FACES

All you see does backward go,
Everything, no matter what.
Imitate the shrimp we do,[10]
Just to do what others do.

In our day one must take care
To have eyes in back, not front,
Even so safe we are not,
For today all traitors are.
Only fools appearance heed.
Often they deceived will be.

So ourselves we do excuse
For this backward going of ours.
We do know all so do go
For it is the only way.
Those who do should then be calm
For we know that all act so.

We believe this better is
Since all do it in the rear.
If one feels that something pushes
One can see where one is leaning,
And before one enters touch,
Since there'll be no shame or hurt.

If the eyes are not behind,
One must turn and so tired get.
She'll receive many great blows,
But for shame will not dare speak.
When it's over she'll pay heed
For she'll then feel how they hurt.

Do not marvel at all this
That all women so will do,

10. Walk backwards.

They are all becoming shrewd,
Their experience doubled is.
They each other now do help
So they all the point will get.

XI

The Baker's Song

My dearest ladies, as you can now see,
Young bakers we all are and highly skilled.

All types of pastry we ourselves do bake,
Also cream puffs with sweetest cream we have.
They are quite big, but may seem small to you,
Inside they're sweet and soft on the outside.

Biscuits and dumplings we also do bake.
They do not please the eye for they are rough,
Hard they do seem outside when you touch them,
But by far better are on the inside.

If some of you now fava beans should like,
The best we have and in small pieces all.
To break them up so fine we use a pestle,
But if too hard we push, it will fall out.

Some leavened breads we make that are the best,
Even more blond than your blond tuft of hair.
We'll tell you how for we do like it so
That all we'd want is dream, make it and talk.

Flour you must from blond and hard wheat have,
Then you must take a sieve and shake it well
So that with water will the flour come out.
Together these you mix and do soak well.

Here you must have a powerful strong back,
For more you knead, the dough better does come.
If for the effort you do some drops sweat,
Just keep on kneading till you have all done.

When once the loaf is shaped, it's put to leaven.
It has then to in some warm place be put;
A little bed could quite appropriate be,
And you will wait until it has well risen.

The oven is now warm and you sweep it.
Do with your broom go back and forth in there.
Since there may be some ashes still in there
For one who bakes a lot can't keep it clean.

The bread does to the heat respond and rise,
It does puff up and does its water lose.
It goes in hard and soft it then comes out,
A mouthful of the loaf you then can make.

To bake some types of pastry or a roast,
Next to the large an oven small there is.
The same door both of them almost do have,
But not all bakers know how to use this.

Beautiful women, this our great art is.
If for your mouth you would now like to taste
Some little thing at once, do speak out now;
We ready are to have you test our art.

Three Epistles

I

Lorenzo de' Medici to Bellincioni, Sending Him to a Certain Place for the Sake of Understanding an Intention of His[1]

O Bellincion, do like Sosia[2] act
Do give wise sayings and all kinds of poems,
Then show how well you can fool one and all
With your quick hand, appearance and your charm.

At times to say some foolish things and then
Their opposite affirm may be quite wise,
So that one may think you're both mad and wise.
In the meantime you do still pluck and take.

Do everywhere act as if deaf and blind,
And do embrace, give praise, laugh and kiss often,
And as a joke do take it if you are stung.

Always do join some little coteries.
To show how little the world's honors are,
Sad stories tell of what great men[3] did lose.

    But do not talk so foolish.
Let your discourse always to the point be.
I told you how: do in Donato learn.[4]

---

1. The first two sonnets were used in a dispute with the poet Bernardo Bellinzone. They are in the traditional style of the old "tenzoni," which were a sort of poetic, but most venomous and scurrilous, correspondence between poets who had taken offense at another's actions or words. Even Dante did not disdain to take part in these. Unfortunately, the ones we have from Lorenzo are practically undecipherable.
2. Sosia is the servant in Plautus's *Amphitryon,* who is used to exemplify one who knows the art of getting along.
3. The "great men" used in the translation are given by Lorenzo in the original as Antiochus and Seleucus. These are probably Antiochus III who lost to the Romans and Seleucus I who was murdered.
4. Told to study grammar in the famous text by Donatus, the celebrated grammarian of the fourth century CE.

II

To Bernardo Bellincioni from Lorenzo de' Medici on His Return from Naples[5]

A certain distance on a scabrous path
With a fierce animal, and there at Prato
A poor and wretched harrow had so shaken
That it did jump so madly from the furrow.

But Nencia mine of it became aware,
And in the sun she put a well-pierced sieve.
A Jew then saw it and was so aggrieved
That they no longer want geometry.

That "giddiup" that the carters always shout,
When with their chests they to Piacenza go,
Make the poor donkeys crazy all become.

Since they have empty heads, so many dogs
For bones do look and all their other food,
And in the morning lazy bones wake up.

And so the Calicioni themselves arm
With a cuirass too weak, which under stress
Does not stand up and brings them to their death.

III

Laurentius Medices Hermellino Equo, Suae Puellae Utendum Misso[6]

If as Jove into a bull himself transformed,[7]
I also could your figure now assume,
My Ermellino, I would spare you now.
My treasure I would want to bear myself.

Never so far nor with such deep misgivings
Nor over the tall waves with such great fear,
I would have taken that pure angel mine,
Who now my lady is, my future glory.

---

5. The second composition addressed to Bellinzone is even less intelligible than the first.

6. Lorenzo de' Medici to Sir Ermellino about escorting his lady.

7. Jove who loved Europa changed himself into a bull, and when she mounted on his back, he kidnapped her by entering into the sea.

But since things so demand, now Ermellino,
You all alone will take this precious load,
And my desire, in safety and with care.

Be sure not to molest her with the rein,
Obey the one whom I also obey,
For Love wants us to love in such a way.

Short Stories

The Story of Giacoppo

As many know, Siena has always had an abundance of jackasses and foolish men. I do not know why this is so, whether it is the air there that naturally produces such men, or whether it is because in the beginning this tree was born of poor seed, and thus it is natural that it produce fruit in accordance with its seed. It is also said that a good son is like his father, and thus it may be that the sons do not wish to shame their fathers, and so try to behave in such a way as not to seem bastards

In any case, not many years ago in Siena there was a citizen whose name was Giacoppo Belanti, a man about forty years old, quite wealthy, but somewhat foolish. It was his fortune, or rather misfortune, to have a wife who was very beautiful. This quality is as natural for the women of Siena, as it is for the men to be somewhat foolish and pretentious. This wife of his was twenty-five years of age and was desired by a handsome young man, as is the case for all beautiful women. This gentle lady's name was Cassandra, and the young man was called Francesco. He was from Florence, but had been in Siena a long time at the university and had been in love with Cassandra all this time. From this it may be reasonable to expect that she should love him no less than he did her, especially since he was very handsome, and she then was old enough to know good from evil and to know whatever a woman can know. For in truth hers was the right age when it is best to love women, for when they are younger they are held back most times by shame and timidity, and when they are past that age they either think about it more than is convenient in such cases or, because they have lost part of their natural warmth, they show themselves to be colder than their lovers would want.

Francesco had followed the spoor all this time, but had never been able to catch the prey, and day and night he thought of nothing but of how he could satisfy this long-held desire of his. What made his desire even stronger was the fact that the only thing missing was the means and the way to accomplish it, for both sides were well disposed. The fact was that Cassandra loved him very much, although this love of hers was curbed by fear for her honor, and also by Giacoppo's jealousy, whose bearing towards her was no different than that of most husbands who have beautiful wives. The more beautiful was Cassandra, the less willingly she could bear these things, seeing that she was married to someone who by now was old, not very handsome and not very virile in love's wars. What gave her cause even more to seek new alternatives was the fact that she knew him to be a bit of a fool. All these reasons were enough to light a fire even where there was no fuel. In addition to all this, when one has a choice between good and evil, it is natural to choose the good. Had she done the opposite, she would have had to be mad and be restrained. It really seems to me that women are very unfortunate and that men have a great advantage, for a man, no matter how worthless or wicked, will always do as he pleases and marry or not marry as he chooses. A woman instead at the discretion of others, without knowing how or why, must accept whoever is given her not to incur any worse, and many are praised for what, for them, is the cause of torture every single day. It is not surprising, then, that misdeeds are discovered every day, and in truth they should be judged in accordance with a different criterion, and with greater mercy and understanding.

To return to our affairs, Cassandra and Francesco lacked only way and means to satisfy their desire. And this caused greater shame since they were the losers in a game in which they competed only with a dolt, although Giacoppo succeeded in obstructing their desires through solicitude rather than through intelligence. And so Francesco, having thought this over again and again and trusting in Giacoppo's foolishness, arrived at a plan that I shall disclose to you. First of all he pretended he had given up his love for Cassandra and continued this pretense for some time so that Giacoppo was almost reassured in this regard. He then made believe he received some letters from some relatives of his in Florence, in which they mentioned he was betrothed. This rumor first spread among his friends and companions, and since in Siena he was well known and liked, it soon spread through most of the city. Giacoppo was among those who heard this, and the news made him happier than he had been for some time, for it seemed to him that his wife was now safe, since he believed that now Francesco would have to leave Siena, or would abandon the thoughts he had had, as is the case with some men when they marry.

While Giacoppo remained without suspicion, Francesco began to say he had no intention of leaving, for he had studied and labored until that moment and did not want to abandon everything now that he was about to achieve his doctorate. He had decided, therefore, to bring his wife to Siena and keep her there until he had conveniently accomplished what he had come for. After announcing this, he rented a house not very near to Giacoppo's, but in a place Giacoppo often passed, so that he could bring his wife there since his previous lodgings were not large enough for both himself and his wife. Not much time then went by before he said he wanted to go to Florence for the wedding and bring his bride to Siena. And this he did.

Once he had come to Florence, he went to see a prostitute who was one of those who practice their profession with greater discretion, but who nevertheless do so no less than streetwalkers. Her name was Meina, and she lived in a section called Borgo Stella. She had a very beautiful face and made a good general impression. They came to an agreement so that for a certain sum she would go and stay with him for some time. She was very happy to do so, and he brought her to Siena accompanied by respectable people and said she was his bride. Since everyone believed this, the gentle ladies of Siena welcomed her and invited her many times. Wicked and shrewd as she was, she well knew how to hide her many stains under a beautiful and ladylike appearance and show herself to be most honest and disgusted by anything deplorable.

She had been well taught by Francesco as to what she should do, and so at times she showed herself at a window that opened on a street through which Giacoppo often passed, as we said, since it was convenient for some of his chores. Since she was often at this window, it was Giacoppo's misfortune to look at her once, for she looked at him kindly and with a happy expression, so that a desire for spring flowers arose in him, although spring had long gone by. And he began to reason with himself: "This is really wonderful. Francesco has been after my wife for so long and has never been able to make her smile at him, and he is young and handsome, while, I, old as I am, have been favored by this woman in such a brief time. It looks as if Francesco will be like Mainardi's proverbial dog that attacked to bite, but was bitten instead."

Moved by conceit no less than by love, he began to go by there often. Since he found a better welcome day by day, he began to boast to young people and would say to them: "The fact is that older men know how to act. You spend all your life courting and will never achieve anything, while I, old as you can see, have lately had such wonderful luck that you would buy at any price. That is all I'll say." But in spite of all these words, he couldn't find a way to approach her and have a one-to-one meeting with her as one does in the confessional. The woman then, who had herself called Bartolomea for the sake of decorum and to hide her past, was forced to act since he did not. She sent a maid with a letter to him in which she said she was dying with desire for him and that he should help her for God's sake for she thought he had cast a spell on her. Giacoppo, beside himself with joy, sent her an answer as foolish as he was himself. Not much time went by before she, after having first shown him that it was very difficult to arrange matters, gave him an appointment one night, saying that Francesco had gone to stay somewhere with a Sienese friend of his.

It seemed to Giacoppo that night took a thousand years to arrive, but when it did and the appropriate signal had been given, Giacoppo found himself in Bartolomea's house. She did not forget any of those things that are done by one who is burning with love and took Giacoppo into a bedroom and made him get under the bed, saying that he would have to stay there until she made a certain maid go to sleep, for she wanted the affair to remain a secret. And he did so and remained there about two and a half hours. When Bartolomea returned to him, she said he had to be patient and showed that she was very sorry for his discomfort. While they were together she would scratch his face, poke him in the eyes, and at times she would bite him, leaving a mark, and would say that she did this through love. Thinking that these were the ways of lovers, he not only remained quiet and patient, but it seemed to him that he was in seventh heaven. When the final point was reached for which lovers pine and endure such travail, Giacoppo, like the old man he was, made a tremendous effort and with great suffering succeeded in his enterprise, and so on. Making believe that she was amazed that at his age he was so virile, she caused the poor fool to risk death and do what did not seem possible at all for him. In conclusion, he would return home more dead than alive, broken and scarred, but thinking he had been in heaven, and he would then have to engage in another battle with his wife. To hide his transgression, he would have to do in one night what at other times would have been not only difficult, but impossible for him to do in a year.

Instructed by Francesco, Bartolomea continued to show the same regard for Giacoppo, for she did not want the game to end there, and although he came there often, nothing much would happen except that he returned home well scratched and bitten. This went on for many months and many a time. It constituted an experience as wonderful in deed as in words. Giacoppo, moved by conceit, kept on boasting of his happiness with young and old. He did not know that he was weaving the net in which he would be caught. Things went on in this way for a good length of time until Lent arrived, and Bartolomea begged Giacoppo to give her a holiday at least during those sacred days, for it was time to think of their souls, although it seemed hard for her to be without him for a while. These words moved Giacoppo to go to confession and give an account of his sins.

Giacoppo's old confessor was a Franciscan friar who was called Brother Antonio della Marca, with whom Francesco had earlier come to an agreement as to what he should do, since he knew that he would be confessing Giacoppo. Of the seven good deeds of charity, Brother Antonio valued helping those in distress, and although he was a friar, he wanted to prove as true the saying that there is no entrapment or betrayal in which someone of this order is not involved, and so he had consented to Francesco's plans without much difficulty. When Giacoppo had knelt before him for confession, he then started to question him as usual. When it came to the sin of luxury, Giacoppo began to tell of his affair with Francesco's wife, as he believed. At which point the friar stopped and said: "Alas Giacoppo, how could the devil's temptation have such power over you that you let yourself fall into this unpardonable sin? Neither I, the pope nor Saint Peter himself, if he were to be reborn, have the least authority to absolve you of this sin." And then Giacoppo said: "But I have heard you say that there is no sin so great that it cannot find absolution." Brother Antonio then answered: "That is true. But one would have to do something that I know you would never accept." Giacoppo then said: "In order to save my soul there is nothing I would not do. I'd even sell myself and my wife." And Brother Antonio answered: "If that is what you think, I'll tell you, but it seems certain to me that you will promise it, but then will never do it." And Giacoppo replied: "I am surprised at you. I love my soul more than anything on earth." And brother Antonio: "Oh well then, I'll tell you. Have you not heard it said that the sin of infamy and of things that man obtains unlawfully cannot find absolution unless restitution is made? And so is this, for having stolen the honor of that woman and her husband, your sin is irremissible unless you make restitution, and restitution cannot be made unless you bring her husband, or if unmarried her closest relative, to stay with your wife as many times as you have been with his. And if you have no wife, then with your closest female relative. And we read that when David committed adultery, he gave his wife to the one whose wife he had taken, and thus he was pardoned. And so you can see what you must do."

When he heard the friar's words, Giacoppo thought he had acted foolishly and said to himself: "I now see that I am the one who will play the role of Mainardo's dog." Then he turned to the friar and said: "O my spiritual father, although it seems most difficult, yet I must love my soul more than anything else on earth, and I must not be ashamed to do what David did, he being a king, and I a mere Sienese citizen. So that by all means I wish to save my soul above anything else." Hearing Giacoppo's holy words, the friar without a word embraced him and kissed his forehead. After holding him for some time, he said: "O my spiritual son, I see that God's grace enlightened you, and I see you proceed in a direction that will accomplish your mind's desire. May you be blessed a thousand times. I see now that the matter will be resolved well, may our Savior be thanked. I let you know that in spite of all this your sin is so grave that it cannot be absolved without a particular penance, and I have decided that you should go to Rome for the remission of this and the other sins of yours. In this manner one gains eternal glory and spends this life happily. So then, my blessed son, go and put into practice what you have promised." And then he gave him his blessing.

Rising from kneeling before the priest, Giacoppo returned home oppressed by his thoughts. He engaged in great debates with himself, but in the end his conscience had the best of it, and he decided to go to Francesco to give him back his honor. Here he was seized by another difficulty, for he did not know how he could tell Francesco all this without incurring great danger. Finally he thought he had found a way to save himself and, overcome by conscience and thinking that it would be safer to do so now during the holy period than at other times, one day he went and said to him: "Francesco, I have always loved you as a son, and by age you could be one. Temptation has now led me to sin in a way of which I deeply repent. Since God will forgive me, I beg you to forgive me also, and before I say anything else promise me and swear that you will not harm me and will forgive me for the sake of our Lord's passion for an injury I have inflicted upon you." Francesco then answered him: "I have always respected you as a father, and for the love of God and the holy period in which we are, first of all, and for the love I bear you next to that, I promise and swear to forgive any injury you may have done me, even if you should have killed my father."

Giacoppo threw himself down before him and said: "I'll never tell you unless on my knees before you." Francesco made him rise with great effort and prepared himself to hear what he knew better than the speaker. And when Giacoppo had told everything in the midst of tears, Francesco said: "You were wise to make me promise, for were it not for that, before I left you I should have done something that neither you nor that whore of my wife nor I afterward would have liked. But I think more of my soul than you have thought of me, and in few words I now forgive you for everything. Now go away from my sight." Thinking that he had accomplished a great deal, Giacoppo then said to him: "You must listen to a few words and help me to have God's forgiveness." And he then told him that it was necessary for him to stay with his wife. Francesco then answered: "I did not promise you this. I do not want to be a ruffian and a traitor like you. It's enough that I have forgiven you for such a serious injury. Don't speak of it for I don't want to hear anything more, and I again tell you to go away from my sight to avoid something worse."

Giacoppo was afraid that something more serious would happen, and so he left and went back to the friar. He told him how things had gone and when he came to the part about Francesco refusing to hear anything about going to stay with his wife, the friar said: "You haven't accomplished anything, for it is necessary that you restore his honor in this way, otherwise it's as if you hadn't done anything." Giacoppo did not know how he could ever go back to Francesco and so he said to the friar: "Perhaps it would be better if you sent for him. I'll be present while you make him understand that it is not a sin. Perhaps he will agree to do for you what he refused to grant me." The friar then said: "This is a good plan. But I don't know him. I'll send one of the young brothers with you, and you will show him Francesco from afar, so that it won't seem that I'm calling him for this." Having reached this agreement, Giacoppo left with the young monk to whom he pointed out Francesco to whom the monk delivered the message.

Francesco came to the church without any remonstrances, and there he found the friar in a certain room next to his cell. He made believe he was having a very heated discussion with the friar, while actually the two of them were laughing about the trick for quite a while. The friar then called Giacoppo and said to Francesco: "You must in any case help poor Giacoppo, not for his sake for he doesn't deserve it, but for the sake of Lord Jesus who will lavish his grace on you and will not consider a sin what you will do for the love you bear him, and I will be obliged to you with Giacoppo." At these words Giacoppo threw himself down at Francesco's feet and begged him to grant him the favor of going to stay with his wife. Francesco made believe he was moved to tears and said: "Oh well, I'll do it. I wish to make God a present of this injury and of the pardon I grant you, and for his love I'll do what you request, although it seems something very hard for my conscience to accept."

While he was most happy at this answer, Giacoppo began to have other doubts, that is, how was he going to convince his wife. Trusting that he could do with her whatever he wanted, he went home, and it seemed to him that he had found a neat trick for putting horns on his own head. Accordingly, as soon as he was home he began to cry and sob loudly so that his wife would have cause to ask him why he was crying. And this happened just as he had planned, for she began at once to ask the reason for all those tears. And Giacoppo explained: "I have good reason to cry for I am damned and cannot save my soul." His wife, who had been informed of all this, began to cry more loudly than him and said: "Oh my, how can this be? What have you done? Is there no remedy?" The husband then said: "There is, but it is very difficult to do." At this Cassandra said: "Why don't you tell me? If it is something that can be done, we'll do it." And then Giacoppo answered: "I'll tell you. It's up to you whether I'll be damned or saved." And he began to tell her about the matter. When he came to the part about what she would have to do, she appeared to be very upset. To make it short, it was necessary for him to kneel before her and beg her for this boon. Once Giacoppo had convinced her, he ran to Francesco in order to receive absolution more quickly and said: "Tonight will be the proper time. You'll come to supper with me and then in God's name you'll begin to help me atone for this great sin."

Francesco had never been as happy, but he pretended that this was a piece of bad news and made him understand that by going there he was granting him an extraordinary favor, but this did not prevent him from feeling that it would take a thousand years for night to arrive. When night did come, he went to Giacoppo's house. After an abundant supper, he left Giacoppo in the dining room and with his so-desired Cassandra went to her bedroom and in her bed. We must all believe that there matters went differently than had been the case when Giacoppo had stayed with Bartolomea. For the atonement of the rest of his sins, it was necessary for Francesco to return there many more times. Since later Giacoppo went to Rome for penance as the friar had ordered, it was a rare night that Francesco was not with Cassandra. Thus was their long-lasting love rewarded. May it please God to give us the same ending for ours.

Thus jealous Giacoppo had to beg on bare knees as a favor what Francesco desired above all else on earth in order to be absolved for an error for which he had done penance before sinning, this through the service of Brother Antonio, who acted as some clergymen are accustomed to act. For while clergymen many times do infinite good, they also at times are the cause of infinite evil because of the excessive faith men foolishly place in them.

The Story of Ginevra

I think everyone knows that Pisa was an ancient and most noble city, for before Fortune was pleased to put an end to its tranquil state and bring it to its ultimate decadence, it did many things in peace and war that for their greatness deserve to be remembered and celebrated among men for a long time. At that time there was in Pisa a most noble family of great fame that bore, and still bears, the name of Lanfranchi. Among the many noble men of that family there was a young man, twenty years old, Luigi by name, who surpassed not only the members of his family, but also all the other young men of Pisa in wealth and beauty, just as he did in nobility of blood. Although the above qualities may be deemed to be goods bestowed by Fortune, he added to them such talents both spiritual and physical that one could deem him to be perfect in every respect. He was so gifted in letters, music, both instrumental and singing, dance and equitation that even if anyone had devoted all his life to one of these subjects, it would have been too little to equal the result of one of Luigi's accomplishments. A necessary consequence of the above was that in his city he was the most respected and beloved young man, not only of his own period, but in all the history of Pisa.

It seemed then that he must have been the happiest man in the whole world, except for the fact that Fortune, always envious of one's well-being, under guise of a great blessing put an end to his happy life and from the happiest man on earth turned him into the most doleful. This misfortune of his came about as will be told. In Pisa, as well as in many other places, it is the custom in the period before the beginning of Lent to indulge in games, feasts and amusements with a view to lessen the discomfort of the abstinence that Lent brings Actually most times this has the opposite effect for the more one enjoys these feasts, the more sorry he is to abandon them and the more he dislikes a tenor of life he must adopt by necessity rather than because he is tired of festivities. It happened then that among other festivities there was a very elegant ball attended by all the beautiful and noble women of Pisa, a city that had many who were most beautiful. It doesn't seem necessary for me to say whether young men were present, for I think that everyone knows that where many beautiful women gather, there will appear many young men. Just as a natural law decrees that iron will be attracted by a magnet, so young men whether for good fortune or misadventure are attracted by those things that most times are the cause of infinite sorrow, rather than any consolation or pleasure, and counterbalance a brief and painful pleasure with long and incomparable grief and sorrow.

Among the other women at this ball there was a fifteen-year-old girl whose name was Ginevra, of the ancient and noble Grifi family. Although there were many beautiful women present, she surpassed all the others in beauty so much that everyone had reason to believe she was divine rather than a mortal. She was adorned with gentle manners and womanly virtues no less than beauty, and she made not only the young fall in love with her, who are naturally so inclined, but also those who, having lost their youthful ardor, scorn or care little for the bouts of love, I know not whether because of age or because of greater experience. It was Luigi's misadventure, then, to find himself with many others at this ball and to look at her like the others and so begin to feel the sting of love and savor a food he had never tasted, while in the past he had scorned and condemned those who indulged in it. Not much time went by until he could think of nothing else and take pleasure in nothing but in examining all the ways and means by which to please this woman and gain her favor. Like most others, in the beginning he wanted to keep his ardent love a secret from others, and this caused a redoubling of his suffering, for as our own Petrarch says: "A secret flame more ardent burns."[1]

As time went by, he no longer could keep secret what no one has ever been able to hide, and so like all wretched lovers, he went from one extreme to the other and with festivities, balls and jousts began to show openly what until then he had kept secret since he had been somewhat ashamed of it. Although everyone knew of his ardent desire, as we said, he acted so prudently and nobly that instead of being condemned for it, as had been the case for many others, he gained greater favor among his fellow citizens. Being wise, Ginevra became aware of all this, and although as a girl she was timid and embarrassed, she nevertheless within herself valued him greatly and secretly felt an honest affection for him. Luigi had never been in love before, and so could not understand this, and therefore grieved, thinking that in her heart she was as pitiless as her face and expression seemed to indicate. He did not know that "No one who's loved can then refuse to love,"[2] and that:

1. Petrarch, *Rime* 207.66, "...chiusa fiamma è più ardente."
2. Dante, *Inferno* 5.103, "Amore a nullo amato amar perdona."

"No heart so hard can be that moved is not
By prayers and tears and love, no will so cold
That never warmed can be by a true love."[3]

Grieving and being in sorrow as much as one can be and not being able to find a remedy for his illness, he decided one day to reveal his situation to a great friend and companion of his. This friend was from Genoa, Maffio Grimaldi by name and a young man of good customs. He had been in Pisa a long time to tend to some affairs of his, and in this long space of time he had developed a real friendship with Luigi, although he was somewhat older than him, for he was about twenty-five. Because of this, one day Luigi, who trusted him completely, went to see him, and after exchanging some words he began to speak as follows: "Maffio, it seems to me that because of our long-lasting friendship and affection we must participate in each other's occurrences, whether happy or doleful, so that what one feels the other will feel also. By making the other participate, we redouble the joy of happy events and find a remedy for the others when possible, or at least diminish the suffering by speaking of it and giving vent to our feelings when there is no remedy. Since at present I am seeking a remedy for an unfortunate event, I should think I had acted against the laws of friendship if I did not confer with you first. I have faith in your prudence and experience, for I know that you have been in this same situation, and no less faith in the love and affection you have for me. I, as you may have noticed, have removed my thoughts and my desire from everything, and I seek and wish for nothing on this earth except to please a woman whom I have made absolute mistress, not only of my will, but also of my thoughts and words, for I can imagine, speak or think of no one except her.

"Love has achieved full sway over me so that it isn't sufficient that I like her above everything else, but he has made me find all other things unpleasant and hateful. And to show that he has all the power he wants over human minds, power that once I thought he did not have, Cupid has made me love a woman who, in exchange for a burning and unrestricted love, bears equal ill will and hatred towards me, as it seems to me.

---

3. Petrarch, *Rime* 265.12–14 "…non è sì duro cor che lagrimando / pregando, amando, talor non si smova, / ne si freddo voler, che non si scalde."

And I, I don't know how, am so bound and blinded that the more she shows her dislike for me, the more does my ardent desire grow. What shows my error even more is that when it seems to me that she is doing something improper in my regards, I am the first to find excuses for her action and justify whatever offense against me. Not to go to great length, I tell you that my situation is as bad as possible and beg you to help and counsel me in the name of the trust that has always governed our friendship.

"My case is different from that of many other lovers who voluntarily fall in love just to pass the time or because they have nothing else to do. In my case we must seek a way to just keep me alive rather than to make me live happily, and I have lost all hope of this, except that which I have in the faithful and wise counsel and help I expect from you. So then, take the helm of this storm-tossed vessel, and assume the cure for the ailing body just as if you had to govern yourself rather than me. I am ashamed of using so many words, especially since deeds are needed, and also because words are necessary with those who either have difficulty in understanding or will grant one's request with ill grace, both things that I have never seen or known in you. From now on, therefore, I'll not waste time in telling you of my suffering, since I am certain that you, having been in love, know what it is. Instead, I shall expect from you your counsel and aid, and if they will not help me, I'll believe that no one can."

Maffio heard the words that Luigi had uttered with many sighs and tears, and being experienced, he understood the source of all this and began to smile to himself. He then turned to Luigi and spoke to him as follows: "You'll think, Luigi, that since I smile at your suffering, either I do not believe what you say or that I do not have much affection for you, and thus can laugh at what I see makes you suffer and cry. Neither of these things is true. The fact is that I have previously fallen in the same error as you and know that your suffering is greater than you have said, and I laugh because the illness is less lethal than it appears. To observe the rule of good physicians who first try and must find a remedy for the patient's major ill and needs, I'll tell you that what you consider the major evil is really the minor one, and those things that now seem to you difficult or impossible, you will with time judge to be possible and easy more than the others, in fact that they cannot but be so.

"If I have understood your passionate words, it seems to me that your greatest and heartfelt suffering is due to the belief that you love without being loved in return. My answer is that you would be right to complain if it were so. But since God and nature ordained that the condition of women is what it is, and since I have had a thousand proofs of this in my time, I cannot believe in any way that only this woman of yours could break or change what until now no other woman has changed. It is natural for any man or woman to love in return on seeing they are loved. It would be a sign of a brutal nature or of a stony heart to do the opposite. You may then conclude that this woman you see as your mortal enemy does not have in her heart the asperity her expression shows. You will agree with me that this woman seems to be most wise and discrete in all other matters, perhaps more than is natural for a woman. Since this is so, you must not believe that she could have no affection for you, since you have never offended her and have always honored her with all your actions and love her as much as it seems to me you do love her. In your case you act like other lovers who have very sharp sight and acute intellect when it comes to looking at their companions' affairs and are blind and unreasonable when it comes to their own. In this matter you are looking at your side of things and not at hers. For since she is of a noble family, wealthy, beautiful as you can see, it would not be proper for her to show that she is in love. You may be certain, however, that secretly you are always in her heart, but she hides her love better than you, for she has greater reasons to do so.

"I remember that once I was in love with a gentle woman, and for a while I thought she was making fun of me and that she scorned me. And then from her own lips it became clear that while I thought she scorned me she had as much affection for me as I for her. There is a natural characteristic in lovers that is lacking in all others. While other men easily believe that things are as they would wish, lovers put the least faith in what they would want most, since every day they feel the many changes Fortune brings about in their affairs. Fortune actually rules universally, but its power is greater over lovers than anything else. Although at times it shows itself to be contrary, it isn't that finally it does not lead one to the desired end. So then, my dear Luigi, I'll remind you of two things: First, since I know that in this enterprise you will encounter a thousand adverse situations, as is the case for all lovers, and these perhaps may make you change your mind and purpose, I ask you to consider these evils as if they were not aimed at you, but at someone else, and to pursue sincerely and with good spirits what you have once well begun. For in the end nothing is difficult for one who really wants it, and he who persists will triumph. We see that men have had the desire to fly, and they have done so. Is it not easier to find what the soul seeks if one wants to be loved, since this is something natural to man? Thus the first precept I offer you is that you pursue your enterprise forcefully.

"The second is that in this love affair of yours you do not leave untried anything that will lead to the satisfaction of your desire. For if you do not leave anything untried, the result will be as I'll now tell you: If your desire is fulfilled, you will have accomplished what you wanted; if it is not, you will at least have satisfied yourself, and the one you love will think the more of you. In conclusion, it seems to me that tonight you and I must see if there is any way or means by which you can let this woman know how you feel. Tomorrow morning I'll see you again, perhaps with some good plan, for the Gospel says that he who seeks shall find, and the door shall be opened to one who knocks. I also hope that Fortune, who never abandons lovers, will let us think of something that could dissipate most of your worries and make you as happy as you are now in grief. Just as the sorrows of love are greater than all others, so also are its joys greater than the rest, and I hope to make you have proof of this before long. Farewell now and go with God."

Luigi heard Maffio's wise words, and his arguments were so successful that he put aside the weight of a great part of the worries that had beset him. Having turned his great sadness into great joy, he returned home happy and lighthearted. Although he had gone to bed after supper, Maffio's words had made such an impression upon him that he, not only could not sleep, but could hardly remain in bed or at home. It seemed to him that daylight was taking a thousand years to arrive, and he thought of all those things that could make time appear briefer. Morning had hardly arrived, when he went to Maffio's house. Finding him still asleep, he woke him up and said: "My dear brother, at what point are we? Have you thought of something with which you'll rid me of my remaining ills?" And Maffio answered: "I think that by chance I've found something you will like very much. The fact is that your lady has a nurse at home with whom I have some acquaintance, and I think that in one way or another she'll do what we want."

Happier than ever, Luigi said: "Brother, I now shall let you think about the remedies needed in my situation. What you will do I'll judge to be well done, and so do what you think best." From this conversation it ensued that Maffio met the nurse who at first made some difficulties, as is their custom, but then in one way or another was convinced to agree to their plans and begin to carry letters and messages back and forth. Since Ginevra was ashamed of these things, she showed that she took offense so much that had it not been for Maffio's daily recommendations, I think Luigi would have abandoned this enterprise more than once. For Maffio spoke harshly to the nurse every day and threatened to have her dismissed and had so dejected her and Luigi that they did not seem to have any courage left for any attempt. This situation made Luigi suffer even more than his former state, for that had seemed hopeless, while this had held some hope. Since it seemed to him that Fortune was exceedingly opposed to every attempt of his, he lived in despair and every day bewailed his adversities with Maffio. He was reduced to such a state that he seemed more dead than alive, and his expression, his solitary ways and his almost changed nature showed what suffering he bore in his heart. Since Ginevra was well aware of these things, she could not help but feel some pity for Luigi, but she was held back by consideration for her honor and thus could not give any sign of affection for him. Since there could be no other satisfaction, Luigi found the only consolation and comfort in one thing only, and this was that neither night nor day did he depart from the vicinity of her house, for unable to see her as he wished, he found much comfort in being able to see at least the house where she lived.

Thus afflicted and grieving, one night near her beloved house poor Luigi heard Ginevra's voice. He listened very carefully to the voice that seemed to come from heaven, and he gathered that singing a certain song all alone she was saying:

> O Love, I see your darts do not allow
> Any defense by anyone at all.
> A girl I am as young as one can be,
> The flame I yet do feel in my heart burn.
> No longer can my heart your blows deflect,
> So much another's sorrow does wound me.
> Since you do now want me in your preserve,
> I shall come there and ready be to serve.

Luigi listened attentively and went over in his mind what he imagined its meaning could be, and from this he regained some of his lost hopes and thus began to try new ways and means to achieve his end. He did not succeed in bringing any of these to a successful end, and thus went to see Maffio in greater despair than ever and said: "I have done everything I could, and since I can no longer find anything that would give me hope of a happy life, I have decided to stay in this city no longer. I shall seek new lands so that after having taken so much pleasure in my ills, at least she will not have that of seeing me die near her. Hearing of my death rather than seeing it will diminish the joy I am certain she will feel at my sorrowful end." Maffio replied to this speech as follows: "I see you did not keep well in mind the precept I gave you, that you should be patient and be strong before Fortune's blows. Perhaps you do believe you have tried everything possible, as you say. But perhaps there is something else you haven't tried. Think about it some more and then you'll be able to speak to me more reasonably. If in one week you do not find another way, we shall then follow a plan that is better than what you now propose." And with these words he left Luigi deep in thought.

Luigi could think about nothing else day and night, and then there happened with him what happens always to those who seek something: that is, after a long search they will in the end find what they wish. Being well acquainted with the disposition of Ginevra's house, he decided to act upon a very dangerous plan, one in character with a desperate man, rather than with a reasonable one. For he preferred to come to a bad end rather than live in such bitterness and torment. Having examined everything well and giving more weight to his desire than to the danger involved, he went with Maffio to Ginevra's house one night when everyone is lost into the deepest sleep. He knew that Ginevra slept in the same bed as her mother....[4] He let a ladder of silken cord hang from the bedroom window and then, having remained dressed in a silver brocade jacket, he began to climb the ladder diligently. Although he was assailed by various fears at every rung, yet he reached the window like one made brave by Love. He found it open, for it was summer, and saw his Ginevra sleeping sweetly on one side of the bed.

The sight upset him so much and made him so fearful that he stepped on the ladder three times in order to go back. But thinking of the long time he had awaited this opportunity and

4. There is a lacuna in the text.

of all the terrible days and nights he had endured to get to this point, he made his heart into a fortress and, once he had decided, stepped down from the window with dexterity. He first of all went to the lamp that was in the room and extinguished it. He then approached the side of the bed where Ginevra was and stayed there some time, not daring to touch her, not so much for fear of being heard, as for the reverence that is always felt by those who are really struck by Love's arrows. But finally he began to find courage and began to touch her lightly above the covers. Having from the covers reached her delicate arms, which she kept uncovered above the covers, because of the heat, he kissed them lightly many times and her face also. At this point Ginevra woke up, and although she thought she was dreaming, yet she opened her eyes and began to look around. Seeing that she was awake, Luigi did not know what to do. He finally covered her mouth with his hand so that she could not cry out, and began to speak as follows....[5]

5. The story has been left unfinished, but it is not difficult to imagine an ending for it.

III. PHILOSOPHICAL AND DEVOTIONAL WORKS

Disputation

Chapter I

By sweeter thoughts attracted and here led,
The bitter civil contests I had fled
To give my soul in tranquil port some respite.

My native city and its sacred walls
I left behind to rest from that dire burden[1]
That so impedes from rising my poor nature,

And brought my heart away from all of that
To this, a life free, tranquil and secure:
The little joy that here on earth is left.

Having arrived in a most lovely valley
By that tall mountain[2] from the sun protected
That does retain its name in spite of age,

I sat there where a laurel tree gave shade,
There almost at the foot of that tall mountain,
And there my heart was cleared of all my worries.

On my left side there rose a limpid spring
Whose cool and sweet clear water gently flowed
Into the meadow there, where I did face.

The tender young green grass was here adorned
By flowers of all sorts, both red and white,
And here my dull tired body I did rest.

More sweet and varied fragrances were there
Than those the phoenix[3] gathers at the end,
When seized at last by pangs of fatal pain.

---

1. Earthly cares.
2. The name of the mountain is Giovi, and Lorenzo plays with the word "giovine" (young). This is where the Medici villa at Careggi was (and is) located.
3. Mythical bird of Arabia that every five hundred years built a pyre of fragrant woods on which to burn itself and then be re-born from the ashes.

In such a heavenly and lovely place
The sky can never threaten with dark clouds,
Nor can there be the signs of storms and ice.

In this most lovely haven all alone,
I did enjoy my company at peace,
Surrounded only by my own sweet thoughts.

In contemplating nature I was lost,
When the sweet sound I heard of a bagpipe
That could induce the player's flock to dance.

To that sweet shade, to that sweet flowing balm
The piper came to spend the warmest hours
And was amazed to find me resting there.

He stopped a while until he did recover
His lost aplomb and then he did greet me
As shepherds do, and thus he spoke to me:

"Do tell me why you have to this place come.
Why have you this harsh path preferred and left
The forum and great palaces and temples?[4]

What do you now contemplate in these woods?
Is it so that our own poor way of life
By contrast will enhance your pomp and wealth?"

And then I said: "No luxury, no wealth,
No honors can life gentle and sweet make
Like you have here away from civil strife.

No treachery or hate can ever reign
Among you peasants and most happy shepherds,
Nor can your furrows let ambition grow.

Wealth is here held without that hateful envy,
For all of you the weakest roots greed has,
Content you are with happiness serene.

Here one does not say what he does not mean,
Nor to the heart contrary the tongue is,
As it is where those who lie best are happiest.

Nor do I think that in this purest air
The heart is troubled while the lips do smile,
As it is where those who best hide are wisest.

4. See Sonnet XXI of the *Commentary*, pp. 144–46.

To those whose nest within the city lies
One who in goodness trusts does foolish seem,
And he seems wise who only cunning is.

Utility of friendship is the measure.
Just think how wonderful that love can be
That Fortune can affect and so vitiate!

How can that heart at any time find peace
That greed can dominate and so torment
And to excessive hope or fear can drive?

But you among these mountains dwell in peace
And have no evil thoughts that you torment,
Nor full of fears do you await bad news.

With greatest ease your thirst a fresh brook quenches,
Your hunger with sweet fruits you do abate.
Of all desires the measure nature is.

In summertime soft leaves your bed do form,
In winter in your humble huts dry hay,
Away from rain and from the season's frost.

Your clothes are not like those that many seek
Beyond the seas in far-away strange lands.
Soft skins and furs do fully you content.

How sweet sleep is among these leafy trees
That worry does not break and with cool streams
That murmuring accompany your snores.

I think that often all the sylvan nymphs
At this so clear and lovely spring do gather
And raise a song that more than earthly is.

At their sweet song so limpid and so soft,
At the sweet sound of pipes and at your verses,
Sweet Philomel[5] or other birds will answer.

If with another should a bull contend,
I think it would no less real pleasure give
Than the fierce jousts in our arenas seen,

Where you, the judge, reward the one who's best
With a green garland while the loser does,
Wretched and angry, with much shame remain.

---

5. Nightingale.

Happy is he who does not more desire
Than what he needs, and not the one who lacks
What his insatiable mind ever covets.

Endless desire from us is never absent,
But grows, and growing does torment us more.
The greater the desire, greater the lack.

Rich seems to me the one who happy is
With only what he has, and not the one
Who values more what he possesses not.

A peaceful poverty, a great wealth is,
If for necessities all is provided.
Rich or not rich depends on what we think.

I do not know how some can blame or scorn
One who of his condition happy is,
While they praise those who do depend on others.

Your life, O shepherd, seems to be to me
The one that most gives peace to human minds,
If such a thing can in our world be had."

No longer did the shepherd wish to hear,
But roaming with his eyes around, at times
He did give sign of a desire to speak.

Then he began with a most friendly sigh:
"I do not know how you can happy deem
This life that really torture is, not life.

Nor do I know why you so much do like
That which you praise, but then you do avoid,
And why you do not seek such restful peace.

Oh, why do you with lies the truth now cover?
If so it seems to you, embrace this truth
That you do so desire with words and covet.

But great the distance is from thought to deed,
And at first sight a path can lovely seem
That trodden then becomes both hard and thorny.

What is there that does not our life so sadden?
Like animals exposed to cold and heat,
This is the sweetness that our life gives us.

In wintertime with frigid cold and snow,
Our clothes do bear on every single hair
Ice crystals that can easily be seen.

At times a storm torments us with such force
That though we shelter seek behind some rocks,
The wind still strikes us and the cruel tempest.

Our so soft mattress nothing is but soil,
Our food the same as that of all wild beasts.
This must us comfort when most tired we are.

If a sweet lamb the cruel wolf should seize
I would then grieve no less than you would, too,
If a great treasure should to you be lost.

You for your greater loss do not grieve more
Than I will do for mine, for in proportion
My little and your great the equal are.

Fortune does me control in lesser things,
But if she should take arms against those things,
Greater my grief would be and have no rivals.

If I should lose a vase of clay or wood,
No less would I then grieve for this cheap thing
Than you for one of gold, that would seem greater.

Nature did not decree of wood and gold
The value. That of them one vile should be,
The other splendid, we ourselves decreed.

If the cheap vase I love as much as you
The gold, then we are both in Fortune's hands,
For equally we love and do desire.

I think that in accord all men can be
That Fortune is our rigid enemy,
For his own cross she gives to each to bear.

An ancient truth I, though a shepherd, know:
No one is satisfied with his own life.
To all of us another's happier seems.

I shall remain where destiny decrees,
You must your star then follow where it leads.
Both will accuse our fate, for every one,

Not only us, dissatisfied must be.

Chapter II

My ears were all intent to catch his words,
When to itself another voice drew them,
And its sweet harmony did then them bind.

So sweet a lyre did it sound like to me
That I thought Orpheus had on earth returned,
Or he who with his lyre encircled Thebes.[6]

"From heaven has perhaps the lyre now fallen
That had among the stars been fixed,"[7] said I.
"The sky will be without its splendid sign,

Or maybe, as that ancient one did say,
The soul of one of these transmigrate did
Into this player as had been ordained."[8]

And while my eyes directed by my ears
Searched deep among the leaves and the thick brush
Of such sweet harmony to find the source,

They all at once did see, the ears did hear
And able was to grasp the noble mind
The doctrine and the music and the player:

It was Marsilio, there in Montevecchio,[9]
Who was endowed by heaven with all virtues
So that in him could mortals heaven see.

The sacred Muses he did always love,
No less did he true wisdom ever love
So that one did the other not exclude.[10]

Worthy he was of our sincere respect
And to us both in common as a father,
So that we stood delighted to see him.

---

6. The sound of Amphion's lyre was such that it moved stones to form the wall of Thebes.

7. Orpheus's lyre had been transformed into a constellation after his death.

8. Perhaps the soul of one of these two has transmigrated into this one, in accordance with Pythagoras's theory of the transmigration of souls.

9. Marsilio Ficino, a famous and revered neo-Platonic philosopher at Lorenzo's court, met with his "academy" at Montevecchio.

10. Did not separate poetic wisdom from the philosophical and religious.

Happy no less, he did stop at the spring,
And when he had been seated on a rock,
The music he did stop and turned to words:

"Already tired I was and oh so weary,
When some most kindly god my steps did guide
And led me here where happily I rest.

But first let me you, Lauro,[11] greet, and you
Alfeo, who by age my father are,
And of all shepherds surely the most wise.

I'm not surprised to see you, shepherd, here
For often do we meet here at the spring
And in the shade of some beech trees at times.

But to see Lauro on this sylvan mountain
To great surprise does now give rise in me,
Not that I am not glad to see you here.

To leave your city, who did counsel you?
Of public life the burden you do know,
And of your family that you must bear."

"To think of them," I did to him then say,
"Those matters cause me suffering and grief,
So great the burden is that I must carry.

From civic burdens I did draw away
To seek some peace for my most weary soul
In pastoral life here that I do envy.

Unbearable is so our way of life
That by comparison much better is
The pastoral, though he deny it does.

That was what our discussion was about,
But when your lyre was heard, its sweetest sound
At once did put an end to our dispute.

But now since God has given you to us,
Do tell of us who the wrong path pursues
And in our lives if the true good is found.

11. Lauro is the name Lorenzo uses in his poems to identify himself. It was also used for Lorenzo by other poets because of its traditional connotations (for instance, Lauro is the tree whose leaves symbolize poetic glory).

Which life is that which the true good adorns,
Even though fate to us it does deny?
Is it God-given or by man bestowed?

Every art, every doctrine, every action,
Every choice seems to this true good to flow,
Just as return does water to the sea.

But what this good may be, you must us tell,
For you do know. So then you must undo
This knot that binds our heart and makes it grieve."

"I must," Marsilio said, "my heart turn there
Where you have turned your own and are intent,
Although it is a steep path to pursue.

For those who truly have the good accepted,
Easier it is to see where it is not
Than it perceive in darkness so enveloped.

So much more light will love this burden make
For nothing to true love can be denied,
For one are all those that true love has seized.

Let no one think before I do go on
He can a perfect good and true now find
While still the soul is to the senses bound.[12]

This has wrought He who power wields supreme
Lest mortals bound in darkness and so blind
Should only to this earth their thoughts confine.

If with of good the image they are blind
And still from the true path they stray, what would
They do if of this earth the good they thought?[13]

True good one is, no more no less than one
That God as a reward does seem to keep
To grant to those whose lives well spent have been.

Those mortals who proud and conceited try
Ahead of time to seek this perfect good
Will be like those who will unripe fruit pick.

---

12. The true good is not to be found in earthly life.

13. Although men on earth have the image or reflection of the eternal good in heaven, they cannot follow the true path. What would they do if they thought the good was of this earth?

If they when sour should eat the ones they picked,
So bitter in their mouths the taste will be
That soon they must their enterprise abandon.

They do not know how sweet they later are,
But sorely frightened by their first attempt
From error to more serious error go.

But to prolong all this you and me burdens,
Nor do I want to be like all those others
Who heaven stretched like one does to a pelt.[14]

This good, I say, this treasure that so many
Have sought and have described in many tongues
God keeps up there in his celestial choir

Where passions and all ardors will die out.
And since so many goods by us are seen,
This is the way it first from others differs.

Three are the types of human goods that may
Be in our minds conceived[15] — thus do begin
Those who would simple make this tangled question.

The first are those that Fortune gives and takes;
Others does Nature to the body give;
The soul does the third type gather within.

The first into four groups divided is:
Dominion, riches, honor and good will[16]:
These last two both the same defect do have.

Just as the sway does of the first grow, so
Suspicion must. The more your subjects are
The more you must as enemies them count.

---

14. Those who speak of heaven at length and in great detail.

15. What follows is to be found in Ficino's *De felicitate,* in which he mentions Lorenzo's "elegant" work on the same subject. The priority of Ficino's work or Lorenzo's is debatable. Although Ficino refers to Lorenzo's work, it does not mean necessarily that Lorenzo's work came first, for Ficino may be making a courteous gesture towards Lorenzo. In any case, it is a fact that Ficino was the philosopher-teacher and Lorenzo his "disciple." Here Ficino begins with the Aristotelian (*Ethica Nicomachea* 1.8) differentiation of goods as of Fortune, physical and spiritual. He then shows the uselessness and precariousness of Fortune's goods until the end of the chapter.

16. "Grazia," the benevolence of others or good will.

It seems that this the true good was for Caesar,
Yet as he lived the truth he came to see:
He who does most command the most does serve.

The second good is to possess great wealth.
Since this desire can sated never be,
Neither can one a peaceful moment find.

Moreover evil taken is for good,
And foolishly ourselves we do entrust
To what will harm us more than it can help.

Not for itself, but for diverse effects
Is gold desired or praised. It is not then
The true good that it did to Midas[17] seem.

So beautiful and splendid honor seems
That many fools in it the true good see,
But it is not the good of which I speak.

What others can control can't a good be.
This all depends from those who honor you.
They often praise but know not whom or why.

In fact, the more the ignorant the wise
Outnumber, so much the less honored is
He who great fame and great rewards does merit.

Often in error do we praise or blame.
Often one we do laud does it ignore.
And if he does, the praise still-born will be.

This then is not that perfect and true sweetness
That a blind man did at one time proclaim,
Whose mind was all befuddled by this error.

He who good will did take as the true good
Mistaken was, and he who did in peace
Rule all the world in this the true good saw.[18]

The danger honor faced this goodwill does
Also incur. It is by others given,
And as they wish these may it back retake.

---

17. Midas obtained the privilege of turning to gold everything he touched (Ovid, *Metamorphoses* 11.85ff.).
18. The emperor Augustus.

Thus we see that in vain we do desire
What beyond reason is in Fortune's hands,
Since all of these precarious and weak are.

In the span of a day, obnoxious Fortune
Blindly apparent goods does give and take.
Wisdom demands that we not set our minds

On what is under cruel Fortune's sway."

Chapter III

Speaking to us, this novel Plato said:
"What Fortune in its power does command
Cannot a perfect good be ever called.

The good of well-proportioned bodies may
Ever divided be in three parts only:
Being beautiful by birth, robust and healthy.

Both strength and health by slight injury struck
That good will lose that the robust Milon[19]
Was pleased to hold as the most perfect good.

Happiness, then, did never in these lie,
Nor does he find himself in tranquil port
One who by birth endowed with beauty was.

In beauty the true good Erillus[20] put.
Though beauty he possessed to an extreme,
One could not with all this deem him content.

If with great beauty is someone endowed,
That beauty without doubt will pleasure give
To others more than him who it possesses.

Nature itself this good gives or denies,
Nor can one let his hopes depend on it:
Time steals it like all flowers and destroys.[21]

19. Milon was a celebrated Greek athlete who won six times at the Olympics.
20. Carthaginian philosopher of the third century BCE. Actually for him the greatest good was wisdom.
21. The Petrarchan theme of time that destroys all things is found throughout Lorenzo's work.

But then our thoughts beyond do pass and flow
And say 'Perhaps the good is in our minds,
Which no one can control except ourselves.'

Our living soul goods has that by the wise
Can in two categories be divided:
One rational, the other that which feels.

Within it reason has a divine part.
Sense is with animals in common had,
And within it there are two diverse paths.

The first is that the senses such should be
As to perfection all their tasks fulfill,
The second sensual pleasures does regard.

Here Aristippus's[22] judgment vain did prove.
He erred and did exceedingly low aim,
Of one and other taking the defects.

Some types of animals do man surpass
Because senses they have that sharper are
Than those of our own fretting, weary souls.

Brutes, he will say, more happy than man are.
Our own sharp senses have, moreover, been
The cause of our displeasure, more than pleasure.

If evil does the good exceed, then must
Our senses with distaste more things perceive,
Nor do I know what good makes up for this.

Eternal wars are pleasures of the senses:
At first their ardor does the heart destroy;
Suspicion rules and their companion is.

Then, when depart does pleasure, comes repentance.
These sensual pleasures for as long endure
As with desire the heart does burn and roar.

For just so long the pleasure lasts of drinking
As taste is by the thirst ensnared. If thirst
Comes to an end, so too will pleasure end.

---

22. Aristippus of Cyrene, philosopher companion of Socrates in fourth century BCE.

No object with its opposite dares stay.
It is not good in fact, it is quite bad
Ever for pain to be with pleasure mixed.

Here with the sensual part we come to an end
And to the other go, if you recall,
More beautiful that rational is called.

Over two parts the rational does rule:
Natural virtue and the acquired one,
And it is thus that we divide it first.

The first is born together with our life.
Of it we all some seeds and light do have,
Just as the soul within the body is.

Sharpness of mind and memory and daring,
Good tools or evil are according to
Their use and custom, whether good or evil.

In fact, the more they're perfect, the more grief
They cause the soul, if evil their use is
As is the case most times in our blind world.

The goods acquired as we pursue our lives
Also divided are into two parts,
Thus we have risen upwards step by step.

Contemplative and active the two are.
Of these the first by far the worthier is,
But with the other humbler one we'll start.

This one does teach us how to live on earth
In company with all the moral virtues
And to prepare us for the others strives.

This part did Zeno[23] and his school pursue,
And over it the horde of Cynics ran,
Affirming that in them the true end is.

Nature did not a brighter light give them.
To live well in accordance with their doctrine
More difficult than stating it would be.

---

23. Zeno (335–263 BCE), philosopher founder of the Stoic School for whom true happiness was to be found in the practice of virtue.

All of these goods subject seem to be
To labor and to harshness and to sweat.
To judge them perfect reason never can.

Since strenuous operations do require
Expenditure of effort and much strength,
The more laborious, the more prized they are.

The end of all things human seems to be
To labor not for labor's sake itself,
But so that then the soul can in peace rest.

Therefore it seems that falsely one does state
That in this good the highest end consists,
That in one's suffering does seek the good.

But is there need to have seen other things,
Since he who does to the true end lead us
Declared the truth, and you by it abide?

An excellent choice did Magdalen make,
Since of two parts we must perforce one choose.
With much disquietude Martha's choice is filled.[24]

This is the truth that never can be changed.
No person can its true judgment appeal.
What it opposes must perforce false be.

Martha is not the one, as you can see,
Who can our thirst for so long suffered quench.
Only the water can that the Samaritan

Woman so humble sought[25]; that do you drink.
Let us Maria follow, who next to
The sacred foot, not restless, but quiet is.

At rest is the contemplative mind, then.
When it the contemplated good approaches,
It asks for nothing but to contemplate,

Then granted is to it its true well-being.
Since ignorant may some of these things be,
I'll say that three divisions it does have.

---

24. Lorenzo wrongly identifies Mary, sister of Martha, with Mary Magdalen (Luke 10.38–42). The identification of Martha as representing active life and Mary the contemplative was traditional.
25. John 4.5.

To contemplate the natural and earthly
The first is, the second is the heavens,
The third that which beyond the heavens is.

Democritus[26] did stop at the first part
And said that Nature did by chance produce
That which beneath the sky will be or is,

And stated that all that on earth there is
The multitude of atoms did create,
Without excepting anything at all.

But the true good beneath the stars is not,
Thus it is not in contemplation found
Of those things that undone are one by one.

To speculate on wonders in the heavens,
As the great Anaxagoras[27] once did,
Content the stars and heavens to admire,

The final good is not. The prize it lost
To one that greater is and up above,
And all the values has the lower lacks.[28]

Just as the sun the other stars does hide
For greater is its splendor, thus this greater
And clearer splendor will obscure the lower.

So much more worthy as it is more rare
To contemplate beyond the heavens is,
As that renowned philosopher did think.

I Aristotle mean, whom all do honor.
But two parts does such contemplation have:
One that the soul performs when with the body;

While in this life, the other can't be had.
It seems that in the first the highest good
Without distinction Aristotle put.

He does affirm, if you his words well read,[29]
That happiness consists in activity
During a perfect life a perfect virtue.

---

26. Democritus (c. 460–360 BCE), philosopher of the Atomistic School.
27. Anaxagoras, a Greek philosopher of the fifth century BCE.
28. The ultimate good is not of this earth, but is in heaven and contains all the values the earthly goods lack.
29. *Ethica Nicomachea* 1.6.

But if the perfect good in two things is,
One being the will and intellect the other,
Of the two neither can perfection reach,

For function well the intellect cannot
While to this body bound and dwelling there
Always desires to greater height ascend.

Anxious it does remain and taken is
With ardent yearning for the good it lacks,
And by confusion weakened is the mind.

Desire and intellect thus tired become.
Our soul, therefore, cannot ever perceive
Pure truth that is so beautiful and white

While it is weighed down by this earthly burden."

CHAPTER IV

Without the help of any other gods,
But only with the favor Pan[30] has shown,
My mellow pipes have harmony brought forth.

All shepherds honor Pan and venerate,
Arcadia does his name well celebrate
For over what is born and dies he rules.

Why is it that when light is at its brightest
And shines in mortal eyes like splendid fire
More dark and with more shadows it does seem?

Like certain animals[31] our soul behaves
That what the more bright is the less they see.
Facing the sun, our eyes are just like that.

And thus does of our intellect the eye,
Because of its imperfection, less well see
What is most manifest and clear appears.

Our mortal feet to greater heights can't rise
So others must lead us to the right path
And must our earth-bound souls to heaven raise.

---

30. In mythology Pan was the god of the woods; he became an important symbol signifying the whole for the neo-Platonists.
31. Pliny, *Naturalis historia* 11.142.

Let the great thunderer's own daughter[32] rise,
Who motherless from his great brow was born.
Let her give wings to my most feeble genius.

With holy love let her desire enflame.
Let her my mind enlighten as is needed
By one who wants of God himself to speak.

Just as the goddess is without a mother,
So let my genius matter now forsake
And from the body separated be.

Let it show me the true and certain path.
Let it be to my intellect the sun
That takes away all darkness and confusion.

My Muse, who is so often by me called,
Now does of being abandoned so complain
And of ingratitude accuses me.

O Muse, my words and verses govern now,
And when Minerva sheds her light on us,
Let's put it down just as from her it comes.

Apollo, if the chaste curls you still love
Of Daphne[33] that you once so much desired,
Do help one who her name does now still bear.

Do give me now of your so sacred furor
Not what is due me, but what needed is
By this high subject that I now must sing.

Your lavish grace let for my lack make up
So that what kind Marsilio did then add
I can in verse enclose as in my mind.

Happy Marsilio looked at us and said:
"The good is not down here, as we can see,
Lauro, my son by age, Alfeo, my father.

While the soul is by bodily chains bound
And does in this dark prison dwell, it will
Ambiguous and full of ardor be.

---

32. Minerva, who was born from Jove's (the great thunderer's) brow, personified wisdom.

33. Daphne, pursued by Apollo who loved her, was saved by being turned into a tree, the laurel. Lorenzo, or Lauro, thus retains her name.

Taken by error, it ignores itself
While in the body, and until the time
When it unbound will be and remain free.

We see then that the soul that is divine,
When from the body separated is,
Perfection reaches of this highest good.

Justice divine that will reward well doing
The triumph does reserve, as I have said,
To the soul that to God devoted is.

But contemplation for our soul is dual:
Of the divine and of angelic nature.
The second will not give us peace or rest.

Impelled by Nature of all things the cause
To find, our intellect does ever move
From cause to cause and with no rest at all.

No respite and no peace it has at all
Until the final cause of all is found
That in God's mystery is shut and locked.

Forever must the will on the move be,
No good can ever satisfy it if
Above there is a greater and new sweetness.

It stops and rests in the divine rays only,
For never satisfied with good it is
Until the highest one it has well found.

In their cause only will all things find rest,
And this is God, so therefore not the angel,
But God this good does give us in abundance.

Although Averroes and Avicenna
And Al-Gazzali[34] disagree in this,
The highest good our beautiful God is.

But to God contemplate there are two ways:
One is to God see through our intellect,
So that this means will let us all know him;

34. Avicenna (980–1037) and Al-Ghazzali (1058–1111) were philosophers and physicians from Persia, while Averroes (1126–1198), also an Arab, was a philosopher from Spain.

The other is the known good to enjoy
Through our desire so that the happy end
So eagerly desired we'll so possess.

The divine Plato, in our world a phoenix,[35]
'Ambrosia' the first vision calls and 'nectar'
The joy we feel for having seen the vision.[36]

Our pure and lovely soul two wings does have:
Desire and intellect by which it flies
Above the stars on high and reaches God.

There on ambrosia at the board divine
And nectar it does feed. No lack is there
Of this supreme, immense, eternal sweetness.

When this our world the soul has left, then nectar
The sweeter is and fuller is the joy,
In what is seen much greater the delight.

For if in our past life to just love God
A greater merit is than knowing him,
Love shall always deserve the fruit of love.

That love is more deserving I shall prove
And that the soul by loving does more merit
On earth acquire than one does by inquiring.

In the first place so weak is mortal sight
That a true knowledge we can't gain of God.
The source of errors it does seem in life.

Perfect the will and true his love of God
Are those of one who always ready is
To sacrifice himself and all for him.

Just as a greater error very clear
Is God to hate than him not understand,
Thus he who loves him more, more merit has.

Nature and reason this do make most clear.
To make my statement stronger and more firm
I shall invoke of contraries a rule.

35. Unique and miraculous.
36. *Phaedrus* 246–47.

The gates of paradise by love are opened,
And when it loves, our soul is never wrong,
But searching for the Truth may lead to death.

Through pride does Science its eyes beyond earth raise
And murky does at times render our sight,
Never to these does God reveal himself.

He hides himself from all the wise and prudent,
As of himself the holy lips did say[37]:
To humble eyes love will make him appear.

Those who did set to study God did not
In this way honor him or venerate.
Perhaps they did in this seek their own glory.

But those who with his beauty are in love,
Themselves and all they have do offer him,
And he in turn himself does offer them.

The soul that is intent in knowing God
Little does profit over a long time;
That which loves him will happiness soon gain.

Thus from what we have stated we conclude
That if love merits more, no one should think
That a more great reward is not ordained.

To him who seeks to see, enough is seeing,
But always will the lover have the joy
Of what he loves enjoying and great pleasure.

Love is that which desire and covet does;
Love is that which most merit does acquire,
So that a worthier prize it does demand,

As we shall demonstrate more clearly yet."

Chapter V

So overwhelmed with sweetness my heart was
That as I listened I seemed to be drawn
To the high good his words were then describing.

Abstracted, separated was my soul
And to myself I said: "What must the real
Good be if happy so can words make me?"

37. Cf. Matt 11.25.

Marsilio, who my thoughts had then read, said:
"In your own self you can now realize
Which of those two the perfect good must be.

To understand that which I said does please,
But when the end has come to this first stage
The good you heard with new delight fills you.

The soul that is in searching all aflame
Searches in order to possess the good
So as the understood good to enjoy.

Enjoying isn't for sake of understanding,
So then the understanding that precedes
Is but a means to the good it desires.

We answer can those who of us inquire
The purpose of our search: it is to enjoy
The good that first our own minds do envision.

No other purpose of enjoyment than
Itself there is, which will forever last,
Nor can the mind a greater good suppose.

Our nature does not flee from any joy.
Those things it deems too irksome or unpleasant,
It often to acknowledge does refuse.

For seeing he who does see has not always
Sweetness received, but he whose mind by joy
Is taken does both understand and see.

Since sorrow does offend our nature more
Than does ignoring, its opposite joy
A greater good than understanding is.

No judgment good is that does not agree
That the supreme good joy must be, if sorrow
Its adversary, the first evil is.

And since it is a part of our own nature
To hold all painful things as a great torment
And to avoid all sorrow in itself,

So does the heart joy want and all things more
That joy do give, and so to that our love
Directed is as to the good supreme.

Just as among the good you can't include
One who the good does see, but does not want,
Though having intellect that choice permits,

Thus must our soul divine perforce then be
By loving God, not just by seeing him,
For then what it had seen it does enjoy.

By understanding God, our soul contracts
Such amplitude so as to fit its limits
And so within itself does God restrict.

By loving we dilate and amplify
Our minds to his immense infinitude.
This then it seems beatitude must be.

By seeing of the immense Almighty we
Only the part do seize that in us fits
And what then present can the soul well see.

By loving you can love what you then see,
But also what your mind did promise you
Of his true infinite and future goodness.

Of heavenly infinity we see
The deep abyss as if by fog enveloped,
Although the soul its eye on it does fix.

But with true perfect love we do God love.
God to himself will draw one who knows him.
By loving to his heights ourselves we raise.

To that which satisfies the mind aspires
As to the good supreme, but it does not
Happiness reach by just admiring God.

For though intense, the vision that the seeing
Soul does receive limited is like all
Created and finite things always are.

And so it must then be if so it's ranked[38]:
If the soul's own potential finite is,
Finite and brief its own creations are,

But the soul that has been from these bonds freed
Entirely happy is and peace does find
In those things only that eternal are.

38. Cf. Ficino, *Theologia Platonica* 18.

Of that good only it desirous is
That through love known always from God proceeds.
The yearning and the joy immense do seem,

For it through love will then with God be joined
And will expand above the God it saw."
And at this point my silence I did break

And said: "This matter do explain some more
For to my mind somewhat confused it is
Because of doubts that have in me now risen."

Marsilio said to me: "If the soul is
beset by errors, I am not surprised,
Nor for this must you now yourself excuse.

So high cannot their sight raise mortal eyes.
But further to enlighten you I shall
A practical example offer you.

A difference there is from taste to tasting.
Of tasting taste must the potential be
And tasting is its only operation.

To move these two to operate the need
There is for savor, that its object is,
What is potential into action move.

The soul is the potential taste that God,
The savor, into action moves, that is,
The tasting that the intellect here is.

When finally it reaches this first object,
With great desire the tasted God enjoys,
And such joy is the savor filled with good.

As good is tasting, as sweet is the savor.
The soul by contemplation God does taste,
And its desire does give it such great joy.

Thus we conclude, as towards our end we go,
That our supreme, true good eternal God
Is, and for him we do all search and strive.

He is that simple, pure, unblemished lamb
Towards whom always our wandering soul moves
In his most holy mansion seeking rest.

The soul's divine beatitude then is
This good to enjoy through its own will, for love
Does move it so that it will towards God journey,

And there it will supreme, great sweetness taste
That it has so invoked and much desired
And that no earthly things can ever give.

If it loves God, God then will it embrace
With holy love and will its mind then turn
Into himself and give it endless joy.

Love is he whom we love and love deserves.
Love for ourselves eternal peace will gain,
Love true well-being is, perfect and so certain.

Paul the Apostle,[39] who so truthful was
By means of this love did to heaven rise,
He who most worthy was of so much grace.

Love did to the third heaven[40] let him rise
Up to the star that love on earth instills,
So that the divine ones his eyes did join.

In that sphere never God himself does hide.
His holy mansion and himself he shows
And his most great and so immense possessions.

For up above there is that most clear fissure
That to our eyes itself and all things shows,
There where God once did put his tabernacle.

Reserved is this reward for our soul that
From its own body freed is, nor can I
Or you find it in this blind world of ours.

Our life on earth is so by evil bound
That happier are the brute and savage beasts
That hidden in some den their life do spend.

The more our mortal eyes the good do see,
The more they grieve if it denied is them,
And greater knowledge greater sorrows gives,

---

39. 2 Corinthians 12.2–4. Also see Sonnet XXXII of Lorenzo's *Lyrics*, pp. 18–19.

40. Venus. Cf. Dante, *Paradiso* 8.1–12.

And then, as long as we alive are here,
We yearn for ever more things in our life,
While grass and streams are all that beasts do need.

Happier is one who is the least in need,
And thus the most unhappy man does seem
While here in life he vacillates and dreams.

Rewarded he will be in future life
That foolish mortals do a sad death call.
Then does man reach his joyful happy end.

Thus our real life is not the one that here
Does not give us an instant's happiness —
For this world does sweetness to us deny —

Nor is it yours, O shepherd, that quieter is,
Or yours that does so beautiful seem, Lauro,
Or any other if it mortal is.[41]

Into the ocean Phoebus sinking is,
And my discourse is ending with the sun.
God be with you, Alfeo, Lauro farewell."

Thus did he of his presence us deprive,
Though we still thirsted for that limpid font
And did wish more his ornate words to hear,

Words that in Lethe[42] never lost will be.
But then the shepherd said: "The hour leads me
To take my humble flock into the pen.

Already does the light from us depart,
So to my ancient labor I'll return,
And you do go where your desire leads you."

Having said this, he with his flock did move,
And I away from him my back did turn,
And with slow steps from him I made my way.

41. This is the answer to Lauro's question (II, 58–63, pp. 387–88) as to whether the shepherd's tranquil life or his own was the ideal. The answer is that they are both false.
42. Lethe is the river whose waters wash away memory.

Thus each of us to his own dwelling went,
And I was burning with that holy flame
And with my mind pursued all those sweet thoughts

And wished to sing the love that all enflames.

Chapter VI[43]

O venerable, immense and eternal
Light that in your own self yourself do see
And all will shine that from your light derives.

Infinite sight that from yourself do move
And for yourself shine, sparkle for you does
All splendor through the light that you concede.

Spiritual eye that none can understand
But spiritual sight by means of which only
You, yes only you, understand and see.

O life of all immortals that do see,
Or of all those who truly well do live
That their desire fulfill that for you burns.

Desire you light and from you does proceed
The flame that does desire all that good is,
For you are all the good, O only hope.

O true and most pure sparkling holy light,
I pray for you to cleanse my darkened sight
Of thick fog and make me most clearly see

So that I shall your pure light clearly see,
Since you do my desire in my heart light
Make the ice that there is enflame and burn.

My weak sight do extend and amplify
So that I shall see you. My lowered eyes
Raise so that beyond the heavens I'll ascend.

Your depth that deeper is than any other,
That more than others lower does itself
Within me does it penetrate and pass.

43. This chapter contains the song of love for God mentioned at the end of the previous chapter. The source for this is Ficino's epistle, *Oratio ad deum theologica.*

Let your sublimeness raise me on high.
That same sublimeness that eminent is
And higher is than any other virtue.

Your marvelous and so great sparkling splendor
Of goodness and admirable beauty
Our soul does penetrate, our mind and body.

This boundless goodness and this beauty warms,
Elates, sets me on fire and forces me
Without my knowing it, splendor sublime.

Desire takes flight, but then the soul slows down
Thinking that all the passions of this world
Are of eternal glory undeserving.

O sole supernal fortress and so lofty
Extend your hand to help my lame desire.
My misery do let your mercy see.

My firmest hope and only refuge mine,
The heart you call to you now guide. Receive,
O God, the one you force to come to you,

The one you do torment, please and elate.
Refresh the one you burn, as is my hope,
For perfect happiness you only are.

Perfect delight, of happiness sole font,
I do know that you only are and that
What our desire thirsts for in you does lie.

For if this or another good may please,
Yet our desire does not seek one of them,
But the true good in them where his peace is.

Of good the essence in all things the heart
Has always asked and for the saving balm[44]
That lives in him and in all things spreads out.

To the font of this balm the heart does rush,
This font eternal it adores and seeks
That is spread out in what below him is.

44. God's infinite goodness.

And since the eyes do nothing see but light
That clearly shows in one or other thing,
Thus a sole good there is that we all want.

But never lacking is our thirst for this
Or that or for both this and that together
Until a greater good does show itself.

The font that does distill the holy liquor
Our thirst does quench. O holy liquor do
My thirst now quench for it torments me so.

Since good all things are only in so far
As you, the final good, in them all are,
Do not let me without your presence be.

O highest mind that without folly is,
O highest wisdom, lofty and profound
That never by insipience tainted is,

From whom it seems that nothing may be hidden
Of what your intellect does order and
Through providence, so infinite, creates.

Not one have you neglected of the things
Which your so infinite mercy does create,
But from perfection the imperfect see.

And yet your ardent charity does all,
For even for those who do it ignore,
It does provide, and this amazes me.

Abundant grace, O intellect most pious,
How can it be that all the slightest things
By you are always fed and fulfilled,

While your most marvelous creation, man,
Who reveres and adores your holy name,
Is left with thirst and with desire that burns?

Do not let man, I say, who honors you
Through faith alone, without peace always live.
To find a final peace in you he hopes.

May that ingratitude perverse and evil
Disappear from that multitude so vast
That does enjoy your charity so gracious.

From you, O truth, let fraud now disappear,
For defrauded the soul would surely be
If after all that thirst, no joy is there.

If the soul does for you a burden bear,
Carries its cross, and worldly things does hate,
With endless glory you must it reward.

O supreme good, so bountiful, eternal,
Wretched is man much more than mindless beasts.
If of your kingdom you the joy deny.

But of your grace the vessel overflows,
So that for my torment I hope that end
That, more than merit, will your grace make mine.

Though for a time we must on this earth sigh
And grieve, our sorrow do for us reward.
Let endless joy all our desires make brief.

For our so little good do give us much.
Give us eternity for our brief time.
Thus you will not defraud or us deceive.

O you who did the world from hell redeem,
O true refuge for us, our sole well-being,
Under your rule you do all things protect;

Highest of all goods, highest of all virtues,
I know you did eternity give me,
So that I should not worse than all beasts be,

Because your ardent charity does love
Instill deep in the vessel of our minds
In order that we may your goodness love.

Thus does our intellect to yours relate.
If we do understand, your intellect
Of deep and lofty things will us enlighten.

As love and intellect from you derive
And your life is eternal, so it must
Be that our share of it to us you give.

You do our life give us, O life, and also
Of some immortal things a true cognition
And our will that on earthly things does rule.

Eternal soul you gave that is related
To your immutable, eternal life
And in us came before the other two,

Eternal made and to endure forever,
Each of these three most capable thus is
Eternal life in its way to enjoy:

Our intellect by understanding; will
By willing; the soul, first given, by living
Eternally without evermore dying.

Since to the other two eternity
Extended was, our soul that did come first
Perforce must then first have been given it.[45]

You will then put an end to my deep sorrows.
Of Heaven to the joys our hearts shall rise
Through our inheritance and grace abundant.[46]

Part of these joys at least do grant us now.
Grant that in this life now we shall enjoy
The certain hope somewhat of your true goodness.

Should it not please you yet because our soul
Yet undeserving is, we do beg you,
Show us the path that to salvation leads.

Grant that we shall ourselves deceived not be
By the corrupt enticements of this world
And lose what certain is for what is vain.

Our hearts do fortify against the threats
Of Fortune and its powerful embrace
To which at times man's senses do respond.

---

45. The argument, which is rather convoluted in the verses, may be paraphrased as follows: Just as intellect and will come to us from you, let your eternal life come to us. We live through you, and you give us knowledge of immortal things and will to govern mortal ones. The immortal life (of the soul) was given us before intellect and will. Thus each of these three, created immortal and to endure forever, is capable of enjoying eternal life in its own way: intellect by understanding, will by willing, and life (of the soul) by living without ever dying. Since eternity has been granted to intellect and will, that came later, it must have been granted to life that came first.

46. By inheritance since man is God's child.

Your kindly face, O Father, do show us.
The arms of your great mercy do now open
To your own children to whom kind you are.

Recrea quos creasti,[47] O supreme good,
Do help us now for of you born we are,
Omnipotent, most lenient Father mine.

Our intellect and most ardent desires
Let your own truth and goodness now appease
Nor think of why we all created were.

Have pity on my sick and tainted soul,
Your child from its celestial home so far,
And in this forest dark and wild exiled.

What keeps my heart from you do now delete,
Have pity for the tears that swell my heart
For the desire of its celestial home.

Where our home is, there only true rest is.
Where Father and home are, there rests the son,
There is our highest good, so true and copious.

Our fretfulness in our exile abides,
And all false good or true and most clear evil.
Oh to your court divine do us elect.

Then only will our hearts some good enjoy,
Then only will we evil thoughts forego,
And the soul will enjoy good that is true

When our hearts willingly and most devout
Of you do think, and the soul seems its good
To reach if to you rise all its desires.

If with its thoughts it happens that the soul
With you is linked, it then can rest. Let then
All vanish that these thoughts from you do keep.

Let diffidence and coldness, and despair
From us depart and after let the soul
In faith and hope and charity find rest

So that divided we never shall be
From you, O life of lives and our true light
That alone can let other lights shine bright.

47. Help us, for you created us.

Without your guide, from the true path we stray,
And following our senses soon shall fall
In the exterior darkness of this world.

So let the soul from the beginning live
Only for you and in your own light shine
When our extreme moment has come and gone.

Let it in your light burn and there rejoice.
When it does come to you, infinite good
And truth that to such good the path shows us.

Your beauty infinite let us love
Without anxiety that us torments,
And you supreme good that our minds attract

May we content and greedy enjoy always.

Devotional Poems[1]

I

O my great God, by means of whose firm laws
And under whose perpetual direction,
This universe is guided and maintained,

Creator of all things, from an eternal
Site, you do make time run its fleeting course,
Just like a wheel that on its axis turns.

Silent always and never prone to change
You do all things create and them transform,
Of all prime mover, still, untiring motor.

Nor do you find outside yourself a cause
That can move you all this matter to form,
Matter desirous to acquire new shapes.

Not because it imperfect is, is matter[2]
by your own goodness ever new forms given,
A goodness that no malice knows or envy.

Nothing but love this goodness moves to make
Things here on earth like models of what is
The great creation that above us is.[3]

Most lovely architect in your own mind
Your beautiful world you did first create,
Then this as image of the one above.

Partially perfect in itself each part
You did, O mighty Lord, contribute make
To the perfection of the universe.

---

1. The subject matter and the imagery of these *Devotional Poems,* or *Capitoli,* show the influence of traditional religious poetry, particularly the *Hymns of Praise,* which found their greatest practitioner in Jacopone da Todi (c. 1230–1306). The influence of the Bible is also noticed. While the *Hymns of Praise* used the poetic form of the ballad, the *Devotional Poems* were in *terza rima.* In the Renaissance the *Devotional Poems* became the preferred form for satirical poetry.
2. God's creative activity brings about a continuous change in all things, not because they are imperfect, but because of his perfect goodness.
3. Our imperfect world is a reflection of the perfect model which is to be found in Heaven. In his platonic orientation Lorenzo was obviously influenced by Ficino, as can be seen in all his works, particularly in the *Disputation.*

The elements you send to their own site
Within their own confines you do bind them
So that they can't impinge one on the other.

In peace you made both fire and ice remain,
The soft and hard by you thus tempered are,
And though contrary, they both union find.

Thus fire more pure and lighter does not upward
Escape, nor does the earth's weight make it sink
Evermore down beneath the darkest center.

Providently you let the soul abide
Right in the center of the universe
From where it seems all matter to pervade.

No other force what moves does activate
Other than this[4] in such a lovely creature.[5]
Three natures in this gentle soul are found[6]:

The worthiest two, more gentle and more pure,[7]
Move from themselves and two great circles make
That will always unto themselves return,

And all around the mind profound they go.
The other straight proceeds, by its love moved
To do those things that from it do depend.

The motor as it moves to heaven does
Motion impart, just like the heart that does
With its own motion move the limbs also.

From you, supreme Creator, life do all
Creatures derive, including lesser ones[8];
Though humbler, this your family, still is.

---

4. The soul.
5. The original has "animali," but the meaning is clearly a living or "animated" being, which in Ficino meant the world.
6. Lorenzo follows Ficino in the matter of the three "natures," which are the soul of the world, that of the celestial spheres, and that of the beings in the individual spheres. (Ficino, *Theologia Platonica* 6.1.)
7. The soul of the world and that of the spheres.
8. Lesser than the celestial beings, with lesser referring to man.

Your endless goodness does to these give chariots,[9]
So light and with the purest fire adorned,
When earth and heaven do invite and call.[10]

When afterwards our mortal days are done,
Your tender rule will kindly let us still
The chariots mount and so to you return.

Do grant, O Father, to my mind to rise
to the so lofty, sacred seat and see
The live true font from whom all good proceeds.[11]

To my eyes do the light that true is show,
And when your beautiful sun I have seen,
The soul's most willing eyes do fix on him.

The fog do dissipate and free me now
Of this my earthly burden. Let your light
Now shine. The good supreme we seek is you.

To you, sweet refuge, we do all aspire,
And you as our true end the pious see.
You are the moving principle and guide;

The path and end, O mighty God, you are.

II[12]

Thanks be to you, supreme and mighty God,
Since by your grace, and not by other means,
We have received the light and so know you.

A sacred name to be adored, sole name
That we must bless and worship and revere,
To which your goodness a response will give.

For you, our Father and eternal goodness,
Charity, mercy and love do give us,
And the most sweet of feelings one can know.

9. The soul, as in Plato's image.
10. That is, when they are born.
11. Lorenzo uses Ficino's image for God, as he also does in the *Disputation*.
12. In this God is thanked for having given man the capability of "knowing" him.

A gift you make of lofty sense and reason,
O most munificent and mighty God,
And intellect to serve you by your grace.

Our lofty sense lets us know what you are;
Reason does doubt and seek, intellect finds,
And I rejoice when I of you do think.

This joy so sweet renewed is when you, who
Did us redeem, yourself do show to us,
O supreme God from whom all good proceeds.

And while we still in our frail bodies are,
We, who poor mortals are, rejoice that we
By you are called to your eternal home.

This is that good that is beyond all ills,
For us sole consolation if your name
most holy we do know and what you're worth.

We have known you, most splendid, brilliant light,
Light that perceived is by the worthy mind,
Only the mind, and not by senses seen.

We do know you, true life, from whom all life
Seems to derive, O lofty and true nature
That does all natures fully impregnate.

We do know you well from the nature that
In you then was and was by you conceived
Eternity that constant always is.

In this my prayer that I to you do offer
As I adore the goodness of your grace,
Only this I from you do beg and want:

For this my humble prayer I send to you
That you will steady me in my firm love
That of my knowing you has been conceived,[13]

And never let my heart divided be
From this so sacred love or such sweet life.
You can supreme, omnipotent, good Lord.

You do want to. Your goodness knows no bounds.

13. Cf. *Disputation* IV and V.

III[14]

Most holy God and Father of all that
This world does fill; most holy God what you
Desire you do fulfill by your own power.

Most holy God, known only to those who
With you familiar are, you holy are
That in the Word to all things you gave form.

Most holy God, of whom an image only
All natures are,[15] you are in essence holy
Since nature never did give form to you.

Holy you are and mightier than might is.
Holy beyond all praise for your own goodness,
Holy you are, more perfect than perfection.

The holy sacrifice your ears let hear
Of my poor prayers that face to face with you
My heart does bring that for being yours rejoices.

Let all who would praise you now silent be;
He who has seen the errors of the world
Praises you well and clearly sees the truth.

Do hear me Lord, and do to me give strength.
Let those also who do not know such goodness
Participate in this our holy fate,

And as on me on them do shed such grace.
Nature, our common mother, did give them
To me as brothers, children dear to you.

O Lord since I in you complete faith have
And I your witness am with everyone,
Life I do gain, and my soul light does see.

O Lord, you are our venerable Father.
You only does man love and with you wants
In holiness forever more rejoice.

---

14. Hymn in praise of the Lord and prayer both personal and for mankind.

15. Cf. *Devotional Poems* I.16–21, p. 413.

Free will you did give him and full dominion[16]
Over all things, and so if he desires
From you to have your goodness, nothing else,

Do touch him, satisfy him, holy God.

IV[17]

Let all of nature listen to this hymn,
Let the earth and the clouds, the fogs and rain,
The strong whirlwinds that all the air do darken.

Be silent, shady, solitary woods.
Be calm, O winds. Do hear, O skies, the song
So that the creatures their Creator know.

I the Creator sing, the All and One.
May the immortal God from heaven grant
What in these sacred prayers I now beg.

I the Creator sing who all the lands
Disposed and did the sky sustain and willed
That the sweet waters from the ocean rise,[18]

So that the human race could nourished be,
For which he does command that the sun shine
For all who God adore and venerate.

With one voice all let us to him give thanks
Beyond the skies. He does create all who
Live, feel and do from him their nature take.

The only true eye of the mind is he,
For our spirit's powers do praise him.
In his true kindness he will our praise accept.

Let all my powers now praise only him.
Let all the powers of my soul[19] this God
Now praise as of them does my will demand.

Holy the knowledge is your light instills.
Enlightened by your clear and lucid light,
My intellect with intense joy does sing.

---

16. Lorenzo, like Pico della Mirandola and humanists in general, stresses man's free will and domination of all things.
17. Hymn of thanks to the Creator.
18. Rain.
19. The powers of the soul that he enumerates in the following verses.

O powers mine, do sweetly with me sing.
O constant spirits mine, do all of you
Sing now of his most constant firmness.

Let me with justice the just One now sing.
O spirits mine, O senses mine, now do
With me together praise the All and One.

Let truth through me the one supreme truth sing
And all the good that ours is his good sing,
Goodness that our desires do all long for.

O life, O light from you to us does come
Your holy blessing, and I thank you Lord,
From whose great power action all derives.

Your Word through me does you, O Lord God, praise.
Through me the world continues to receive
The holy words of my most pious prayer.

My powers do invoke and this demand.
They sing the All and One and thus fulfill
All high desires by you in them inspired.

Desire inspired by you reflected is
In you. Accept, O holy King, the words
Of piety that we all send to you.

O Life, do save what all in me is now.
The darkness where my soul to wander seems
Illumine, O light, for you are the light.

O God, your Word the human mind sustains.
Holy Font that to all spirit instill,
You the God are that all things rule alone.

Your creature does invoke you at all times.
For fire and air, water and earth he prays,
For the spirit and all you did create.

From the eternal I received a blessing,
And my hope is, as I so much desire,
To find in love of you a tranquil state:

No rest there is away from you, O God.

V[20]

Blessed are they who from those impious councils
Do keep away and in the sinners' path,
So evident, they do not step or stay.

Nor do they stay in that contagious lair,
But day and night the Lord's law in their heart
They do desire and in their minds they keep.

They're like a plant that near the water is;
Its fruit in proper time it will then bear.
It will not bend nor will its leaves all wither.

The things that they will do will always prosper.
Not so, not so for all the impious sinners
Who will like dust before a strong wind be.

The impious won't at the Last Judgment rise,
Nor will the sinners then the council join
Of all the just who their duty fulfilled.

God knows the pious path of all the just,
The evil's path to ruin always leads,
For you the life now are, the truth and way.

Glory to you always, almighty God.

VI

Poem in Which I Exhort and Excite Myself

Wake up, you lazy mind, from that deep sleep
That seems your eyes to cover with a veil
With the result that you the truth can't see.

Do wake up now and contemplate your deeds.
See how they are fallacious, useless, vain
Since your desire did reason overrule.

Just see how men mistakenly do love
Utility and glory and their pleasure
And how most do affirm in them is peace.

Never your mind's high dignity forget.
It was not given to pursue the earthly,
But so that Heaven would its object be.

---

20. This is a paraphrase of Psalms 1.

You do well know through personal experience
The worth of that which others call the good,
From the truth further than East is from West.

The charms that Love did to your eyes present,
Starting when you of tender years still were,
Have you deprived of happiness in life:

Brief, fleeting, false, and with all sorrows filled,
Lovely to see, but monstrous in reality,
With wolves and dolphins hidden by the clothes[21]

Just think what our poor life now would have been,
If that which always must in firm charge be
Had the path taken that I did show you.

Just think if so much talent, time and skill
You had towards a desire more just directed,
You could now well in peace console yourself.

If towards yourself your will more pious were,
What you desire and hope perhaps you would
Know better now if it is just or evil.

Of all your years, the fresh green spring you wasted,
And so perhaps the rest will also be,
Until the last nightfall of winter comes.

With false pretexts and under a false shadow,
You did yourself convince that all this was
What gentle heart will in a man propose.

It's time to break these evil bonds right now.
Do now remove that chain from your poor neck
That a false beauty did around it keep,

And from your heart remove that most vain hope
That leads you on, and let that part of you
Most lovely and serene your guide now be.

With greater force and with still better counsel,
Let it with its sharp claws force to submit
Desires that ever dare its will oppose,

21. Wolves and dolphins, that is, fierce animals, which here stand for spiritual torment and sin. Cf.Virgil, *Aeneid* 3.428 where the poet describes Scylla: "delphinium causas utero commissa iuporum."

So that once beaten its most evil foe
Never again will dare its head to raise,
But a vile slave and mercenary be.

Four winds[22] on the high seas will tempests blow
And strike our fragile bark[23] on every side,
From stern to prow and with no rest all sides.

These do with ignorance the boat load down
So that perforce it rushes towards perdition,
While of all good the refuge it should be.

It seems that thus it sails on its own way,
And in those dearest places where are stored
Most precious things there now is only ballast.

The first of these strong winds that wants to strike
The so-desired vessel is most vain hope.
The course it interrupts from the prow striking

With greater force and fury from the stern.
Fear comes and strikes the ship with greatest force
That does the wretched vessel keep in peril.

From one side comes the good that on this earth
Little endures, vain happiness that strikes
With force the boat and in dire straits puts it,

And from the opposite side, present grief
Comes that makes all grieve and does them torment.
This does our life with all its pain death seem.

One or the other of these winds does strike
The wretched vessel in so dire a storm.
Now all, now only some do it invest.

The guiding star's sight do all these impede
To the good helmsman, the dark clouds do cover
The air that was most beautiful and clear,

So that he can but grieve and be inert,
With the poor ship at the waves' mercy left
That seem to swallow it at any moment.

---

22. Hope, fear, joy, and grief, which according to the Stoics were the four perturbations of the soul.
23. Bark, that is, the soul. Cf. Petrarch, *Rime* 132, 189, 235.

If grace divine does not soon intervene
And save the helmsman, I seem him to see
Struck down and dead and by the waves well covered.

I see him call in vain or hope for shore,
And those in vain repent who were the cause
Of his pursuing such a mortal course,

For of the great Neptune[24] the most just will
Is rarely bent by all the prayers of one
Who is with ignorance and malice filled.

Let an example be the ruin of others
Or of yourself, for you can say in truth,
"In such a pass I, too, was at one time."

You are and still will be for as long as
Your chariot guided is by him who sits
Where a most faithful driver should now be.

The more desire does get, the more it wants,
And since it endless is there is no peace:
He cannot rest so well who never sits.

The more you will recur your thirst to quench
To that most evil font, the more you will
Then see it grow until you cross the Lethe.[25]

Reason tells us that so must matters be.
The soul, which is created for perfection,
Cannot be satisfied with imperfection.[26]

It must then search, and never does it rest
Until what it desires it has then found,
That it as target put for its own bow.

But often while it does the path pursue,
Led by an evil and unfriendly guide,
Before its good it reaches, it falls down.

It must well judge in whom its faith to put,
And to whom it the horse's reins entrusts,
Before it searches or the path does enter.

---

24. The great Neptune is God.
25. Lethe is the river whose waters give oblivion. Cf. Dante, *Purgatorio* 31.
26. That is, with the imperfection of earthly things.

It must well know what is excess and lack,
For on each side of their dividing line
The truth is never found to be complete.

Though purpose and intention may be good,
And the same be that in all minds exist,
Yet over various paths does one proceed.

Many and different the ways all are
And what one searches for is only one
And so most difficult it is to find.

A little pebble in the path, a thorn
That pricks the slow and fragile foot will then
Of food so wonderful deny the taste.

And so a great misfortune will occur,
For the soul will another way then take
And hold as good what to damnation leads.

Befuddled then and in thick fog enveloped,
So much it suffers trying to see the light
That visual power will abandon it.

So it must be that it must burn and suffer,
For through long usage evil ways have taken
Control of what its natural course is.

But if I have a harmful course pursued,
Before in you this evil should then grow
Stronger than reason's power to restrain.

Before you for yourself that grave do dig
In which you later would most sinful fall,
From which some bones and nothing else would rise,

Look at the sun in heaven that bright shines,
Look at the fruit that does from it descend
That once you've tasted it, no other pleases.

Oh leave the sinful path you have long trodden,
To heaven's beauties do now turn your eyes,
So much more beautiful in that they are rare,

False beauties they are not, like those ornate
Ones that so much have troubled you and grieved
And to the stars the path have from you taken.

These ways of yours have shame and harm both brought.
The others to eternal peace and glory
After the weary way will lead the soul.

Blind must be he who does not easily see
How great the distance is between the sun's
Great splendor and a lantern's weak, false light.

My ardor does not let me to more say.
This only to the purpose will I add:
If the heart should some good desire or seek,

It should do so without itself forgetting.

VII

Written for Giovanfrancesco Ventura on His Daughter's Death

My amorous sweet style, my song so sweet
That as my destiny so blind decreed
Was happy once, but now it turns to tears.

Feeble and sad my verse has now become
Through that most bitter grief that to me gave
A true desire, a love pious and holy.

This flame of love that in my heart did burn
Did not permit my eyes to dry remain
Or me to silent be at such a blow.

But in the face of your adversities,
Of them and of your grief a share it took
That showed that everything in common was.

So that, my friend, my heart was struck and pierced
By your so ill, unfortunate, dire fate,
For to its own your grief was added on

When it did hear of the so premature
Death of your dear and most beloved daughter,
Whose threads of life too short did Clotho make.[27]

27. One of the three Fates, of Parcae, whose functions controlled a person's life: Lachesis assigns the lot, Clotho spins the thread of life. And Atropos severs it.

But then the thought into my mind occurred
That with your torment there was also prudence
That to your current grief a brake should put.

In trying to counsel you to be resigned,
I could not give you what in me was not,
So much your sorrow did me overcome.

If ruled you are by your own better part,
With reason that is common, though most true,
The grief that is too strong take from your heart.

One looks in vain, desires and does cry for
What Death that knows no mercy ever steals:
In vain one fears and flees from what must be.

Unmovable always and firm she is;
Complain you mustn't if she to her has done
What she by nature does to all of us.

No pact she ever made or violated,
Nor does the ancient law allow exceptions
That all who here are born will be undone.

Since the great Lord who over all does rule,
Because of his most ardent, burning love
Did not exclude himself, no one will be.

You will tell me: "Her green and tender years,
Her character, what all did think of her,
The sudden blow do this more horrid make."

Let reason your desire now overcome,
For love divine does better know than us
When for salvation has the time arrived.

If this our mortal journey a death is,
Then at an age immaculate and pure
To leave the bounds of earth is to gain life.

If our brief span eternal were and perfect,
Then our deep grief misplaced might not now be,
But who could ever think he could have this?

So then if all who born are must then die,
Whether our journey long or short will be
Has no significance before eternity.

The longer you are subject to earth's mercy,
The more your candid soul risks to be stained,
And you add wood to the infernal fire.

So you must not now grieve if in her youth
To greater good she rose, for then you would
Your loss more value than another's good.

A brief joy for you, an eternal torment
Her life was then that on that day did end
And to a better one a start did give.

If you for her with tears your face do cover,
Let the tears cease, for to a greater good
He who took her from you did then call her.

Nor should you grieve because you had a hope
Of future joys, for from the sweetest flower
Will oftentimes the fruit most bitter be.

If your own loss grieves you, it will not last,
But infinite her glory is, so that
Envy your grief would be, not a true love.

Let your grief, then, depart from you right now
And if you must still cry, cry for yourself,
Not her, for she to better life has gone.

For your harsh fate do cry, for it did not
Let you her guide be now on this her journey,
But she'll yours be when granted it will be.

And do take comfort in your own self now,
If this example will you more wise make,
So you will not so much love what is dead.

Fortune did not offend you in this way.
What in her was potential, she fulfilled
When of her journey had the end been reached.

But why did you a mortal object love
When it so fragile was and so ephemeral,
As if eternal could the pleasure be?

Our highest good, our own true guide does often
Our mortal journey block and bring to an end
So that his light will in our dark shine more.

All memory of him would then be lost,
For mortals are so prone to lose the way
Unless misfortune did awaken them.

This is the way his love does spur us on
And our supine minds does to heaven raise
So that they will not in the end be lost.

This cruel grief do from your heart remove.
Do not your health endanger for an event
That, if not now, in future would have come.

Do not grieve now if she more things didn't see,
Or that more time she has not here received.
For always filled with evil old age is.

You now experience it and if your fate
Will more time grant, you will know it much better,
For happiness in life comes at the end.

The longer on our journey we proceed,
The harder do the path our slow steps find
And crushed we are by an increasing burden,

And when we do arrive, tired, at the end,
When to go back or to repent is useless,
We clearly know that we our steps have wasted.

Oh what an insupportable fierce evil
That sad repentance is that cannot help,
And he who further rises, further falls.

Mad is he who almost at every hour
Derided or deceived is by this world
And every time he seems to be surprised.

Where love is less, so less is also grief.
Where less is hope, less will be sorrows, too.
What one does value less, less harm will do.

Desire too ardent and too uncontrolled
For your dear daughter's welfare has your heart
Of sweetness all deprived and swept all bare.

From this example do conclusions draw
For all events: remember to be "viro,"
A word that comes from "virtue" and so worthy.

More hard is the condition of that virtue
That has for long proof given of itself
Than that which hidden is, unknown, and new.

More diligence and effort we expect
From him whom general opinion holds
That firmer and more sure his virtue is.

More we expect from him who proof has given.
In fact, as if it were an obligation,
We moderate, grave actions, wise demand.

Since your good fate did virtue give to you,
If in yourself it first does not now act,
One then cannot believe it can help others.

Then let the best part now that is above
Remove the fog of sighs from your eyes and
Of tears the rain so that the sun will out.

With its warm rays and brilliant let the sun
Reveal your guide, your most dear missing one
There where she is with other saints most happy,

As proper is for a deserving soul.

Sonnets to Ginevra de' Benci[1]

I

Do follow, pious soul, that fervent passion
That holy goodness does in us inspire,
And when the shepherd's voice so sweetly calls
And you invites, do go O little lamb.

In this new ardor so devout of yours
There is no envy or wrath or suspicion,
But hope that does aspire to the high good,
Sweetness and peace and fame for holiness.

If in your happy and most holy madness
You should at times plant pious tears and sighs,
The harvest will then be sweet and eternal.

"Populi meditati sunt inania."[2]
Let people talk. To Jesus's voice you listen,
O you new citizen of Bethany.[3]

II

When Lot and all his family did flee[4]
The city that God's judgment set aflame,
His wife looked back at the just punishment,
And so became a lifeless pile of salt.

You have now fled the city that with vice
Does ever burn, and this a marvel is.
Do know, you gentle soul, that now your duty
Is not to turn and never more look back.

His flock the good eternal shepherd leaves
To find you once again, you poor lost lamb.
He does and so takes you back in his arms.

---

1. Ginevra de' Benci was a Florentine noble lady portrayed by Leonardo and praised by Vasari as a beautiful woman.
2. Psalm 2.1: "the people imagine a vain thing" (Authorized King James Version).
3. The site where John the Baptist baptized Christians.
4. Genesis 19.1–26. Lot fled Sodom, the city that was punished for its sinful ways. His wife disobeyed the divine command not to look back and was turned into a salt statue.

Orpheus did lose Eurydice when he,
Almost free at the gates, turned back to look.[5]
So then do not turn back to look at hell.

5. Orpheus with his song moved the god of Hades to release Eurydice from the dead. But he, like Lot's wife, disobeyed the command not to look back, and so lost her once again. See Virgil, *Georgics* 4.453–527; and Ovid, *Metamorphoses* 10.1–85.

HYMNS OF PRAISE[1]

I

TO BE SUNG LIKE "THE SONG OF THE FARMER WIVES"[2]

Oh how great your beauty is,
O my holy, sacred Virgin.
Let us all praise you, O Mary.
Let us all so sweetly sing.

With your beauty that great is
You made beauty[3] fall in love.
O eternal holy beauty
For the Virgin you did burn!
With your love, Love[4] you did bind
Holy Virgin sweet and pious.
Let us all praise you, O Mary.

That great love that all does burn,
Beauty high and infinite,
Did your womb a sweet fruit bear,
Mortal womb whose fruit is life,
Perfect goodness so complete
Is your good O holy Virgin.
Let us all praise you, O Mary.

The great power that all does
In you did his force then find.
You the sun did make your light,
Hidden light in you did grow.
He to whom we all do owe
Is your debtor holy Mother.
Let us all praise you, O Mary.

---

1. The Songs or *Hymns of Praise,* or *Laudi*, are in the tradition of the genre that was cultivated by religious minded poets and found its greatest exponent in Jacopone da Todi (c. 1230–1306). They sang the praise of Christ, the Virgin, the virtues, etc. Practitioners of this genre included Lorenzo's mother, Lucrezia Tornabuoni, and some of his friends. The meter for this type of composition is that of the ballads.
2. *Carnevale Songs* VI, pp. 350–51.
3. Beauty, the highest beauty, is God by antonomasia.
4. Love, like beauty above, is God.

In your holy breast before
All that good was in you born,
In great sorrow and in tears
Would have died who God would see.
Bitter death to life was changed
By your child, O holy Virgin.
  Let us all praise you, O Mary.

Mortal eyes did then look at
This eternal highest good.
To be seen and to be touched,
He did will to all give life.
Happy mortals whose sins he
Just so lightly punish does.
  Let us all praise you, O Mary.

Though by ancient sin and error[5]
Man is stained, he happy is
Since God did let us all see
Such a wonderful Redeemer.
This does show how the Almighty
Such a love for us does bear.
  Let us all praise you, O Mary.

If it weren't for that first tree[6]
That once tasted did us harm,
This vile world would never have
Of the Cross the triumph seen.
From that shameful sin of man
Holy goodness glory drew.
  Let us all praise you, O Mary.

You, O Virgin, the one were
Who such goodness did man give,
Your humility did please:
One were creature and creator.[7]
With pure minds let us then praise
This most pious holy Mother.
  Let us all praise you, O Mary.

---

5. Original sin that God punished "so lightly," since man was redeemed by Christ's sacrifice.
6. The tree of good and evil whose fruit was prohibited, and one taste of which condemned mankind.
7. Cf. Dante, *Paradiso* 33.4–6.

To praise you, O Virgin Mary,
Let all come who burn with love.
Let no one think he's a sinner
Though he has our God offended.
All our burdens she has put
On the shoulders of her Son.
Let us all praise you, O Mary.

Do not doubt of your salvation
Though a sinner you now are.
This most merciful of mothers
To her Son her breast does show,
And the highest pious goodness[8]
Does show her his bleeding wounds.
Let us all praise you, O Mary.

She does say, "O holy son,
This my breast did nurse you once."
And he says, "I with my blood
Did my ribs all color once.
Pity for ungrateful man
Pity does to mercy move."
Let us all praise you, O Mary,
Let us all so sweetly sing.

II

To Be Sung Like "The Song of the Perfumes"[9]

O you wicked stony heart,
Source of all that evil is,
Why don't you in my breast break?
Why aren't you by grief dead struck?

Do no longer comfort seek,
O my heart of hard stone made.
Since sweet Jesus did now die,
The earth trembles, the sun darkens,
From their graves the dead arise,
In the church the veil is torn.[10]
Earth and heaven both do cry,
But you're deaf, my heart of stone.

---

8. Christ crucified.
9. *Carnevale Songs* II, pp. 344–46.
10. Cf. Matt 27.51ff.; Luke 23.45ff.

Do you now all melt like wax,
O you wicked and vile heart.
Since now dying is true life,
Our kind Lord, your own sweet Jesus,
Do my heart on that hard wood
Crucify yourself right now.
May that lance just now you pierce
That the heart of Jesus pierced.

O my heart all full of wounds,
Of your tears a torrent shed,
Just like Jesus from his side
Let your blood a long time flow.
A great sweetness, O my heart,
Feels one who with Jesus is.
If the pain such sweetness gives,
Sweeter yet is with him dying.

From a font that bitter is
Such sweet waters do spring forth
Since you did death like, O God,
Death is now both sweet and dear.
O my heart from Jesus learn.
Your own cross do you take up,[11]
And yourself on it do hang.
No one dies who with Him dies.

III

To Be Sung Like "The Song of the Backward Faces"[12]

O you sinners do come all,
Let us all now cheerful be.
This day God himself did make,
So let's sing and happy be.

Listen sinners death is dead,[13]
This death does to us give life.
Jesus's passion does us comfort,
Sweetest passion and good death.

---

11. Cf. Matt 16.24.
12. *Carnevale Songs* X, pp. 356–57.
13. The death of the soul. Christ's death has redeemed man. This hymn is for Easter.

On this day the slave is freed,
And from hell do saints come forth.[14]

Jesus's death down here on earth
Up in heaven does bear fruit.
If he hadn't on earth here died
There would not a fruit have been,
And this fruit the tears does comfort
Of the Virgin up in Heaven.

The grain Jesus did then bear
Now has grown and bread become,
Holy bread that feeds us all
At the altar every day.
Human minds that happy are
For they're fed the bread of saints.[15]

O blind night that are so holy
That did then see him reborn,
In your darkness so deep there
Came a light of such great splendor
That your shadows clearer were
Than the sun's most brilliant rays.

In the darkness of the night[16]
Did the column show the way
To the people in the desert.
The Egyptians were so frightened,
Hell does tremble at the light,
And in heaven sing the saints.

Holy night that was so worthy,
Your Creator does you love!
Though the sun may angry be,
You did see a clearer sun.
With our words we cannot praise
Such great glory or it sing.

Let us all the cover drop
Of the darkness of the night.

---

14. The slaves of sin are freed from sin, and those who would have been damned in hell are now pure.

15. Cf. Proverbs 9.5.

16. From verse 29 to 34 Lorenzo refers to the cloud of fire that led the way for the Hebrews in their exodus. Cf. Exodus 13.21–22.

Let us all light's armor wear.
In us all let light be bright.

Let our lives hidden in Christ,
In God's light always now be.

IV

To Be Sung Like "The Song of the Cicadas"[17]

That ungrateful wretch am I,
A great sinner who has erred.

I the prodigal son am[18]
To my father I'm returning.
In great danger I have been
When I you did leave, O God,
But so merciful you are
That you don't at my sins look.

I'm that lost and little lamb[19]
That did stray from its own flock,
And you Shepherd, you for that
The flock left and me did follow.
O sweet infinite love, I
That lost was you have now saved.

Woe is me, on a frail ship
I myself and wealth did trust.
Bitter storms goods and ship wrecked,
The survivor on a plank
Has just now safe harbor reached.

Healthy I and handsome was,
I was wounded in my breast.
That knife did so much pain me
And did fear of death give me.
Great physician that you are,
You did heal this body well.

My pure soul with you in love,
God its father and spouse, too,
By the devil blinded was,

---

17. *Carnevale Songs* IX, pp. 355–56.
18. Cf. Luke 15.11–32.
19. Cf. Matt 18.11–14; Luke 15.4–7.

And its lover did then slay.
And for this it cannot rest.
This is then its wretched state.

Since to you, and only you,
Does it come and there find rest,
Nothing else can on this earth
Of much help to my soul be.
So it must always go round
Till it you, O God, does find.

A safe harbor our life finds
When to you, God, I return.
There the mortal wound is healed,
There it finds its most sweet spouse.
The lost son the Father has,
The lost lamb the Shepherd finds.

All dissolved is by your Word
The stone hardness of the mind.
From your spirit a wind comes
That of tears a torrent brings.
I shall happily then harvest
What my tears have here all sown.

O you wonderful God mine,
How do you me so affect?
I do like to cry so much
That I nothing else would do,
O sweet sorrow that now did
With sweet Jesus so bind me.

O most sweet chain that there is
That God did put round my neck,
O immense and so full sweetness
That God gives those who love him.
He does not this grace give often,
So be grateful you have it.

I do see in an imperfect way,
And you make me like what
I see. All that I dream
And imagine is so sweet that
It makes me melt. What will it be
When I will see your face in heaven?[20]

---

20. Cf. Petrarch, *Trionfo dell'eternità* 144–45.

Mortal is my heart still now
Till it goes where it came from.
Give it, God, wings of a dove
So it rises and peace finds.[21]
You, O God, are that sweet food
That has sated my desire.

V

To Be Sung Like Tanta pietà mi tira[22] — *"So Much Does Love Draw Me"*

Since I did taste your sweetness, O my Jesus,
Never more my soul desires
The pleasures of this blind, sad world of ours.

Since your love did my poor afflicted heart
Burn with the ardent flame you did there light,
Nothing does please or does attract me now.
All other goods to me seem pain or grief,
And other peace trouble and war does seem.
Since so inflamed with your deep love I was,
Nothing else will me satisfy or please,
And I can't my thirst I now quench,
If not at your most blessed sacred font.[23]

What made me fall in love so much with you,
O Pelican,[24] was your great charity:
That to give life to others, you chose death,
And to make me divine, human became.
The state and fate of slaves you did then take
So I wouldn't be a slave[25] or live in vain.
Since your great love does not know any bounds,
Not to be to you ungrateful,
I do love you so much and all else scorn.

When my own soul does with you now find rest,
The earth's false goods into oblivion sends.

21. Cf. Petrarch, *Rime* 81; Psalms 55.6.
22. "Tanta pietà mi tira" is a *lauda* by Feo Belcari. See above, p. 41, n. 44.
23. Cf. Disputation VI, 49ff., pp. 407–12.
24. Pelican: traditionally Christ was figured as the pelican that opened its breast with its beak to nourish its young with its own flesh.
25. A slave of sin.

Our life so full of woes and tribulation
Comfort does find in this desire alone.
Of nothing else at all it can now think
Or speak or see, but you alone, my God.
Only one grief remains that does it tear:
The sad thought that its defect
Too often the sweet thought does let escape.

Your sweetness now let bitterness allay,
Let your bright light this world of mine illumine,
So that your love that I hold dear and sweet
Will in the future never part from me.
You were not miserly with your own blood,
So then do not deny me one more gift:
Let your sweet fire always my own heart burn,
So that slowly over time
No one but you will in my heart remain.

VI

To Be Sung Like La canzone del fagiano — *"The Song of the Pheasant"*[26]

O God, O highest good, what are you doing
That only you I seek, but never find?

Alas, if I do seek one thing or other,[27]
In them I do you seek, O sweet Lord mine.
All things through you are beautiful and good,
And since they are all good, I them desire.
You are in every site and in all things,
And never can I find you anywhere.

My poor sad soul to find you anxious is.
All day I grieve, at night I do not rest.
Alas the more I seek, the more you flee,
Oh sweet and much desired rest for my soul.
Oh do tell me, my Lord, where does it hide,
I am so tired, O Lord, do tell me now.

If to seek you, my Lord, I ever move
In wealth, in honors or in pleasures still,

26. See Charles S. Singleton, *Canti carnascialeschi del Rinascimento* (Bari: Laterza, 1936), p. 130; also *Tutte le opere,* ed. Orvieto.

27. For verses 3–8, cf. *Disputation* VI, 49–57, p. 407 and *Sylva I,* 10, p. 224.

The more I do you seek, the less I find,
So that dead tired my vain love never rests.
You set my heart afire with love for you,
Then you did flee, and I do not you see.

My sight that to a thousand things does turn
Looks but does not see you, and yet you shine.
My ears also to many voices listen,
And though your voice is there, they don't hear you.
With all my senses I that sweetness seek
That I don't find, but yet for all is there.

O why do you, my poor sad soul, still seek
A happy life amidst such pain and grief?[28]
Do look for what you seek, but it is not
Where you do ever search for this great good.
You seek a happy life where death resides.
And life you seek where life there never was.

From these vain eyes do let all light be gone
So I can then see you, true friendly light.
My ears do deafen so I shall then hear
That voice I so desire that will tell me:
"O you who labor or so burdened are
Do come and rest in me,[29] 'tis now good weather."

Let this so wretched life in me now die
So I shall live in you, O my true life.
Death in an endless multitude[30] appears,
Only in you life is, for you are life.
When I leave you and look at me I die,
When I to you do turn, I shall not die.

Then will the eye invisible light see,
The ear will hear a sound that has no voice,
Light and sound that alone the mind perceives.
Excess does not offend or a sense harm.
While the feet still remain, the soul will race
To that good that with it will always be.

---

28. For verses 27–32, cf. *Disputation* V, 142–44, p. 404 and VI, 178–80 p. 411.

29. Cf. Matt 11.28.

30. The multitude of earthly things in opposition to God one and eternal.

I shall then see, O beautiful sweet Lord,
That this or that good is not meant for me,[31]
But as I'll take away these[32] from the good,
The good that will remain will sweet God be.
This true and only sweetness he will feel
Who seeks the good and never will this fail.

The running waters of all other streams[33]
Can never quench our great eternal thirst,
But to our flaming passions firewood add;
Only the font of life eternal can.
O sacred waters if your font I reach,
I shall then drink and never thirst again.

Such great desire should never be in vain.
Our ardent love to you does ever rise.
With mercy do reach out with both your hands.
O Jesus mine, infinite love you are.
Since you so sweetly did my poor heart wound,
Do You yourself now heal what you have done.

VII

To Be Sung Like Amore Io vo fuggendo — *"Love I Am Fleeing"*

O you sinners come to me[34]
For with open arms I'm waiting.
From the holy breast does flow
Water and blood and love, as you can see.

As the staff did in the desert[35]
From the rock make water spring,
Thus Longinus opened wide
All my side with his sharp lance.
Do come now ungrateful people,
Come now and drink the deathless holy water.

---

31. Cf. *Disputation* VI, 52–54, p. 407.

32. The imperfect earthly good as opposed to the true good of God.

33. For verses 57–62, cf. *Disputation* VI, 67–69, p. 408.

34. Christ speaks from the cross.

35. As he guided the Hebrews towards Palestine, Moses made water spring from a rock by striking it. Cf. Exodus 17.6.

All the people who did thirst
In an arid spot then were.
From the rock there did come forth
A great spring of running water.
Let the people here then drink:
The rock is Christ from which the water comes.

Let those who have thirsty been
To the sacred water come.
Also those whom others scorn
At the spring here welcome are.
Let them here in these fresh waters
Happy and gay their thirst and ardor quench.

Holy Noah this now is
Who the grapes did so well crush.
Inebriated he was so
And uncovered without fear;
His son Cam, that evil seed,
Laughed at him, while his shame the others covered.

Just so naked on the cross
Jesus, filled with burning love,
Does not care for all the sneers
Of those who did him deride.
Nicodemus him did take
And then with sheets our Savior he did cover.

With great love all filled Isaiah,
Thus did he the Lord then see.
His clothes did all red then seem,
With wine wet and all red stained.
From the press wine did then flow.[36]
This and the pain the cross does represent.

"Sacred breast and holy feet
Everywhere do blood there shed.
Hands and head suffer you see,
And of this the fruit is yours.
Though so stained with blood I am,
O you repentant sinners to me come.

36. Cf. Isaiah 63.2.

O come now, do me approach.
Do not fear that I'd you stain,
You my son dear always are
That I call in many ways.
These nails here will not me hold
From to my heart so hard embracing you.

Do not fear the cruel thorns
That are wound around my head,
Or that will my lips so taste
Strong of vinegar and bile.
My poor face do now you kiss.
Do not disgusted be by your true Lord.

This blood that I now shed
Does not stain, instead it cleanses.
This great font eternal is
All man's thirst does ever quench.
Greater then would my torment be
If this great love of mine should unknown then be."

VIII

To Be Sung Like "The Song of the Farmer Wives"[37]

O sinners, your eternal God I am
And I do call just to keep you from hell.

O come do think who does love you so much
And who so sweetly does call you today,
And who are you whose health he does so want.
Just think of this and you won't ever die.

I am the God who has created all.
A man you're not, but a vile mortal worm.
In many ways I ever touch your heart.
You do not listen and do hell prefer.

So that my holy voice will move you more,
I do upon the cross for you then die.
With my own blood your awful sin I wash,
So much do I regret your own damnation.

O come to me, you poor and wretched sinner,
For I do you await with open arms

37. *Carnevale Songs* VI, pp. 350–51.

To let you cleanse your sins in my own blood
And to embrace and rescue you from hell.

With loving and sweet voice I do you call
So that your sinful ways you will amend.
O come, my yoke do take, it is not heavy,
It is so light and gives eternal life.

I do well see that your old sins do make
You shut your ears against my voice that calls,
And here my grace I do for you make ready,
But you from it do flee and hell prefer.

Tell me what fruit you reap now or what pleasure
From this that may seem life, but torment is —
Unless it is repentance, shame and woes —
And you for this will lose eternal life.

With love all filled, with pity and deep mercy,
I call on you, O sinner, to repent,
But if you should wait for the final judgment,
Too late it would then be. Hell doesn't redeem.

Do not wait for that final cruel sentence,
For then all pity must be set aside.
Do not now wait for death to close your eyes,
For it comes fast and may eternal be,

IX

A hard heart he must well have
If he at times our Savior forsakes.

His heart evil must then be,
He must for sure himself hold in contempt
If at once he does not go
Where blessed Jesus does to us all call.

He does say, "Come now I'm waiting
For I am dying just to save you, O sinner."

He does not for his health care
Who by this voice does still unmoved remain.
Neither grace nor virtue has
One, who the love of the Cross does forget.
He does much himself to injure
Who does not see how great is Jesus's love.

Blind you are if you don't see
Your own eternal good, O wretched sinner.
You must have your hearing lost
If here the voice that comes you do not hear
So from hell you will be saved,
If you will want an end to error put.

He made you without your will,
But he will not save you if you don't act.
If you didn't yourself remove
From all your sins there can be no excuse.
If self love is not in you,
The fault is yours, the damage and the grief.

Oh do you now turn to him
He'll satisfy you with eternal good.
Your will isn't your own if you
Do others let with your life interfere.
You do not very far see,
If you do not see who your real Lord is.

He did die to give you life
And mortal did become to make you good.
Suffer does his glory great
To now save you, an evil, wretched sinner.
If he is both good and pious,
Let not ingratitude be your repayment.

Oh do you his path pursue.
His holy yoke do take that is so sweet.
Do begin and do decide
To live with that sweet yoke that so light is.
So much pity does he have
That at all times he will you happy make.

The Mystery Play of Saints John and Paul[1]

List of Characters

Angel (announcer)
First relative of Saint Agnes
Second relative of Saint Agnes
Third relative of Saint Agnes
Constantia
A servant of Costantia
Saint Agnes
Constantine (Costantia's father)
Gallicanus
A daughter of Gallicanus
Another daughter of Gallicanus
Attica
Artemia
John
Paul
Angel (apparition)
Trumpeter
Trumpeter
King
Prince
Messenger (to Constantine)
Constantine (son of Emperor Constantine)
Constans (one of the brothers)
Constantius (other brother)
Emperor (the new one)
A servant
A soldier
A comforter
An accuser
Julian the Apostate
Terentianus
Saint Basil (bishop)
Virgin Mary
Treasures
Astrologers

The angel announces and says:

Silence, O you who have now gathered here. 1
A new and holy story you will see.
Diverse and pious things you will see here.
Examples of how Fortune varied is.
Without a word do please remain in silence,
Especially when singing we shall be.
For us work now, for you to watch with joy,
Please do make sure we can all this enjoy.

Saint Constantia, who of leprosy was 2
Cured, you'll see here as she converted is.

---

1. The play was probably presented for the first time on February 17, 1491. Lorenzo, who had written it to celebrate his son Giuliano's election to "messere" of the group that presented it, attended. The play, then, was written specifically for a particular occasion. While there are some specific sources for the material used (e.g., the *Legenda aurea* of Jacobus de Voragine), the play depends more on the tradition of the miracle plays in Italian. Moreover, among Lorenzo's friends or courtiers there were some who had written sacred plays and other works of that nature.

In the fierce battle that most furious is,
You will see many there killed or taken.
A second time the scepter will change hands,
And there will be of John and Paul the torture.
The death you'll see of Julian Apostate,
So to avenge the martyrs killed of late.

The company this is of our Saint John. 3
We shall recite here, but we are so young[2]
So if the verses should be poorly read,
Do us excuse for our so tender years.
Also if we don't have of lords the bearing
And can't old men and women so well play,
We shall our best with love do for your sake.
Think of our age, excuse every mistake.

First relative of Saint Agnes:

If I didn't tell the truth I'd wiser be 4
Than telling it to you and seem a liar,
But since of the same line we are relations,
I shall not be so careful as I talk,
For if in talking a mistake I'd make,
Mistaken I am not to trust you now.
The blood relation that is very close
Is such that the truth now I'll disclose.

The case I wish to tell you this one is: 5
On this last night that has already fled,
Fully awake I wasn't, but not asleep.
The dead and holy virgin did appear,
Agnes who just six days ago did die.
She was all dressed in white, happy, devout.
With her there was a lamb, humble and white,
And many other virgins crowded tight.

With her soft words and sweet she did console 6
Us for our grief at her most holy death.
"You are quite wrong," she said, "to grieve for me,
For great the glory is that I have reached.
Beyond the earth's shadow the sun I see

2. The company of Saint John the Evangelist had actors between the age of thirteen and twenty-four. Lorenzo's children, Piero, Giovanni and Giuliano, were all members of the company.

And the angelic choir I do hear sing.
So then, my dear relatives, do be brief:
If you do love me an end put to grief.

SECOND RELATIVE:

Do not continue. You have just narrated 7
What I to say did want, but was afraid,
For something foolish I didn't want to say.
While I was at her grave to make sure that
No one would dare to touch it, to me, too,
This holy and pure virgin did appear.
With the lamb and the virgins she did come,
And I saw her as if she were at home.

No one will it believe, but yet it's true. 8
I did see her, and I did hear her speak,
Not while I slept or in imagination,
But with my eyes wide open and well focused.
I did begin to speak, but could not finish:
"O holy beautiful virgin,..." but then
She moved away from there as I did fear.
Happy I stayed and with many a tear.

FIRST RELATIVE AGAIN:

Although to such fallacious visions one 9
Not very holy must never believe —
For often they are but the devil's tricks —
This one from God himself could truly come,
Since this vision to more than one appeared.
We must thank God and his mercy implore,
For us it is both lucky and so wise
To represented be in paradise.

CONSTANTIA:

Oh woe is me! What good is it to be 10
The daughter of one who the world does rule[3]
And have so many servants and hand maidens,
Be rich and young? What good does it do me
To be so honored and be so much loved

3. Costantia is the daughter of the emperor Constantine; the scene is now the imperial palace.

If leprosy does stain my youthful limbs?
I'll not my father give any grandchildren,
For by my body's ulcers it's forbidden.

Better it would have been if this my soul 11
Had never in my body nourished been,
Or if, once there, it would have soon decided
In my young years from this body to flee,
For a real death by much the sweeter is
Than in this life to die at every hour
And give my father one grief in this way
Than make him so much suffer day by day.

A SERVANT OF CONSTANTIA:

Presumptuous I may be or importune, 12
But what I thought I must to you now say:
When for an ill no remedy there is,
To new and strange things then recur one must.
Since no one, no medicine or effort,
This evil can now take away from you,
I think new remedies then must be found:
Where art is lacking, there does God abound.

By many people I have heard it said 13
That Agnes, who had suffered martyrdom,
Had recently appeared to her relations,
And thus it is believed she is a saint.
I should now there with much devotion go
Where buried is this holy woman now.
Do ask protection with a humble voice.
What cannot harm can't be so bad a choice.

CONSTANTIA:

I have in vain so many things now tried 14
That I this so short distance will soon try
If to my body it should health restore.
A burden small this is that I shall bear.
Perhaps my journey will not be in vain.
I now do feel my heart burn with devotion:
It seems my health now to predict already.
Let us now go with a few friends but steady.

Constantia, having arrived at Agnes's grave, says:

O holy virgin, enemy of pomp 15
And luxury and filled with love of God,
In the name of your chaste blood that was shed,
I beg you to consider my desire.
Have pity for my young but tainted body.
Have pity for that old father of mine.
O holy Virgin, though I don't deserve,
For my old father's sake cleanse me and preserve.

Constantia sleeps and Saint Agnes appears to her and says:

Be of good heart, O blessed daughter mine, 16
Your prayer was heard by God whom it did please,
And your desire has fully granted been,
For rise your prayer did from a true devotion.
You are now free, your body is all cleansed.
Give thanks to God for you real reason have.
Always love mighty God for his great grace
And from vice do ever turn your face.

Constantia awakens and says:

It is so true, I can't believe it yet, 17
But with my eyes and hands I see I'm cleansed.
Gone is the evil that defaced my limbs.
I am all clean just like when I was born.
O God so marvelous, why such great grace
For me? And how shall I to this respond?
My old merits it was not or my goodness,
But Agnes that did move your bountifulness.

The fragrance of her holy chasteness did 18
Into your presence like incense then rise,
And I, who have so thoroughly been cured,
The vow do take before you, blessed Jesus,
That while this brief span of years does endure,
For you my breast I'll keep all chaste and clean.
The body that I now feel clean outside
With your grace I will keep the same inside.

She turns to those who are with her and says:

My dearest friends, these limbs you can now see 19
That the supreme physician has thus cured.
With me together let us all give thanks
To God for his so great mercy divine.
Such fruit with sweetness all those harvest will
Who God respect and in his path do walk.
Let us return, to God singing our praise,
And father's sadness all away to chase.

While returning home:

O God, who do not even human sinners 20
Leave destitute of your bountiful grace,
Who could have ever thought that from dire evil
Like leprosy so many goods would rise
That my so awful illness useful was?
I must now say that my ill good has brought.
Oh holy illness that on me was urged
That cleanse the body did and the soul purged.

Having arrived, she says to her father:

Here is your daughter who a leper was 21
Who comes to you with body cleansed and cured,
Now healthy with most perfect and true health,
For both her body and her mind are well.
Too happy am I and perfect is my joy
Because of you, O sweetest father mine,
For God so graciously health to me gave
And did from so much grief you, father, save.

Her father Constantine answers:

So much sweetness I feel, dear daughter mine, 22
That my joy now seems sure to overflow,
And I can't help myself with such emotion
If from my eyes sweet tears I now will shed.
O my dear, sweetest hope for my old age
I can't believe all this, let me touch you.

As he says this, he touches her hand:

Oh wonder of wonders, it is all so true!
But daughter mine, do tell me, who cured you?

CONSTANTIA ANSWERS:

Of this infirmity no doctor cured 23
Me, but divine intervention did so.
I went so much contrite and so devout
Of Agnes to the holy burial place.
There I did pray and was in heaven heard.
I then did go to sleep and woke all cleansed.
O father mine, I then did take a vow
That God my spouse and your new son is now.

CONSTANTINE ANSWERS:

A most great wonder this certainly is. 24
Who did it I don't know, nor does it matter.
Enough. If well my daughter does remain,
Whoever did it a great thing did do.
Come, let us happy be and celebrate.
O majordomo, do set up the table
At once. Let come right here just before me
Singers and players for feasting will there be.

IN THE MIDST OF THE FEAST, GALLICANUS[4] RETURNS VICTORIOUS FROM PERSIA AND SAYS:

I have to you returned, O great Augustus, 25
I don't know how for many were the perils.
That fierce and strong people I have subjected.
Never again will it against you rise.
In Persia is your scepter high and just
Now held, and with my sword I made the rivers
Filled with blood all run as if painted red.
Vanquished and tamed they're all, or else they're dead

With fire and steel around us, the dead and 26
Wounded, we did victory seek with our
Swords, I and your strong and audacious knights.
Memory of our deeds the world will keep.
I do well know that you do realize
How important this is to state and glory,
For the reverse would have been at high cost:
Your state and Roman name would then be lost.

---

4. That Gallicanus was Constantine's general is apparently Lorenzo's invention.

Though glory and to serve a worthy lord 27
To noble hearts a great reward must be,
Yet the endeavor, the courage and mind,
Even if I didn't, would reward demand.
If half your kingdom you would offer me,
It still would not suffice, as I believe.
But I'd be happy if you less gave me:
Do just Constantia let my own wife be.

Augustus, that is Constantine, answers:

Welcome to my great warrior and my captain, 28
Welcome to the sole pride of my empire,
Welcome to my faithful Gallicanus,
Tamer of that most proud, ferocious people.
Welcome to him who is my strong right hand,
Whose strength and valor give me cause to hope.
Welcome to him who while in life does last
Our great empire and glory will stand fast.

Our deeds and efforts all require reward, 29
And your deserts with me are great, indeed.
If you expected a most just reward,
I never could your merits have repaid.
My daughter to give you a great thing is,
And you do know how much I do love her.
Great is a father's love that cannot fail,
But great your merit is and must prevail.

The daughter of an emperor who rules 30
The world she wouldn't be, were it not for you.
If some, however, should show surprise and
Blame me, I should then with these words respond:
"I think that she and all my family
And all the people will most happy be,
And I from this will get great happiness,
No less than I have had from your success."

I now do wish to go, O Gallicanus, 31
To tell some things to my daughter Constantia.
I shall return at once with all resolved,
You must not mind to wait here until then.

As he goes, he says:

O foolish man! O most vainglorious mind!
O pride to wonder at! O arrogance!
For me to have won now has a false ring,
If victory with it does this home bring.

What shall I do? Shall I then to a subject 32
My beautiful daughter give who dear is?
If I do not I'll put the state in danger,
And who is there who will then help us out?
Oh, woe is me! No rose without thorn is,
So much does Fortune to her goods hold on.
Those who do think Fortune has favored me
Much better off than me must often be.
I come to see you with my eyes, dear child, 33
As I always with my heart do see you.

Constantia:

O father, I do see upon your brow
A sign that tells me that your heart is grieving
And that surprises me and gives me grief.
Sweet father mine, if I your love do have,
Do tell me what this grief to you does bring
And if I can for you do anything.

Do tell me father, do not hold it back. 34
I am your daughter and I want you happy,
And after God you only count for me,
And I do wish to give your life some cheer.

Constantine:

I'm loath to tell this news, so I delay.
I am most sorry for my own old age
And for your body that a cure did find,
So Gallicanus would you have in mind.

Constantia:

O father, do your grief now hold in check. 35
I fully understand what you are saying.
Almighty God a generous Lord is
And will not now his grace from us withhold.
I see what so much grief is giving you:

If you give Gallicanus what he wants,
You'll offend us. If I will not him take,
The kingdom will in peril be and quake.

When every choice will just the same one harm 36
And not so sure and clear the matter is,
I've heard it said a wise man will delay,[5]
Promises he gives, but lets time go by.
Although my mind cannot soar to great heights,
I'd say that me you promise him, O father.
Do him assure he will soon get his prize,
And then send him on some new enterprise.

Although perhaps I may presumptuous seem 37
If I still young, a woman and your daughter
Should in this matter of mine counsel you,
So prudent and experienced, also aged,
You could tell him how dangerous the war
In Dacia is, and that all that he wishes
You will grant him. You will not him deceive.
Paul and John[6] you'll give him, so he'll believe.

These hostages let him now take so he'll 38
Know that his I'll be since this he now wants,
But do let him respond by giving you
Attica and Artemia, his own daughters.
Much will there happen in this war, and time
Does have a way to fix so many things

Constantine:

I do so like what you have now just said
And happy, soon with it I'll go ahead.

To himself as he returns to Gallicanus:

Blessed be he who in you does inspire 39
Goodness and prudence and love, my dear daughter.
No longer am I angry or afraid,
And so let Gallicanus content be.
Honor is safe that does all else involve,

5. This is what Machiavelli calls the "benefit of time," but condemns the Florentines for the belief as a sign of weakness and prefers to react forcefully to crises.

6. Costantine's children.

Although at times these things are paid for dear.
When time has passed and days are put to rest
We shall then see what to do will be best.

To Gallicanus:

Happier than when I went do I return 40
For now Constantia does agree your wife
To be, and I can also happier be
For then I had so many doubts in mind.
She seemed to want a tranquil and quiet life
Without a husband and away from people.
Cured of her ill, as if now born anew,
Lovely and happy she consents to you.

I should say let the wedding now take place 41
And let the nation with all this rejoice,
But let us now, if you agree, just wait,
For rebel Dacia all around us presses,
And you well know how hard we are beset.
It is not right to have weddings in war.
Once we have won, and if you are content,
The wedding we'll hold, as is my intent.

I know you do so much Constantia want, 42
But first your honor comes, and so my state,
Or rather yours, for yours the empire is,
For your own valor has this state preserved.
As proof that I speak true, O Gallicanus,
John always dear to me, Paul so beloved
You'll take with you as my own guarantee,
Artemia and Attica stay here with me.

Father you will to the ones I love be, 43
Constantia will be mother to your own,
Not stepmother. Be certain that she will
Always treat them as if her own they were.
I hope the gods will offer me their help,
But in your valor so much more I trust.
So then a great victory must soon come:
Constantia is yours, and we shall feast at home.

Gallicanus:

O great emperor, nothing does my heart 44
So much desire as to make you content
And to preserve your state and my own honor.
Without all this I could not face Constantia.
I hope I'll soon a conqueror return.
I know this fire will soon extinguished be.
To their own damage the barbarians will
See how my hand and sword know how to kill.

When an action dire peril does entail, 45
One must then undertake it all at once.
It must be planned with care and all due thought,
But then it must at once be executed.
So then I shall move out without delay.
Paul and John will with me now always be,
Like brothers or my sons as I intend,
And to you my Constantia recommend.

O trusted Alexander go at once 46
And here Attica bring and so Artemia.
And you Anthony[7] to the money see
And all my people gather here at once.
O my brave knights that never were defeated
While you were with me, O most valiant knights
Brought up in arms by you never forsaken,
Once more we'll conquer. I am not mistaken.

When his daughters arrive Gallicanus says to Constantine:

My eyes cannot remain dry while I say 47
What I should like of my dear and sweet daughters.
I do leave them to you to be your own.
Fortune in war over all things holds sway.
I shall now go so very far away
Against a people that to win desire.
Though I believe victorious I shall be,
Returning safe is not all up to me.

And you my daughters, since my lord it pleases 48
That I this enterprise do undertake,

---

7. Alexander and Anthony are officers of Gallicanus.

Pray Jove that I unharmed come back with peace
Or victory, and do return with honor.
If dead and buried I should there remain,
The emperor will be your own new father.
For him I do my life willingly spend,
And you to my Constantia do attend.

One of the daughters:

When we do think that you, O dearest father, 49
Perhaps we never shall see once again,
Our saddest hearts our eyes do fill with tears.
And where, dear father, do you leave us now?
A thousand times and more I have arms cursed
And war and he who is the cause of it.
Although you have proposed a worthy father,
We would our own so sweet always have rather.

The other daughter:

O mighty, worthy lord, why do you now 50
Want that we should like orphans here remain?
In this dire enterprise do spare our father
If you now can: thousands you have like him,
But other father we surely don't have.
Make us content, give us our peace of mind.

Constantine:

I tell you now your father, come don't cry,
Will soon return with victory and spry.

Gallicanus turns to Constantine and says:

I wish to kiss your foot, O mighty lord, 51
Before I leave, and my sweet daughters' faces.
Do now believe your faithful Gallicanus:
I shall over your sons John and Paul watch.
One on my left, the other on my right
I shall keep them so they will not be harmed.
If you hear that to harm them some contrive,
You can be sure no more am I alive.

He turns to his knights and says:

O knights of mine all by the sun burned black, 52
The Persian sun that hot and flaming is,
Our emperor our mettle wants to try
Amidst the snow and ice of Dacia now.
Valor does heat and cold soon overcome,
Peril and Death like nothing it defies,
But first of all to Mars let's sacrifice.
Worthless without a god is man's device.

Having said this, he conducts a sacrifice in a place that can't be seen; he then leaves with his army for the Dacian enterprise.

Constantia to Attica and Artemia, whom she converts:

My dearest sisters and of God beloved, 53
O my sweet Attica, my dear Artemia,
I think your father didn't give you to me
As guarantee or company for me,
But so that happy, gay and by God blessed
I should give you to him when he returns.
I do not know how I can all this do,
Unless by God blessed I make you, too.

My dear sweet sisters, I now must tell you: 54
My body once by leprosy was stained,
And now these limbs have been all cleansed and purged
By God almighty who all good creates.
To him my chastity I did then vow
Until my body is by death embraced.
With all my heart to him serve I desire.
It is not hard, just love and him admire.

With my example I do you encourage 55
To dedicate to God with a good heart
This life that so brief is and so fallacious
And to avoid what this blind world does love.
If you do turn to him all your desires,
You will in life true peace of mind then find
And for defeating Satan you'll have grace
And in the next the glory of God's face.

Artemia:

I do not know, my lady, what you did. 56
The holy words that you just now did say
Have made me feel as if my heart were melting,
And my chaste breast with love of God all burn.
And all at once I was all moved as you
Your mind did open with your sacred words.
In love with God, I am all ready now
The holy path to take and make my vow.

Attica:

And I, my lady, now do this world hate, 57
As if it were my deadly mortal foe.
I promise God to keep my body pure.
With my lips and my heart I tell you this.

Constantia

May God almighty ever more be blessed,
And in his name I now do bless you both.
True sisters we now are. Let us now raise
Our voice on high and give our God full praise.

Constantia, Artemia and Attica sing together:

O perfect charity, praise be to you 58
For you have filled our hearts with charity.
The love that our sweet prayers do now contain
Do let, O Lord, to your own ears arise.
Do welcome now three virginal chaste hearts,
And do their flames of love keep ever burning.
Our Virgin Mother, you loved at one time
O most dear Spouse, our hearts are now all thine.

Gallicanus speaks to his soldiers:

O my brave knights, when planning in his tent 59
The captain prudent must and careful be,
But when the time for fighting does arrive,
Let him be strong and brave and without fear.
Those who propose in victory to triumph
Do not give thought to arrow, sword and lance.
There is our enemy, and he shows fear.
Let us attack, our victory is near.

(In the battle with the enemy his army is routed.)

Having remained alive with John and Paul, he says:

This is the victory that I have gained, 60
Thus have I saved my emperor's great state.
Alas, it would better have been if I
Had died in Persia then with honor bright.
But Fortune has preserved me from my death
To make me suffer so much grief and sorrow.
That I didn't die today I rue and pine
For how can I return to Constantine?

John:

When with our purpose Fortune interferes 61
One must always believe it's for the best.
If you today have lost your knights and army,
Give thanks to God, for this from him does come.
Never will one triumph against his foes
Who over his own self has not prevailed.
No triumph over others we obtain,
If we know not how to ourselves restrain.

Perhaps today God brought you to this pass 62
So that you would yourself right now reform.
Though in the past you have your foes defeated,
Know that no leaf can turn without our God.
What man, corrupt and mortal, can himself
Do, nothing else is but to sin and suffer.
Yourself reform and do to God return:
From him all good and in him love does burn.

Paul:

Do not believe that your own strength and glory, 63
Your power and your mind, O Gallicanus,
Did give you all your triumphs and your honors.
God it was who in your hands power put,
And since too proud you grew and so vain, too,
God all at once honor from you did take
So that he would to your boastfulness show
That he does give and take, as all should know.

If from your rout you would some fruit derive, 64
Return to God, to Jesus, our sweet Lord.
Decide that never more you will adore
The idol Mars that so fallacious is.
You will then see an army here anew,
More numerous and of much greater power.
Humble yourself before Jesus's great might
For he himself did so from his great height.

Gallicanus:

If I myself humble as you propose 65
I do not know how it will Jesus please,
For from necessity I'll seem to move
That has brought me to this most wretched state.
Some Christians have I heard who did then say
That if one does his heart to God donate
God will reciprocate if voluntary.
My wretchedness shows only the contrary.

John:

In every place and at all times God will 66
All workers in his vineyard well receive,
And the devout and sweet family head
His money also gives to one who's late.[8]
Entirely do give him your full desire
And you will harvest then for one a hundred.
To God with heart and body do now bow,
Honor and army he will render now.

Gallicanus kneels and says:

O mighty God, your power I adore, 67
And I confess I'm nothing but a worm.
If it may please your great magnificence,
Permit me on this day to be triumphant.
If it does not please you, I'll patient be.
In your hands, O my God, I've placed myself.
Firm and decided I am, I'll no more
Any but you, sweet Jesus, now adore.

8. Cf. Matt 20.1–16.

Once they are all kneeling, John says:

O God, who did Joshua the daring give 68
And the great grace also the sun to stop,
And before one you made a thousand flee,
And made but two ten-thousand chase away,
And made the fatal stone from the sling hurl
That did the giant Goliath then strike dead,[9]
Do grace and strength give Gallicanus's hand
Who humbled is and before you does stand.

A lamb bearing a cross appears to Gallicanus and says:

A contrite heart, O humble Gallicanus 69
A sacrifice is that does God so please,
So then your humble prayer he has now heard
And merciful has your desire just granted.
Be of good heart and bravely do proceed,
For your foe will his kingdom surely lose.
A greater force you'll have and all so brave,
The cross on your flag is, so let it wave.

Gallicanus kneeling:

This did not merit Gallicanus's heart 70
So full of pride and his so great vainglory.
Your word has hope in me now re-awakened,
So that as certain triumph I now see.
O God I will my sincere faith in you
Preserve and all false gods from my mind chase.
But where is this new force now coming from?
From him, who my God is, it does now come.

Turning to the soldiers who had miraculously arrived, he says:

O soldiers so relentless and so brave, 71
We shall at once the enemy besiege.
Let all the bombards be brought here at once —

---

9. Joshua was given the power to stop the sun during a battle so that he might complete his victory. David and Saul are the two mentioned: the former killed one thousand enemies, and the latter ten thousand. Goliath, a giant Philistine warrior, was killed by David.

God is with us, no remedy they'll have —
And right away do bring all our firearms[10]
So that they will not dare to bother us,
Sappers and faggots, too. The town will fall.
It is surrounded as if by a wall.

Do the defenses ready, get the shelter, 72
Shields for all our guns, do make the bridge strong,
The bombardiers securely do protect
So that artillery will not them kill.
And you, O knights, in armor do remain,
Careful and vigilant do all escort
So that to spike all our bombards the thought
Our enemy does have will come to naught.

And you, O John, the straw and hay provide 73
So that it won't be lacking in our camp.
Have them make bread and check all our provisions.
Paul will help you and always with you stay.
Have ladders made that climb our soldiers will.
When the time comes for battle to begin,
For his own task let each one ready be,
And only I to everything will see.

Do all the trumpeters here gather now, 74
The usual proclamation let be made,
For our attack I'll launch so very soon.
For my commands do all of you be ready.
Whoever will be first the wall to mount
Will be rewarded with a thousand ducats.
Five and one hundred are for the next two,
And double pay is there for all of you.

Those who around there are have just been told 75
That their brave leader has let it be known
That should the city not give up at once
It would be sacked and to the ground all razed,
And Gallicanus wouldn't show mercy then,
Let the axe fall wherever it may be.
To those who first mount he'd give, them to thank,
One thousand, five and one hundred by rank.

10. Obviously there were no fire arms at the time.

(The battle is fought, and the king is taken prisoner.)

The king says:

Let those who put their trust in reigns or states 76
And with great pride the mighty gods do scorn
The wasted city see and me in chains,
And let them learn from my so dire example.
These are the reigns I've given you, my sons.
This is our father's legacy to us:
One chain, alas, does you and me now bind.
The conqueror now does drag us behind.

Turning to Gallicanus, he says:

You in whose hands now Fortune has decreed 77
To put our lives, our future and our fate
Let it suffice that you did me defeat,
The city burn and a brave people kill.
Do not desire that I at my age spared
Have been to witness my own children's death.
All power and all means are just to win,
Not to have mercy after is a sin.

Noble and generous I know you are 78
And in a noble heart mercy does grow.
If my old age does not at all you move,
Let tender years and innocence so do.
To kill one who bound is a vile thing is,
And mercy is by all so praised and lauded.
The reign is yours. Our lives to spare do deign
In which for me just a few years remain.

The prince, one of the king's sons, says:

Since Fortune has so hard all of us struck, 79
We who his sons are, innocent and wretched,
Beg you the life to save for all of us,
If you so please, but if this cannot be,
Do let at least our aged father live.
If so, we then won't mind this world to leave.
If to kill all of us you do so thirst,
The grace extend to us that we die first.

Gallicanus:

Pity for all of you my heart has touched 80
So that almost I do regret my winning.
In every game the victor is but one,
The vanquished must then well themselves resign.
For young and for old age I pity feel.
Fortune's example I do well remember.
To spare your life I willingly command
Until before Augustus we do stand.

The messenger who brings news of victory to Constantine speaks:

My emperor, good news I do bring you, 81
Your Gallicanus has the city taken.
The king was either taken or is dead.
I saw the city burn all filled with flames.
So I'd be first to bring you such good news,
All the details I could not ascertain.
That ours is the city I did observe,
A good drink do give me, I it deserve.

Constantine:

I do not want to make some great mistake 82
By thinking that this news is really true.
This man no letter has from Gallicanus.
Lies on their lips, the truth they keep inside.
Do not waste time, put him in jail right now:
If these rose bushes are, they will soon flower.
If what you said is true, you'll have your drink,
If not your trip you will regret, I think.

Gallicanus returns and speaks to Constantine:

Here you see me. From a most cruel war 83
To you triumphant I do now return
With honor bright and prisoners and booty.
Here is the king who once that city ruled.
But know that things at first did not go well,
For he who much does can also much err.
Yet with the help that God did to us give
We did a glorious victory achieve.

The captive king speaks to Constantine:

O emperor, a lord I, too, was once; 84
Captive and slave I'm now and so my sons.
If Fortune, God's minister, does this want,
Then let all note this as a great example,
And fully warned by what to me has happened,
Let no one be surprised by adverse blows.
God's gift does us with victory regale,
But once triumphant, pity must prevail.

Constantine answers:

The soul that does aspire to worthy things 85
Like God does try to be in what it can.
It strives to win and evermore to rise
Until its high desire contented is.
But then the wrath and ire it had conceived
And the offense it soon does put aside.
I pardon you and do all wrath disdain,
I do not blood want, but glory and reign.

He then turns to Gallicanus:

When you to me return, O Gallicanus, 86
Even in dire defeat you would be welcome.
Just think how dear you must then be to me
When you return in triumph and in glory.
To see before my eyes a king in chains
Is something I will never more forget.
Where does that cross come from, do now tell me.
You have religion changed, how can that be?

Gallicanus answers:

Deny you something I could never do, 87
How could I then the truth refuse to you?
No noble heart could ever even think
Of truth denying to anyone at all.
I have just now thanked God here in Saint Peter's
For the most glorious fortune I've enjoyed.
Since Christ my victory did then ordain,
The sign I wear that does to Christ pertain.

In my first words I did mention to you 88
That broken and defeated I had been.

Of all of us just three remained alive,
I and these two dear ones here by my side.
All three of us did do what others do
Who down are hurled into a low, vile state.
Though very late, it does to those occur
As a last remedy to God recur.

As you from Paul and John will soon now hear, 89
We won through miracles and God's own grace.
I now have learned how the false gods deceive.
The armor of God's faith I have now donned.
I'm ready to devote my life to him
In peace away from this world's noise and tumult.
To give me Constantia it did you please,
But from that promise I now you release.

Constantine:

You don't bring me one victory alone 90
Or one joy only from this latest war.
A kingdom you gave me, also a daughter
More dear to me than any conquered land,
And since you now believe in Christian doctrine
And do one God adore who's never wrong,
You can say that you now yourself do know:
On you did God all these triumphs bestow.

And to increase your joy so much right now 91
I will give you some news that better is,
For Constantia, my own so holy daughter,
Your lovely daughters has to God converted,
And you are now all branches of one tree,
And all bright stars you will in heaven be.
You and your daughters God wants as his own.
Through grace he does reward, as is well known.

Gallicanus:

O mighty and worthy lord, better news 92
You now give me than what I you did bring.
Though I defeated have a king and kingdom,
Much happier am I for my daughters who,
To God converted, a pledge do now have
Of life eternal that does peace one give.
No triumph is kings and lands to subject,
But all the world and its ways to reject.

To subject Satan and defeat the world 93
Is to real glory gain then in the future,
And the world is far more than the said provinces
And of this world the devil is the king.
Only our faith does victory permit
Over the world and him to subjugate.
So then true victory, it does seem clear,
Is that which will eternal glory bear.

If it should please you then, O mighty lord, 94
I should like to remain in solitude,
The world abandon and by myself live,
And leave the court and what the world does offer.
My life I have for you in peril put
And labored have for you throughout my life.
My blood I've shed for you many a time,
So let me now well serve this God of mine.

Constantine:

When of my state I think and of my honor, 95
Most difficult it seems to give you leave,
For if without his captain, like a man
Without a hand the emperor would be,
But when of my affection I do think,
Thoughts of myself do all then vain become.
More than my peril I do you esteem,
And your decision laudable I deem.

Although I much do grieve at your departure, 96
You to content I do my leave you grant,
But since God does to his true good invite,
Do well proceed as you did well decide.
Life treacherous and brief is, in the end
Nothing but labor, troubles and vexation.
Your holy plans do put into effect.
Others to follow you will soon elect.

(Gallicanus leaves and there is no further mention of him.)

Constantine leaves the empire to his sons and says:

O Constantine, Constantius and you Constans, 97
My sons, who of my great empire heirs are,

You see my limbs and how they all do tremble,
And my white head and my unsteady feet.
After so many labors my age wants
That at long last some rest it granted be.
The labors are so heavy and so dire:
I am too old to now rule an empire.

If to remain I were here on the throne, 98
It would tire me and do the people harm:
Age rest demands. The people need a ruler,
And as for me, I don't deceive myself.
And let the one who will the heir be know
That all that reigning is sheer peril is —
Of body and mind efforts it requires —
Nor is it ever sweet to rule empires.

If you should ever wish a state to govern,[11] 99
You must the people's welfare keep in mind.
He who from error others wants to wean
Must first himself always the right path take,
So then he must a just life choose and lead,
For his example will the people move.
What the lord does, so many will then do,
For all the eyes will surely be on you.

Self-interest and pleasure set aside, 100
And think of universal well-being first.
Your eyes you must always wide open keep,
For others while they sleep on them rely.
The scales of justice you must keep well-balanced.
Alien to you must greed and lust now be.
Affable, mild and grateful yourself show,
Servant of servants the lord is, you know.

Anxious always, the empire I did rule. 101
From day to day always new things I faced.
My sword victorious I now lay aside
For Fortune I no longer wish to test
That never long does in one pose remain.
He who does seek is bound to find all things.
You will see how vexatious is and dire
Empires to rule, that you so much desire.

---

11. In 99ff., there are lessons of governing that are of interest particularly because of Lorenzo's position. Machiavelli cites parts of these.

(Having said this, the father leaves in secret and does not reappear.)

Constantine, the son, speaks to his two brothers:

You have just now, my dearest brothers, heard 102
Our father's words that filled with wisdom are.
He has decreed he will no longer rule.
To this empire one only must succeed,
For were it not most firm and all united,
Divided it would be and so then fall.
I am the eldest. Nature does make me
The ruler be, and reason does agree.

Constantius, one of the brothers, says:

For my part I do willingly consent 103
That you the ruler be as being first-born,
And if I now your servant do become,
By God and fate it was decreed, my brother.

Constans, the other brother:

I shall be glad to this solution have,
For I do think you'll be both mild and liked.
My elder cedes, and I, his minor, too,
So on the throne as ruler will be you.

The new emperor:

O my dear brothers, since it did you please 104
That from mere brother I your lord become
And that tribute the whole world shall pay me,
And that I rule so many varied peoples,
Brotherly love always among us reigned
And it shall so remain, not otherwise.
If Fortune gives me greater state and fame,
All of us here from the same parents came.

A servant:

I now, my emperor, must tell you what 105
I rather now would hidden keep from you:
A part of your empire is now your foe
And has rebelled and makes a most great tumult
Because your father does not wish to rule.

They your officials gravely have insulted
No more do they to your commands attend.
At once out there an army you must send.

The emperor:

My father did predict just this when he 106
Told us that ruling was with perils fraught.
I've hardly in his place now been installed
That I to my great sorrow find it true.
In God I trust on this my first occasion
That these vile wretches all shall punished be.
O Constantius, O Constans go at once
With my own knights and on the wretches pounce.

Captains than you more trusted I don't have. 107
You do well know that this empire yours is.
Since you yourselves did put it in my hands,
You can with truth then say, "Our own this is."

Constantius and Constans answer:

All your commands shall not in vain be given.
We shall proceed, as you have chosen now.
To quell the flames at once we now shall race.
The army will then follow us apace.

The emperor:

One his own people must have everywhere, 108
For bound are they by love and are more faithful.
Do one or two of you now go at once
To the high temple where Mars always reigns
And have them sacrifice both sheep and oxen,
For great we can all see the tumult is.
From the dire peril that we face we pray
That God will us save and keep it away.

A soldier says:

O emperor, I'd like to bring you news 109
Of happy things, not of sad tears and death.
Whether from me or others you must learn
What happened has, this time did fate choose me.
You must then know your army routed is,
The strongest warriors prisoners or dead.

Your own two brothers who the army led
Fallen to earth are with the others dead.

THE EMPEROR:

O father Constantine you did your crown 110
And your empire now leave right just on time.
I do not know what heart to face this evil
Is good and constant or what bastion strong.
This now the scepter is, the pomp and splendor,
And here is fame with which my name resounds.
That the world does rebel it isn't enough,
My brothers' life fate now did have to snuff.

SOMEONE COMFORTS HIM AND SAYS:

O my great lord, if ever aches the head, 111
So will the body's other parts ache, too.
To lose so quickly heart at first one mustn't,
From evil one must seek to draw some good.
Who can tell what best is? Discord at times
Is among brothers born and will then grow.
Fortune perhaps did them refuse to spare
So that with them you would not have to share.

Do to your throne return, the scepter take, 112
Prepare yourself to face the situation,
The reins of your empire do take in hand
And do thank God you did alone remain.

THE EMPEROR SAYS:

I'll take the counsel of my faithful subject
As my own reason now does recommend.
To my throne I'll return as you have said,
Who's alive is alive, the dead are dead.

I do know that all my vexations are 113
Caused by a great mistake that I have made,
For in my jurisdiction I support
These most vile people that believe in Christ.
If this the cause is, I'll remove it now,
I'll persecute all of this useless faith,
I'll seize and kill all those I come to know.
Alas, my poor heart, this is the last blow.

(With these words he dies. Those who remain take counsel.)

One of them says:

We have been left without a head or guide, 114
For the empire this surely will not do.
The people roar and all the world does shout.
We must an heir find and bring here at once.
If anyone of you here does believe
He knows to whom the throne should now belong,
Speak out for on the throne we must him see,
For my part, I don't know who it might be.

Another speaks:

Julian[12] there is, of Constantine the nephew. 115
Though sorcerer and monk he once has been,
He most courageous is and of keen mind
And is by birth of the imperial blood.
Though far away he is in remote parts,
He will come here when called to reign he is.

A third one says:

This I do like.

A fourth one says:

And it does please me, too.

The first one:

Let one of us then go call him, please do.

Julian, the new emperor:

When I do think who on this throne has been, 116
I don't know whether to rejoice or grieve
That I'm the heir of Julius and Augustus,
Nor do I know whether to reign I want.
In their own time where seen this eagle was

12. Julian the Apostate, stepbrother of Constantine, reigned from 361 to 363. He was deemed to be both a monk and a magician, but was neither. These assertions had their origin in the fact that he had received a religious education.

The world did tremble like a leaf in wind.
In the empire so shrunken in our care
Every vile city to rise up does dare.

There in the heavens where the sun does rise 117
Until where tired it then does seek some rest,
The Roman deeds always gave rise to fear.
We now are of the world a bitter joke.
Since banned the sacrifices to Phoebus were,
To Mars, Minerva, Jove, Juno and then
To Victory the altar[13] put away,
Of this empire the glory went astray.

By all these sure examples fully warned, 118
I now decided have and am disposed
That in its place to Victory the altar
Be now restored and all the temples opened.
From Christians do their property now take
So that they can much better contemplate,
For Christ to those of his faith did announce,
"All that you now possess you must renounce."

This surely is in their own Gospel written[14]; 119
A Christian I once was and that I heard.
So have this edict public made at once:
"No property shall Christians from now hold.
(Of this no one should very much now grieve
If they in truth joined really are with Christ)
The goods of those who in Christ do believe
To those shall now belong who them retrieve.

Someone who accuses John and Paul:

For many years, my emperor, in Ostia 120
Two Christian brothers, John and Paul by name,
Have owned much property and great possessions
And never to your edict paid attention.

---

13. The altar to victory had been removed by Constantine. From 116 to 118 we have another favorite theme that is later found in Machiavelli: the glory of the ancients Romans and the lack of moral strength of most Europeans, particularly the Italians, a catastrophe brought about by Christianity.

14. Cf. Matt 19.21, Mark 10.21, and Luke 18.22.

The emperor:

Those two are wolves all in lamb's clothes arrayed,
But we shall shear them as you will soon see.
Do you go there and with much diligence
See that they're brought right here in my own presence.

What good a lord is who by all his subjects 121
Obeyed is not, especially at first?
Whoever power holds in any office
Will show his mettle in his first four days.
One must always his own domain protect
By having it esteemed and feared by force.
Since here I've risen, I now do intend
To be obeyed and so I will pretend.

To John and Paul, brought before the emperor, he says:

I grieve for you since I have heard it said 122
That you true Christians are and both baptized,
For though I was a child, I well remember
How dear you were to Constantine, my uncle.
Yet I must value more my own commands,
For reputation does the state maintain.
Now in few words, your property surrender.
If not you must to Jove now honor render.

John and Paul:

As you do like, O lord, of all our goods 123
You can dispose. Our lives in your hands are.
From us you can this take when you do please,
But all you do against our faith is vain.
Those who to Jove, a most false god, recur
Mistaken are. True faith all Christians have,
Christ's way we'll follow as he does require.
Do what you like. This is our own desire.

The Emperor Julian says:

If I your obstinacy did consider, 124
I would most cruelly let them torture you.
I pity you and do compassion feel,
Else of your pain I'd never sated be.
But time does often help man to decide,

So then I shall now give you ten days' time
In which you will your foolish faith abjure,
Else that you lose your life you may be sure.

Now, Terentianus,[15] go and with you bring 125
That beautiful small statue of our Jove.
For these ten days do well these two encourage
To this adore and let their Christ go away.
If they insist the wrong path to pursue,
Their heads do from their shoulders separate.
Do think that once life taken is from you
Never can you return to earth anew.

John and Paul:

O emperor, you give us time in vain, 126
For we always will Christians good remain.
Zeal for our faith and love of God always
Does burn in us and will until the end.
That seed will sprout that in the earth does die:
Death will not, therefore, to repent us bring,
And even if we could ever repent,
Not to, we'd love to have our poor lives spent.

So then with us what you do want just do, 127
A bitter death does not give rise to fear.
Do look! Our neck we shall all happy offer
For him who on the cross his body offered.
You were, once you were, of his faithful ones.
Now deaf, his voice you do no longer hear.
Pretend the ten days have to the past driven,
The body's yours, the spirit to God given.

The Emperor Julian:

With force one can with greatest ease one harm, 128
But to do good by force is not permitted.
In Christ's own law a saying there is that states
That God will not save you without your help.
Most natural and true this saying is —
Though I will not that faith as true confess.
Since all my prayers your will cannot now bend,
Do, Terentianus, to all this attend.

15. An officer.

For you I do feel sorry who still young[16] 129
Are now like sheep to your own slaughter going.
Oh do you now repent you wretched men
Before you feel the knife on your own necks.

John:

If we elected are to die like this,
Remember that the Lamb did also suffer.
You must not think of our so tender years.
Death will us spare of woes and future fears.

Terentianus:

This golden figure that I now do bear 130
Does Jove omnipotent well represent.
Is it not better to adore this figure
Than die since this the emperor permits?

Paul:

O Terentianus, you are quite mistaken.
When one does say that Jove god is, he lies.
Jove is a planet that its sphere does move.
God does Jove move, so greater he does prove.

John:

But you, O Terentianus, you'd do well 131
If Jesus, our sweet God, you would adore.

Terentianus:

In fact, this is what Julian really wants.[17]
Better it is no more to waste our breath.
Do let the headsman come, and you at once
Get down so that you can right here be killed.
Come, master Peter, do their eyes blindfold,
For their decision I do see will hold.

16. They could not have been very young since they lived in Ostia for many years (above stanza 120, v. 1, p. 476), and Julian remembers, although he had been a child, how Constantine had loved them (122, vv. 3–4, p. 477).

17. That is, this clear statement of their conviction.

On their knees, blindfolded, they together say:

O merciful and bountiful sweet Jesus, 132
Who the most sacred wood with blood did stain,
Your own most innocent and precious blood,
Man to redeem and heaven offer him,
Your merciful eyes do on two men turn
Who hope they will see you in your own kingdom.
Blood you did shed once, blood to you we render.
We do ask you to now accept our tender.

The Emperor Julian:

He who does rule a state and wears a crown 133
To rule seems not when reputation wanes.
Nor can one say he is a private person.
True rulers do all subjects represent.
Ruler is not he who the state neglects
And tends to gather wealth or look for pleasure.
These he accumulates, the state neglects,
The people's misery all this reflects.

If a great income he has, it is given 134
To be distributed freely with reason.
Let him see that the people are not harmed
By enemies, and let him keep an army.
If wheat is costly, he must subsidize
So that the people won't of hunger die.
Also the poor must be in his good care,
And thus of piling wealth he must beware.

The empire's wealth and power his are not 135
But fully to the people they belong.
Though it may seem the lord all this does own,
Possess he doesn't nor usufruct is his.
A true lord is but the distributor.
The sole reward for all his labor is
Honor that ever comes of all things first,
For which a noble heart will always thirst.

The spur of honor urges me on always, 136
The flame of glory always burns in me
And does spur on the horse that gallop does
And urges me to try new enterprises
Against the Parthians who are far away,

By whom Rome was so many times offended.
The blood that many Romans nobly shed
Vengeance awaits by armies by me led.

So let my people now all ready be 137
To come with me to this of glories highest.
So volunteer and have no doubts at all:
To glory, we proceed, not to a war.
Your prowess guarantees we'll be victorious.
Old injuries do all still haunt my mind.
The blood of those old noble Romans thus
Let it finally be avenged by us.

They were our fathers; we are their descendants. 138
To avenge the fathers, sons the duty have.
Do get your arms all ready here at once.
Do every effort make. This is my plan:
Two birds we'll catch with but a single stone.
Basil the Great[18] in Cesarea now is —
My enemy he is, of Jesus friend —
When I'll there be to writing he won't tend.

O treasurer do come, enroll the people, 139
Four rates in money, two in clothes and cloth,
And do make sure their pay all good will be.
One here and now must act. Do not waste time.
Let the astrologers be brought here now
So that we'll know the most propitious time.
Mars to the others must be well related.
Tell me when is the moment I've awaited.

The bishop, Saint Basil says:

Eternal Father do my lips now open 140
So that I shall you praise as proper is.
The grace give me to make my prayer now be
Sincere and pure without my sinful thoughts.
Your church that is our own most saintly mother
I see on every side is persecuted —
Your church that you did as your bride elect —
See that at least some vengeance you effect.

---

18. Saint Basil the Great, a learned Byzantine theologian and writer of the fourth century.

The Virgin Mary appears over the grave of Saint Mercury and says:

O Mercury come out from your dark grave, 141
Take up the sword and arms you laid aside.
Do not await the trumpet of the judgment.
Do you avenge the injuries done me.
The most foul name of Julian does resound
Above in heaven and his wicked deeds.
Innocent Christian blood avenged should be,
The Virgin Mary I am. You must heed me.

Julian the emperor through here must pass, 142
Through this same road, O my most blessed martyr.
Of justice with the sword do strike him down.
Show no compassion, in the breast do strike.
I do not wish such infamy should last,
For pity for my people does move me.
Do kill this poisonous and wicked snake,
To sate his thirst, he Christian blood does take.

The treasurer returns and says to the emperor:

Victorious emperor, your soldiers are 143
Now ready and your orders they await.
With sparkling armor covered they all are
And cannot wait the battle to engage.
I have supplied them with sufficient money;
Content you'll be when you will them all see.
Soldiers more flourishing you never saw,
All armed and ready are their sword to draw.

The astrologers called by the emperor say:

O emperor we do to you report. 144
According to the heavens only one
Peril there is that from a dead man springs.
Perhaps our counsel you will now deride.

The emperor says:

If only this I face I can be glad.
If a dead man can harm I'll be surprised.
Let Mars protect me from all swords and lances,
Gossip alone astrology advances.

Sages and kings above the stars all are 145
So that these laws so vain affect me not.
A favorite conjunction or right time
Is what a man does by himself elect.[19]
Let these strong handsome warriors now start out,
I shall them follow, shepherd to this flock.
O my brave soldiers all for honor rife,
Always with you I'll be in death or life.

(Julian moves out with the army.)

Mortally wounded on the way by Saint Mercury, he says:

That in the army's midst my life safe wasn't 146
Something it is to be much wondered at.
Of the fierce Parthians these are not the snares.
Death I received before I could feel fear.
A single man avenged has all these Christians.
Deceitful life, O our most foolish cares,
By now the spirit leaving is my breast.
O Jesus Christ, you do so win at last.[20]

19. Lorenzo speaks against astrological beliefs here and elsewhere; cf. *Sylva II,* 74, p. 246.
20. According to tradition, these were Julian's last words.

BIBLIOGRAPHY

Editions

Complete Works

Opere di Lorenzo de'Medici. Ed. Attilio Simioni. Bari: G. Laterza, 1914, rpt. 1939.

Tutte le opere. Ed. Gigi Cavalli. 3 vols. Milan: Rizzoli, 1958.

Opere di Lorenzo de' Medici. Ed. Mario Martelli. Scrittori classici italiani. Turin: G.A. Caula, 1965.

Opere di Lorenzo de' Medici. Ed. Luigi Cavalli. Naples: F. Rossi, 1969–70.

Opere. Ed. Tiziano Zanato. Turin: Einaudi, 1992.

Tutte le opere. Ed. Paolo Orvieto. Rome: Salerno, 1992.

Selected Works

Scritti scelti. Ed. Egidio Bellorini. Collezione di classici italiani con note. Serie 1.41. Turin: Unione Tipografico-Editrice Torinese, 1922, rev. ed. 1927.

Le piu belle pagine. Ed. Roberto Palmarocchi. Milan: Treves Treccani Tumminelli, 1933.

"Scelta delle poesie di Lorenzo de' Medici." In Giosuè Carducci, *Opere*. Edizione nazionale. Bologna: Zanichelli, 1935, 6:105–60.

Lorenzo de' Medici e Angelo Poliziano: Pagine scelte. Ed. Giuseppe Citanna. Verona: Mondadori, 1941.

Scritti scelti di Lorenzo de' Medici. Ed. Emilio Bigi. Turin: Unione tipografico-editrice torinese, 1955 (2nd rev. ed. 1965).

"Scelta di opere." Ed. Vincenzo Pernicone. In *Antologia della letteratura italiana* 2. Ed. Maurizio Vitale. Milan: Rizzoli, 1966.

Scritti spirituali. Ed. Luigi Cavalli. Milan: Rizzoli, 1958.

Opere scelte. Ed. Bruno Maier. Novara: Istituto geografico de Agostini, 1969.

Selected Poems and Prose. Ed. and trans. Jon Thiem. University Park: Pennsylvania State University Press, 1991.

Selected Writings. Ed. and trans. Corinna Salvadori. Dublin: Foundation for Italian Studies, University College, Belfield Italian Library, Dublin, 1992.

Ambra

Ambra, Chansons de carnaval, L'altercation et Lettres à Frédéric d'Aragon. Ed. and trans. André Chastel. Paris: La Colombe, 1947.

Ambra (descriptio hiemis). Ed. Rossella Bessi. Florence: Sansoni, 1986.

Commentary

The "Comment" of Lorenzo de' Medici. Trans. Murray Linwood Marshall. Washington, DC: The Marshalls, 1949.

Comento de' miei sonetti. Ed. Tiziano Zanato. Florence: L.S. Olschki, 1991.

The Autobiography of Lorenzo de' Medici the Magnificent: "A Commentary on My Sonnets." Ed. and trans. James Wyatt Cook and Tiziano Zanato. Binghamton, NY: Medieval & Renaissance Texts & Studies, 1995; Tempe, AZ: Arizona Center for Medieval and Renaissance Studies, 2000.

Canzoniere

Canzoniere. Ed. Paolo Orvieto. Milan: Mondadori, 1984.

Canzoniere. Ed. Tiziano Zanato. 2 vols. Istituto Nazionale di Studi sul Rinascimento. Studi e testi. Florence: L.S. Olschki, 1991.

Carnival Songs

Canti carnascialeschi. Ed. Paolo Orvieto. Rome: Salerno, 1991.

Canti carnascialeschi. Ed. Enrico Baj. Milan: Ed. Sedd, 1992.

Carnival Songs. Ed. and trans. Anthony Oldcorn, William T. Wiley, Mimmo Paladino and Jörg Schmeisser. New York: Raphael Fodde Editions, 2001.

Letters

Protocolli del carteggio di Lorenzo il Magnifico per gli anni 1473–74, 1477–92. Ed. Marcello Del Piazzo. Florence: L.S. Olschki 1956.

The Epistolario of Lorenzo de' Medici. Ed. and trans. Cecil H. Clough. Florence: Tipografia Classica, 1966.

Lettere. Ed. Nicolai Rubinstein, Melissa Meriam Bullard, Lorenz Böninger, Riccardo Fubini, Michael Mallett. 16 vols. to date. Florence: Giunti-Barbèra, 1977–2011.

Apologia e lettere. Ed. Francesco Erspamer. Rome: Salerno, 1991.

Nencia

Corinto, La caccia col falcone, La Nencia di Barberino e passi scelti e collegati di tutte le altre opere. Ed. Giovanni Necco. Milan: Vallardi, 1935.

"Una nuova redazione della *Nencia da Barberino.*" Ed. M. Messina. *Mica* 28 (1951): 174–80.

Il testo della "Nencia" *e della* "Beca" *secondo le più antiche stampe*. Ed. Vito R. Giustiniani and Luigi Pulci. Florence: L.S. Olschki, 1976.

La Nencia da Barberino. Ed. Rossella Bessi. Rome: Salerno Editore, 1982.

POETRY

Poesie. Ed. Giosuè Carducci. Florence: Barbèra & Bianchi, 1859.

Poesie. Ed. A. Castaldo. Piccola Biblioteca Utile 45. Rome: O. Garroni, 1912.

Poesie Volgari di Lorenzo de Medici. Ed. J. Ross and Edward Hutton. 2 vols. Edinburgh: Ballantyne, 1912.

Capitoli e altre rime. Ed. Attilio Simioni. Bari: Laterza, 1913.

Lorenzo il Magnifico: Dichtungen. Trans. Carl Stange. 2 vols. Bremen: H.M. Hauschild, 1940.

Poemetti e Canti carnascialeschi. Ed. Alberto Tallone. Paris: A. Tallone, 1947.

La poesia di Lorenzo de' Medici. Ed. Bruno Cicognani. Florence: Le Monnier, 1950.

Poesie. Piccola biblioteca Longanesi 76/77. Ed. Giuseppe Prezzolini. Milan: Longanesi, 1953.

Scritti d'amore. Ed. Gigi Cavalli. Milan: Rizzoli, 1958.

Poemetti & canti carnascialeschi. Alpignano: A. Tallone, 1966.

Poesie. Ed. Ilvano Caliaro. Milan: Garzanti, 1996.

MYSTERY PLAY OF SAINTS JOHN AND PAUL

La rappresentazione di San Giovanni et Paulo composta pel Magnifico Laurentio de' Medici. Florence: Francesco Bonaccorsi, 1491/2, with 14 subsequent editions to 1606.

Rappresentazione di SS. Giovanni e Paolo. Ed. Federico Doglio. Rome: Coletti, 1987.

Rappresentazione di SS. Giovanni e Paolo. Ed. Franco Molè. Viterbo: Centro studi sul teatro medioevale e rinascimentale, 1987.

Rappresentazione di San Giovanni e Paolo. Ed. Paolo Orvieto and Guido Davico Bonino. Parma: Pratiche Editrice, 1992.

Rappresentazione di S. Giovanni e Paulo. Ed. Paolo Toschi. Florence: Libreria editrice fiorentina, 1992.

Rime spirituali: La rapresentatione de San Giovanni e Paulo. Ed. Bernard Toscani. Rome: Storia e Letteratura, 2000.

OTHER WORKS

Laude. Ed. Bernard Toscani. Florence: L.S. Olschki, 1990.

La quadreria di Don Lorenzo de' Medici. Ed. Karla Langedijk and Annamaria Petrioli Tofani. Florence: Centro Di, 1977.

Scritti giocosi. Ed. Gigi Cavalli. Milan: Rizzoli, 1958.

Simposio. Ed. Mario Martelli. Florence: L.S. Olschki, 1966.

Stanze. Ed. Raffaella Castagnola. Florence: L.S. Olschki, 1986.

Il tesoro di Lorenzo il Magnifico. In *Catalogo della Mostra, Palazzo Medici Riccardi, Firenze, 1972.* Ed. Nicole Dacos et al. Florence: Sansoni, 1973.

Trionfo di Bacco e d'Arianna. Arco: Maryla Tyszkiewicz, 1960.

Studies on the Works

Bigi, Emilio. "Sulla cronologia dell'attività letteraria di Lorenzo de' Medici." *Atti dell'accademia delle scienze di Torino* 77 (1952): 154–69.

Branca, Vittore. "Per le *Canzoni a ballo* di Lorenzo il Magnifico: Problemi di tradizione e di autenticità." In *Miscellanea in onore di Roberto Cessi*. 3 vols. Rome: Storia e Letteratura, 1958.

Chiari, Alberto. "Sul testo della laurenziana *Uccellagione.*" *Rinascimento* 9.1 (1958): 1–41.

Cotton, M.S. "La sacra rappresentazione di Lorenzo de' Medici e il Gallicanus di A. Hroswith." *Giornale storico della letteratura italiana* 111 (1938): 77–87.

Dempsey, Charles. "Lorenzo de' Medici's *Ambra.*" In *Studies in Honor of Craig Hugh Smith*. Ed. Andrew Morrogh, Eve Borsook, Piero Morselli, Fiorella Superbi Gioffredi. Florence: Giunti Barbèra, 1985, 177–89.

Eisenbichler, Konrad. "Confraternities and Carnival: The Context of Lorenzo de' Medici's *Rappresentazione di SS. Giovanni e Paolo.*" In *Medieval Drama on the Continent of Europe*. Ed. Clifford Davidson and John H. Stroupe. Kalamazoo, MI: Medieval Institute Publications, 1993, 128–39.

Freedman, Luba. "*Apollo and Daphne by Antonio del Pollaiuolo and the Poetry of Lorenzo de' Medici.*" *Memoirs of the American Academy in Rome* 56/57 (2011/12): 213–42.

Graziano, Stefano Andrea. "Lorenzo de' Medici's *Canzona dei Confortini, Canto dei Profumieri, Canzona dei Sette Pianeti and Trionfo Di Bacco: Their Historical Contexts and an Analysis of Their Texts and Music.*" M.A. Thesis, School of Music, University of Utah, 2004.

Huss, Bernhard. *Lorenzo de' Medicis "Canzoniere" und der Ficinianismus: Philosophica facere quae sunt amatoria*. Tübingen: Narr, 2007.

Leporatti, R. " Sull'elaborazione del *Comento* di Lorenzo de' Medici." *Interpres* 7 (1987): 45–102.

Lipari, Angelo. *The "dolce stil novo" according to Lorenzo de' Medici: A Study of His Poetic Principio As an Interpretation of the Italian Literature of the Pre-Renaissance Period Based on His* Comento. New Haven: Yale University Press, 1936.

Maier, Bruno. *Lettura critica del "Corinto" di Lorenzo de' Medici*. Trieste: F. Zigiotti, 1949.

—. "Lorenzo de' Medici." In *Classici italiani nella storia della critica 2*. Ed. Walter Binni. Florence: La Nuova Italia, 1956.

Marchia, B. *Libro di ricordi*. Ed. Mario Martelli. Florence, 1954.

Martelli, Mario. "La tradizione manoscritta dell'*Uccellagione di starne.*" *Rinascimento* 5 (1965): 51–88.

—. "Per l'edizione critica del *Comento dei sonetti di Lorenzo de' Medici*: Restauro preliminare al testo vulgato." *Rinascimento* 7 (1967): 53–138.

—. "Per la storia redazionale del *Corinto.*" *Studi di filologia italiana* 33 (1975): 221–40.

—. *Politica e religione nella "Sacra Rappresentazione" di Lorenzo de' Medici.* Rome: Centro Studi sul teatro Medioevale e Rinascimentale, 1988.

—. "Savonarola e Lorenzo." *Memorie Domenicane* ns 29 (1998): 75–98.

—. "72 restauri preliminari al testo del *Canzoniere* laurenziano." *Interpres* 11 (1991): 182–294.

—. *Studi laurenziani.* Biblioteca di lettere italiane 2. Florence: L.S. Olschki, 1965.

Messina, Michele. "Sconosciuti delle *Rime* di Lorenzo il Magnifico: Appunti per una edizione critica." *Studi di di filologia italiana* 16 (1958): 296–77.

—. "Rime inedite di Lorenzo il Magnifico o del Poliziano?" *La bibliofila* 53 (1951): 23–51.

Momigliano, A. "La poesia del Magnifico." In *Ultimi studi.* Florence, 1954.

Phelps, Ruth Shepard. "The Sources of Lorenzo's *Sacra Rappresentazione.*" *Modern Philology* 23 (1925): 29–42.

Rubinstein, Nicolai. *The Letters of Lorenzo de' Medici and of the Medici Bank: Problems of Authorship.* Florence: Sansoni, 1982.

Santoro, Mario. "II Poliziano o il Magnifico?: Sull'attribuzione dell'*Epistola* a Federico d'Aragon." *Giornale italiano di filologia* 1 (1948): 139–49.

Simioni, Attilio. "Intorno alle *Canzoni a ballo* e ai *Canti Carnascialeschi* di Lorenzo de' Medici." In *Raccolta di studi e critica dedicata a Francesco Flamini.* Pisa: F. Mariotti, 1918, 495–536.

—. *La materia e le fonti del "Corinto"di Lorenzo de' Medici.* Perugia: Unione tipografica cooperativa, 1904.

Sturm, Sara. *Lorenzo de' Medici.* Twayne's World Authors series. New York: Twain, 1974.

Shapiro, Marianne. "Petrarch, Lorenzo de' Medici, and the Latin Elegiac Poets." *Romance Notes* (1973): 172–75.

—. "Poetry and Politics in the *Comento of* Lorenzo de' Medici." *Renaissance Quarterly* 26.4 (1972): 444–53.

Wadsworth, James B. "Landino's *Disputationes Camaldulenses,* Ficino's *De felicitate,* and *L'Altercazione* of Lorenzo de' Medici." *Modern Philology* 50.1 (1952): 23–31.

Zanato, Tiziano. "Gli autografi di Lorenzo de' Medici: Analisi linguistica e testo critico." *Studi di filologia italiana* 44 (1986): 87–207.

—. *Saggio sul "Comento" di Lorenzo de' Medici.* Florence: L.S. Olschki, 1979.

—. "Sul testo del *Comento* laurenziano." *Studi di filologia italiana* 38 (1980): 71–152.

—. "Un nuovo codice del *Comento* laurenziano." *Studi di filologia italiana* 39 (1981): 29–55.

General Background

Acton, Harold. *The Pazzi Conspiracy.* London: Thames and Hudson, 1979.

Baron, Hans. *The Crisis of the Early Italian Renaissance* Princeton, NJ: Princeton University Press, 1966.

Bec, Christian. *Cultura e società a Firenze nell'età della Rinascenza.* Rome: Salerno editrice, 1981.

Beschi, Luigi. *La Toscana al tempo di Lorenzo il Magnifico: Politica, economia, cultura, arte.* Pisa: Pacini, 1996.

Bing, Gertrud, ed. *La rinascita del paganesimo antico: Contributo alia storia della cultura.* Florence: La Nuova Italia, 1966.

Brown, Alison. *Medicean and Savonarolan Florence: The Interplay of Politics, Humanism, and Religion.* Turnhout: Brepols, 2011.

—. *The Medici in Florence: The Exercise and Language of Power.* Florence: L.S. Olschki, 1992.

—. "Platonism in Fifteenth-Century Florence and the Contribution to Early Modern Political Thought." *The Journal of Modern History* 58 (1986): 383–413.

Burke, Peter. *Culture and Society in Renaissance Italy 1420–1540.* New York: Scribner, 1972.

Burckhardt, Jacob. *The Civilization of the Renaissance in Italy.* Trans. S.G.C. Middlemore. Harmondsworth: Penguin Books, 1990.

Cantimori, Delio. "Rhetoric in Humanism." *Journal of the Warburg Institute* 1.2 (1937–38): 83–102.

Cerretani, Bartolomeo. *Storia fiorentina.* Ed. Giuliana Berti. Florence: L.S. Olschki, 1994.

Chastel. André. *Art et humanism a Florence au temps de' Lorenzo de' Medici.* Paris: Presses universitaires de France, 1959.

Clarke, Paula C. *The Soderini and the Medici: Power and Patronage in Fifteenth-Century Florence.* Oxford: Clarendon Press, 1991.

Connell, William J. ed. *Society and Individual in Renaissance Florence.* Berkeley: University of California Press, 2002.

Conti, Elio, Alessandro Guidotti, and Roberto Lunardi. *La civiltà fiorentina del Quattrocento.* Florence:Vallecchi, 1993.

Cronin, Vincent. *The Florentine Renaissance.* New York: Dutton, 1967.

Dempsey, Charles. *The Portrayal of Love: Botticelli's* "Primavera" *and Humanist Culture at the Time of Lorenzo the Magnificent.* Princeton, NJ, 1992.

Field, Arthur. *The Origins of the Platonic Academy of Florence.* Princeton NJ: Princeton University Press, 1988.

Garin, Eugenio. *Italian Humanism.* Translated by Peter Munz. Oxford: B. Blackwell, 1965; rpt. Westport, CT: Greenwood Press, 1975. Originally published as *L'umanesimo italiano: Filosofia e vita civile nel Rinascimento.* Bari: Laterza, 1952.

—. *La cultura filosofica del Rinascimento italiano: Ricerche e documenti.* Florence: Sansoni, 1961.

—. *La letteratura degli umanisti.* Milan: Garzanti, 1966.

—. *Portraits from the Quattrocento.* Trans. Victor A. Velen and Elizabeth Velen. New York: Harper & Row, 1972.

Godman, Peter. *From Poliziano to Machiavelli: Florentine Humanism in the High Renaissance.* Princeton NJ: Princeton University Press, 1998.

Goldthwaithe, Richard A. *The Building of Renaissance Florence: An Economic and Social History.* Baltimore, MD: Johns Hopkins University Press, 1980.

Gombrich, E.H. "The Early Medici as Patrons of Art." In *Italian Renaissance Studies.* Ed. E.F. Jacob. London: Faber and Faber, 1960, 279–311.

Grayson, Cecil. *A Renaissance Controversy: Latin or Italian.* Oxford: Clarendon Press, 1960.

Greenfield, Concetta Carestia. *Humanist and Scholastic Poetics.* Lewisburg, PA: Bucknell University Press, 1981.

Hale. J.R. *Florence and the Medici: The Pattern of Control.* London: Thames and Hudson, 1977.

Hankins, James, ed. *Civic Humanism: Reappraisals and Reflections.* New York: Cambridge University Press, 2000.

—. *Plato in the Italian Renaissance.* Leiden and New York: E.J. Brill, 1990.

Hibbert, Christopher. *The Rise and Fall of the House of Medici.* Harmondsworth: Penguin Books, 1985.

Jones, P.J. *The Italian City-State: From Commune to Signoria.* Oxford: Clarendon Press, 1997.

Kent, D. *Cosimo de' Medici and the Florentine Renaissance.* New Haven: Yale University Press, 2000.

Kraye, Jill. *Cambridge Translations of Renaissance Philosophical Texts.* New York: Cambridge University Press, 1997.

Kristeller, Paul Oskar. *Il pensiero filosofico di Marsilio Ficino.* Florence: Le Lettere, 1988.

—. *Le Thomisme et la pensée italienne de la Renaissance.* Montreal: Institut d'études mediévales, 1962.

—. *Renaissance Thought II: Papers on Humanism and the Arts.* New York: Harper & Row, 1965.

—, and Michael Mooney. *Renaissance Thought and Its Sources.* New York: Columbia University Press, 1979.

—. *Studies in Renaissance Thought and Letters.* Rome: Edizioni di storia e letteratura, 1985.

Martines, Lauro. *April Blood: Florence and the Plot against the Medici.* Oxford: Oxford University Press, 2003.

—. *Power and Imagination: City-States in Renaissance Italy.* New York: Knopf, 1979.

—. *The Social World of the Florentine Humanists.* Princeton NJ: Princeton University Press, 1963.

Rubinstein, Nicolai. *The Government of Florence under the Medici.* Oxford: Clarendon Press, 1966.

Taddei, Ilaria. *Fanciulli e giovani: Crescere a Firenze nel rinascimento.* Florence: L.S. Olschki, 2001.

Trexler, Richard C. *Public Life in Renaissance* Florence. New York: Academic Press, 1980.

Literary and Cultural Background

Bembo, Pietro. Prose della volgar lingua, Gli Asolani. Ed. Carlo Dionisotti. Bergamo: Nuovo istituto italiano d'arti grafiche, 1989.

Binni, Walter, ed. *I classici italiani nella storia della critica.* Florence: Nuova Italia, 1954.

Croce, Benedetto. "Poesia poetica e poesia letteraria." *Quaderni della Critica* 6.16 (1950): 91–93.

Dall'accademia neoplatonica fiorentina alla riforma: Celebrazioni del V centenario della morte di Lorenzo il Magnifico.Convegno di studio, Florence, Palazzo Strozzi, 30 ottobre 1992. Florence: L.S. Olschki, 1996.

Dempsey, Charles. *The Portrayal of Love: Botticelli's* Primavera *and Humanist Culture at the Time of Lorenzo the Magnificent.* Princeton, NJ: Princeton University Press, 1992.

De Robertis, Domenico. "L'esperienza poetica del *Quattrocento." In Storia della letteratura italiana 3.* Ed. Emilio Cecchi and Natalino Sapegno. Milan: Garzanti, 1966, 357–784.

De Sanctis, Francesco. *Storia della letteratura italiana.* Ed. Niccolò Gallo, intro. Giorgio Ficara. Turin: Einaudi-Gallimard, 1996.

Francastel, Pierre. "La fête mythologique au Quattrocento." *Revue d'esthétique* 5 (1952): 376–410.

Fubini, Mario. *Studi sulla letteratura del Rinascimento.* Florence: La Nuova Italia, 1971.

Jeanroy, Alfred. *La poesie lyrique des troubadours.* Toulouse: E. Privat, Paris: H. Didier, 1934.

Lanza, Antonio. *Polemiche e berte letterarie nella Firenze del primo Quattrocento.* Rome: Bulzoni, 1971.

Levin, Harry. The Myth of the Golden Age in the Renaissance. Bloomington: Indiana University Press, 1969.

Lewis, C.S. *The Allegory of Love: A Study in Medieval Tradition.* Oxford: Clarendon Press, 1936.

Lucchi, Lorna de', ed. and trans. *An Anthology of Italian Poems.* New York: Biblo and Tannen, 1967.

Machiavelli, Nicolò. *Istorie fiorentine.* In *Tutte le opere 2.* Ed. *Carlo Cordié and Francesco Flora.* Verona: A. Mondadori, 1967.

Maier, Bruno. *I classici italiani nella storia della critica 1.* Ed. Walter Binni. Florence: Nuova Italia, 1954.

Mutini, Claudio, ed. *La cultura a Firenze al tempo di Lorenzo il Magnifico.* Bologna: Zanichelli, 1970.

Nencioni, Enrico. "La lirica del rinascimento." In *La vita italiana nel Rinascimento.* Ed. Ernesto Masi. Milan: Fratelli Treves, 1893, 178–204.

Panofsky, Erwin. *Renaissance and Renascences in Western Art.* New York, Harper & Row, 1972.

Petrarca, Francesco. *Canzoniere.* Ed. Gianfranco Contini and Daniele Ponchiroli. Turin: G. Einaudi, 1966.

Pompeati, Arturo, ed. *Storia della letteratura italiana.* Turin: UTET, 1944–77.

Poncet, Christophe, and Germana Ernst. *La scelta di Lorenzo: La Primavera di Botticelli tra poesia e filosofia.* Pisa: Fabrizio Serra, 2012.

Ponte, Giovanni. *Il Quattrocento. I classici italiani 6.* Ed. Walter Binni. Bologna: Zanichelli, 1966.

Proclus. *Theologie Platonicienne.* Ed. and trans. Henri-Dominique Saffrey and Leendert Gerrit Westerink. Paris: Les Belles Lettres, 1968–97.

Rho, Edmondo. "Il Quattrocento e i suoi critici." In *Primitivi e romantici.* Florence: G.C. Sansoni, 1937, 59–72.

—. *Lorenzo il Magnifico.* Bari: Laterza, 1926.

Rinaldi, R. "Il principe e la letteratura." In *Storia della civiltà letteraria italiana.* Ed. G. Barberi-Squarotti. Turin: UTET, 1993.

Sapegno, Natalino, ed. *Antologia della storia e della critica letteraria 1.* Rome: Oreste Barjes, 1968.

—. *Compendio di storia della letteratura italiana: Dalle origini alla fine de Quattrocento.* Florence: La Nuova Italia, 1964.

Savonarola, Girolamo. *Prediche e scritti.* Ed. Mario Ferrari. Milan: Hoepli, 1930.

Spongano, Raffaele. *Due saggi sull'umanesimo.* Florence: Sansoni, 1964.

—. *Un capitolo di storia della nostra prosa d'arte.* Florence: Sansoni, 1941.

Torre, Arnoldo della. *Storia dell'accademia platonica di Firenze.* Florence: G. Carnesecchi, 1902.

Toschi, Paolo. *Dal dramma liturgico alla sacra rappresentazione.* Florence: Sansoni, 1940.

Trinkhaus, Charles Edward. *In Our Image and Likeness: Humanity and Divinity in Italian Humanist Thought.* Chicago: University of Chicago Press, 1970.

—. *Adversity's Noblemen.* New York: Octagon Books, 1965.

Varese, Claudio, ed. *Prosatori volgari del Quattrocento.* Milan: R. Ricciardi, 1955.

Verdon, Timothy, and John Henderson, ed. *Christianity and the Renaissance: Image and Religious Imagination in the Quattrocento.* Syracuse, NY: Syracuse University Press, 1990.

Villari, Pasquale. *La storia di Girolamo Savonarola e dei suoi tempi.* 2 vols. Florence: Le Monnier, 1930.

Vossler, Karl. *Italienische Literaturgeschichte.* Leipzig: G.J. Göschen, 1908.

Weinberg, Bernard. *A History of Literary Criticism in the Italian Renaissance.* Chicago: University of Chicago Press, 1961.

Weinstein, Donald. *Savonarola and Florence: Prophecy and Patriotism in the Renaissance.* Princeton, NJ: Princeton University Press, 1970.

—, and Valerie R. Hotchkiss, ed. *Girolamo Savonarola: Piety, Prophecy and Politics in Renaissance Florence.* Dallas: Bridwell Library, Perkins School of Theology, Southern Methodist University, 1994.

Weiss, Roberto. *The Renaissance Discovery of Classical Antiquity.* Oxford: Basil Blackwell, 1969.

Lorenzo and His Life

Ady, Cecilia M. "The Quincentenary of Lorenzo de' Medici." *Italian Studies* 5 (1950): 55–66.

—. *Lorenzo dei Medici and Renaissance Italy.* New York: Collier Books, 1966.

Altomonte, Antonio. *Il Magnifico.* Milan: Rusconi, 1982.

Armstrong, E. *Lorenzo de' Medici and Florence in the Fifteenth Century.* New York: Putnam, 1896.

Barfucci, E. *Lorenzo de' Medici e la società artistica del suo tempo.* Florence: Gonnelli, 1945.

Bérance, Fred. *Laurent le Magnifique, ou la quête de la perfection.* Paris: La Colombe, 1949.

Bizzarri, Edoardo. *Il Magnifico.* Milan: Mondadori, 1950.

Brion, Marcel. *Laurent le Magnifique.* Paris: A. Michel, 1937.

Brown, Alison. *Lorenzo and Public Opinion in Florence: The Problem of Opposition.* Florence: L.S. Olschki, 1994.

Buck, August. *Der Platonismus in der Dichtungen Lorenzo de' Medicis.* Berlin: Junker u. Dünnhaupt, 1936.

Bullard, Melissa Meriam. *Lorenzo Il Magnifico: Image and Anxiety, Politics and Finance.* Florence: L.S. Olschki, 1994.

—. "The Magnificent: Between Myth and History." In *Politics and Culture in Early Modern Europe: Essays in Honour of H.G. Koenigsberger.* Ed. Phyllis Mack and Margaret C. Jacob. Cambridge: Cambridge University Press, 1987, 25–58.

—. "Medici, House of." *The Oxford Encyclopedia of the Reformation.* Oxford Reference Online. Ed. Hans J. Hillebrand. New York: Oxford University Press, 1996.

Cardini, Franco, and Giovanni Cherubini. *Lorenzo il Magnifico.* Rome: Liberia dello Stato, 1992.

Cecchi, Emilio. "Lorenzo il Magnifico." In *Ritratti e profili: Saggi e note di letteratura italiana.* Milan: Garzanti, 1957.

Cloulas, Ivan. *Laurent le Magnifique.* Paris: Fayard, 1982.

Daniels, Tobias. *La congiura dei Pazzi: I documenti del conflitto fra Lorenzo de' Medici e Sisto IV. Le bolle di scomunica, la "Florentina Synodus," e la "Dissentio" insorta tra la Santità del Papa e i fiorentini. Edizione critica e commento.* Florence: Edifir, 2013.

De Sanctis, R.E. "Lorenzo il Magnifico: L'allegrezza incompiuta." In *Il letto di Procuste.* Milan, 1943.

Fabroni, A. *Laurentii Medicis Magnifici vita.* Pisa: Jacobus Gratiolius, 1784.

Fletcher, Stella. "Lorenzo de' Medici." *Oxford Bibiographies.* Ed. Margaret King. New York: Oxford University Press, 2010.

—. "The Medici Family." *Oxford Bibiographies.* Ed. Margaret King. New York: Oxford University Press, 2013.

Fusco, Laurie Smith, and Gino Corti. *Lorenzo de' Medici: Collector and Antiquarian*. Cambridge: Cambridge University Press, 2007.

Garfagnini, Gian Carlo. *Lorenzo de' Medici: Studi*. Florence: L.S. Olschki, 1992.

—. *Lorenzo il Magnifico e il suo tempo.* Florence: L.S. Olschki, 1992.

—. *Lorenzo il Magnifico e il suo mondo.* Florence: L.S. Olschki, 1994.

Garsia, Augusto. *Il Magnifico e la Rinascita*. Florence: L. Battistelli, 1923.

Hankins, James. *Lorenzo de' Medici as a Patron of Philosophy.* Florence: L.S. Olschki, 1994.

Hook, Judith. *Lorenzo de' Medici: An Historical Biography.* London: H. Hamilton, 1984.

Kent, F.W. *Lorenzo de' Medici and the Art of Magnificence.* Baltimore, MD: Johns Hopkins University Press, 2004.

—, and Carolyn James. *Princely Citizen: Lorenzo de' Medici and Renaissance Florence.* Turnhout: Brepols, 2013.

Lang, Jack. *Laurent le Magnifique: Essai*. Paris: Perrin, 2002.

Lebey, André. *Essai sur Laurent de Médicis, dit le Magnifique.* Paris: Perrin, 1900.

Loth, David. *Lorenzo the Magnificent*. London: Routledge, 1930.

Maguire, Yvonne. *The Private Life of Lorenzo the Magnificent*. London: A. Ouseley, 1936.

Mallett, Michael Edward, and Nicholas Mann. *Lorenzo the Magnificent: Culture and Politics.* London: Warburg Institute, University of London, 1996.

Morandini, A. "Contribute ad una bibliografia laurenziana." *Archivio storico italiano* 107 (1949): 216–35.

Orvieto, Paolo. *Lorenzo de' Medici*. Florence: La Nuova Italia, 1976.

—. "Lorenzo de' Medici e l'umanesimo toscano del secondo Quattrocento." In *Storia della letteratura italiana*. Ed. Enrico Malato. Rome: Salerno, 1996, 295–403.

Palmarocchi, Roberto. *La politica italiana di Lorenzo de' Medici: Firenze nella guerra contro Innocenzo VIII. Biblioteca Storica Toscana 8*. Florence: L.S. Olschki, 1933.

—. *Lorenzo il Magnifico.* Turin: UTET, 1946.

Pancrazi, Pietro. "Attrattiva del Magnifico." In *Nel giardino di Candido.* Scritti letterari 4. Florence: Le Monnier, 1961.

Perini, Leandro. *Lorenzo politico: Dal Pulci al Burckhardt*. Roma: Bulzoni, 1992.

Rochon, André. *La jeunesse de Lorenzo de' Medici, 1449–1478*. Paris: Les Belles Lettres, 1963.

Romagnoli, Sergio. "Lorenzo de' Medici." In *Momenti di vita civile e letteraria*. Padua: Liviana, 1966.

Roscoe, William. *Life of Lorenzo de' Medici Called the Magnificent*. Liverpool: J. M'Creery, 1795.

Rubinstein, Nicolai. "Lorenzo de' Medici: The Formation of His Statecraft." *Proceedings of the British Academy* 63 (1977): 71–94.

Stapleford, Richard, ed. and trans. *Lorenzo de' Medici at Home: The Inventory of the Palazzo Medici in 1492*. University Park: Pennsylvania State University Press, 2014.

Stevenson, Angus, and Christine A. Lindberg. "Lorenzo de' Medici." *Oxford Reference Online*. New York: Oxford University Press, 2010.

Tateo, Francesco. *Lorenzo de' Medici e Angelo Poliziano*. Bari: Laterza, 1990.

Toscani, Bernard. Lorenzo de' Medici: New Perspectives. Proceedings of the International Conference Held at Brooklyn College and the Graduate Center of the City University of New York, April 30–May 2, 1992. New York: Peter Lang, 1993.

Unger, Miles. *Magnifico: The Brilliant Life and Violent Times of Lorenzo de' Medici*. New York: Simon & Schuster, 2008.

Viti, Paolo. *Studi su Lorenzo dei Medici e il secolo XV 1*. Florence: L.S. Olschki, 1992.

Von Reumont, Alfred. *Lorenzo de' Medici il Magnifico*. Leipzig: Duncker & Humblot, 1883.

INDEX OF FIRST LINES

A beautiful and gentle, graceful nymph 35
A bitter thought at times possesses me 52
A certain distance on a scabrous path 360
A hard heart he must well have 445
A little wood there is amidst a valley 331
A lovely, pleasing work our eyes do see 63
A simple little bird that nature guides 15
A thought that does of Love so often speak 57
A young woman did desire 333
Aflame am I with love and I must sing 263
Aflame am I with love and I must sing 268
Afraid that Jove again to love would fall 5
After such sorrow and so many sighs 231
Against the power of those proud new eyes 65
Alas, how beautiful were all those tears 62
Alas, how much desire Love has now placed 57
Alas, I do not know what I should do 192
Alas, poor me, when in the presence of 103
All happy places to my heart do bring 67
All red the eastern sky already was 279
All you see does backward go 356
Alone my lovely lady never is 194
An impious fury now in Janus's temple 39
Annoyed with Love, my lady did pretend 63
As Love had wished, reduced almost to ashes 77
As once you seemed to me, O eyes, you are 52
As soon as Bartolin had told me this 295

Blessed are they who from those impious councils 420
But a short time ago you did know joy 40
By Love conducted, I the top had reached 20
By sweeter thoughts attracted and here led 381

Clear, sparkling waters, I do hear you murmur 134
Come nymphs, the glorious mountain now adorn 220
Complain I don't of you nor of myself 316

Daughter mine, do all you can 335
Delicate, beautiful and candid hand. 121
Do follow, pious soul, that fervent passion 430

Enough it was that you my freedom stole 39
Ever from us time flies 31
Eyes of my love that are within my heart 107

Faster than Jove can make the heavens bright 38
Five times the sun its course completed has 13
Fled is the season that had then transformed 209
Fortune with ease could happiness bestow 4
From many sides am I attacked by Love 43
From my breast light and fast 75
From our abode we planets do here come 354

Give me peace now, O ardent sighs of mine 138
Growing in me from day to day I feel 14

Have pity all of you for my deep sorrow 319
How can I leave you or you stay with me 49
How can I then with cheerful heart now sing 328
How foolish to desire or hope for what 109
How I do envy you, my blessed heart 127
How many times for having too much hope 8
How vain it is for us to ever hope 30

I can no longer see those saintly eyes 185
I did my lady see among green leaves 16
I did once cry as Love commanded me 33
I did stand there just like a man who dreams 292
I do not know of anything more vexing 327
I do not know what destiny of mine 11
I do not know who is my greatest foe 15
I do thank you, O Love, for all my woes 68
I ever used Endymion to deride 49
I feel returning that so sweet a time 18
I thought, O Love, that now the time had come 16
I wish and seek what I do most dislike 7
If all intent it happens that my sight 59
If as Jove into a bull himself transformed 360
If in my eyes at times my lady looks 65
If in some sunny, sweet and lovely site 47
If Love should happen some brief joy to offer 18
If Love their lovely sun to my eyes shows 40
If my tired eyes now here or there I turn 179

If one is not in love 327
If one should have so powerful a sight 50
If someone tunes two instruments so that 48
If when I'm close to her so lovely face 49
If when most close to you, my dearest lady, 116
If with my sighs that from my breast do come, 114
I'm leaving you, O sweet dear thoughts of mine 28
In a serious argument 334
In happiness I live and in sweet peace 317
In my poor heart my soul does seem to move 61
In shadow through long, steep and savage ways 55
In Thessaly a mountain tall there is 203
In this carnival, alas 350
In your swift waves you carry away with you 58
Is there anyone among you ladies now 323
It does not honor you, O Love, that you 68
I've received so much good counsel 336

Just as a lantern in the early hours 34
Just as in spring the sun and morning dews 34
Just like a falcon for the launch raised high 301

Ladies and girls, I do my faults all heed 339
Ladies and maidens please do listen well 340
Leave your beloved isle so dear to you 35
Let all of nature listen to this hymn 418
Let not the earth that did well nourish you 54
Let those who wish great pomp and highest honors, 144
Like in a pail full of half-curdled milk 312
Like when a bell does toll a long, long time 305
Look here you women, biscuits, cookies, too 343
Love did, on that triumphant day that still 61
Love has so held me tight from time to time 29
Love in my heart the lovely image put 158
Love promised me at peace one day I'd be 12
Love that is ever paired with jealousy 12
Lovely ladies a long time 326

More beautiful than ever but less proud 27
Most holy God and Father of all that 417
Most tenderly does Love beg me at times 47
My amorous sweet style, my song so sweet 425

My dearest ladies, as you can now see 357
My ears were all intent to catch his words 386
My eyes could not withstand at any time 4
My eyes were firmly fixed on this Steccuto 298
My heart is filled with bitter sweetness now 329
My lady's sacred feet Love did then guide 53
My poor sad heart in my afflicted breast 177
My tender thoughts together all the time 50
My thoughts always and only do admire 53
My tired and moist eyes often do tell me: 57

Never a cruel god, O Love, you'll be 62
Never to taste your sweetness, O my Love 21
No sweeter sleep nor more untroubled rest 160
Not from the well-cared-for, ornate, green gardens 54
Now I must the truth tell you 332

O Bellincion, do like Sosia act 359
O blessed home that then accustomed were 19
O brilliant star that with your own bright rays 93
O charming flowers, O green fragrant grass 161
O cruel Fortune, where have you led me? 322
O eyes, I ever sigh as Love decrees 111
O gentle lady mine, who all surpass 5
O God, O highest good, what are you doing 440
O happy countryside, green fields and woods 2
O happy land where still my lady dwells 3
O hill so proud, though humble in appearance 60
O lady mine, how vain it is to think 315
O lady mine, in your most lovely eyes 156
O Love hold me forever close and tight 330
O Love, if in my heart you'd wish to be 324
O Love, I see that satisfied you're not 9
O Love, so many trials you set for me 36
O Love you well do know all thoughts of mine, 315
O lovely hand of mine that charming are, 124
O lovely violet, you were born there 59
O loving sighs that now do come to me 171
O memory so harsh, why don't you leave 66
O my dear image, you the haven are 22
O my great God, by means of whose firm laws 413
O my poor tired eyes, stop your woeful tears 146

O nights so brief and clear, days long and dark 64
O purple, fresh and lovely violets 131
O servitude so sweet, my heart you freed 224
O sinners, your eternal God I am 444
O sleep most peaceful, do to me come now, 141
O truly sacred and most happy night 51
O venerable, immense and eternal 406
O you sinners come to me 442
O you sinners do come all 435
O you wicked stony heart 434
Oh how beautiful is youth 352
Oh how great your beauty is 432
On a cold rock and hard I often sit 68
On reaching us, one at my guide does look 309
On that most happy day I left you here 136
Of grafting we are masters, my good ladies 347
Of life the sweet light I would now abandon 97
Of that so loving breast the lofty sighs 60
Of Valencia we are youths 344
Of your uncertainty, O Love, am I 28

Silence, O you who have now gathered here 447
Since I did leave, O Love, your kind domain, 323
Since I did taste your sweetness, O my Jesus 439
Since that dire time when my well-ventured" heart 118
So beautiful my lady is and such 62
So cruel and inhumane the first wound was 1
So many are the charms and such the beauty 164
So overwhelmed with sweetness my heart was 400
So sweetly does my lady call for death 150
Some time ago I was a poor sad lover 51
Sorrows and tears I pray that God will bring 321
Speaking to us, this novel Plato said 391
Sweet thoughts of mine, do not as yet depart 22

Thanks be to you, supreme and mighty God 415
That graceful sweetness Love was pleased to place 44
That noble heart that Love as pledge gave me 169
That proudest look so lethal to our eyes 27
That sudden amorous and candid pallor 189
That ungrateful wretch am I 437
The ardent rays I flee of my bright sun 41

The dress, the time, the place where I at first 105
The jeers of Fortune ever follow me; 14
The moon among so many lesser stars 197
The One who lifted was on up to heaven 21
The only paradise I can foresee 325
The sun had risen to its midday point 313
The sun has now its ancient course resumed 13
The sun that your dark way did brightly light 3
The time I've waited for is now approaching 20
The tree Apollo once did love so much 7
The year's sweet time had come when old Tithonus 1
The young and tender leaves in warm springtime 56
There can be no game so lovely 337
There where her splendid eyes my lady turns, 174
These eyes of mine will ever have no tears? 6
This animal, my ladies, perfect is 349
This weak and frail poor little bark of mine 4
Those beautiful and perilous bright stars 56
Those first sweet thoughts that nourish did my heart 33
Those lovely eyes that give or take away 15
Those tearful stars to my own eyes have given 53
Those who await the morrow will repent: 320
Though I laugh and sing and dance 315
Through many paths and many varied ways 23
Tithonus seven times our hemisphere 2
To follow Love excuses I don't need 329
To open once again an ancient wound 72
To Pisa on the way, at night I strayed 339
To this beloved place I often come 6
To you I do return, bright lovely stars, 187

Unto itself the spirit draws at times 41

Wake up, you lazy mind, from that deep sleep 420
We are women as you see 355
We are young, but as you'll hear, we are masters 346
What do I feel, alas, in my breast move? 166
What I once loved with my most strong desire 28
What is, alas, my lovely lady doing? 182
What wonder can it be if evermore 78
When a warm ray of light 69
When for my greater sorrow blind desire 64

When from her lovely face my soul had left 55
When I do think of lodging some complaints 153
When in the season that their green leaves lose 289
When Lot and all his family did flee 430
When the horizon sees the sun descend 95
When the light of her eyes to me arrives 65
When will Hope die, sweet enemy of mine 58
Where shall I go where I shall not find you 99
Who can that be there in my lady's eyes? 46
Why be surprised, O my gentle Cortese 66
Why in my heart do you return, O Love 48
Why is my lady not here with my thoughts 67
With bitter sighs and deepest sorrow filled 8
With heavy steps and slow and troubled mind 26
With one farewell content I cannot be 77
With promises and with so much hypocrisy, 318
Without the help of any other gods 396

You with others play at love, 319

This Book Was Completed On November 1, 2015
At Italica Press, New York, New York.
It Was Set in Bembo and
Bembo Expert.

www.ingramcontent.com/pod-product-compliance
Ingram Content Group UK Ltd.
Pitfield, Milton Keynes, MK11 3LW, UK
UKHW041632190726
13854UKWH00006B/2454

9 781599 102313